SAFE SPACE

Perverse Modernities

A series edited by Judith Halberstam and Lisa Lowe

Christina B. Hanhardt

SAFE SPACE

GAY NEIGHBORHOOD HISTORY
AND THE POLITICS OF VIOLENCE

Duke University Press   Durham and London   2013

© 2013 Duke University Press
All rights reserved
Printed in the United States of America on
acid-free paper ∞
Designed by Heather Hensley
Typeset in Chaparral Pro by Copperline Book
Services, Inc.

Library of Congress Cataloging-in-Publication Data
Hanhardt, Christina B.
Safe space : gay neighborhood history and the
politics of violence / Christina B. Hanhardt.
pages cm — (Perverse modernities)
ISBN 978-0-8223-5457-4 (cloth : alk. paper)
ISBN 978-0-8223-5470-3 (pbk. : alk. paper)
1. Gay liberation movement—New York
(State)—New York. 2. Gay liberation
movement—California—San Francisco.
3. Gentrification—New York (State)—New York.
4. Gentrification—California—San Francisco.
5. Community policing—New York (State)—
New York. 6. Community policing—
California—San Francisco. I. Title. II. Series:
Perverse modernities.
HQ76.8.U5H37 2013
306.76'609747—dc23   2013013825

CONTENTS

ACKNOWLEDGMENTS

First and foremost I thank all of the activists from whom I've learned. It is no exaggeration when I write that their vision and labor has given clarity of purpose not only to this book but to my own life. The activists whom I interviewed include, in order of appearance, Del Martin, Phyllis Lyon, Randy Alfred, Hank Wilson, Ben Gardiner, Michael Shernoff, Ali Marrero, Ruth Mahaney, Maggie Jochild (Meg Barnett), Pamela David, Lois Helmbold, Lenn Keller, Joan Gibbs, Bran Fenner, and Krystal Portalatin. Extra thanks to Maggie and Lenn for their exceptional generosity and memory, and to Joan Annsfire, with whom I had invaluable exchanges as well. I also thank those who chose to remain anonymous and the many individuals whose interviews did not make it into this narrative, including Rickke Mananzala, Yasmeen Perez, and others. I am thankful to all of the members and staff of Fabulous Independent Educated Radicals for Community Empowerment (FIERCE), past and present. Those active in the early 2000s deserve special mention, such as Krystal, Bran, and Rickke, as well as Aries Dela Cruz, Lucia Leandro Gimeno, Jesse Ehrensaft-Hawley, Mervyn Marcano, J. D. Melendez, Justin Rosado, and many more. I am also thankful for exchanges with other former and present FIERCE staff members, including Emerson Brisbon and Naa Hammond. Many thanks to FIERCE allies and other fellow travelers, especially Kai Barrow, Kenyon Farrow, and Joo-Hyun Kang. I have been honored to work alongside more people than I could mention here who are involved in social movements inside and outside New York and Washington, D.C. I thank them all.

I am tremendously grateful to the archivists, staff, and volunteers at the Gay, Lesbian, Bisexual, Transgender Historical Society (GLBTHS) in San Francisco; the Division of Rare and Manuscript Collections of Cornell University; the Lesbian Herstory Archives in Brooklyn; the Sexual Minority Archive of Northampton, Massachusetts; the New York and San Francisco Public Libraries; the June Mazer Lesbian Collection in Los Angeles, now at the University of California, Los Angeles; the ONE National Gay and Lesbian Archives in Los Angeles, now a part of the University of Southern California; the Fales Library of New York University; the Bancroft Library of the University of California, Berkeley; and the National Archive of Lesbian, Gay, Bisexual, and Transgender History of the LGBT Community Center in New York. Special thanks go to Susan Stryker, who pointed me to many of the sources on which the first and second chapters of this book are based and whose research on San Francisco's history has been so foundational. I owe extra recognition to Brenda Marston, curator of the Human Sexuality Collection at Cornell; Rebekah Kim and Marjorie Bryer, archivists at the GLBTHS; and the entire collective of the Lesbian Herstory Archives.

I am lucky to have had the opportunity to study at the Program in American Studies at New York University (NYU). I am most grateful to have learned so much from Lisa Duggan. It is because of her example that I sharpened my feminist and queer analysis, first thought conceptually about the state, pursued historical research, and believed that one day I would be done. Andrew Ross was also an important guide, who gave me knowledge and confidence that inspired me to identify as an urbanist, taught me invaluable lessons about writing clearly, and cheered me on with genuine encouragement. They are exemplars of engaged scholars, and they understood what was at stake for me as I pursued this path. Without them, none of this would have been possible. Phillip Brian Harper was a key advisor, especially in my first years of graduate school, when he encouraged me to direct my close readings at the social world. I am thankful for Adam Green's example of historical analysis joined by cultural critique. In those years, I learned from a remarkable group of faculty members, including Arlene Dávila, Steven Gregory, Robin D. G. Kelley, Anna McCarthy, Toby Miller, José Esteban Muñoz, and George Yúdice. It was in a class with Cathy Cohen, then a visiting faculty member at NYU, that I first began to think about the ideas that would become this book. I will be forever grateful for Alyssa Burke's expertise during the years she served as the administrative head of the Program in American Studies. Madala Hilaire combined humor and generosity, making me laugh as she assured me that smooth sailing was ahead. I cannot thank them enough.

My coconspirators from NYU are many, and I thank in particular Alyosha Goldstein, Laura Harris, Richard Kim, Sujani Reddy, Mariel Rose, and Emily

Thuma. Rich Blint, Rebecca Sumner Burgos, Sybil Cooksey, Carlos Ulises Decena, Mireille Miller-Young, and Alison Redick were also invaluable thinking partners. I have appreciated the opportunity to continue to learn from people I first met at NYU who were years ahead of me in the program, such as Davarian Baldwin, Tanya Erzen, Alondra Nelson, Julie Sze, Thuy Linh Tu, and many more. The year I wrote my dissertation proposal was a very lucky one for me. It was then that I met Dayo Folayan Gore, who was finishing her dissertation in history at NYU. Ever since, she has been my most important colleague and friend. Her sharp thinking, kind patience, and great fun have kept me out of trouble and in this game.

A network of scholars has inspired, supported, and challenged me. In particular, I am tremendously grateful for the example and generosity of Jack Halberstam, Regina Kunzel, and Siobhan Somerville. Through visits to the University of Maryland, invitations for me to speak at their institutions, on panels and in the rare breaks of various conferences, and via other exchanges and collaborations I have been inspired by the scholarship and collegiality of Eduardo Contreras, Beth Currans, John D'Emilio, Kirstie Dorr, Roderick Ferguson, Gill Frank, Ruth Wilson Gilmore, Laura Gutiérrez, Yukiko Hanawa, Gillian Harkins, Scott Herring, Lucas Hilderbrand, Colin Johnson, Miranda Joseph, Sara Clarke Kaplan, Roshy Kheshti, Larry La Fountain-Stokes, Ian Lekus, Adela Licona, Martin Manalansan, Joanne Meyerowitz, Nick Mitchell, Kevin Murphy, Tavia Nyong'o, Marcia Ochoa, Jasbir Puar, Jordana Rosenberg, Nayan Shah, Svati Shah, Andrea Smith, Sandra Soto, Dean Spade, Marc Stein, Karen Tongson, and Ara Wilson, and many more (as well as others whom I mention elsewhere). Extra appreciation goes to Mimi Thi Nguyen and Hiram Perez. Three people are owed special mention for their close engagements with this book: Emily Hobson, Kwame Holmes, and Emily Thuma. Their respective, and shared, knowledge about the history of the left, sexual and racial politics of the city, and vexed terms of antiviolence have been invaluable, although, of course, all errors remain my own. I also give thanks for astute research assistance from Aaron Allen, Douglas Ishii, Emerson Brisbon, Abram J. Lewis, Justin Maher, and Mary White.

I was fortunate to have amazing colleagues and students when I taught classes at Barnard College and Hampshire College while finishing my dissertation. Tally Kampen (at Barnard) and Barbara Yngvesson and Margaret Cerullo (at Hampshire) were supportive as I balanced teaching and writing. While I was in western Massachusetts, Kara Lynch and Wilson Valentín-Escobar brought me good politics and conversation. E. B. Lehman magically made a year at the Five College Women's Studies Research Center productive and relaxing. I am very fortunate that Janice Irvine had just become the center's new director; she is now an important friend.

At the University of Maryland, I benefit from the support of many individuals, programs, and other units. The chair of the Department of American Studies, Nancy Struna, has been a stalwart source of support and humor; I am also very happy to work alongside my colleagues John Caughey, Jason Farman, Perla Guerrero, R. Gordon Kelly, Jeffrey McCune, Jan Padios, Sheri Parks, Jo Paoletti, Mary Corbin Sies, Psyche Williams-Forson, and Janelle Wong. Nothing would be possible in the department without the skills and acumen of Julia John and Betsy Yuen. In the LGBT Studies Program, I have benefited from the leadership of Marilee Lindemann and affiliates Martha Nell Smith, Katie King, Luke Jensen, and Jason Rudy. J. V. Sapinoso, assistant director of LGBT Studies, is an ideal colleague. I also thank other close colleagues at the University of Maryland, most especially Hilary Jones, Keguro Macharia, Michele Mason, Randy Ontiveros, Sangeeta Ray, Tara Rodgers, Michelle Rowley, and David Sartorius. Bill Cohen has been a very important (and patient) mentor. I miss seeing Kandice Chuh and Laura Mamo on campus. In addition to those already named, I acknowledge my colleagues in the Department of Women's Studies and those associated with the Consortium on Race, Gender, and Ethnicity: Lynn Bolles, Elsa Barkley Brown, Seung-kyung Kim, Debby Rosenfelt, Ashwini Tambe, Ruth Zambrana, and Bonnie Thornton Dill, dean of the College of Arts and Humanities. The students in American Studies, LGBT Studies, and Women's Studies make it all worthwhile.

I recognize various institutions for the economic resources that made this research possible, from dissertation through book: the Graduate School of Arts and Sciences at New York University for the MacCracken Fellowship, Summer Predoctoral Fellowship, Dean's Dissertation Fellowship, Penfield Award, and travel grants; the Social Science Research Council for the Sexuality Research Dissertation Fellowship, with funds provided by the Ford Foundation; the Phil Zwickler Charitable and Memorial Foundation and the Human Sexuality Collection of the Kroch Library of Cornell University for two Phil Zwickler Memorial Research Grants; the Five College Women's Studies Research Center at Mount Holyoke College for the support of the Research Associateship; the Graduate Research Board and the Consortium on Race, Gender, and Ethnicity for research grants and the office of the Dean of Arts and Humanities, especially Associate Dean Sheri Parks, and the Department of American Studies, all at the University of Maryland, for grants to help cover publication costs; and the Bill and Carol Fox Center for Humanistic Inquiry at Emory University, then directed by Martine Watson Brownley, for a one-year residential fellowship. I also thank Keith Anthony, Amy Erbil, and Colette Barlow at Emory.

The D.C. Queer Studies Consortium has been a source of intellectual debate, fun, and more. The group includes many of my colleagues from Maryland whom I have already mentioned, as well as scholars from across Washington, D.C. I have enjoyed spirited conversations and friendships with Libby Anker, Kristin Bergen, Mandy Berry, Fiona Brideoke, Kate Drabinski, Lázaro Lima, Dana Luciano, Carla Marcantonio, Robert McRuer, Ricardo Ortiz, Craig Willse, and more.

Many thanks go to Ken Wissoker, who has supported this book since before it was one and who was essential to making its final realization possible. I have no doubt that without Ken's prodding, this book would not have been done in the time frame it needed to be. I am also indebted for his selection of two very helpful readers; I can only hope to have done justice to their excellent feedback. Many thanks, too, to Jade Brooks, as well as to all of the Duke University Press team, including Liz Smith, Jeanne Ferris, Heather Hensley, and Katie Courtland.

I have terrific friends who indulge my neuroses, buoy my spirits, and, most important, are inspiring thinkers and makers. Yoruba Richen has long provided astute breakdowns of the personal and the political, and I have eagerly awaited the completion of this book so that we might return to late-night drinks and talk. Renee Gladman gives me perfect words and long walks that promise intimacy even though we are so often far apart. I have learned the most about history, politics, and friendship from Dayo Gore; although she and Arianne Miller now live quite far away, the promise of conversations, cocktails, and card games with them both will always get me through. The first years of graduate school were aided by the smarts and enthusiasm of Julia Bryan-Wilson. I have been lucky to enjoy lengthy talks on Brooklyn stoops with Stephanie Pope; I hope for many more. I will always cherish my memories of conversations and adventures with Kyle Goen, both characterized by his steadfast care. Other invaluable friends in New York include Lucia Leandro Gimeno, Judy Yu, Laurie Prendergast, Leyla Mei, and Amaha Kassa. The best aspects of my life in D.C. are my friends. I would be lost and lonely if it were not for Bill Cohen's sharp wit and kind heart, David Sartorius's camaraderie and cookery, Carla Marcantonio's long walks, and Salvador Vidal-Ortiz's good humor. I have relished and look forward to many more outings with Craig Willse and Dana Luciano, and I always learn from Johonna McCants. My friends at Different Avenues throughout the years—in particular Kelli Dorsey, Darby Hickey, and Skytrinia Berkeley— made me laugh, worry, and feel less unmoored.

The love, support, and intellectual influence of my family—my father, John G. Hanhardt; my mother, Eva B. Hanhardt; and my sister, Lydia B. Hanhardt, brother-in-law, Jeremiah Dyehouse, and their children, Chloe and Asa—are reflected on every page of this book. My mother's vision of a just city provided the ethical base of this project. My father's expansive understanding of cultural politics focused its analytic lens. My sister's no-nonsense sensibility tethered me to the ground where she, Jeremiah, Chloe, and Asa continue to provide me with loving care. I grew up in the New York neighborhoods about which I write. I am deeply grateful to my mother, for taking me to protests in support of public institutions as well as broad-based social movements, and to my father, with whom I spent long hours in book-stores and galleries. It was in these contexts that I first learned the values of that which is unfamiliar and often uncomfortable and the importance of being curious and generous. With them I have walked more city blocks than I could count, learning about people, places, and politics through genuine interest and engagement. My family members are excellent cheerleaders, al-though I am a terrible athlete. Their enthusiasm and endurance are true gifts.

I am so very fortunate that Jane Hageman has shared her love and care with me, not to mention her home, car, and some really great food. Her generosity was exceptional as she housed me during my more-than-annual research visits and invited me along to join her friends for coffee and donuts before I took off for long days at the archive or doing interviews. Her quilts keep me warm in all the places I consider home.

By the time this book is published, it will have been over ten years since I first met Eva Hageman at a political protest against the U.S. bombing of Iraq. Her brilliance and passion have taught and sustained me. It is her analysis of the world from which I most learn, and it is her hand that I most want to hold on protest lines. It is difficult to express how much I admire her insight, wit, determination, and beauty; but it is also she who has taught me that words—of which I am mightily fond—are just that. It is a life of action, of movement and change, with her that I most cherish.

INTRODUCTION

On May 6, 2002, residents, business owners, and politicians staged an anticrime rally called "Take Back Our Streets" in Christopher Park, in New York City's Greenwich Village.[1] The location chosen was symbolic; the park is located at what had been the center of the uprising at the Stonewall Inn bar, the famed riots of June 1969 that have been central to many legacies of lesbian, gay, bisexual, and transgender (LGBT) political organizing.[2] Yet in recent years the memory of "Stonewall" (as the riots are now called) as a long overdue, passionate expression of selfhood often omits the facts that it was a collective challenge to the police and that it was just the latest clash in an ongoing struggle. Furthermore, the gay liberation organizations that arose in the aftermath of the riots believed that protection from the police would depend on their forming coalitions with other social movements, including Black Power, radical feminisms, and Third World decolonization. This was in contrast to the approach adopted by their immediate predecessors, homophile activists who largely advocated for police accountability through liberal reform measures. Consequently, the refusal of Stonewall's participants to collaborate with dominant institutions not only marked a rejection of social assimilation (in which, for example, the adoption of gender norms might promise protection) but was also in defiance of the partnership solutions to urban conflict that had been popular with policymakers in the 1960s, such as community policing and War on Poverty initiatives.

Over thirty years later, the 2002 rally had a very different aim in mind.[3] It was linked to a broad, ad hoc campaign for the enforcement of quality-of-life laws, which target low-level offenses such as noise and loitering and had been the hallmark of former New York mayor Rudolph Giuliani's anticrime policy.[4] Proponents included Residents in Distress (RID; the name was inspired by an insecticide), the Christopher Street Patrol (a neighborhood anticrime group supported by the Guardian Angels), block associations (representing residents and business owners), and officials from the local community board (New York's neighborhood-based governing structure). Supporters claimed that boisterous crowds and sex and drug trades were fomenting a threatening culture of crime and violence in their neighborhood, that part of Greenwich Village also known as the West Village.[5] In meetings, rallies, and media blitzes that would stretch throughout the first decade of the 2000s, residents complained that their neighborhood had been taken over by "the Bloods and the Crips," "the dealers, the hookers, the pimps, the johns,"[6] "vicious drug dealers and hostile transgender prostitutes," and "rowdies,"[7] all of whom constituted "an army of occupation" (fig. intro. 1).[8]

The most public members of the campaign were white, and the areas they cited as needing to be cleaned up were the very same places where people of color—many of whom identify as LGBT—long have socialized.[9] Residents' primary focus were the neighborhood's waterfront piers at the end of the famed Christopher Street, the place of an active, largely black and Latino social scene that had been pushed out of nearby Washington Square Park under resident and police pressure during previous decades.[10] Residents also cited what they considered undesirable activity outside the entrance to the Port Authority Trans-Hudson (PATH) train station, which connects the New Jersey cities of Newark and Jersey City (both of which are significantly black and Latino in population) with lower Manhattan;[11] some residents were also involved in a campaign against the expansion of PATH exits into a designated Stonewall Historic District.[12]

The fact that residents' primary opposition was to LGBT youth and adult transgender women of color was not only coded in the choice of targeted geography. One public resolution explicitly named the problem as "rowdyism resulting from large crowds of young people, mostly lesbian, gay, bisexual, and transgender youth of African-American and Hispanic origin."[13] Although in public venues residents denied that their complaints were "racial," almost all media coverage of the situation—both sympathetic and critical—made it clear that those considered a problem were people of color and that those presumed to be engaged in prostitution were also transgender.[14] Yet residents were also insistent that their efforts were not anti-LGBT. This claim was supported by those who called for the protection of the Stonewall Historic District as well as by those who invoked the history of antigay violence to bolster their fight against undesirable street life. Moreover, resi-

CITY OF NEW YORK
COMMUNITY BOARD NO. 2, MANHATTAN
3 Washington Square Village • New York, New York 10012-1899 • (212) 979-2272 • FAX (212) 254-3102
Greenwich Village • Little Italy • SoHo • NoHo • Hudson Square

Aubrey Lees
Chair

Arthur W. Strickler
District Manager

Carol Yankay
1ᵗ Vice-Chair

Ann Arlen
2ⁿ Vice-Chair

Jeanne Wilcke
Treasurer

Robert Rinaolo
Secretary

Martin Tessler
Assistant Secretary

NOTICE OF
PUBLIC HEARING

TAKE BACK OUR STREETS

Date: Monday, May 6, 2002
Time: 6:00 p.m.
Place: Sheridan Square Park
7ᵗʰ Ave. & Christopher St.

RE: Summer's coming! Fight Back against our
new neighbors; the Bloods and the Crips
plus our old neighbors, the dealers, the
hookers, the pimps, the johns, etc. etc.

Sponsored by the Sixth Precinct
Community Council, Chelsea, Greenwich
Village Chamber of Commerce and
Residence in Distress (RID).

ALL ARE WELCOME TO ATTEND.

Please come and be heard. We need your input. If you are unable to
attend, please submit your comments in writing to the Community
Board #2, Manhattan office, 3 Washington Square Village, Suite 1A,
New York, NY 10012.

Aubrey Lees, Chair   Arthur W. Strickler
Community Board #2, Manhattan   District Manager

Blane Roberts,
Community Board Liaison
Man. Borough President's Office

FIGURE INTRO.1 "Notice of Public Hearing: Take Back Our Streets," City of New York
(COMMUNITY BOARD 2, MANHATTAN, NEW YORK)

dents advocated for the use of strategies that have been promoted by LGBT antiviolence activists since the 1970s, from safe streets patrols and community watch efforts to calls for increased police presence and enhanced criminal penalties—tactics that also parallel shifting approaches to urban crime control during these same years. The result is that the demands of Greenwich Village residents and a mainstream LGBT antiviolence movement can look strikingly alike.

Safe Space asks how this neighborhood-based convergence of anticrime and LGBT rights strategies came to pass, and why it matters. Far from coincidental, these overlapping responses to perceived threats bring into focus an entwined history of LGBT activism, urban development, and U.S. policy responses to poverty and crime. By treating the construction of violence as central to both U.S. LGBT and urban politics, I ask how the ideal of safe space has shaped the transformation of LGBT social movements and the administration of cities where related policies often coalesce.[15] I explore how interpretations of violence and safety have influenced changing concepts of LGBT identity as well as urban policy and social science research on neighborhoods and social deviancy—ranging from War on Poverty programs to quality-of-life laws, and from debates about the so-called culture of poverty to the idea of homophobia. Thus, this book is not a history of gay neighborhoods per se but an urban history of the encounters between *gay* and *neighborhood* in U.S. cities and social movements over the past fifty years.

Stonewall Redux?

On the surface, the challenge championed by Greenwich Village residents at the start of the 2000s appeared to be a return to the conditions that had given rise to Stonewall in the first place. In the late 1960s, Christopher Park had been a hangout for youths—many queer and some of color—who used drugs, hustled, and found themselves in trouble with the law. Unlike many other Greenwich Village gay bars, Stonewall opened its doors—if only by a crack—to those active in street economies, as it also did to a steady if small number of the gender nonconforming.[16] These groups stood outside a normative gay culture—often standing outside its literal doors—and they were frequently the recipients of Greenwich Village residents' ire.[17] Right after Stonewall, many gay men and lesbians disassociated themselves from the riots, and reform-oriented organizations like the homophile Mattachine Society beseeched fellow "homosexuals" to "maintain peaceful and quiet conduct on the streets of the Village."[18] It was within this context that Stonewall provided the impetus for the founding of a radical organization, the Gay Liberation Front, which sought to forge gay politics within a multi-issue left.[19]

Similarly, in the Greenwich Village of the early twenty-first century, many white, middle-class lesbian and gay residents remained silent or absent during community meetings or supported organizations like RID and the Christopher Street Patrol. No major LGBT groups came out on behalf of those targeted, although residents' efforts were countered by the birth of a radical queer youth of color organization, Fabulous Independent Educated Radicals for Community Empowerment (FIERCE), which became a loud and unrelenting foe. The neighborhood was still seen by many to be a magnet for queer life, but during the day children's strollers had become more visible than hustlers, and Two Potato—once a gay bar with a significant black and drag scene—would become Bar Nocetti, owned by and catering to those native West Villagers who were a part of the Italian community that has long been another dominant aspect of the neighborhood's identity.[20]

But these two moments are also very different, for reasons that are both obvious and counterintuitive. First, in the 1960s, antisodomy laws still existed in many states, including New York, and crossed racial and class lines—in their letter, if not in their uneven enforcement; in addition, laws against lewdness, vagrancy, solicitation, and cross-dressing were routinely used to target a wide range of sexual and gender nonnormative people.[21] Thus, an imagined solidarity existed between many of those arrested at the Stonewall Inn.[22] Although in its early years the homophile movement had pursued some high-profile campaigns against the entrapment of homosexuals using such charges, gay men and lesbians were still considered a criminal class, and homophile efforts were dedicated to distinguishing them from others in that category.[23]

In the years following, things changed. Decades of activism produced innumerable organizations and agencies to deal with "homophobia"—whether expressed by police misconduct, antigay violence, or even unneighborly hostility. Laws against private, consensual sodomy were eliminated as a general criminal category, and LGBT activists largely succeeded in dissociating the generic terms of homosexuality—and, to a lesser degree, transsexuality—from the broad category of the criminal. The enforcement of laws against lewdness, loitering, and solicitation continued to be used against LGBT people, but most often they were applied to those also targeted along other lines—significantly, race and class but also age, gender expression, and sexual subculture.[24] Insofar as these laws disproportionately affected LGBT youth, low-income people, and people of color, they were not necessarily still seen years later as shared concerns of white, middle-class, gender normative gay residents. Thus, in the early 2000s there were more organizations than ever prepared to respond to an anti-LGBT situation in an environment that did not appear to many to be anti-LGBT.

Second, during the late 1960s, solutions to the problems of so-called juvenile delinquency were still at least somewhat influenced by the analysis of poverty put forth by Richard Cloward and Lloyd Ohlin's differential opportunity theory, which was the basis of the 1961 Juvenile Delinquency and Youth Offenses Control Act. The theory argued for structural rather than individual solutions and called for increasing institutional opportunities for low-income youth.[25] It was first put into practice in the organization Mobilization for Youth, which was based in New York's Lower East Side, not far from Greenwich Village. The organization provided the model for the Community Action Program that was part of President Lyndon B. Johnson's War on Poverty. The program exemplified the ongoing call for "community control" that was central to the War on Poverty; this ideal also led the charge for the development of neighborhood-based community boards in New York City during the mid-1960s.[26]

Although by the end of the decade War on Poverty programs were under attack, and, in many cases, critiques of unequal social and economic structure were cast as indictments of unhealthy kinship and intimate relations (and used to uphold the normative valuation of liberal citizenship), the Stonewall-era response to youth and crime stands in contrast to the conservative rational choice approach that has supported the "zero tolerance" youth policing and education policies popular since the 1990s.[27] Furthermore, the broad influence of ideologies based in the primacy of the free market have worked in neighborhoods with rising rents to further secure the use of liberal institutions like community boards as mechanisms to protect property rights. As a result, community board members in Greenwich Village in the early 2000s often used the terms of community in order to restrict membership in the neighborhood. In addition, programs that serve LGBT youth have been unevenly developed across race and class lines in school districts and neighborhoods and are often concentrated in white, middle- and upper-income areas like Greenwich Village.[28] Thus, although youth who socialize on the streets of Greenwich Village have always been racially and economically mixed, by the last decades of the twentieth century the neighborhood was serving a crucial function for young people from areas without LGBT services from across the New York City region. The fact that this neighborhood was the ground zero for new draconian policing strategies—for example, quality-of-life policing in the city was initiated in Greenwich Village—must be understood as part of this broader cultural and economic geography.

Third, after Stonewall, Greenwich Village's reputation as a gay enclave grew, despite the fact that its queer history long preceded the riots.[29] By the end of the 1970s, the area's gay identity was not only a product of its gay residents and nightlife denizens, but also of its commerce, as more gay-owned and gay-oriented businesses were established there. Since then, Greenwich Village's gay identity has lasted despite the fact that many gay businesses have not, pushed out since the 1990s by rising rents and antisex zoning restrictions.[30] In 2007 the *New York Times* declared on its front page that gay neighborhoods were "passé" and had, in places like San Francisco's Castro District, "gone from a gay-ghetto mentality to a family mentality."[31] Nonetheless, for many of these neighborhoods, their gay reputations have been durable enough to continue to attract local visitors and tourists. New York

City's largest LGBT community center is based in Greenwich Village, and when the city's tourism marketing agency launched the international Rainbow Pilgrimage campaign centered on the fortieth anniversary of Stonewall, its website heavily featured Greenwich Village spots.[32]

As a result, although the neighborhood's gay identity continues in some ways to decline and many (although not all) of the residents who spoke up against LGBT youth in recent years were not publicly identified as gay, many observers saw the actions of the local community board as representing the viewpoint of a gay neighborhood.[33] Thus, regardless of the actual identities of the key actors, the dominant identity of the neighborhood supported both a broad assumption that a residents-based campaign against LGBT youth and transgender adult women of color was not anti-LGBT as well as a counteractivist argument that residents' efforts fundamentally represented white, middle-class, lesbian and gay interests that collude with those of the police.[34] The fact that residents deployed the same tactics as LGBT antiviolence activists—and often declared their actions to be in the name of gay protection—further cemented the latter association. It is this dualism—in which LGBT politics and property politics can be so indistinguishable—that outlines the history between the 1960s and the contemporary moment that I tell here.

Although the cross-temporal juxtaposition of the growth of radical liberation movements and the entrenchment of rearguard actions on behalf of property owners in Greenwich Village does not tell the whole story behind the politics of sexual identity, violence, and neighborhood, it does point to a significant overlap. The call for safe streets has been a rallying cry of social minorities and property owners in the eras of postwar urban decline and neoliberal development in the United States. In the early twenty-first century, this call became louder as national protection entered the center of U.S. public debate. The increased attention paid to security has revealed the disparate understandings of threat held by those considered representative of and marginal to the national body politic. This disjunction points to the need for deeper knowledge about violence and the quest for safety within local communities and contemporary social movements.

Whether to prevent crime, allay political uprisings, or assert the right to equal mobility, the fight against urban violence has been waged by the state and the disenfranchised alike—crossing lines of race, class, gender, and sexual identity—and has inspired much urban research since the tumult of the 1960s.[35] Scholars have focused on the conditions leading to and following the riots of the 1960s: some frame the problem of violence in terms of police repression and the conditions of racism and poverty; others cast the city as the site of violent crime with, since the 1970s in particular, women, out-of-towners, and a generalized white, middle-class populace as its victims.[36] Studies on formal LGBT efforts to combat violence have been few. Historians have discussed the informal ways in which LGBT communities have fought back against physical threat as well as the legacy of homophile and gay liberation opposition to zealous policing, but the latter has been in the frame of entrapment more than violence, and there has been little coverage of the response to violence since.[37] Sociologists have given some attention to the official LGBT antiviolence movement begun in the 1980s and its advocacy of laws against hate crimes (crimes motivated by bias), and psychologists' studies of the rates, causes, and impacts of violence have supported policy efforts to name and address the problem of anti-LGBT violence.[38] Yet this empirical research is more likely to assess the effectiveness of advocacy than the ideologies of activism, and it almost never considers the broad context of the urban environment in which most of these movements have been staged.[39] Queer theory has provided a key framework for understanding how violence or the claim of injury has structured left and queer politics. Nonetheless, the majority of this scholarship is based on readings of narrative or visual representation, the law, and normative political claims.[40] Although this approach has been invaluable, there is less work that provides a kind of "thick description" of how grassroots and national movements construct the agents and victims of the violence that they hope to prevent and the spaces that they aim to protect.[41]

An analysis of the goal of LGBT safety in the city is important to understanding not only the transformation of LGBT politics since the 1960s, but also the development and management of space at various scales during the decline of a certain model of liberalism in the United States.[42] Since the late 1960s, the state-based policies of social welfare and economic regulation that characterized postwar liberalism have been targeted by the ideals (if not always the practice) of a pure free market championed by neoliberalism.[43] One feature was the continued decimation of and then selective reinvestment in central cities, a process that has been repeated over the years.[44] Recurrent, too, in this cycle has been the declaration by policymakers and political pundits that (white) gay populations might hold the key for the rejuvenation of struggling metropolitan areas. In the 1970s, gay men were extolled for saving declining cities as vanguard members of the vaunted back-to-the-city movement; in the late 1990s and early 2000s, gay populations were invoked as enticements for the creative class of workers to settle in, and thus revitalize, restructured urban regions.[45] In each example, gay men (and, to a lesser degree, lesbians) are seen as the arbiters of risk, their vulnerability to violence—or their protected presence—a measure of an urban region's vitality.[46] Thus, central to this history is the assessment of risk—the risk of violence associated with gay vulnerability that calls for crime control, as well as the risk of lost profit associated with real estate speculation—and how it shapes the conditions of possibility for normative gay community belonging and the land market.

Ultimately, this book argues that in mooring a dominant understanding of sexual identity to place, the promotion and protection of gay neighborhoods have reinforced the race and class stratification of postwar urban space. As I show, this has been enabled by the simultaneously flexible and fixed language of threat, in which violence is imagined as the central risk—and thus the defining feature—of gay visibility: the key term of mainstream LGBT politics since the 1970s. It is therefore impossible to understand LGBT political history outside of the social and spatial restructuring of U.S. cities during this time.[47] Nor can one fully understand changing spatial development patterns apart from LGBT politics, especially as white gay men continue to be invoked as arbiters of quality in urban life. Finally, these dynamics are not restricted to cities or to the United States, as they speak to both the global processes and the local effects of uneven development alongside the travels of U.S.-centered models of LGBT identity and social movements.

But this book is not only a story of the vexed legacies of postwar liberal policy and triumph of neoliberal ideology; it is also an analysis of organizations that struggled with and against each of those in imagining LGBT and queer futures in all sorts of places. Although I assert that mainstream LGBT political discourse has substantively transformed the category of anti-LGBT violence from the social to the criminological, and that this shift was grounded in privatized claims to neighborhood, the process was neither foretold nor total. Activists debated different definitions of violence and staged their critiques in varied contexts—in cooperation with civil rights leaders and in solidarity with revolutionary nationalists, alongside feminists as well as crime victims, through public agencies and in radical collectives, in the name of state-based redistribution and for the end of the U.S. nation-state. Although my coverage is far from complete, I signal the existence of a wide mix of LGBT and queer-identified urban activist responses to the pointed theme of violence.

Sex and the City

Recent scholarship in queer studies has rightly set the city to the side, underscoring that the central place afforded to a privileged urbanity in dominant lesbian and gay cultures and their historiography has created, to use

Judith Halberstam's term, a "metronormative" ideal that is applied to all other places not at equal scale.[48] Scott Herring specifies the operations of metronormativity as based in "the narratological, the racial, the socio-economic, the temporal, the epistemological, and the aesthetic" and argues that it "facilitates the ongoing commodification, corporatization, and de-politicization of U.S.-based queer cultures."[49] Depoliticization might be interpreted as a rather precise form of politics—one that, in this case, values an exclusive cosmopolitanism or consumer power.[50] In addition, as Herring agrees, those excluded from—or critical of—the metronormative promise often live well within city lines. A critical analysis of a politics of the city not only goes out of town; it also asks to whom the city belongs.

The narrow dominance afforded to the city (and to only certain cities, at that) is also reflected by the fact that many contemporary national LGBT organizations trace their roots to groups or campaigns founded in two U.S. urban centers—New York and San Francisco—in the 1970s and 1980s. This is particularly so in the case of violence: in the 1970s, the prevailing story may have held that the so-called gay ghetto provided salvation from an inhospitable small town and alienating suburb, but to many this also made it a clear target. Lesbian and gay activists took on the problem of street violence and developed theories and strategies that shaped the national approaches still in use today. This line of influence has been sustained even as some of the most well-publicized cases of anti-LGBT violence in recent years have taken place in small cities situated in more rural and midcontinent regions, such as the murders of Brandon Teena in Humboldt, Nebraska, in 1993 and of Matthew Shepard in Laramie, Wyoming, in 1998.[51] In many ways, these events affirmed the dominant movement's claims of coastal urban refuge while confounding its reliance on models of protection based in threats imagined to lurk in East and West Coast central cities.[52] Although this might be explained as the very contradiction of the metronormative, the facts that Shepard and Teena were white, their killers' hatred of them explained as products of self-perpetuating cultures of poverty, and their deaths used to advocate for the passage of hate crime laws and the application of the death penalty—all features of the history that I tell here—demonstrate that these issues are less related to urban form per se than to other modes of differentiation.[53] Nonetheless, the stubborn focus on the urban in early national movement building has meant that a variety of local responses to anti-LGBT violence—which have their own, albeit less institutionalized, histories—often have had to contend with models forged far from their social worlds.[54] These activist solutions are sometimes perpendicular, rather than parallel, to the story I tell here.[55]

Today many national activist visions look not only metronormative but also homonormative—Lisa Duggan's term for gay politics rooted in the ideal of privatization—insofar as they focus on individual rights, ask the state to adjudicate, and maintain faith in the equalizing power of the free market.[56] This is the case despite the fact that many of the first activists to challenge violence did so as part of movements in the late 1960s and 1970s that highlighted systemic inequality. Moreover, prior to that period, homophile organizations did not strategize to address individual violence as much as they responded to police abuse and broad anti–lesbian and gay sentiment. And among sexual and gender outsiders not in organizations, the reaction to one-on-one street violence was often more informal, with a direct return of violence such as that described by Elizabeth Lapovsky Kennedy and Madeline Davis in their study of working-class lesbians in Buffalo, New York, in the 1930s through 1960s; or by Susan Stryker about trans women at San Francisco's Compton's Cafeteria in the mid-1960s.[57] In other words, even as a dominant, national movement has sought privatization through the homogenization of people and state- and market-based solutions, a wide mix of individuals inside and outside the city have pursued safety through strategies of discretion, individual self-protection, and varied, often unofficial group measures.[58]

This book argues for the centrality of the city, not as a natural or preferred place for homosexuality or for LGBT identities, but as a critical nexus for analyzing how politics, policy, and property have indelibly shaped LGBT social movements, in particular in response to violence. And it also contends the reverse: the defining function of violence within LGBT politics has influenced the life of U.S. cities.

There is a rich archive to draw on here. Since at least the nineteenth century, cultural production, academic research, and social policy in the West have associated sexual nonnormativity with the urban vice and alienation assumed to be negative by-products of industrialization. Julie Abraham describes Charles Baudelaire's *lesbiennes* and *flâneurs* in the streets of nineteenth-century Paris and Friedrich Engels's fear that industrialization's factories might turn women into prostitutes (even as he defended cities themselves).[59] In his famed essay "Capitalism and Gay Identity," John D'Emilio argues that it was the growth of the industrial city that produced the conditions of possibility for homosexual identities and, later, gay and lesbian communities.[60] And artists, scholars, and politicians have continued to hold up the vice-ridden city as the preeminent site of sexual perversion. This characterization has not only been used to discipline; the traction of the urban-homosexuality connection was also used to forge a sense of community. George Chauncey writes: "The men who built New York's gay world at the turn of the century and those who sought to suppress it shared the conviction that it was a distinctly urban phenomenon."[61]

Yet homosexuality is not the only marker of identity presumed to be in a relationship of equivalence with the city, especially in the United States since the late nineteenth and early twentieth century. *Black* and *urban* are often treated as interchangeable adjectives, based on a correlation that has been most strongly asserted in periods of urban growth (such as the Great Migration); contraction (such as postwar urban renewal and suburbanization); and crisis (such as the uprisings of the 1960s). As Hazel Carby, Roderick Ferguson, Kevin Mumford, and Marlon Ross have shown, the enterprises of urban sociology and progressive charity emerged in part by interlocking sexual, racial, and gender regulation in efforts to control the forces of social disorganization in the city.[62] Reform and research took family and neighborhood as key sites of intervention for a variety of supposed deviancies, and racial hierarchies were often asserted through sexual discourses of normalization. As Ferguson notes, these associations also drove professionalized approaches to mapping the city: "While sociology established an epistemological proximity to blackness and homosexuality, vice districts helped to render them as materially proximate."[63] Siobhan Somerville charts the entwined and contradictory discourses of racial and sexual deviance that were present not only in social research and the law at the start of this period, but also in diverse forms of cultural production, such as literature and film.[64] Unsurprisingly, then, sites of leisure were among the most studied and targeted; but, as Shane Vogel demonstrates in his look at the cabarets of the Harlem Renaissance, they were also places in which performances that refused the paired imperatives of respectability and knowability were, quite literally, staged.[65]

From the late nineteenth century onward, the U.S. city also was a preeminent site for the regulation of other racialized migrant populations, and the impoverished neighborhoods to which they were confined were often described by those in power as spatial expressions of residents' "true nature." Nayan Shah shows how places like San Francisco's Chinatown were treated by municipal managers as physical manifestations of the "perversions" of Chinese immigrant men and women—whose domestic patterns were, in part, shaped by the restrictions mandated by the 1875 Page Law and 1882 Chinese Exclusion Act.[66] And starting in 1952, the Urban Indian Relocation Program of the Bureau of Indian Affairs moved Native Americans into urban centers just as the white middle class was taking flight to the suburbs.[67] Arriving in cities like Chicago and Los Angeles with limited economic opportunities, many Native people would soon be living near to or in—and then increasingly associated with—areas described as skid rows. These are but two of numerous examples of how racial segregation and economic stratification have been charted as biological and cultural phenomena.[68]

Although the correlation between homosexuality and vice has appeared in many contexts, most organized activism on behalf of lesbians and gay men has been dedicated to tearing this association apart. After World War II, homophile activists slowly—yet inconsistently—moved to distinguish homosexuality from other forms of social deviancy, especially those associated with the racialized poverty of the city. By the 1970s, in the midst of a much-hyped crime crisis, activist efforts to assert that lesbians and gay men were victims rather than perpetrators of crime widened the distance. Although this book argues that the process of distinguishing between gay identity and racialized ideas of urban disorder must be understood in the context of the restructuring of central cities and the expansion of the penal state, it also outlines this dynamic as a product of activist engagement with federal policy. As Margot Canaday demonstrates, it was during the World War II era that the federal government began to constitute homosexuals as an explicit category to be regulated in immigration, welfare, and military policy. Prior to that point, homosexuality had been policed by the state alongside other social problems such as "poverty, disorder, violence, or crime."[69] In this book, I trace how the disaggregation of homosexuality from other social problems was pursued by activists eager to create a new political identity in similarly separate terms—a strategy adopted, for example, by early homophile organizers who directed their actions both against and in collaboration with federal powers. Furthermore, the emergence of homosexuality as an autonomous regulatory category did not mean that others marked deviant, such as the racialized poor, were no longer criminalized and subject to policing. Nonetheless, these *other* outsiders were not uniformly considered a part of a new social movement that would largely be cast in terms of identity, respectability, and rights—rather than the refusal of normalization that might be in affinity with what Cathy Cohen describes as "deviance as resistance."[70]

Thus *Safe Space* looks to the city not only because of its connection to the now dominant LGBT movement it studies, but also because of whom this movement has defined itself against. When the antigay-marriage Proposition 8 passed in California in November 2008, many white gay commentators suggested that it was African Americans' fault. The assumption that people of color of all economic classes are more *homophobic* than whites has been durable within mainstream LGBT politics—a view often held across racial lines—and this book argues that these ideas are linked to how LGBT organizations imagined their relationship to low-income people of color within urban centers in the early years of the consolidation of the LGBT rights movement.[71] Furthermore, this association was sutured in place by the central role of social science research in postwar liberal politics, which provided an explanation—and a mode of quantification—for inequality in cultural pathology and damaged psychology and thus outlined its terms of proper social and personal remediation. The result today is that even as organizations and scholarship have expanded to include the experiences of LGBT and queer people of color in the United States and around the world, the idea that poverty and/or nonwhiteness is at the crux of homophobia and thus outside of idealized LGBT identities has been central to mainstream LGBT political discourse.[72]

The implications of this cultural map for homophobia within antiviolence politics cannot be overstated; two of the primary activist solutions to anti-LGBT violence since the 1970s—the establishment of protected gay territories and the identification of anti-LGBT violence as a designated criminal category—must be paired with two of global capital's own "spatial fixes": gentrification and mass imprisonment.[73] These are processes that have involved the containment and exclusion of the racialized poor: in neighborhoods marked for cycles of disinvestment and then selective reinvestment, and, as Ruth Wilson Gilmore has shown, in prisons built to absorb surpluses of labor, land, and capital.[74] By the 1980s anti-LGBT violence had become most recognizable as hate crimes, and the risk of anti-LGBT violence was increasingly understood as the risk of being a crime victim. In gentrifying neighborhoods in which the speculative risk of investment was lessened by the elimination of those deemed criminal, the fight against anti-LGBT violence might achieve such an effect. As the dynamics of criminalization are not reducible to economic structure alone, those indicted by mainstream homophobia discourse constitute a simultaneously broad and precise group that accommodates shifting dynamics of racialization. Furthermore, spatial-temporal fixes operate as part of uneven development on a local and a global scale. Thus, although laws against hate crimes emerged in the context of the primacy of antiblackness within devalued U.S. central cities, they also have become a part of efforts to outline as a threat racialized migrant and religious groups in multiple spatial contexts across the globe.[75]

This is not to say that anti-LGBT violence is not a problem, nor is it to downplay the effects of violence, especially among those who are left out of dominant LGBT politics. The violence of poverty and white supremacy carry a brutal force for those who also stand outside heterosexuality or gender conformity, and the very acts of consolidating and parsing identities can constitute a kind of epistemic injury. Furthermore, I do not mean to suggest a mere reversal: that low-income or of color communities are never homophobic, or that LGBT organizations should not fight various forms of anti-LGBT violence. What I hope to stress, instead, is that the history of criminalization and spatial development must be considered as part of the equation. This is because as the category of what constitutes a crime has grown to become more inclusive, it has also condensed what counts as violence so that those things that are not legible within juridical modes are not acknowledged at all.

Thus, another key piece of this book is to analyze the role empirical evidence has played in legitimizing injury. One of the antiviolence movement's most significant contributions was the formalization of independent and U.S. Department of Justice mechanisms for reporting hate crimes. These annual reports both replace and supplement narrative understandings of violence. The effect is to narrow the field of focus through a figuration of all that it hopes to make "visible"; as Mary Poovey writes of statistical representation, "it . . . both limits what it will depict and necessarily produces an uncontrollable excess."[76] The consequences I explore include the ways in which the social science of cause and effect can transform the field of radical politics into a rubric for social service delivery. Furthermore, in a liberal analytic that sees group inequality to be based on an enumeration of individual injuries, key terms of distinction—such as between individual self-help and group self-determination—become increasingly blurred.[77] This book narrates the history of LGBT liberalism as one fundamentally indebted, then, to the elaboration of the social sciences.

A Tale of Two Cities

My critique of empiricism follows José Esteban Muñoz's call for a "utopian hermeneutics" as I reach across time and geography to mark the past in the present, and to find the future there as well.[78] As a result, this book is not a singular, progressive history of the formal LGBT antiviolence movement founded in the early 1980s, nor is it a comparative urban study. Rather, the book sketches a light and jagged line for analyzing LGBT activism against violence as framed by questions of neighborhood and crime. Through case studies, I examine campaigns against violence since the 1960s—the years in which organized lesbian and gay activism against the police began to gather broad, public momentum—and outline their ideological and organizational links and breaks. I highlight moments in which violence functioned as the principal term of organizing, as well as when it was used as shorthand for other concerns. In addition, I focus on aspects of the formal LGBT antiviolence movement that have rarely been included in the secondary literature, such as the influence of small, grassroots activist groups as well as related forms of urban crime control and economic policy. Although I ultimately trace the emergence of a mainstream LGBT movement, I set it within a complicated history of political developments that imagined a variety of solutions to the problem of violence. This includes homophile activists who considered poverty and state violence as important points of intervention. I also look at organizations from the late 1970s and early 1980s that inverted the terms of antiviolence organizing by critiquing calls for gay territory and refusing the promises of police protection. Often centered in people of color and lesbian feminist collectives, these efforts developed across the country and pursued goals outside the visibility mandate. Finally, I consider contemporary groups that draw on the legacy of antiracist, multi-issue organizing and that maintain a troubled relationship to the goal of inclusion. As much of the scholarship on LGBT movements has emphasized visibility, coalitional groups or those with other goals have received less attention. Indeed, an unintended development of the literature on homonormativity is the overshadowing of long-standing challengers to homonormative political visions. Thus, although its full scope is beyond the reach of this book, I gesture toward a genealogy for activism against violence that has sought strategies outside of state protection and property and that has been forged in small collectives, often outside my featured cities.

That noted, the book *is* focused on New York and San Francisco, the two cities most key to the career of mainstream U.S. LGBT antiviolence organizing. Although Los Angeles has played an equally significant role in LGBT activist history as the other two cities, it was not as central to the antiviolence movement's origins and subsequent national consolidation. This is due, in part, to the status of San Francisco and New York as pedestrian-oriented cities with strong community responses to street violence. In neighborhoods across New York and the San Francisco Bay Area, 1960s social movements were bound up with local solutions to violence and crime.[79] Activists and residents alike responded to the call of President Johnson's Great Society, hoping that the promise of militancy might be realized alongside local liberal reform. It is interesting, then, that it was during this period that some of the earliest sustained LGBT activist efforts to challenge violence in designated urban areas began. Other cities that shared San Francisco's and New York's dense development, neighborhood campaigns, and active LGBT politics—such as Chicago and Philadelphia—did not make as early a mark on the national antiviolence movement.[80] This is not to say that responses to violence, both formal and informal, did not flourish in these and other cities, small towns, and rural regions. Rather, it is to highlight the fact that the formal movement was initiated in the cities that would continue to be so centered in LGBT political activism and history. To this day, New York's and San Francisco's antiviolence projects are among the largest and most developed, and the National Coalition of Anti-Violence Programs shares an office with the New York Anti-Violence Project.[81]

There are many risks to my approach. First, it keeps the field of what constitutes politics narrow, excluding a range of activities that do not announce themselves as LGBT activism. This book, for example, does not analyze the broad range of cultural productions that radically rearticulate the political sphere.[82] It also does not include activism that advocated for sexual justice without ever naming LGBT subjects.[83] It thus accepts the limited terms of social movements, even as it does so to gesture toward and even highlight other interpretations. In many ways this tack can affirm that which the dominant approach has already affirmed: to tell a story about the mainstream and its critics is to leave the former in the center.[84] These are some of the dynamics Karen Tongson describes through which the literature of LGBT studies creates the very parameters by which it recognizes the queer subject in space. Tongson points to the narrow dominance of New York and San Francisco in LGBT history, and she shows how easily a description of a given city's particular features can slip into a naturalization of that city's supposed "cultural style" and its "quality of queer life" as "a prototype for the exemplary queer."[85] This book addresses this issue by considering the antiviolence movement as a locus for the institutionalization of a "special character" of gay politics—which I dub militant gay liberalism—that found particular momentum in the 1970s around the question of violence in the gay enclaves of New York and San Francisco.[86]

Tongson's critique highlights the limitations not only of a mainstream lesbian and gay politics but also of a queer antinormativity that figures itself in opposition to the *other* of the suburbs. Pointing to suburbs as not only homogeneous spaces of white wealth but also as home to working- and middle-class people of color, Tongson questions the neat divisions made between that which is supposedly critical versus the allegedly complicit, between the fashionable and the out of it. Although not the focus of this book, Tongson's observation here is crucial, given that the waves of gentrification in U.S. cities since the 1970s have been in part responsible for the flip (often via the "flipping" of real estate) in land values between urban core and periphery. Cities like San Francisco and Washington, D.C., for example, are small seas of speculative growth marked by pockets of intense poverty, both of which are defined along racial lines. Inner suburban rings have become the sites of capital flight and the places where poor and working- and middle-class people, both of color and white—and inclusive of LGBT people—increasingly may be found.[87] (In New York, the core of Manhattan and near parts of Queens and Brooklyn are contrasted to the outer boroughs, which also function somewhat like close suburbs.) These are also the places where strip bars, prostitution and drug houses, adult bookstores, and gambling clubs are increasingly located. Thus the investment in a hip queer urbanity must be seen as a rejection both of purportedly earnest and unfashionable suburbanites and of those other queer subjects that tend to be deemed *risks* for capital investment and *at risk*, in need of social intervention.[88] In these cases, the race and class markers associated with the city are shown to be less about urban form than about patterns of racial segregation and capital investment that prescribe who lives where; this is in part why the word *ghetto* is now used as often as a free-floating, derogatory term for a racialized class position as it is for a race- and class-bounded urban area.

As a national political agenda item, antiviolence activism has not been primarily associated with neighborhood history or spatial development regimes. Rather, since the 1980s, the LGBT movement has combated violence by demanding the inclusion first of sexual orientation and later of gender identity as protected categories under local and federal statutes against hate crimes. My research considers the history of cities alongside the move to legislate violence and, in doing so, argues for a link that is rarely acknowledged. Here I hope to demonstrate that the connection between neighborhood transformation and antiviolence ideologies is both conceptual and organizational. Conceptually, I show that urban politics since the 1960s has hinged on the operation of violence as an individualized threat that then justifies calls for forms of state violence, such as criminalization and privatization. Thus, certain lesbians and gay men, as they move out of the category of criminal and turn to the language and strategies of state protection (in the call for rights or responsive policing) necessarily play a key role in this urban transformation. These links between neighborhood and antiviolence activity have also been demonstrated on the level of the activist organization: the earliest movers and shakers of the formal antiviolence movement learned from the examples of safe streets patrols in the so-called gay ghettos of New York and San Francisco in the 1970s.[89] Founded in opposition to homophile activists who had followed a more quietist approach to piecemeal state reformism, as well as to gay liberationists who refused a gay-only focus, these efforts inaugurated a shift from multi-issue organizing against state abuse to a vigilant concern with individualized threats found on the streets. The fact that this fear and strategy continued to circulate in gay enclaves like New York's Greenwich Village and San Francisco's Castro demonstrates the central role violence has played in defining neighborhood as one of the most prized expressions of LGBT community.[90] In unraveling this history, this book asks some of the less common questions put to these movements: How is violence assessed? What counts as safety? Who is part of the LGBT community? And in what social collectives and physical spaces does belonging bring security?

The book is structured to engage key moments in LGBT activist history without drawing a straight or progressive line between them (both puns intended). It also brings together a range of literatures, including the history of U.S. LGBT activism, postwar cities, and left/liberal social movements; the sociology of urban development and crime; critical debates about race, capital, and space; and queer theoretical takes on identity, normativity, and political cultures. This approach manifests the benefits and limits of a mode of scholarship that leads with questions and seeks answers across disciplines. My hope is that a wide variety of readers might find themselves in conversation with me, although I invariably do not do justice to the full breadth of scholarship on each topic or from a given field. My goal, instead, is to forge connections between areas of study and to elaborate what emerges from those intersections. Thus, rather than provide an introduction to the book with an overarching framework for any one or all of these contexts, I open each chapter with a review of the most relevant background needed for the reader to understand its case studies. Nonetheless, the book's key arguments are cumulative, so although each chapter stands alone, it refers to the histories and analyses outlined by the previous ones.

It is also important to note that insofar as I tell and dislodge a story of homonormativity, this book is in many ways a gesture of recovery, itself a visibility claim made legible by historical narrative in particular. Indeed, that is the structure that organizes and propels this book; one of the main contributions I offer is a historical, social movement–centered analysis of questions that are often taken up by more literary-critical queer studies scholarship. But should you make it through to the end of this book you will find yourself in another register of academic ordering, one that tries to address the moment in which it is written. As I describe later in this introduction, the book's research began near the point at which it ends, and thus it constitutes not only improper history but, I hope, a push back at social movements' singular end-driven impulses.[91] Along the way, I strive to make the road bumpy, refusing stories of constant improvement as well as those of determined demise: claims that LGBT or queer activism has gotten more inclusive or more exclusive, less radical than ever or less strategic than it could have been. I try to paint a picture that is at once messier and more in focus, not only so that I may mix my metaphors and my methods, but also so that I might ask what has changed, what has remained the same, and why we might care.[92]

My first chapter features two campaigns from the mid- to late 1960s that included the leading participation of homophile activists in San Francisco's Central City. In the first, homophile activists collaborated with other social reformers to demand that the neighborhood be designated a target area under the Community Action Program of the Johnson administration's War on Poverty. They did so in part by asserting that one part of the Central City—the Tenderloin—was a "white ghetto" of "prostitutes," "transsexuals," "hotel loners," and "homosexuals" who faced the same problems as did people in low-income areas where people of color were the majority. In the second case study, homophile activists were among those who banded together to found Citizen's Alert, one of the nation's first citywide, homosexual-inclusive police watchdog organizations. In this chapter I show how the mid-1960s San Francisco fight against poverty and state violence provided an opportunity for white homophile activists to participate in forms of cross-identity coalition at the same time as they leaned on a limited analogy between the social regulation of (white) sexual "outcasts" and people of color. In particular, I examine how the focus on psychology central to the legacy of postwar racial liberalism facilitated these connections and provided the groundwork for a model of gay liberalism that would prove lasting in the decades to come. The chapter also considers the activities of a small radical youth organization, Vanguard, which both inverted and replicated many of the terms of homophile activism.

Because none of these coalitions were exclusively focused on homosexuals and they took place during the years that the homophile movement has been described as fading, they have received little attention until recently.[93] Moreover, the combination of social justice theology, Saul Alinsky–style community organizing, countercultural expressions, and varying degrees of state-sponsored uplift delegates these efforts to an indeterminate, if also familiar, place in 1960s left/liberal politics. This is especially the case since the key players did not abide by many of the standard definitions of *radical* and *conservative*, collaborating with activists who called for the end of state institutions at the same time as they forged state-participatory solutions, or advocating assimilation while assailing cultural norms. To be sure, these seeming oppositions were a product of the conflicted promises posed by the War on Poverty's emphasis on community participation. They also reflected many of the debates that marked the history of the civil rights movement, which Central City activists held as a model. Ultimately, I argue that these dynamics demonstrate the contradiction involved in consolidating gay identity while gaining recognition from a federal antipoverty program; a process that unhooked, even as it depended on, the links between homosexuality, transsexuality, and other categories of deviancy associated with urban poverty as well as the shared experience of state violence among a variety of marginalized city dwellers.

In contrast to the homophile drive for state recognition, gay liberationists at the end of the 1960s refused to accept what they saw as the placating efforts of urban social policy, despite a shared conviction that violence was linked to unchecked police power. Early gay liberation was closely linked to the New Left and, in general, stood in solidarity with anti-imperialist, revolutionary nationalist, and radical indigenous activisms. These political movements tended to focus on a critique of state violence and to support self-determination and place claims. Gay liberationists extended this stance through an interpretation of violence as that both practiced and sanctioned by the state, and they trumpeted the reclamation of gay neighborhoods from Mafia and police control. But as this was increasingly conjoined by a call to see gay men and lesbians as on the side of the law rather than as criminals, individual violence remained an amorphous category, as did the potential locales (urban and rural) for new gay territories. Chapter 2 opens with a discussion of the shifting definitions of and approaches to violence held by gay liberationists, and it shows how, in particular, analogies between race and sexuality were used to theorize the problem of violence and to stake land claims.

As the 1970s continued, lesbian and gay organizations multiplied, as did divisions between them. Activists debated core ideological issues, including multi-issue versus gay-centered approaches, the place of communist and socialist visions, and the role of race and gender in structuring anti-LGBT oppression. Chapter 2 considers the growth of a new gay rights model in the mid-1970s that I call militant gay liberalism, which combined the militancy and countercultural performativity of gay liberation with a gay-focused, reform-oriented agenda. Neither far to the left nor complacent in their liberal goals, these organizations arose to address a range of issues that activists understood to directly and uniquely affect all gays and lesbians, such as street violence and the need for designated neighborhoods. The chapter focuses on a series of gay safe streets patrols—such as the Lavender Panthers in San Francisco's Tenderloin, the Butterfly Brigade in that city's Castro, and the Society to Make America Safe for Homosexuals in New York's Chelsea—that postdated the heyday of gay liberation and predated the consolidation of national civil rights organizations. These patrols ranged from quests for self-determination to ad hoc gatherings of self-proclaimed vigilantes, all of whom hoped to assert and protect *gay space*.

Here the book also explores the parallels between social-scientific studies of urban violence and poverty and the growing circulation of the term *homophobia*. I examine how the lasting influence of the psychological bases of postwar liberalism—in particular, their sedimentation in the culture of poverty thesis—shaped the consolidation of the new discourse of homophobia through a shared emphasis on the psychopathologies of damaged masculinity and low self-esteem. During these same years, community policing in the form of neighborhood patrols became popular among both middle-class communities and gay activists. I consider how these patrols were inspired by the participatory ideals of postwar liberalism but took shape in the 1970s in the context of the rising influence of conservative rational choice theories, which take crime as a given and shift the focus to punishment and the management of victims. Thus, gay safe streets patrols were part of a broad process that saw the transformation of gay spaces from places of residential concentration to expanding visible niche markets for retail commerce and real estate speculation, each firmly in place by the end of the 1970s.

Gay safe streets patrols learned from feminist models, in particular anti-rape activism. Yet at the time, many lesbian feminist organizations were taking a very different approach to issues of violence and urban space. Around the same years as militant gay liberal visions were congealing and achieving some power—most famously with the 1977 election of gay supervisor Harvey Milk in San Francisco—others were pointing to the contradictions inherent in trying to solve street violence by relying on crime control and the protection of gay neighborhoods. This was a critique sustained by a variety of organizations, especially LGBT groups whose members were also active in other movements, including the black freedom struggle, radical feminisms, anti-imperialism, and Marxist-Leninist and Maoist parties. Chapter 3 begins by returning to the time of Stonewall and then moving quickly through the 1970s to identify organizations that focused on analyses of race and gender in their explanations for LGBT marginalization. The chapter then homes in on 1980, around when many of these trajectories merged and gained traction in a series of organizations that theorized the place of race, gender, and sexual identity in public contestations over antigay violence and gay participation in gentrification. I show how these groups pointed to the contradictions of militant gay liberalism as part of the history of criminalization and uneven development, while they also posited models of activism outside the instrumentalism of scientific measurement, social reform, and dominant leftist visions.

Organizations such as the Third World Gay Coalition in Berkeley, Lesbians Against Police Violence in San Francisco, and Dykes Against Racism Everywhere in New York, among others, were also key for how they challenged economic programs that pushed ahead with the election of Ronald Reagan. Reagan's policies of privatization and market freedom helped to formalize the U.S. role in the global ascension of neoliberalism. Neoliberalism not only transformed the structure of accumulation under capitalism, but it—along with the attendant growth of financialization—also reshaped the ideologies of everyday life to naturalize the market and downplay group inequality. The organizations featured in this chapter claimed identity while disavowing its singularity, called on structural analyses while refusing the will to tabulate, and, therefore, helped to point to the crisis in liberalism during those years. Furthermore, I show that these examples of radical lesbian and gay organizing should not be dismissed due to their admittedly short life and small scale. Rather, by considering these groups cumulatively, I suggest that they constituted a social movement that has not only been lost in the archive, but that has been disaggregated in its narration into false camps that place identity and culture on one side and class structure and organized movements on the other. The groups profiled in this chapter insisted, for example, that white identity held economic value in an urban land market, while they also saw a sweaty softball game to be part of the struggle. Activists would follow a protest against the police with a poem, not only so that they could then hand it out at the next rally but also as a way to talk about how language makes history.

Also at the start of the 1980s, activists who had become frustrated by the limits of grassroots organizing—including some members of the street patrols described in chapter 2—were central to the founding of a new wave of policy-oriented antiviolence organizations, such as Community United Against Violence in San Francisco and the Chelsea Anti-Crime Task Force (which eventually became the New York Anti-Violence Project). Chapter 4 marks the birth of these organizations and their influence on the founding of the national antiviolence movement in the 1980s. Although the impetus for local campaigns came from on-the-ground action, the institutionalization of antiviolence politics was fueled by a reliance on social research. The inspiration for many studies was the National Gay (and Lesbian) Task Force and their (Anti-)Violence Project, which was established in 1982 to address the issue of antigay violence nationwide. Federal policies and agencies protecting crime victims also first came into effect during these years—for example, the federal Office for Victims of Crime was established in 1983. Fighting for laws that target hate crimes soon became a top priority of the antiviolence movement. In this chapter, I sketch a history of this movement, considering how advocacy for sexual orientation–inclusive (and, later, gender identity–inclusive) hate crime laws took center stage.

One of the ambiguities of hate crime designations is proof of intent; language tends to be the main determinant. Yet another factor is geography, and how the location of violence, coupled with the identity of the accused, might prove violence has been spurred by bias. As a result, hate crime designations are effectively in the position to label certain areas as "gay" and certain individuals as insiders or outsiders. Chapter 4 looks at how gay visibility was cast as a goal and a risk of neighborhood growth, and how this dual set of assumptions helped to define the essence of antigay violence as a crime. This convergence of ideas was aided by two of the leading partnerships formed by the lesbian and gay antiviolence movement in the 1980s: with the National Organization for Victim Assistance and the Anti-Defamation League of B'nai B'rith. The former group helped to provide a framework for understanding that the injury of the individual crime victim was also an attack on a broader group, and the latter developed the model legislation for hate crime laws. It is also important to note that the antiviolence movement's collaboration with the Anti-Defamation League occurred at the same time that the league expanded its campaigns on college campuses to assert that many emerging critiques of Zionism constituted anti-Semitism. The National Gay and Lesbian Task Force's talking tours during these years gestured at this link, citing as shared between gay and Jewish people the experience of the Holocaust, life with invisible marginalized identities, and the need for safety in protected territories. I analyze the implications of these connections to the development of a national antiviolence movement.

Also central is the fact that although the first hate crime statutes mandated government documentation of bias, by the early 1990s the thrust had shifted to the enhancement of punishment. Chapter 4 analyzes the significance of empowering the state to arbitrate hate. By considering hate crime laws as but one strategy of constructing uneven geographies, this chapter forces discussions of violence in a culture of bias to include—in the plainest of terms—a history of real estate. The chapter ends in the early 1990s, highlighting how the understanding of anti-LGBT violence as first and foremost a crime had become so widespread as to be central to otherwise varied political visions. Specifically, I look at the activities of groups spun off from the organization Queer Nation that were modeling new patrols after the Guardian Angels in the streets of gay enclaves and gentrifying countercultural zones in San Francisco and New York (among other cities). I mark here the founding of another safe streets patrol—the Christopher Street Patrol—that remained active in New York's Greenwich Village in the decades to follow. Primarily run by residents and business associations, the Christopher Street Patrol emerged as nonaffiliated yet often complementary to activist-oriented patrols like the Queer Nation–affiliated Pink Panthers.

Over the next decade the Christopher Street Patrol's targets narrowed. By 2000 Greenwich Village residents were making heated claims that social service providers and nonresidents were to blame for residents' low quality of life and lack of safety, and calling for police crackdowns on minor infractions like noise and loitering. Those most targeted were LGBT youth and transgender adult women, both of color—who saw gay enclaves as providing the safety of community and anonymity. But Greenwich Village residents were not without opposition; chapter 5 looks at the challenges put to them by activists associated with the group Fabulous Independent Educated Radicals for Community Empowerment (FIERCE). The 1990s saw the founding of numerous community-based organizations in the United States dedicated to racial, sexual, economic, and gender justice that often kept issues of violence and neighborhood at the top of their agendas. This was also the period in which there was a substantial growth in transgender activism, and the vulnerability of trans and gender nonconforming people to violence became a major activist theme. Organizations such as the Audre Lorde Project in New York and TransAction in San Francisco were initiated in 1994 and 1997, respectively, just as the national antiviolence movement was sharpening its focus on penalty-oriented hate crime laws. In the early 2000s groups such as FIERCE, the Sylvia Rivera Law Project, and the Trans-Justice Project of the Audre Lorde Project—all in New York—and, later, a retooled Community United Against Violence in San Francisco, provided alternatives to the dominant script of violence and safety circulating in the mainstream movement. This chapter looks closely at FIERCE and its campaigns in Greenwich Village, demonstrating how activists extended the kinds of critiques of violence featured in chapter 3.

Chapter 5 also considers how FIERCE activists rewrote (and sustained) many of the terms of urban reform that frame this book. Specifically, the chapter places the debates between residents and activists over who can make claims to Greenwich Village within a history of neighborhood-based governance. It demonstrates how the 1960s liberal reforms with which the book opens can provide the very mechanisms through which marginalized populations continue to be excluded from an increasingly privatized urban landscape. I analyze this in the context of policy claims that gay tolerance—presumably a measure of safety—increases the success of the so-called new (now old) economy in U.S. cities. Ultimately, I show that the uneven value attributed to safety by activists and residents in Greenwich Village underscores the tenuous, rather than commonplace, understanding of violence and the unstable link between individual and group benefit behind both hate crime laws and neoliberalism. In the book's conclusion, I examine how some of the primary themes of this book—place claiming and uneven development, risk and speculation, social services and social movements, vulnerability and visibility—continue to be mobilized together and torn apart, and I speculate about how queer organizing that takes on the terms of violence and safety might redefine those structures of injury and belonging that I have traced.

Looking "Backward"

Although the book's case studies unfold in chronological succession, they were captured through a process of tracing history backward and of marking what some would deem to be backward or shameful history.[94] My interest in the topic first began with two small case studies of lesbian bars in gentrifying neighborhoods—the first in San Francisco, in 1996; the second in Brooklyn, New York, in 1999—that were using the terms of safety to advocate for new development and policing, respectively. Several years later, I again found myself in community meetings that were debating the same issues in New York's Greenwich Village. I set out to find the backstory, so to speak, of these recurring conflicts. This investigation would send me on innumerable trips to archives to find the records of earlier activist campaigns. These archives included collections at both New York City's main public library and its Lesbian, Gay, Bisexual, and Transgender Community Center; crowded repositories of lesbian "herstory" and new transgender movement artifacts in lived-in homes from Brooklyn, New York, to Northampton, Massachusetts; established archives at New York University and Cornell University; early community archiving projects such as the June Mazer Lesbian Archives and ONE National Gay and Lesbian Archives, both in Los Angeles, and the Rainbow History Project, in Washington, D.C.; the massive collections of the San Francisco Public Library and that city's Gay, Lesbian, Bisexual, Transgender Historical Society; and the small holdings of nonprofits like the Women of Color Resource Center in Oakland, California, and those of numerous individuals.[95] Along the way, I interviewed Del Martin and Phyllis Lyon, who founded the first lesbian organization in the United States; gay safe streets activists from the 1970s, many of whom became leading players in the fight against AIDS in the 1980s and 1990s; lesbian feminists from the 1980s who have traveled down roads much wider than I could have ever imagined; LGBT policy advocates from the 1990s who continue their hard work in diverse milieus; and contemporary queer youth organizers who are, to this day, reinventing the politics of gender and sexuality. I also had discussions with activists, archivists, nonprofit workers, and fellow researchers—on phones, in homes, on panels, and on street corners—whose stories enlivened the policy documents, correspondence, meeting minutes, and other ephemera I found. Throughout this process, I would return to my home in New York, attending rallies and direct actions and helping organizers carry bottles of water to youth-run speak-outs and protests.

When I began to write up this research, I found the following words I had written in italics and set aside from my innumerable pages of notes taken while I was in various archives: *"There is no way to deny the intense emotional response of someone's murder, their lover's loss, a sense of community injury. I'm trying to capture this feeling."* The desire to capture this feeling was not because emotions were absent from my research process. More often than not, feelings of anger and upset would alternate with those of excitement and optimism as I moved between studying political cultures that I found deeply troubling and those that I found incredibly meaningful (and, of course, those that were not so simple to categorize). Rather, I wrote these words because it had become easy to minimize the pain of individual violence while crafting a critique of what I often understood to be organized retribution, and I needed to remember that these two things were not the same. In refusing to write a singularly celebratory story of LGBT history, I also wanted to resist a drive to shame those whose actions I might analyze in ways different than they do.[96]

This is not only because of a desire to maintain empathy in the context of study. Rather, many of the political actors I encountered were passionate about the rights not only of LGBT people, but also of numerous individuals at the dominant culture's margins. Although this book sometimes differs in its analysis of the consequences of certain movement actions, it does not doubt the genuineness of activists' individual intentions. It is thus necessary to state clearly that this is not a history of individual activists per se, but a historical study of collective, public action. I conducted original interviews with twenty-one individuals, and I draw on additional interviews done by others.[97] I use this material to highlight activists' individual experiences, which are often downplayed by the collective form of activism. But those of us who have participated in social movements know that many actions do not represent individual beliefs, and that in retrospect good ideas can seem . . . well . . . less so.[98] This is one of the risks of the model of participatory democracy that most of the organizations I studied followed.[99] Furthermore, I spoke with a broad political spectrum of individuals whose interpretations of events—let alone memories of them—can diverge and have changed. For all of these reasons and more, the majority of my narrative is culled from archived documents and ephemera, as I focus my lens on actions, mission statements, meeting minutes, correspondence, strategy sessions, manifestos, and policy reports.[100] That noted, in those cases in which there is an absence of accessible written materials, I rely more heavily on interviews, including activists' narration of their own private collections.[101] In sum, this book hopes to avoid an approach that flattens the dynamic struggles of movement actors and that takes frozen targets out of context, while also contending that a focus on the individual activist's intention too can provide for a limited reading. And, importantly, I want to note that many of the people I interviewed have since died and others fight in political struggles with marginal support every day.[102] They plan actions with limited resources, and they do not always get the opportunity to debate analyses with each other, let alone with academic audiences.

The method I adopt also extends into the final chapter, which features political campaigns that are still ongoing. In 2003, while a graduate student, I affiliated with FIERCE as an "ally," meaning someone who is supportive of the group's aims but not a member of its named constituency—in this instance, queer youth of color. My role mostly involved administrative support in the office and logistical assistance at events, which were useful tasks for someone with the skills and schedule of a full-time student. I also participated in the planning (mostly silently) and execution (often loudly) of rallies, marches, and other actions. But I did not do a sustained study of the organization and its members. Furthermore, the organization assigned me, in my role as ally, the task of speaking to other researchers about how we might work to support rather than only advise or study the group. As a result, this final chapter is based in a combination of observations I made at public protests as well as public meetings hosted by residents and business owners (with and without the presence of FIERCE), in addition to municipal documents, journalistic coverage, and interviews, many conducted years after I was most actively involved with the organization.[103] I also draw from the extensive written and visual materials produced by FIERCE. Thus, this chapter, like the others, does not seek to be a representative look at the lives of those creating political arguments in the West Village but, rather, a study of how those arguments took shape in the public sphere.[104]

Violence, Safety, and Risk

This book is fundamentally concerned with the tricky character of both queer and left politics and, especially, the messy places in which they meet. The liberal state has denied homosexuals some of what full citizenship implicitly promises, and for many activists otherwise committed to a leftist critique the terms of equality have been hard to refuse.[105] In turn, leftists have not in general incorporated a critique of normalization and of the family and have, as a result, supported liberal gay agendas despite the contradictions they represent to anticapitalist analyses.[106] Moreover, the assault since the 1970s on the institutions central to liberal democracy have been joined by the rise of what Wendy Brown, among others, calls "neoliberal rationality," with its voracious appetite for "all aspects of social, cultural and political life."[107] One outcome is that LGBT and queer leftist visions vary widely between seeing liberal political reforms such as rights or social welfare programs as complicit with neoliberal agendas or as something that must be saved. This also underscores the fact that the supposed line that marks what is included in the category of neoliberalism cannot be drawn so neatly. A key theme of this book, then, is to trace the transformation of liberal politics as they have found expression in LGBT/queer social movements. I begin with a look at the influence of racial liberalism on homophile advocacy in the 1960s and the emergence of militant gay liberalism in the 1970s; I also examine how LGBT politics transformed itself, and was challenged, first in the context of Reaganism and later in the current security era.

Political responses to violence are particularly difficult here because, as Frantz Fanon and others have noted, violence is the means by which power is often both asserted and resisted.[108] And because of violence's ability to undo a person, the response to violence can often cloud its scenes of address. In this book, I do not theorize the paired concepts of violence and safety as much as I trace their variable use. That said, I strive to be consistent, but the contradictory mentions of these terms in other sources means that I am at times precise and at others admittedly vague. In general, I use *violence* for acts that cause immediate bodily harm. LGBT antiviolence activist discourse frequently folds hateful language into its definitions of hateful violence or recasts both under the general category of *victimization*. When discussing such examples, I try to parse language from physical acts without denying either the fact that a verbal threat can be the first stage of physical violence or the injurious power of words. To not acknowledge the latter would be to accept the dominant epistemology that constructs the psyche and the body as separate, even opposite, affects. Furthermore, the logic of cause and effect, a product of this same worldview, has itself shown that emotional harm can lead to bodily disintegration; thus, to imagine the distinction between immediate and delayed harm is significant is to forget that time is but a constructed relation. In addition, the structure of language is itself part of the administration of knowledge and power. All that noted, in order to effectively show how different activisms have built their arguments, these distinctions are helpful. In addition, while the aggregation and disaggregation of data that claim to distinguish among categories of injury is more often than not the ruse of statistics, I want to avoid leveling particular harms into universalized claims of shared vulnerability.

My use of the term *state violence* is similarly both straightforward and complicated. I use it to mark the routineness of police and prison brutality as well as the fact of incarceration through the circuit that runs from the law to policing to imprisonment. The inclusion of law and incarceration might confuse some readers, since both are within the terms of the state's social contract and many of my other examples of violence point to acts outside those terms. I say *many* here, since much violence is tacitly accepted; for violence to count as violence against a person, those bodies must be understood as belonging to humans, and we cannot assume that all people are granted their humanity. And the immediate enforced immobility and stolen bodily autonomy involved in arrest and caging cannot be made null by arguing that it is justified, for that is to accept the belief that crime categories and the idea of crime itself are just.[109] Finally, I describe racism and poverty (together and separately) as premised in the promise of injury. Most effective is Gilmore's definition of racism: that which puts certain groups at greater "vulnerability to premature death."[110] Vulnerability to death that is premature but not always immediate is a much better way to get at exploitation and harm and its temporal features than the word *violence* alone; nonetheless, I often do refer to these structures as *violence*.

Safety, and by extension *safe space*, are even trickier concepts. James Baldwin often spoke about safety and its status as an "illusion" on which the dominant society depends.[111] I, too, am not convinced that safety or safe space in their most popular usages can or even should exist. Safety is commonly imagined as a condition of no challenge or stakes, a state of being that might be best described as protectionist (or, perhaps, isolationist). This is not to say that the ideal of finding or developing environments in which one might be free of violence should not be a goal. Most liberation movements call for freedom from such exploitations of power, and Baldwin saw the role of the artist as one who must "disturb the peace."[112] Ultimately, I argue that the quest for safety that is collective rather than individualized requires an analysis of who or what constitutes a threat and why, and a recognition that those forces maintain their might by being in flux. And among the most transformative visions are those driven less by a fixed goal of safety than by the admittedly abstract concept of freedom. This is all, I might add, to say nothing about the benefits or limits of a stance of nonviolence.[113]

Safety is a key term in LGBT politics, colloquially as well as in political organizing and social service provision. At many colleges and universities the mere words *safe space* on a sticker on a door may signal that those inside are sympathetic to LGBT students without naming those very identities. And then there is *safe sex*: some public health advocates like to clarify the point that no sex is without risk and thus prefer the term *safer sex*.[114] Yet this nomenclature does not displace the idealization of safety; for sexual conservatives, it can translate into a call for abstinence (the only truly safe sex is no sex); for sex-positive activists, as they are often called, sex is then cast as a project of risk management.[115] Tim Dean takes on the politics of risk as it relates to HIV as part of a broader cultural "imperative of health" that finds its roots in a moral discourse of responsibility over oneself. Moreover, as Dean argues, the elaboration of scientific knowledge has "not produced a greater sense of security but, on the contrary, a heightened sense of risk."[116] Today, life in the so-called West is full of risk; as Anthony Giddens puts it, there have long been hazards, but this "is a society increasingly preoccupied with the future (and also with safety) which generates the notion of risk."[117] At the same time, risks as dangers are more and more uneven in their distribution.[118] One result is that individuals are asked to manage their own risks while relying on the rule of the expert to determine what is a threat.

The call for self-control and deference to the sciences of social explanation must be considered alongside another use of risk: as the central term for economic regimes that have led to the financialization of everyday life.[119] Here risk taking is both celebrated and stigmatized: you are either a successful speculator or a stupid spender. (Take, for example, the narrative of the mortgage crisis in which the deregulation that fostered wild market speculation, that in turn inflated the housing market bubble, is cast as a lost gamble, while those people who were sold subprime mortgages and later lost their homes to foreclosure are represented as having made irresponsible purchases.) As a result, marking the queerness of risk taking is difficult. Is it displacing the very idea of risk by dispensing with the idealization of futurity or safety? Or is it embracing risk so as to reap speculative rewards?[120]

Given all this, a central contention of this book is that violence and safety have been the not-always-spoken-about yet defining motors of mainstream LGBT political life since the 1970s. Paralleling the approach of this book, this claim is based in history and in theory. First, as I show in chapters 2 and 4, the antiviolence movement was the first model of gay activism to receive public and corporate monies, and it was following these initiatives that other forms of LGBT politics entered the streams of nonprofit and private funding.[121] Second, throughout this book I outline how the threat of violence has functioned as a sort of moral bookend to queer deviancy that promises redemption, if only for some. The dual insistences that the lesbian or gay man is not the criminal and that antigay violence is the act of the criminal have largely succeeded in making lesbians and gay men not otherwise associated with criminality into legitimate subjects, although it has not removed the threat of violence for many people who identify as gay or who participate in same-sex sexuality.[122] I exclude transgender here since those so identified have not achieved the same legitimacy; nonetheless, transgender activism too can claim a totalizing experience of abjection and violation, with similar if not parallel political results.[123]

The resorting of criminality has happened while leaving intact its attendant categories and geographies, in particular those defined by race and class. The result is to quite literally secure the definition of *lesbian* and *gay* as those threatened by illegitimate violence and to find solution in risk ne-gotiations: as calls for self-regulation, scientific experts, and open financial markets. Furthermore, the assessment of rational choice has been central to liberalism's individualism and profit motive. Thus, of central impor-tance to this book is the argument that LGBT political goals based on the terms of protection and safety are inextricable from spatial development and crime control strategies in which U.S. urban regions have played a lead-ing role. This is not to suggest that gay identity per se is complicit with urban-centered capital accumulation and criminalization—here it is worth remembering that D'Emilio's field-defining argument about the industrial city and gay possibility concludes with a socialist feminist vision—but that political goals that call for these forms of state protection must be under-stood at least in part as expressions of the risk management that is central to those processes.[124]

The dynamics of risk are also why the comparison to AIDS activism is so useful. In the late 1980s and 1990s many chapters of the AIDS Coalition to Unleash Power (ACT UP) focused on vulnerability, by highlighting whose bodies were vulnerable to the vagaries of the medical establishment and fed-eral policy but also by using the vulnerability of their own bodies in dramatic direct actions. Of course, vulnerability can be used as another word for risk, but it doesn't have the same link to probability and thus statistics. Judith Butler has argued that being human involves a primary vulnerability—one present even before individuation—and so the recognition of vulnerability might, in a way, be an acknowledgment of one's status as human.[125] ACT UP's die-ins, in which activists lay as if dead in public streets, or their political funerals, in which the bodies of recently passed loved ones were brought to protests in caskets, could be seen as making a demand for such a recogni-tion. Butler argues that in critiquing humanism, one need not dismiss the question of who is made human; yet the example of ACT UP also raises the question of how those excluded from the category might make a variety of political claims that exceed the limited terms of recognition.[126]

The issue of recognition is important, though, because the majority of people who are most vulnerable to violence are not held up by policymakers, LGBT organizations, or even queer collectives. Furthermore, the experience of violence is often invoked as an equalizing mode of identification even as different LGBT people are made more or less vulnerable to it. And the it of violence remains an amorphous category, the definition of which may, in turn, define who is included in LGBT.[127] In an early interview, Butler praised ACT UP's die-in model as resisting a kind of easy legibility: "The act posed a set of questions without giving you the tools to read off the answers."[128] In the context of antiviolence organizing, contemporary grassroots organizations continue to try to create alternative systems of protection, but they often struggle to understand vulnerability in ways that neither flatten difference nor rely on the impulse toward knowable identity. In other words, the solidarity of a more inclusive *we* may collapse important differences when the act of naming identity as contingent is done only to reorganize it, or when the celebration of actions demeaned as inchoate transforms them into types of affirmation that are just as distancing.

To turn one more time to Baldwin: "Any real change implies the break up of the world as one has always known it, the loss of all that gave one an identity, the end of safety."[129] I must repeat that this is not a book about the history of violence against LGBT or a range of other sex/gender nonconforming or nonnormative people, on the street or by the state. I do not restage scenes of brutality experienced in schools, homes, workplaces, and other institutions, or on street corners. But it is through the effort to write a history of activism and not an account of violation that I strive to contribute to broad-based efforts to make the operations of violence legible for critique, without fixing those whom violence targets.[130] And I consider that which is driven by the confident promise of what is simply not yet.[131]

CHAPTER 1

"THE WHITE GHETTO"

*Sexual Deviancy, Police Accountability,
and the 1960s War on Poverty*

Every great city has a dumping ground, a plot of land it allocates to the people it will not tolerate anywhere else. The Central City performs this function for the city of San Francisco. Into the target area have been moved all the people and problems our society, at some time in the past, decided it would ignore; the older person, the homosexual, the alcoholic, the dope user, the black (and just about every other minority group), the immigrant, the uneducated, the dislocated alienated youth.
—**Tom Ramsay**

The observation quoted in the epigraph was made by Tom Ramsay, a political organizer active in San Francisco's Western Addition neighborhood after he was asked in 1968 to assess the viability of San Francisco's downtown Central City area for mass community action. In turning to the Western Addition for advice, Central City activists—many of whom were associated with homosexual advocacy groups then known as homophile organizations—hoped to build on a connection that they had already suggested existed between the two areas. Two years earlier, the Central City activists had won their fight for a piece of the meager benefits provided by President Lyndon B. Johnson's War on Poverty and its Community Action Program. The War on Poverty had been implemented as a part of the Economic Opportunity Act of 1964, passed the same year as the Civil Rights Act, and its approach reflected an increasing public recognition that people of color lived in disproportionate poverty in U.S. cities. The San Francisco neighborhoods originally chosen for the program, such as the Western Addition, were areas so identified. Yet the demographics of the Central City hardly matched: the majority of the Western Addition's residents were African American, but the dominant identity of the Central City, especially the section known as the Tenderloin, was as a place of white homosexuals, sex workers, itinerants, and drug users.

Advocates for the Central City argued to the San Francisco Economic Opportunity Council (EOC), established as part of the federal War on Poverty, that the stigmatization of social deviancy, in particular nonnormative sexuality, might—like racial inequality—be implicated in producing urban poverty. At the core of their argument was the contention that it was the conditions of the so-called ghetto—rampant poverty, inadequate infrastructure and services, and police misconduct—that promised this result: what they would call a "white ghetto," to be exact. In addition to seeking funding to address poverty, homophile activists collaborated to found Citizens Alert, a citywide police watchdog organization. And during these same years, Vanguard, a group of youth active in downtown street economies, mobilized those who lived on the fringes of urban policy and homophile organizing. None of these campaigns took violence as their primary point of challenge. Yet their focused critiques of abusive policing and profit-oriented development—rather than street crime, a key target of gay activism in the following decades—meant that accusations of violence were more consistently directed at what they called dominant society than at private individuals.

Focusing on the years 1965 through 1969, the years just prior to the Stonewall rebellion in New York City and the avowed birth of a gay liberation movement, this chapter looks at a moment in which homophile and affiliated activists focused their aim at poverty and policing and, in doing so, found an opportunity to fight systematic forms of inequality faced by a variety of San Francisco's most marginalized. Multiple forces converged to shape these campaigns. The first was an existing legacy of gay activism in the San Francisco Bay Area that had gained momentum in response to police arrests following a 1965 New Year's dance in the Tenderloin. The incident is credited with changing the tenor of activism by drawing more pointed attention to the problem of unjust policing and solidifying ties between religious and homophile advocates.

In addition, 1965 was the year of the uprising in the Watts neighborhood of Los Angeles—one of many confrontations between the police and African American residents in cities across the United States—an event that secured the place of police and interpersonal violence on activist and policy agendas. Three years later, in 1968, the concern about police abuse of African Americans would be both aired and contained with the publication of the Report of the National Advisory Commission on Civil Disorders, better known as the Kerner Report. Although the report noted the existence of "two societies, separate and unequal," it also narrated a crisis of violence among black residents and social movement actors.[1] Also in 1968 the Omnibus Crime Control and Safe Streets Act was passed, establishing the Law Enforcement Assistance Administration. The bill expanded federal policing powers while distributing funds for state-based antidisorder initiatives; it also further formalized the newly prioritized place of victims and social research within police practice.

The third primary context for Central City activism in 1965 was provided by the aforementioned War on Poverty, which had started seeding programs in San Francisco by the start of that year. The Economic Opportunity Act mandated "maximum feasible participation" of the poor in economic development programs. Local initiatives soon were engaged with a constellation of social movements dedicated to the varied goals of rights, redistribution, or, even, revolution: from civil rights to welfare rights, from the New Left to Black Power.[2] Indeed, the War on Poverty was the scene for many negotiations between radicalism and liberalism in the late years of the civil rights movement, and Central City activists' efforts to analogize sexuality to race reflected many of the same contradictions—such as between calls for the end to an unjust market economy and the opportunity for greater participation; between an indictment of the police and a call for their protection; between the goal of freedom and that of equality; between claims for the group and those for the individual. Furthermore, the structure of the War on Poverty provided an opportunity for state administrators and activists to ground—and rework—abstract concepts about culture and identity diagnosed by social scientists affiliated with the lasting project of postwar liberalism. In sum, the mid- to late 1960s saw both the creeping expansion of the penal state and local calls for empowerment. The election of President Richard Nixon in 1968 would extend the former and reroute the latter, casting the poor and their advocates as criminal and the white middle class as in need of and central to regimes of protection.

Centered on the seedy streets of the Central City, the campaigns for War on Poverty funding and Citizens Alert each framed sexual oppression as a product of discrimination but also of unchecked profit motive enforced through violent state forces. This analytic opening allowed for collaborations between homosexuals (and, less so, trans people) and other social minorities; in forming these coalitions, activists did not always parse identities nor distill antigay sentiment from other expressions of social domination. Neither did this approach present an individual's place in the economic structure as transcending exploitation based on race, gender, or sexuality. The approaches of these campaigns were therefore in contrast to the more privacy-oriented solution to entrapment that was most associated with homophile activism of the era. Yet in line with the prevailing liberal framework, activists ultimately sought explanation for nonconformity and exclusion in individual psyches and found remedy in the expanded role of proper citizen: a mode of analysis and strategy that would prove durable in the years to come.

1965: Central City

In order to understand these campaigns, it is essential to first place them in the history of U.S. homophile activism and on a map of San Francisco. The origins of the homophile movement are most associated with the Mattachine Society, founded in Hollywood, California, in 1951. Modeled on the Communist Party USA—of which its founder, Harry Hay, was a member—the society initially adopted a secret cell structure for sponsored discussions. Members also pursued a few high-profile campaigns, such as when Mattachine formed the Citizens' Committee to Outlaw Entrapment in 1952 in support of Dale Jennings, a member who had been arrested for indecency. In the years that followed, Mattachine members debated ideology and strategy while focusing on the pursuit of legal reforms (such as the decriminalization of sodomy and an end to police entrapment, vagrancy charges, workplace discrimination, and censorship) and a shift in popular values (via mass culture and the word of the expert). Chapters opened across the country, and other homophile organizations were founded; in San Francisco these included the Daughters of Bilitis (1955), League for Civil Education (1961), and Society for Individual Rights (1964).[3]

Notwithstanding its later centrality to the LGBT movement, the issue of street violence was not at the top of homophile organizations' agendas, even if it was a sustained concern of their members. To be sure, violence was a structuring feature in the lives of many who lived outside dominant heterosexuality in the United States in the mid-twentieth century. Be it domestic, vigilante, or state-practiced, violence was common, especially for women and men who refused gender norms or those who lacked the privileges that came with wealth or whiteness.[4] By the 1950s, white racial violence had long been a mode of controlling sexuality; the targeting of black men in the name of protecting white women is but the most cited example. And although sexual entrapment in bars was less common for women than for men, women's bars were often targeted for antiprostitution raids. Yet these kinds of violence fell outside the bounds of the homophile movement, which tended to target the disproportionate enforcement of laws against homosexuals specifically, or to challenge the inclusion of homosexuality in otherwise uncontested regulations. Those who might be charged with sodomy, lewdness, or vagrancy, or who experienced violence, for reasons that were not singularly perceptible as antihomosexual—such as for cross-race sexual contact, sexual commerce, or itinerancy linked to poverty—were not necessarily included in homophile campaigns.[5] This division was not only conceived by activist strategy; the separation of homosexuality from other forms of urban disorder was also a new aspect of regulatory state administration during these years.[6] Although it is difficult to determine whether the omission of violence as such from activist agendas was substantive or tactical, it is significant that violence per se was not primary. For homophile activists, the main predicament was how to publicly acknowledge and protect homosexual practice and identity (what would later become known as coming out or becoming visible), rather than negotiating embodied displays of difference or multiple marginalized identities.[7]

Despite the lack of focus on antiviolence in their organizations' formal plans, lesbians, gay men, and trans people did act collectively to resist violence, especially in places considered less respectable by many homophile organizations. Informal group dynamics were strongest in what Elizabeth Kennedy and Madeline Davis call "street bars" that catered to, in the words of one person they interviewed, "straights, colored, pimps, whores, and gay people."[8] Bar patrons often responded to violence through everyday refusals, be it by fighting back, breaking a window, or boldly flouting a law. Bar owners, too, organized to protect these spaces, forming business alliances to safeguard their property interests from state interference. Nan Alamilla Boyd argues that one result in San Francisco is that lesbians and gay men often depended more on each other and on bar owners for their safety than they did on homophile organizations, and thus bar culture—rather than incipient activist groups—might be seen as the early foundation of unapologetic lesbian, gay, and transgender political communities.[9]

Yet this profile of the homophile movement would change in San Francisco after the 1965 New Year's Day arrests at California Hall. A costume ball fund-raiser had been organized by the Council on Religion and the Homosexual, which had been founded in 1964 by homophile and religious activists hoping to build a broad coalition for local action. Police officers photographed attendees, and the lawyers who challenged them were among those arrested.[10] Homophile and religious leaders were outraged, and a group of ministers, many associated with Glide Memorial Church in the Tenderloin—a Methodist congregation that had been largely responsible for the founding of the council—spoke out, while the group further homed in on the problem of policing. The church's urban mission had been concretized in the Glide Urban Center for community outreach, founded in 1962 by Rev. Lewis Durham. Durham and the head of youth outreach, Rev. Ted McIlvenna, both played a central role in the council.[11] In the years that followed, Glide ministers and homophile activists would continue to be key partners in the Central City area, as the church's ministrations to the urban poor melded well with the homophile movement's dedication to providing social services. Phyllis Lyon, cofounder of the Daughters of Bilitis, worked for years at Glide, first as McIlvenna's assistant and later helping to found the National Sex and Drug Forum, in 1968. Glide Publications released Del Martin and Phyllis Lyon's classic 1972 book *Lesbian/Woman*.[12] In 1963 an African American activist minister, Rev. Cecil Williams, joined the majority-white congregation and soon became head pastor. Under his leadership, Glide would sustain church and homophile cooperation and further cultivate cross-constituency organizing.

Glide's location in the Tenderloin put it at the literal crossroad of San Francisco politics and culture. Physically speaking (see appendix), the Tenderloin was in the broad impact zone of some of the most sweeping urban renewal projects of the time, including the neighboring Yerba Buena Center plan, a convention complex. As Chester Hartman describes in his history of San Francisco's growth machine, the groundwork to build the Yerba Buena Center had been laid in the 1950s, when corporate and city interests first prepared to expand the city's central business district to serve a restructuring service economy. (This would also include the building of the Bay Area Rapid Transit system in the 1960s, to link the suburbs with downtown.) The area chosen for the center was the Central City neighborhood known as South of Market, which included, as Hartman explains, "hundreds of acres of flat land with low-density use, low land prices, and, to the corporate eye, expendable people and businesses."[13] The neighborhood was home to a growing number of Filipino families as well as many who depended on single room occupancy housing, such as elderly people and male dockworkers—ranging from longshoremen to merchant marines. South of Market also included Sixth Street, San Francisco's skid row, and South Park, an isolated, economically impoverished neighborhood with a sizable population of African Americans and new immigrants.[14] The other areas close to downtown were hilly and thus less amenable to office development.[15] The broader Central City area was also affected by an ongoing renewal plan for the Embarcadero area to the north and the so-called slum clearance of the nearby Western Addition. The San Francisco Redevelopment Agency had sponsored two major urban renewal projects in the Western Addition: the project called A1 was approved in 1956 but did not go into effect until the early 1960s; A2 followed in 1966. Together, they displaced thousands of residents and businesses.[16] As James Baldwin described it after touring San Francisco in 1963, it was, in essence, a program of pointed "Negro removal."[17]

This made the Tenderloin section of the Central City in the North of Market area, like the nearby Chinatown, one of the few neighborhoods with affordable housing near the demolition zones. (Chinatown had also been designated as blighted, and the famous decade-long effort to evict the residents of the International Hotel began in the late 1960s.[18]) Although dealing with its own encroaching hotel development to service the upgrading downtown, the Tenderloin was not (yet) considered prime real estate. This was due, in part, to its hills that proved a geographic block, but it was also because of its status as the area's red light district. The Tenderloin was a neighborhood of prostitution, strip bars, and other forms of scandalous nightlife. As Susan Stryker observes in her defining analysis of the Tenderloin during this period, the neighborhood was to absorb much of the "exodus" of socially and economically marginal people and activities forced out of the surrounding areas.[19]

These were the political, social, and geographic contexts in which homophile activists, in conjunction with church and neighborhood leaders, would take on the violence of poverty and the police. The San Francisco EOC had chosen the neighborhoods of Hunters Point, Mission, Chinatown, and Fillmore/Western Addition as designated target areas for the War on Poverty and its Community Action Program.[20] Absent was Central City, which ran from parts of downtown through South of Market and the Tenderloin.[21] Glide ministers, activists, and community members immediately decided to start a campaign to rectify what they saw to be a clear oversight. Cognizant of the growing understanding of urban poverty as racialized—all of the other target areas were neighborhoods whose residents were mostly people of color—activists would argue that the issues at stake placed the socially nonnormative in a similar relationship to neighborhood inequality. And in the very same August as the Watts riots, Reverend Williams and others associated with Glide founded the police watchdog group Citizens Alert to emphasize the problem of police brutality—an organization that built on know-your-rights initiatives already in use by homophile leaders. Although Glide was dedicated chiefly to the Central City, Citizens Alert would develop as part of the church's effort to broaden its citywide impact. The organization would highlight police violence as endemic to the U.S. city and argue that homosexuals and other sex and gender nonconformers were among those targeted by that abuse.

The campaigns for these two goals provide important examples of homophile activism that contrast with the focus of the homophile movement then, and much LGBT activism since: on visibility and single-issue strategies. The campaigns also showcase interpretations of violence developed in the context of neighborhoods that saw sexual and gender minorities as vulnerable while sustaining a broad-based critique of exploitation. In starting with these examples, I aim to displace ahistorical analyses of gay politics as premised simultaneously in atomized and universalized understandings of harm. Yet these case studies also highlight some of the conflicts inherent to the goals of state participation, policy reform, and individual remediation, especially as these solutions were outlined by the political economy and cultural geography of San Francisco. The fact that the federal government responded to popular demands with new forms of both accountability and control is among the contradictions that mark this period, yet remain so misunderstood. Furthermore, by placing political debates about sexual and gender identities at the center of this history, the chapter also reveals an exceptional example of how critiques of normativity shaped challenges to, and the local administration of, the War on Poverty. That said, despite reaching out across lines of difference, homophile organizers would ultimately stumble over addressing the most marginal: those who were unable or refused to assimilate. Although some of those who remained outside the bounds of formal incorporation did act collectively—such as the organization Vanguard—they also demonstrated the challenges that life on the street posed to the ideals of self-possession and organization.

Race and Sexuality in San Francisco's War on Poverty
REFORM AND REHABILITATION

Zones of vice have long been the concern of social and religious reformers, who read urban degeneracy as manifest in selected residents and seek their moral uplift as a means to achieve a polished urbanity.[22] The Glide clergy who roamed the streets of San Francisco's Tenderloin in the 1960s also saw such a crisis, but they cast this in terms less of perversion than of isolation. For them, the Tenderloin was the archetype of urban life as loneliness amid agitation and excess. Glide ministers hoped to provide the care of food and shelter and the respect of one-on-one ministry to those whose lives on the street the dominant society often saw as throwaway. The assessment made in 1965 by Rev. Edward Hansen, then a young student from the Claremont School of Theology who had come to Glide to train in a combination of pastoral work and social service provision, provides a prime example. In the opening to a document he penned about his first night there, "Night Ministry in the Tenderloin," Hansen describes the neighborhood as follows:

The "Tenderloin" is in the heart of the downtown area of San Francisco. It is notorious for prostitution, "gay" bars and hotels, drunkeness [*sic*], sexy news stands, and other "evils." It includes such key places as the Greyhound Bus Depot, the YMCA, several blocks of Market Street, hamburger stands, numerous restaurants, bars, and hotels, and the Glide Memorial Methodist Church. During the day the sidewalks are crowded with people hurrying everywhere; and the streets are jammed with cars, cable cars, trolley cars, and buses. The clamor of so much activity drowns out the distinctive human sounds of individual persons, and one is easily lost into anonymity, subdued in the evening, and individual sounds begin to take on more importance. Slow footsteps on the sidewalk and conversation at the street corner mark the beginning of night-life in the Tenderloin.[23]

Evoking the classic 1903 essay by the sociologist Georg Simmel, "The Metropolis and Mental Life," Hansen's description presents city life as a struggle to maintain individuality under the attack of heightened stimuli.[24] For Hansen, the alienation of the market system crystallized in the Tenderloin—where the exchange of sex for dollars produces, as he continues, young people both hardened to and desperate for attention. The large numbers of young *queer* men and women—hustlers, prostitutes, homosexuals, transsexuals, and addicts—were, to Hansen and fellow reformers, a sort of lost children of Babylon. In response, Hansen and others associated with Glide worked to form a network to combat what they dubbed the "Tenderloin problem." Drawing attention to the voracity of the urban renewal economy pressing on the area from all sides (and, as Simmel would have put it, the threat of "self-generating" profits that land garners by merely existing[25]), Glide clergy and others associated with the area—including Council on Religion and the Homosexual activists and other religious figures, homophile activists, and social service and public health providers—decided to demand a piece of the money promised to the downtrodden of the modern city. Together, they turned to the War on Poverty's local EOC.[26]

The group began its campaign to be added as the fifth target area of the antipoverty program, working together with activists from across downtown's Market Street divide, including Calvin Colt, the former interim director of the Mission Area board.[27] Together they formed the Central City Citizens Committee,[28] which held its first meeting at the offices of the Mattachine Society.[29] In fact, homophile members played a major leadership role in the campaigns that followed, most especially Donald Lucas, a long-term Mattachine member, and Mark Forrester, a cofounder of the Society for Individual Rights, both of whom were also involved in the Council on

Religion and the Homosexual. The Central City Citizens Committee's strategy included not only picketing the EOC offices, but also releasing a series of reports that highlighted the problems of the Central City in general, and the Tenderloin in particular. The report called "The Central City Ghetto of San Francisco" presented the area in the broadest terms and pronounced a dire diagnosis: the neighborhood was the final resting ground for all those destined never to assimilate, including the elderly, immigrants, and single parents unable to adjust to changing technological forces, as well as sexually wayward youth, prostitutes, and addicts shunted aside by social norms. Emphasizing the devastation of economic restructuring that made upward mobility unattainable to these people, the authors of the report wrote: "It is a true central city ghetto—that segment of a city from which only death can remove the individual."[30]

The Central City report was joined by another: "The Tenderloin Ghetto: The Young Reject in Our Society."[31] The main difficulties experienced by the protagonists of "The Tenderloin Ghetto" (referred to in the report as homosexuals, hustlers, female prostitutes, pill users, young lesbians, and single young adults) were those commonly associated with the populations of other low-income areas: health problems, limited housing opportunities, unemployment, inadequate education, and, mentioned toward the end of the report, police brutality. The proposed programs focused on skills training, civic participation, tutoring and vocational centers, health clinics, coffeehouses, information clearinghouses, a police watchdog group, high-school classes, a legal aid center, and a halfway house, all to be planned by the community. In short time, the writers of the report would found the Tenderloin Committee, an organization focused on this area of the Central City, which would release its own report, "Proposal for Confronting the Tenderloin Problem" (fig. 1.1).[32] This report homed in on the "emotional needs" of Tenderloin youth "outcasts" with "confused sexual identit[ies]" and recommended therapeutic solutions as well as alternate kinship networks to help create proud and productive citizens.[33] The Mattachine Society also released a report by the same title that replicated much of the other reports' language and emphasized the need to not stigmatize homosexuality and to mentor young people against a "preoccupation with sex" and "promiscuity."[34]

Much like the social scientists associated with the Chicago School of the 1920s and 1930s, who likened the city to a biological organism and elaborated techniques for its study based on participant-observation, the writers of the Mattachine report described what they saw in terms of pathology, calling the neighborhood "a human ash heap" and a "cancerous sore" that threatened to spread across all of San Francisco. They also de-

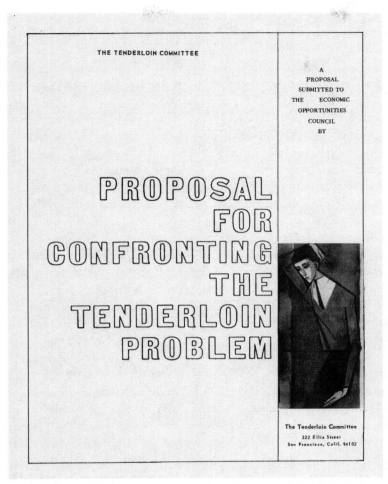

FIGURE 1.1 The Tenderloin Committee, "Proposal for Confronting the Tenderloin Problem"
(COURTESY OF THE GAY, LESBIAN, BISEXUAL, TRANSGENDER HISTORICAL SOCIETY)

scribed their project as "of distinct interest to many sociologists and behavioral scientists."[35] Despite the reports' pessimistic look at the urban condition, the solutions the reformers sought did not overlap with dominant solutions for rejuvenating the inner city. The members of the Tenderloin Committee made it clear that "at no time is it proposed that the Tenderloin be 'cleaned up,' 'redeveloped,' or that these people be 'relocated' elsewhere."[36] Focusing instead on the rehabilitation of people, the reformers cast sex work, drug use, thievery, and some expressions of homosexuality as situational outcomes produced by economic conditions and social rejection. Nonetheless, the media headlined the scene as "The Cops Vs. City's

Sin Jungle," "Tenderloin's Exiles of Sin," and "Stories of 'Boys for Sale,'" emphasizing the uncontrolled and defeatist spirit of the Tenderloin.[37] Some members of the neighborhood, such as Guy Strait—of the League for Civil Education, who published the papers *Citizens News* and, later, *Cruise News and World Report*—declared that the reports' sensationalistic language encouraged media coverage in those same terms and would, in turn, anger the police and increase harassment and brutality. Strait also concurred with those who called Mattachine opportunistic, accusing its members of exploiting the area for federal money.[38]

The Tenderloin Committee's focus on Central City residents as troubled outcasts may have fostered a kind of opportunism, but it also reflected the influence of the Glide ministry's commitment to a social justice theology that had gained currency in the civil rights era. Individual churches of many denominations had been key to mobilizing constituencies in the North and South; as David Hollinger argues, ecumenical Protestants, including Methodists, played a significant role in racial and sexual justice advocacy and secular collaboration among white churches during these years.[39] The Tenderloin Committee's focus on outcasts also had much in common with popular liberal ideas about inequality based on theories of cultural repudiation, damaged personality, and the need for integrationist remedies. Like the so-called Negro problem diagnosed by Gunnar Myrdal in his 1944 *An American Dilemma*, the "Tenderloin problem" was considered by reformers to be a symptom of the unrealized promises of American democracy—what Myrdal idealized as "the American Creed."[40] Myrdal's indictment of racism was joined by a call for the inclusion of African Americans in the institutions of nation and economic opportunity and was central to what would become a common diagnosis made by social scientists in the postwar era: that African Americans' problems were due in significant part to "damaged psyches."[41] Racial liberals used this research in the fight against segregation and discrimination, and some studies—such as those done by African American scholars like Kenneth Clark and E. Franklin Frazier—drew on a legacy of scholarship that challenged racial reductionism and posited institutional critiques.[42] Yet considered collectively, this research tended to pose narrowly predictive relationships between structure and psychosocial effects and were imbued with moralistic notions of what counted as a good community, highlighting the problems of failed nuclear families and sexual and gender nonconformity.

The social-scientific research that shaped racial liberalism did, on occasion, also speak directly to the question of homosexuality. As Joanne Meyerowitz outlines, some scholars associated with the "culture and personality" school of the 1920s through the 1950s wrote about race and homosexuality, and a few—concerned that the "repression of sexuality caused psychological problems"—advocated for the acceptance of homosexuality.[43] Other researchers of homosexuality in the early to mid-twentieth century also argued against draconian policing and advocated preventive measures for halting public and commercial sex, rather than advocating for the wholesale condemnation of homosexuality.[44] Although these viewpoints would make their way into popularized research and social policy, they did not have the same wide-ranging influence on antipoverty policy as did the literature on race and racism.

By 1965 few viewpoints on urban poverty would have as much sway as that of one of the key architects of the War on Poverty, Daniel Patrick Moynihan—then President Johnson's assistant secretary of labor. Moynihan's 1965 *The Negro Family: The Case for National Action*, better known as the Moynihan Report, offered an analysis of racialized poverty that described black families as caught in a "tangle of pathology."[45] At the center of its indictment were female-headed households and the damage they supposedly caused to the development of normative masculinity. In sum, the report argued that poor black families were ravaged by pathologies that kept them moored in place, stuck in neighborhoods of social and psychological stagnation. Moynihan's ideas met with outspoken criticism, but the report still had major influence among liberal reformers then and for years to come. In fact, the related "culture of poverty" thesis—that poverty begets poverty through a generational, community-based transmission of undesirable behaviors (a theory that Moynihan advocated)—has proven lasting across the political spectrum.[46]

Kevin Mumford demonstrates that a concern about homosexuality shaped the report's research and realization; nonetheless, its broad reception ignored or subsumed these terms.[47] Yet Tenderloin activists mobilized the language of pathology, self-fulfilling cycles, and failed families in their outreach to youth, many of whom were homosexual. This surely was also informed in part by the approaches to juvenile delinquency outlined by Richard Cloward and Lloyd Ohlin in their differential opportunity theory, which had become a basis of the War on Poverty's Community Action Program.[48] Cloward and Ohlin's model aimed to increase access to what the authors called legitimate social avenues while restricting access to illegitimate ones, staged on the level of neighborhood. Although its programmatic application focused on institutional opportunity, the theory also drew on the concept of anomie, or the breakdown of social norms. In the case of the Tenderloin, this would have included efforts to understand the dynamics of sexual waywardness. To make their case, reformers turned to these popular liberal explanations for inequality in order to account for sexual marginalization, adopting concerns about self-esteem and damaged personality to explain the self-destructiveness of sexual outsiders. From there, they proposed programs of opportunity.

It is important to note that although the Tenderloin Committee supported social opportunities for area youth and spoke out against the rigid renunciation of homosexuality and the economic contexts that forced people into prostitution, they did not see all sexual and gender nonconformity as affirmative. The goal of the committee was to provide the conditions of possibility for people's assimilation into dominant society. Hence the solutions sought—social services, job training, therapy, and education—constituted the kind of social engineering advocated by Myrdal and other researchers who looked to culture and personality rather than biology, but who still individualized social problems. Thus the activists' plans valued the opportunity for individual self-help central to the War on Poverty over the risky effects of group self-determination (then significantly associated with the growing dangers supposedly posed by race-based cultural nationalism) and they would bolster campaigns for youth opportunity with an assertion of the importance of sexual minority identity.[49] In this way, the problems in the lives of those youth supported by Central City advocates would be increasingly separated from other forms of disorder associated with urban poverty and radical social movements. This distinction would be made manifest via a discourse of likeness, as activists analogized, often subtly, racial and sexual minorities in a way that nonetheless kept the two separate. And the terms of violence and crime would be key to marking their distance.

"THE WHITE GHETTO"

One of the alternate titles for "The Tenderloin Ghetto" report was "The White Ghetto," although it does not seem to have been extensively circulated.[50] In general, organizers occluded the explicit mention of race, including, but not remarking on—as was the case in "The Central City Ghetto" report—the fact that at most 17.5 percent of Central City residents were people of color.[51] But the use of this alternate title demonstrates that the organizers understood race to be a primary framework for explaining urban poverty, although how they analyzed the relationship between marginalized sexual and racial identities is open to interpretation. One reading is that organizers sought to argue that sexuality constituted an axis of inequality like race, and that the status of these areas as majority white was an almost incidental feature that invited the label "white ghetto." This explanation seems to be the one most probably intended by Tenderloin organizers, given that the reformers cast themselves as in solidarity with the civil rights movement—

some had even marched the previous year in Selma, Alabama—and not in opposition. In this scenario, the need for homosexual inclusion is described as similar to the call for African American civil rights, and thus the movements as much as the identities are made parallel. Near to this argument is one made by Kathleen Connell and Paul Gabriel, who have suggested that implicit in the reformers' strategy was an antiracist critique of the premise that nonwhite racial identity and poverty went hand in hand; the authors describe the "assumption that peoples of color necessarily correlate with poverty" as having "latent racist underpinnings."[52] Conversely, the move to call the area a "white ghetto" might be seen as an expression of backlash intended to restore to poor whites the benefits many assumed that they had lost to civil rights activism; examples of this response from the period include the attacks on the 1964 and, later, 1968 Civil Rights Acts (including the Fair Housing Act).[53]

All of these perspectives have merit. Among homophile activists—the majority of whom were white—metaphors based in marginalized sexual and racial identities were salient in their efforts to use the African American civil rights movement as a model for homophile mobilizations, which I explore later in this chapter. That said, any investment in whiteness might be seen as a backlash in response to affirmative nonwhite racial identifications—although, as Daniel Martinez HoSang has described, the concept of "backlash" itself sidesteps the continuous history of white supremacy.[54] Some Central City target area activists were among those who accused community-based programs intended for people of color of being preoccupied with narrow self-interest rather than the supposedly generalized concerns of the poor, and they pointed to the large number of African Americans in positions of power in San Francisco's EOC structure.[55] In addition, confusion about how racism—rather than racial difference—governs social inequality was a feature of the War on Poverty, but Connell and Gabriel's argument cited above leaves out the fact that activists had fought hard to get the federal government to acknowledge that a disproportionate number of people of color were living in poverty, however contested the reasons. Finally, it is worth stating the obvious: the use of the term *white* ignored those who were not, as well as those whose identities defied pat definitions. For example, many of the broader area's denizens were Filipinos and African Americans, and one cannot presume a uniform heterosexuality for the residents of other Community Action Program target areas.

What is most compelling is how the concept of the "white ghetto" helps us to analyze how homosexuality increasingly became constituted as a respectable form of sexual nonnormativity—one dissociated from the criminalized and disorderly of the city—insofar as it was associated with whiteness, and how this identification would be made possible by way of a popular psychology found within poverty policy shaped by racial liberalism. The term *white ghetto* was used to modify the Tenderloin area only: that part of the Central City most linked to forms of deviance such as homosexuality and sex commerce. Other parts of the larger Central City were also home to those who lived outside of normative heterosexuality, such as transient male workers, multiple family households, and single mothers; furthermore, gay nightlife and a sex trade existed in other parts of the Central City as well. But it is in the reports on the Tenderloin that activists provided a detailed look at the problem of antihomosexual discrimination and its effects on one's psyche. (And in one of his letters home at the time, Hansen wrote of how he and another author of the report, Mark Forrester, had taken a group of psychiatrists and psychologists from Langley-Porter Psychiatric Hospital and San Francisco General Hospital on a tour of the neighborhood.[56]) The reports named homosexuality as something that should be accepted and described other nonconformities, such as sex work, promiscuity, drug use, and nonconventional gender, as symptomatic outcomes of rejection. Although activists did warn against stigmatizing youth who participated in these activities—and individual organizers in the antipoverty program often questioned the privileged valuation of citizen—in general, the reformers treated these acts as blocks to the modes of integration and participation they most idealized. In this way, the "white ghetto" is both the place where white people might be consumed by the city's worst pathologies and a marker of the promise of assimilation through a certain kind of white (homosexual) identification.[57]

The understanding that homosexuality might stand outside of other forms of deviance reflects a stance that Margot Canaday has asserted was consolidated by the state's administration of social welfare policy during and after the World War II period. She argues that although during the 1930s homosexuality was regulated as part of the perversions associated with transience, by the 1940s programs such as the GI Bill would further concretize the valuation of "settlement" over "mobility" manifested by New Deal policies and move to explicitly exclude homosexuals.[58] It is also important to note that the full benefits promised by the GI Bill also were not accessible to many African Americans because of discrimination, segregation, and disproportionate poverty. In this way, the GI Bill assumed not only heteronormativity, modeled in settlement, but also whiteness. This suggests that homophile efforts to achieve full inclusion in state welfare programs was shaped not only by the dissociation of homosexuality from other social deviances identified with poverty, in general, but also by the racial exclusions at these policies' ideological cores. Thus although idealized homosexuality was a middle-class position, a product of gay liberalism's investment in productive citizenship, the concept of a "white ghetto" made explicit the fact that this was necessarily a racial project.[59] This model of citizenship was also a feature of those parts of the African American civil rights movement most committed to middle-class respectability, a tie that served homophile analogies between gay and African American rights struggles (even as each did not necessarily include the other). But the limited reach of the GI Bill, as but one example, demonstrates how tightly knitted race and class were in social welfare policy; middle-class respectability was not a guarantee of mobility for all.

Furthermore, the target area campaign didn't need the appellation *white* in order to draw on its benefits (to repeat, the report title was later dropped). The ideology of gay liberalism does not simply borrow from racial liberalism through metaphor, but it is also an expression of liberalism in general that is "always already racial," in terms fundamentally shaped by citizenship, labor, and class.[60] Drawing on W. E. B. Du Bois, Cheryl Harris, and George Lipsitz, HoSang calls this "political whiteness": an investment in the material and symbolic rewards granted to those designated as white that also "disavows its own presence and insists on its own innocence."[61] At the time of the Tenderloin Committee's activities, the Tenderloin—or any other neighborhood, for that matter—could only tenuously be called a *gay ghetto* in empirical or conceptual terms.[62] When, just a few years later, such neighborhoods would emerge, their defenders would cite models of inequality based on gay exclusion from equal opportunity but would also invest in the assumptions of black criminality and pathology that would remain a durable feature of urban discourse.

Indeed, in research and policy application, not all aspects of racial psychology were presumed to apply to sexual nonconformers living in "white ghettos"—most evidently, in the operation of violence. Alongside the literature about black dysfunction and low self-esteem was a body of writing that ascribed violence to African Americans. The correlation between blackness and violence was not only the product of lasting biological theories of black inferiority, but it was also pursued by liberals who had for years variably promoted cultural and psychological response theories that oppression led to fear, aggression, and rage. These ideas would be used to discount racism in the North by detailing it as a Southern phenomenon, or to argue against black nationalism as an unhealthy—even psychotic—reaction. As Khalil Gibran Muhammad shows, these ideas were all framed by a long legacy of racial statistics that outlined what became understood as "black criminality." Black alterity would remain a defining core of statistical imaginaries mobilized for social policies and activism, including the LGBT movement as it later assumed a national stage.[63]

But in the 1960s personality damage and cultural deficiency were put forward less as explicitly disciplinary forces than they had been in previous years (and would be again in later years). Rather, they were described as psychic and social blocks to the goal of assimilation, an approach that tended to discount structures of racism and class stratification. That noted, there were others who moved to call racism itself—rather than the experience of it—psychotic, and they posed violence as one of the few rational responses one could take.[64] Needless to say, these theories were not taken up in social policy or reform-oriented activist models, although some activists did critique the discourse of modern psychology. For example, in 1963, Martin Luther King Jr. appropriated the concept of maladjustment as a refusal to normalize oppression and violence rather than as a stigmatizing diagnosis.[65] Although there was a sociological and literary tradition of naming homosexuals (a category that then often included transsexuals) as violent predators, such violence was not figured as a rational response, but neither was it named a cultural or psychological adaption to inequality.[66] Instead, it was considered a manifestation of homosexuals' inability to control private impulses. (In a warped inversion, the "homosexual panic" defense emerged instead.) The longer history of psychoanalysis as enemy to affirmative homosexuality meant that activists more often than not sought to distinguish homosexuals from sexual predators, even if they might still figure homosexuals as suffering from psychological injury. In this way, homophile activists also hoped to align themselves with those African American civil rights activists who asserted their respectability in opposition to people assumed to lack moral righteousness (nothwithstanding a critique of homosexuals). But the imminent success of the Central City in winning designation as a War on Poverty Community Action Program target area would also showcase how an investment in whiteness would make comparisons between marginalized race and sexuality—and collaborations between their increasingly cordoned-off advocates—difficult to sustain, especially in the stratified spaces of the city.

ANALOGY VERSUS ALLIANCE

The use of the term *white ghetto* was short-lived, yet the suggestion that sexual marginalization was akin to racial exclusion continued to be deployed by organizers, a move that was not well received by many of the city's African American political leaders. For example, the Central City organizers sought the support of other area boards in their quest for target area status. Chinatown and the largely Latino Mission District both responded positively.[67] Yet the Western Addition and Bayview–Hunters Point—African American neighborhoods—did not. When Central City activists staged a protest at the main offices of the EOC, over 100 residents of the Tenderloin walked out of a meeting run by African American municipal officials, while singing the song "We Shall Overcome." Hansen wrote in a letter to his parents: "This council is controlled by the Negro leadership of San Francisco, and they are very fearful of losing control so this works against us when we try to become a part of the total program." He continued: "The Negro people sat quietly and watched us leave singing *their* song."[68] The campaign to demonstrate that race was not the only element that shaped economic marginalization wavered between strategies that signaled alliance and those suggesting competition. In addition, African American activists had reason to be wary about the Central City designation. First, any additional target areas would not bring more money, but simply redistribute previously allocated funds.[69] Second, the Central City activists received more favor—and considerably less scrutiny—from officials than did the activists of the Western Addition and Bayview–Hunters Point. In the latter neighborhoods, organizers—many of whom were involved in the growing Black Power movement—would be increasingly accused of "anti-white" bias and extremist politics.[70] One issue of the local EOC newsletter from a few years later described the "venomous racist jargon and invective" directed at the citywide council by "disident [sic] poverty agencies" such as the Hunters Point Young Men for Action and Head Start.[71] (Young Men for Action had been founded after the neighborhood rebellion in response to the murder by police of sixteen-year-old Matthew Johnson in 1966.[72]) Indeed, years after the Central City board had been approved, African American organizers there faced more charges of impropriety and incompetence than did other, nonblack, participants.[73] One member, Genie Bowie, whom Don Lucas (the Mattachine Society member and Central City activist) described as a friend of the Black Panther Kathleen Cleaver, organized mostly black youth in the Central City's South Park area and advocated for a community center. Yet she also faced vague criticisms of her management skills.[74]

Such contentiousness did not plague the majority of white Central City activists. Many officials supported the Central City designation, which presumably bolstered the argument that other antipoverty activists were "anti-white racists." The few black activists in the Central City, together with sympathetic nonblack radicals, simply did not have a strong power base. Many white Central City activists also supported the complaint made by some politicians that African Americans were using the antipoverty program as a means to grab power in the city. Thus it was not surprising that the Central City organizers prevailed on May 25, 1966, when the San Francisco EOC voted in the new target area.[75] The decision surely was made possible by the support of Joseph Alioto (then board chair of the San Francisco Redevelopment Agency and soon to be the city's mayor), Harry Bridges (head of the powerful longshoreman's union), and other local politicians and federal Office of Economic Opportunity officials.[76] The programs to be funded were based on those detailed in "The Central City Ghetto of San Francisco" report, and the area would be eligible to receive services from existing citywide Community Action Agencies, such as those providing low-cost legal services and youth programs. The proposed initiatives would eventually be administered via a Central City Multi-Service Center, whose official board structure would include street outreach workers, health and human services providers, and a police community relations officer.[77]

The triumph of Central City activists in achieving funding for a majority white urban neighborhood highlighted some of the less well-addressed dynamics in the federal antipoverty program, including the geographic aspects of the policy's racial politics and its vexed status vis-à-vis social movements. Johnson's War on Poverty had built on initiatives developed under President John F. Kennedy; as stated earlier, the Community Action Program was modeled on the Mobilization for Youth project based on Cloward and Ohlin's differential opportunity theory. The growth of Mobilization for Youth in New York was accompanied by parallel developments in urban planning, especially the adoption of broad-based systems reform. This approach not only extended long-standing Chicago School concepts of social disorganization and the natural ecology of the city, but it was also instrumentalized to more directly address issues of economic development and the restructuring of urban labor markets. Of central concern were "gray areas" of "cultural deprivation"—home to both new migrants to the city and those left out of technological changes—exactly those people imagined to live in the vice districts and skid rows of San Francisco's Central City.[78] The National Institute of Mental Health and the Ford Foundation would not only support much of this research, but they would also merge youth opportunity and urban renewal plans in future initiatives. Moreover, they would do so in a way that maintained race as a less spoken, more neutral category, even as activists and community members would note the uneven challenges faced by different populations.[79]

Ultimately, the realization of Community Action Agencies was the result of a professionalized approach to the problems of the so-called ghetto, and racial difference was at once disavowed and understood to mark a distinction between program administrators and the poor—and, in a different register, between the country and the city, the West and the rest.[80] Thus the tug of war between approaches that took the Community Action Program's mandate of community control at its word and those that called for its tight administration was necessarily a series of racial conflicts, although they were often described as reflecting the difference between radical demands for the end of the establishment and liberal reforms within the given structure, and even though people of color found employment in the program on both the federal and municipal levels. This is how white Central City activists could garner the favor of high-level administrators at the same time as they could assert an opposition to black politicians and antipoverty workers as an expression of militancy. Furthermore, the War on Poverty was far from a city-only program; its vision had been influenced by Kennedy's Appalachian Regional Commission, and Johnson had announced the program from a house in Kentucky. As Wendell Pritchett shows, Johnson initially sought to deemphasize the racial aspects of the proposal and to focus on poverty among rural whites.[81] But any models forged to address white poverty in Appalachia (or so-called Third World countries of underdevelopment, another focus area of antipoverty policy) were not really considered applicable to the sexual outcasts of the U.S. city, although these places of poverty had also been noted for their sexual deviancy and were the sites of some of the first culture of poverty research. The homosexual—increasingly cast as an affirmative and a white identity, rather than a symptom of pathology—was considered a person of the cosmopolitan city. And the discussion of the sexual outcast—like that of youth—often sidestepped racial identification, as each category was described as mired in psychological or developmental crises.

This is not to suggest that white homophile activists were blind to or wholly supportive of the racial dynamics between white Central City and other activists. One regular critic was Mark Forrester, a feisty and contentious Central City activist who had been involved with the Tenderloin Committee and would stay on as an organizer after the Central City won target area designation. Earlier, Forrester had drafted the first versions of the Council on Religion and the Homosexual's "A Brief of Injustice," which had been published after the California Hall arrests, and he was a regular columnist for *Vector*, the magazine of the Society for Individual Rights (SIR).[82] Part of the reason Forrester later left SIR was due to its dedication to a homosexual-only political agenda that prioritized courting institutional favor. *Vector*'s tag line then read: "Responsible action by responsible people in responsible ways" (fig. 1.2). In an interview by John D'Emilio in 1976, Forrester explained that he felt distanced by both the Mattachine Society—whose members he described as protected by their white identity from the kind of marginalization faced by black people—and by SIR for its single-issue stance.[83]

Homophile supporters of the antipoverty campaign hailed from Mattachine and SIR; some were members of both groups. Mattachine would go

FIGURE 1.2 *Vector* magazine tagline (COURTESY OF THE GAY, LESBIAN, BISEXUAL, TRANSGENDER HISTORICAL SOCIETY)

defunct soon after its endorsement of the EOC project;[84] SIR, which counted Mattachine members as among its founders, would last longer but would reject the Central City plan. Former SIR director William Beardemphl explained that Mark Forrester "left SIR and asked if he could use the SIR Center for these [EOC] projects. They were not gay projects. I said we will not deviate or add to that area. I am a firm believer that combining the homophile, homosexual revolution, gay liberation or anything else with the black community or the Asian community or with anything else or any other level except homosexual rights is wrong."[85]

Mattachine's participation in the EOC and SIR's rejection of the EOC are in many ways a reflection of the limited numbers of individual homophile activists involved in the antipoverty campaign, but it is also interesting to consider those alliances in the context of the historiography of the LGBT movement that has named SIR a more radical development, following Mattachine. This position tends to take as examples SIR's "bold language" and uncompromised focus on electoral politics and rights (SIR provided the founding members for the nation's first gay and lesbian Democratic Club, the Alice B. Toklas Club); this analysis also suggests that SIR's politics were most like that of the African American civil rights movement.[86] The historian Martin Meeker has challenged the designation of the Mattachine of this period as not "radical" for its adoption of strategies based in respectability; instead, Meeker suggests that respectability was a tactical "mask" that allowed Mattachine to participate in a range of forward-thinking, nonconventional activities—including the Central City campaign during the organization's final years.[87] Although confusion about the word *radical* is primarily semantic, it also signals what have become multiple, often contradictory, registers for measuring radicalism in LGBT—and much left of center—political history. In LGBT history, the designation of radical is most frequently used to mark an organization's militancy, strong break from conventional sexual mores, or embrace of public identities over the protection of privacy. Marc

Stein uses the helpful terms *militant respectability* and *sexual liberationism* to describe two different political positions that might both be dubbed radical; in the first case, for its nonapologetic, identity-affirmative stance, in the second, for its more transgressive rejection of traditional sexual mores and roles, manifested in strategy and goals.[88]

But radical is also used to mark the far ends (or the wholesale rejection) of a left to right spectrum, measuring perspectives on the merits of different forms of political economic structure. In the case of 1960s lesbian and gay activism, this would include leftist and other critiques of liberalism. Thus it is important to note that Mattachine's focus on the just distribution of welfare benefits or SIR's uncompromising position on individual rights are both part and parcel of a broad but shared investment in the promises of liberal citizenship. Although it is true that SIR's strategies could have been more singular and hard-hitting in achieving the goals of a gay-rights focused agenda, an emphasis by Mattachine and SIR on equal access to social services and cultural production makes the two organizations more complementary to each other than adversarial. In addition, to compare SIR—which would reject the EOC project—to the African American civil rights movement also risks emphasizing a limited, albeit popular, narrative for the movement that, in Jacquelyn Dowd Hall's words, "distorts and suppresses as much as it reveals."[89] The comparison ignores the history of civil rights as a movement of movements that included campaigns for the poor, for unionization, and against the Vietnam War—a model that might see homophile activists' demand for inclusion in the EOC as part of this broad constellation rather than as a separate movement linked to civil rights only through metaphor.[90] Although the assertion that the Central City campaign might be considered as part of the black civil rights movement is a stretch—especially given the forms of racial animosity and competition that I have just suggested and the debates between privatized and public forms of inclusion—it is significant that Central City activists' goals of redistribution and their interpretation of marginalization were invoked in affinity with civil rights activism and that they represent some of the issues that have been downplayed in the historiography of both LGBT activism and the civil rights movement.

The liberalism of the 1960s, especially as represented by the War on Poverty, was quite varied in its integration of economic explanations and its advocacy for widespread systemic reform. As Alice O'Connor argues, American Keynesianism was shifting from its New Deal model to one more guided by market-based social policy during these years, and thus a wide variety of interpretations influenced diverse state players and programs.[91] In addition, as Jonathan Bell asserts in an assessment of this same Central City campaign, homophile participation in the War on Poverty was an example of how the economic liberalism central to the welfare rights movement provided a context for fights for individual sexual rights. The challenge to the moralism of antiwelfare politics melded well with homophiles' rejections of moral reproaches to homosexuality because both modeled the need for economic as well as social inclusion (even as both also depended on distinctions between pathological and healthy sexuality). Bell highlights this coalition so as to underscore a moment when "economic redistribution" and "civil rights liberalism" worked together.[92] But the coalition also demonstrates the limits of codifying civil rights politics, in general, as divested from redistributive and even radical economic concerns. This was particularly the case since the on-the-ground programs of the War on Poverty included Alinsky-style reformers and Black Power activists among others; although they may have fought more than they collaborated, this fact blurs efforts to neatly map political processes.[93]

Among the ways homophile activists would help to recast these political boundaries was through the support of critiques of morality and normalization within citywide reform. Although one of the lasting implications of the target area campaign would be the assertion of (white) homosexuality as a path out of urban deviancy, the fact that homophile advocates named their solidarity with the poor is significant. Furthermore, that tactic was an exception for homophile activists, who tended to seek respectability through claims to privacy to which the poor were not entitled. Nonetheless, the approach would not last long in dominant gay politics. But in its time, it would allow for the creation of motley affinities between activists and would make unique demands on federal powers. Considered in retrospect, this history decenters normative assumptions about the allies and constituencies of gay politics in the city.

INSTITUTIONAL CHALLENGES

The Tenderloin Committee continued after the Central City had been designated a target area, even seeking official nonprofit status of its own.[94] The group established a hospitality house that they named after Hansen and that hosted programs on relations with the police—many featuring Elliott Blackstone, a well-liked police liaison between the Central City and the Community Relations Unit who was assigned to work with the area's homosexuals and transsexuals.[95] Yet far from limiting their concerns to the Tenderloin, homophile activists continued to be fundamental to the larger Central City program, ensuring that sexual politics remained at the forefront. Within a year after the Central City target area was founded, Calvin Colt, the area board's first director, stepped down; he was replaced by his assistant Don Lucas, of Mattachine. Colt was an EOC insider who had served on the board of the Mission target area; Lucas's roots were firmly in the Central City.[96]

The participation of activists like Lucas demonstrates the important and unusual influence of homophile activists in mid-1960s San Francisco city politics, but also San Francisco's status at the vanguard of broad-based efforts to redefine public morality through an interpretation of the exclusions inherent to bureaucratic structures committed to social norms. Only months before the approval of the Central City as a target area, and before Lucas was appointed to his leadership role, members of the San Francisco EOC disseminated a press release to protest two federal memos from the Community Action Program in 1966. Memos 23 (March 3, 1966) and 24 (March 7, 1966) regarded personnel regulations and included sections that prohibited the hiring and promotion of those convicted "of a crime involving moral turpitude" as well as limiting salaries. The San Francisco EOC fired back at federal officials, asking how one defines and establishes the standards of "good character, good reputation, and moral turpitude."[97] The EOC explained that such a regulation was directly counter to the goals of a poverty program because it imposed "middle-class standards" on an area whose criminality was due to the "sociological factors" that cause poverty. Although the EOC did not explicitly say so, the rules also were a problem for a new target area whose primary constituency often broke moral codes in their everyday gender expressions and sexual practices. Despite the fact that this argument abided by an analysis of behavior as an expression of economic class, the concern with "middle-class standards" also suggests that the very idea of morality was constructed. The challenge to the federal memos was made by San Francisco's citywide EOC, but there is reason to believe that the arguments made by those advocating inclusion of the Central City as a target area influenced this stance. The fact that a municipal agency might understand those disciplined by "morality" to include sexual minorities is a remarkable piece of the War on Poverty's history that has been understood as far detached from lesbian and gay politics and community. It also demonstrates the key status of critiques of normativity alongside identity-affirmative visibility politics within gay organizing before Stonewall.

Another provision capped entry salaries for new workers in the poverty program at 20 percent, or $2,500, more than the workers' previous wages. The San Francisco EOC pointed out that when one's previous salary is near zero, these rules perpetuate rather than alleviate poverty and discourage the participation of those low- and no-income people for whom the War on Poverty had been designed. Memo 24 mandated that boards maintain moral standards to decide basic eligibility for those making policy. The San Francisco EOC rejected this provision in its entirety:

> The implementation of Memo 24 would necessarily take the form of an investigatory committee be [sic] set up by each area board and neighborhood council to delve into the background of persons who are willing to serve in a policy-making position. The creation and operation of such committees would serve absolutely no useful purpose but rather as a deterent [sic] for everyone, regardless of qualifications, from giving of their time and effort to serve on these voluntary policy boards. The idea of having to appear before a so-called fact finding committee to determine one's character rating, criminal past or sympathy with the E[qual] O[pportunity] Act would serve [as] the gravest form of intimidation ever imposed on poverty people.

Following this complaint, the initial Central City Interim Area Board decided that it would accept federal funds only "under protest," so that it might hire a staff to get started. The board decided that such restrictions could be applied according to its own interpretation.[98]

Although the Interim Area Board of the Central City spoke up against the moralism that would limit the participation of the most marginal—and assured residents that their initial administrators were temporary, to be replaced with low-income residents later—many members of the neighborhood as well as activists felt that the Central City board was still too top-down and failed to incorporate local participation. One critic was, again, Mark Forrester. Forrester promoted the Saul Alinsky model of organizing, as did many others associated with Glide and other area churches. Urban neighborhood campaigns across the country, including those sponsored by the War on Poverty and the Model Cities Program, adopted the Alinsky method, which was favored for its multi-issue and local emphasis. Alinsky had been trained by Chicago School urbanists and the Catholic Church, and his commitment to the ideals of liberal democracy and opposition to left-identified solutions translated into a populism that found strong support in many community churches. Furthermore, even though Alinsky described the War on Poverty as a "prize piece of political pornography"—aptly, if inadvertently, pointing to another analysis of the sexual economy of poverty policy—he, too, took part in its programs.[99] Nonetheless, many critiqued Alinsky, arguing that although he stressed the power of the grassroots, this did not always involve seizing full control from below rather than relying on the skills of trained middle-class organizers who were community outsiders. In San Francisco neighborhoods such as the Mission and the Western Addition, this resulted in tensions between radical Latino and African American activists and the white-dominated, church-based Alinsky camp.[100] In the Central City, where such activists were more limited in number, Forrester's leanings cast him as radical. His "A Workplan for Community Organization" for the Central City Citizens Council detailed the need for "indigenous" and "representative" leadership and self-determination and concluded with a warning: "If the above realities are not recognized, our people will either blow their tops—as they did in Watts—or just withdraw and exist chloroformed out of their individual freedoms, which is what most Americans seem to be doing."[101]

Although Forrester's Alinksy-inspired vision did overlap with values held by the Central City and Glide leadership (he and they alike called for greater acceptance and local reforms), Forrester's concerns point to challenges that were regularly put to War on Poverty programs. Residents and activists accused the antipoverty program of being a top-down bureaucracy that benefited only the social reformers who had become federal employees.[102] The board members attempted to defend themselves against accusations that they were tainted bureaucrats, reminding residents that they did not hold the funds but were merely a conduit for fighting for them.[103] Nonetheless, employees of EOC area boards often publicized their complaints in the *Gadfly*, a publication of the San Francisco Poverty Workers Association. In one issue, an organizer with the Central City Multi-Service Center agency announced his resignation and proclaimed that "this office in its day to day, month to month functioning is but yet another enemy of and to the poor like the Welfare Department, Slum Landlords, Bigot associations, institutions in our society."[104] Other issues of the *Gadfly* highlighted federal Office of Economic Opportunity regulations that limited employees' participation in demonstrations and San Francisco rules limiting "unfounded and disloyal remarks"; the paper instead advocated campaigns such as one in solidarity with Black Panther Huey P. Newton.[105]

The Central City board did hire an outside consultant from the Western Addition Community Organization, Tom Ramsay, to assess the viability of mass organizing in the Tenderloin; he concluded (in the quote that opened this chapter) that the area was ripe.[106] Nonetheless the recommendations of Ramsay—who had also been a project director with the Student Non-Violent Coordinating Committee[107]—to use organizers already there, to train them in the Alinsky method, to require of them no other organizational affiliation, and to alter many day-to-day operations—seem to have gone unheeded, since the service-center model remained. Indeed, Forrester's attempt to initiate a "mass-based" organization was questioned as "red flag" language that would prove unfeasible.[108] Although other target area neighborhoods provided fertile grounds for campaigns for self-determination and revolutionary promise—albeit ones that were often later appropriated by municipal machines—these did not as effectively take hold in the Central City, although one organization profiled later in this chapter, Vanguard, was somewhat an exception.[109] This suggests that although Central City advocates could be unapologetic in their challenges to the normative demands of social policy, they did not all agree about the goal of increasing access to state institutions.

Many of the community programs put into place by the War on Poverty continued into the start of the next decade, in spite of the shrinking of funds that would lead to Nixon's essential dissolution of the Office of Economic Opportunity by 1974. In 1973 Robert Edward Cruz and Michael B. Music, two employees of the Central City branch of the San Francisco Neighborhood Legal Assistance Foundation, a Community Action Agency, sent out a press release in a last-ditch effort to stop the closing of the foundation's branch office:

> On behalf of our Gay, Lesbian and Transsexual brothers and sisters in San Francisco, who for seven years have felt at ease to utilize the services of the *only* Neighborhood Office in the Foundation that has unreluctantly encouraged them to utilize our services, and that has handled enormous numbers of service and class action cases either referred to us by the various Gay Community Organizations or which successfully derived representation by our office through clients who were not afraid, intimidated, or embarrassed to approach us because of their knowledge that this office specifically delivered services to eligible members of the Gay Community, WE EMPHATICALLY OPPOSE THE CLOSING OR CONSOLIDATION OF THIS OFFICE WITH ANY OTHER OFFICE OR DEPARTMENT OF THE FOUNDATION.[110]

Lamenting the loss of a long list of legal services—including reforms against police brutality and harassment, transsexual name changes, representation in cases of housing and employment discrimination, and welfare rights—Cruz and Music asserted the importance of a "Gay neighborhood office." This is significant because, as I explore in the next chapter, in 1973 the Castro, and not the Central City, would be considered San Francisco's gay neighborhood. In 1973 the broadly defined Central City was still best known as home for many of San Francisco's low-income Filipino families, the elderly, and single people, as well as a place for transient queer uses. The call to save the "gay neighborhood" of the Central City reflected the newly popular use of the word *gay* and the large concentration of gay life in the area. However, in the years that followed, the idea of defining a gay neighborhood as a place of gay users would soon be replaced by a focus on such a neighborhood's gay home- and business-owners.

The organizers of the Neighborhood Legal Assistance Foundation also worked with the support of Filipino organizations, two of which—Sandigan and the Pilipino Organizing Committee—brought seventy-five people to the meeting of the foundation's board of directors at which the decision was reached to keep the office open.[111] Yet this too was not simply a story of triumphant cross-racial solidarity. Although by 1973 the service organizations of the Central City were divided between Filipino and what were named as gay, lesbian, transsexual, and transvestite groups, the opposition to the closing of the foundation's office also reflected a hesitancy to consolidate the Central City with the African American Western Addition. As Elliott Blackstone, the Central City Community Relations Unit officer, was reported to have said at this meeting: "I can't see those militant Black men from Western Addition mingling, let alone sharing the same reception room, with my nelly faggots."[112] Assumptions about the hypermasculinity and antigay sentiments of black activists would linger, as would the separation of the categories *black* and *gay*—and both would frame repeated conflicts in the next decades, staged in the terms of neighborhood, policing, and crime.

Strikingly absent in both the Central City campaign and its efforts to learn from the Western Addition was any recognition of African American lesbians, gay men, or other sex/gender outsiders, although it is worth noting that activists did take on the San Francisco Police Department's aggressive response to economies of prostitution in both neighborhoods during these years.[113] Furthermore, the lack of explicit attention to the intergroup dynamics involving Filipinos demonstrates the centrality of black/white racialization to the dominant discourse about poverty, militancy, and homosexuality during these years.[114] Finally, although the call of the Neighborhood Legal Assistance Foundation in the name of "Gay, Lesbian and Transsexual" communities reflected changing lingo—*outcast, variant,* and *deviant* were terms no longer favored in the post-Stonewall years—it also demonstrated that such terms might constitute accepted forms of minority identification deserving of state welfare funding. Central City organizations continued to provide services for other outcasts struggling with the challenges associated with addiction, isolation from families, extreme poverty, or the exchange of sex for dollars, but these practices would not—at least in these years—consolidate into affirmative identities that might be cultivated in prideful (and privatized) claims to neighborhood. Instead, they would continue to be targeted by state policing and be exposed to associated violence, as would the area's low-income Filipino community. Although other organizations would be founded in opposition, they, too, would struggle with how to understand the dynamics of race, poverty, and nonnormativity in the restructuring spaces of the U.S. city.

Police-Community Relations and Citizens Alert
FROM LOITERING TO BRUTALITY: THE FOUNDING OF CITIZENS ALERT

In 1961 San Francisco abolished its law against vagrancy, substituting it with regulations associated with disorderly conduct. Antivagrancy laws targeted people on the basis of their status and gave police great discretion in making arrests; by contrast, laws against public drunkenness, loitering, sexual solicitation, and prostitution were conduct-specific and supposedly more precise in their reach. Nonetheless, these laws—especially those against loitering—continued to be used to target homosexuals in particular. Boyd shows that antivagrancy laws had united homophile and bar-based communities across lines of difference because of the way the law made vulnerable a range of people who walked the streets.[115] Although by the 1950s homosexuality was, in the eyes of the state, clearly a target of directed regulation, laws such as those against vagrancy still might make diverse activist collaborations salient. Although some homophile activists pushed for the removal of the homosexual from the category of the vagrant, it is arguable that in many ways conduct-specific laws would actually aid a parsing process that would later make it easier to distinguish homosexuality from disorderly conduct.

Nonetheless, many Central City activists, including members of homophile organizations, saw unjust policing as a shared and unifying experience for the range of people who lived or socialized in the broad territory of the downtown neighborhood. Although some of the antipoverty reforms in the target area were restricted to subareas—South Park needed a community center, for example, and South of Market proposed new parks and services for the elderly—policing was considered a common concern. As a member of the Tenderloin Committee and an organizer in the target area, Mark Forrester helped to spearhead challenges to police harassment and the zealous arrests of prostitutes promoted by San Francisco Police Chief Thomas Cahill.[116] At a press conference in 1968, Forrester and supporters criticized the police for promoting sporadic arrests, using specious charges (such as "obstructing sidewalks"), targeting people of color and those of low income, and using arrests to instill fear and even foster prostitution. The group's press release concluded with a declaration that incarceration had no role in rehabilitation: "arrests do not strike at the same conditions leading to prostitution; the role of the pimp, the effects of living in a ghetto, of discrimination, and of poverty."[117]

Activists maintained that the use of antiloitering laws to target homosexuals and those working in the sex trades was linked to the redevelopment of the South of Market area of the Central City, and they made this a primary issue at a series of contentious Police Community Relations meetings in 1967 and 1968. At a meeting on February 14, 1967, residents, activists, and the police explicitly debated the issue of urban disorder, crime, and so-called deviant street life. The police detailed the concerns of business and property owners—"Complaints of not being able to walk the streets safely, thieves, robbers, assaults, litter, the side walks being blocked"—and asserted businesses' privileged claim to the neighborhood. Activists from the Tenderloin Committee and other Central City groups, including homophile activists, protested and were joined by social workers and sympathetic residents. One member of the Central City Neighborhood Association, Elizabeth Finn, started the meeting by asking those present: "Could those who are blemishes please stand up?" Larry Littlejohn, a member of SIR, added: "What is a criminal?" And Forrester reminded the group: "There is more to life than property values."[118]

Opposition in the Central City to the policing of vice was supported by many local agencies, including the Family Service Agency and the Neighborhood Legal Assistance Foundation—which was then headed by the gay attorney Herbert Donaldson, who had been among those arrested at California Hall.[119] But despite sharp rhetoric and the participation of individual radicals, most activists advocated for top-down reform.[120] They pushed for the arresting of so-called johns as well as of some prostitutes, and for better police relations rather than an end to policing or the criminalization of prostitution. That noted, Central City activists were also keenly aware that the topic of policing might present an opportunity for collaboration with other populations in the city, and they were particularly eager to make connections with San Francisco's African Americans. To do so, they expanded their concern with the uneven policing of vice in the upgrading Central City to include other expressions of police misconduct in a changing San Francisco—namely, police brutality. Within the boundaries of the Central City, these connections would be manifest through expressions of solidarity with the small South Park and its black community. But to take on this bigger framework, organizers also collaborated with an existing, albeit still new, initiative: Citizens Alert.

Citizens Alert was officially founded in 1965 and, like the target area campaign, was also developed under the auspices of Glide. Also like the antipoverty project, Citizens Alert included the participation of homophile activists (and was among those organizations proposed to receive War on Poverty funding). The Council on Religion and the Homosexual's "A Brief of Injustices," published after the New Year's Day California Hall arrests, had charged the police with numerous abuses, including intimidation of homosexuals and their supporters, entrapment, and enticement, and also had complained that criminal attackers of homosexuals "go free because too much police manpower is used to harass, entice and entrap suspected homosexuals."[121] The original proposal for Citizens Alert came out of a model developed by SIR, which had been hosting public programs on homosexual and police relations. These meetings often featured Community Relations Officer Elliott Blackstone.[122] SIR also distributed "Pocket Lawyers" pamphlets to gay men facing entrapment arrests—an act funded by the Tavern Guild, the gay bar association—and had published in *Vector* a preliminary plan for a "Homophile Alert System."[123] (During this time, *Vector* had also begun to occasionally list incidents that it labeled "police brutality."[124]) SIR's proposal included a twenty-four-hour telephone service to provide quick referrals to bail bondsmen and sympathetic lawyers. Yet unlike the "Homophile Alert System," Citizens Alert was to be geared toward *all* those who were socially marginalized—across race, sexuality, and even lifestyle—and counted among its goals not only advice and referrals but a criticism and reform of the police department and an increase in minority civic participation.

The organization's first public statement of purpose, published in *Vector*, focused on the problem of institutional ignorance and the role of the citizen in rectifying that:

> The purpose of Citizens Alert is to establish an organization and procedures to be used to collect, analyze and channel to responsible governmental and social agencies accurate and reliable reports of police misbehavior, including brutality, intimidation, harassment and the unequal enforcement of the law, to establish other means for constituting remedial action as may be necessary, to alert the general public, and to educate individuals in their rights and obligations as citizens. Recognizing that unequal enforcement of the law, based on income, color, national origin, sexual identification and minority status, exists, Citizens Alert has been formed with the realization that the law enforcement bodies, local and national, need the full cooperation of all citizens to attain the high standards necessary in the role of law and order.[125]

The supporters listed were Freedom House, the Committee for Racial Equality, Bay View Community Center, and Rank and File Labor Union.[126] SIR announced in a sidebar that it soon would consider joining. This widely distributed statement of purpose varied slightly from one more modestly distributed that focused instead on the problem of institutional denial: "One of the most basic problems cited as causing the recent Los Angeles riots has been police brutality and harassment. The newspapers have been unable to report this area to the public adequately and city officials deny or ignore that it exists, yet the problem grows and grows."[127] This suggests that even as the organization was created in the name of just enforcement, activists were on some level motivated by a stronger criticism of policing writ large. Although its original leaders were clergy, Citizens Alert was largely staffed and funded by activists or organizations central to the homophile movement, including Daughters of Bilitis members Del Martin (who served as chair of Citizens Alert in 1969 and then as a board member until 1972), Phyllis Lyon, and Barbara Deming; Larry Littlejohn and Dorrwin Jones of SIR were also involved. Large donations came from the Tavern Guild. Mattachine members Don Lucas (also occupied with the EOC campaign) and Hal Call were also supporters.[128]

Lucas, Martin, and Lyon each recalled in subsequent interviews that Citizens Alert and the Central City target area campaign were the only examples they remember of homosexual-inclusive, cross-race organizing in the pre-Stonewall years in San Francisco.[129] The reasons they suggested were twofold. First, they explained that the main problems that inspired the founding of Citizens Alert were police violence against gay men at the Park police station near the cruising ground of Golden Gate Park and the much publicized violence in Watts. Lyon said: "We all decided, wait a minute, we don't need to just do something for gays. Because other people are having problems, too, and obviously the riots down in Watts were telling us that something else was going on." In addition, they had a keen sense that a collaborative effort might gain more favor with mainstream organizations like the American Civil Liberties Union (ACLU). According to Lyon, "we were pretty sure that if CRH [Council on Religion and the Homosexual] or just a group of gay citizens called a meeting and invited the ACLU and—all the other groups and so on—that they wouldn't come."[130] On the surface, these answers suggest that homophile activists considered racial and sexual minority identities as autonomous and that their pursuit of coalitions was at least somewhat opportunistic. That view is not untrue, but it also points to a moment in which violence would be invoked less as a leveling strategy than as an alternative to the privatization and polarization of gay vulnerability.

One way that Citizens Alert developed a broad base was by hosting rallies and meetings in neighborhoods the group wanted to tap for organizing. Between February and September of 1966 it sponsored events at the American Indian Center in the Mission, the EOC office and a coffee shop in the Western Addition, churches in Haight-Ashbury and North Beach, and the Bay View Community Center in Hunters Point.[131] The group also coordinated training for those who wanted to handle calls, interview victims, and collect documentation.[132] One report released around 1968 explained: "Citizens Alert is . . . made up of a unique blend of people . . . the Negro, Mexican-American, Japanese, Chinese, Jewish, homophile and religious communities."[133] Members included Nassar Shabazz, a Western Addition activist who had been targeted by the EOC for his radicalism; Robert Gonzales and Mary Salazar of the Mexican-American Political Association; George Ishida of the American Friends Service Committee; Charles McClinton of the Congress of Racial Equality and the Western Addition EOC; Agnes McFaddin of the Student Nonviolent Coordinating Committee and Women for Peace; and C. J. Wellington of the NAACP.[134] Eventually over fifty groups from around the city had joined Citizens Alert, and the organization would settle into a strategy initially based on volunteerism and data collection.[135]

DOCUMENTING ABUSE

In its first year of operation, Citizens Alert received over 1,700 calls.[136] The vast majority of the calls were for information or to make vague complaints, but a handful specified details of particular incidents. Of the twenty-two complaints the organization filed with the police, half were for brutality and the rest were for harassment and unequal enforcement (or a combination of all three). Citizens Alert calculated that about half of the complainants were African American, followed by hippies, homosexuals, and members of "motorcycle clubs." The largest number of incidents took place in the Central City, followed by the Western Addition, Fillmore, and Haight-Ashbury. Of those complaints that Citizens Alert considered valid but did not file with the city, the majority were for harassment, targeting hippies, and based in Haight-Ashbury.[137] By 1968 the number of calls had risen to about 4,000, the majority of which were for referrals and information, and the complaints processed were roughly equally distributed between physical force, illegal arrest, and verbal insults. At that point Haight-Ashbury, a neighborhood known for its mostly white counterculture, far and away topped the list, surpassing black neighborhoods like Hunters Point. The authors of the report explained:

> It is unrealistic to assume that there is more police misconduct in the Haight-Ashbury than in Hunter's Point. Part of this statistical anomaly can be explained by the fact that C.A. [Citizens Alert] is better known in the Haight than in Hunter's Point. But another reason for the discrepancy may be that there is a willingness to complain through official

channels in the Haight, whereas there is an overwhelming suspicion and distrust of the system in Hunter's Point. People in Hunter's Point have known for a long time that the system doesn't work. But those in the Haight-Ashbury, many of whom are recent emigrants from the middle class, are just now earning their cynicism.[138]

Organizers were caught in a bind. They did not want to undermine any complaints against the police but did not see their primary constituency to be the white downwardly mobile middle class. Furthermore, the lack of evidence counted as a kind of evidence; in other words, nonreporting was symptomatic of the depth of African American exclusion. Yet rather than shift operations to Hunters Point or the Western Addition to focus on black participation or design other modes of demanding accountability, Citizens Alert instead increased its emphasis on policy oversight reform.

Despite this shift in focus, Citizens Alert noted some of the limits of serving only a watchdog function as a citizens' police review board; the group argued that acting in such a role inevitably prioritized the participation of "the big fat cats" and stifled community voices. This was a concern shared by other homophile commentators at the time Citizens Alert was founded; in the same issue of the gay paper *Town Talk* that announced the consolidation of Citizens Alert was the headline "Cops Loathe Brutality, Hate Queers Equally." The article exposed a police officer newsletter that had included the following comment: "To most police officers brutality is heinous and avoided as a homosexual would be." With the homosexual described—like brutality—as something to be avoided (lest exposure as a brutalizer lead to job loss), the article in *Town Talk* suggested that reform might ultimately buffer the police's reputation more than alter its mode of operation.[139] In August 1968 Citizens Alert released its "Eight Point Plan for Better Police-Community Relations in San Francisco," which called for a standard set of comprehensive police reforms including reorganization, a citizens' complaints bureau, police training on urban issues, a rumor control center, group discussions for police and citizens, a formal policy on firearm use, a system of citations rather than arrests for misdemeanors, and the assignment of black officers to black communities.[140] In subsequent years, Citizens Alert focused on building citizen participation in the altering of San Francisco judicial policy more broadly. For example, the group joined a coalition to stop the paramilitary Tactical Squad; pushed for Rodney Williams, an African American, to be made head of Police Community Relations;[141] continued to advocate for a citation system that would supplant arrests for misdemeanors; opposed a proposition which the group said unfairly distributed police power among those of top ranks;[142] sponsored a conference on prison reform; and campaigned for the restructuring of the Department of Corrections.[143] Although the mission of Citizens Alert shifted, the group's emphasis on changing local policy distinguished it from the National Legal Defense Fund that was also housed at Glide and that was concerned more with litigation.[144]

Citizens Alert's diverse constituency and hard-edged reform vision was unique. Similar campaigns in other cities were less sustained or did not include as wide a mix of members or goals. In New York, for example, activism against police abuse was also one of the few issues that tied the local Mattachine Society to nonhomosexual organizations, but activists there shied away from rather than embraced the category of police brutality as relevant for homosexuals. During the same years as Citizens Alert's activities, Dick Leitsch, president of the New York Mattachine, joined representatives from the NAACP, New York Civil Liberties Union, Puerto Rican Bar Association, and religious groups to form the New York City Review Board Conference to advocate for a civilian complaint review board.[145] Yet in many versions of the proposal for a review board, New York activists opposed the rhetorical emphasis on police brutality, which they felt did not adequately address the criminalization of sodomy and entrapment of homosexuals, and they supported a proposal, ultimately successful, to provide the option of privacy—for officers as well as those arrested—in complaint hearings.[146] Unlike the members of Citizens Alert, who expanded the fight against harassment and entrapment to include brutality, New York activists reversed the order, claiming that a focus on brutality excluded homosexual concerns.[147] Although this clarified the facts that entrapment was not necessarily violent and that police abuse came in multiple forms, in a way it also specified the vulnerability of homosexuality to state power as a particular and privatized experience.

San Francisco activists' work with the poor, for whom privacy was so systematically denied, may have helped to broaden their understanding of violence as well. This is not to say that definitions of homosexual vulnerability or police brutality were shared among homophile activists in San Francisco, nor is it to suggest that everyone was in agreement about what kinds of policing might or might not be justified.[148] In the August 1967 issue of *Vector*, William E. Beardemphl—the publication's editor and the head of SIR who opposed the antipoverty project—wrote an article supportive of Citizens Alert but added: "We are now confronted with an increasing crime rate, much of which is outrageously perpetuated against homosexuals. The police are busy on rooftops chasing ballet stars or are adamant in some cases and unable in other instances to meet the need of protection of homosexuals. Maybe the time has come for us to reconsider another proposal we advocated 3 years ago. Let us consider setting up a homosexual citizens protective force."[149] This points to how early homosexual activists diverged on the importance of challenging police power compared to calling for police protection, as well as on their judgment of whom self-protective measures would guard against.

One of the most prolific public thinkers on issues of violence and collaboration was Del Martin, of the Daughters of Bilitis and Citizens Alert, who drew particular attention to issues of gender within the homophile movement. In her years as chair of Citizens Alert, Martin wrote a column titled "The Police Beat" for *Vector*, in which she updated readers on Citizens Alert campaigns and on incidents of police harassment and brutality toward individuals and organizations,[150] decried the racist and antihomosexual "yellow journalism" of the mainstream news outlets,[151] honored police officers who had sought internal change,[152] informed readers of their legal rights,[153] and reported on general homophile and police news in town.[154] Yet the aspect of Martin's journalism that most stood out was her outspoken criticism of both the immorality of police practices and the sexism of the homophile movement. Much has been made of the homophile movement's stance on proper decorum and respectability, including the positions taken by the Daughters of Bilitis, which Martin helped found. Yet as a member of Citizens Alert and as a police beat journalist, Martin showed no tolerance for police stings staged at public sex spots—from beaches to the restrooms at Macy's—demanding that at least the officers wear uniforms and inform people about surveillance.[155] She treated as laughable Supervisor Dianne Feinstein's support of police licensing of movie theaters, emphasizing that homophile and black communities were very familiar with the arbitrary "judgment" and "discretionary power" of the police. She spoke out against the legal category of "obscenity" writing: "Movies do not constitute 'crime in the streets' that the police purport to be doing something about. Movies, like books, are a matter of private choice and taste. Obscenity is in the eye of the beholder." She then proposed lifting all obscenity laws.[156] In sum, Martin insisted on making the construction of normative desire and propriety central to concerns about police abuse of power.

But perhaps Martin's most hard-nosed opposition was to the misogyny and sexism of male homophile activists. Martin stopped writing for *Vector* in October 1970, when she announced that she was resigning from all homophile politics. Her farewells—including "Goodbye to the wasteful, meaningless verbiage of empty resolutions made by hollow men of self-proclaimed privilege"—assailed SIR and Mattachine and other homophile groups as using women as "window dressing" and for "secretarial work."[157] Yet her sign-off from the police beat was confusing. Although she did not resign from Citizens Alert, she did proclaim a "good bye" to "the defense of washroom sex and pornographic movies." "That was never my bag anyway," she explained.[158] Indeed, Martin's defense of public sex and lewdness came from the standpoint of alliance with gay men and not from a sense of lesbian inclusion. She and other members of the Daughters of Bilitis wrote articles for *Vector* and letters to the editor of the *San Francisco Examiner* repeating that entrapment does not affect lesbians, and that male "switching" and "swishing" had better soon come to an end.[159] Lambasting the fact that the homophile movement had room only for white men, she concluded her resignation with the stunning: "I will not be your 'nigger' any longer. Nor was I ever your mother."[160]

As a clarifying addendum to that article, Martin published "Sexism and Lesbians" for *Vector* readers in January 1971. Most of her examples clearly resonate with the evidence of homophile activist history: male-dominated meetings, ignorance about lesbian lives, gender-stratified labor, and self-centered behavior. Yet Martin's first specific example of male sexism was the absence of men at a lesbian-organized meeting with the police, an assistant district attorney, a public defender, and a judge to discuss the problems of police entrapment and harassment.[161] Confined herself to a largely white and middle-class lesbian culture, Martin seems unaware of the fact that lack of interest in police matters might reflect something more than, but inclusive of, male chauvinism. By 1971 police relations had improved considerably—although problems had far from disappeared—for white middle-class gay men. But for gay people of low-income or of color or for the gender nonnormative, policing was a tangible problem that activists continued to fight. In addition, Martin herself had written about how uneven policing linked (white) homophile and (heterosexual) African American concerns together. Martin's failure to get an audience for the meeting may have reflected white men's lack of interest in issues they no longer felt concerned them. Furthermore, by aligning herself rhetorically with African Americans at the same time as she considered heightened policing to be the issues of "others" (not white lesbians), Martin adopted a racial epithet to describe those with a lack of power, rather than those with a specific place in a racial hierarchy with whom one might act in solidarity.

Citizens Alert ended after some years, but these competing concepts of analogous, allied, and shared issues well capture the conflicts of sexual, gender, and racial politics in the late 1960s Central City. Siobhan Somerville outlines for later legal political contestations the effort to draw analogies between sexual and racial marginalization as at least somewhat informed by the primacy of African American exclusion in the rectifications sought by the Constitution's Fourteenth Amendment. Somerville shows how equal protection as a goal has driven sexual minority movements and that one result of the use of the "sexual identity is like race" metaphor is that it can exclude other categories of comparison (such as sex or gender) or of complexity (in which sexuality would be entwined with race).[162] It can also limit the possibilities of imagining political challenges outside the terms of liberal citizenship. Nonetheless, at least one group in the Central City did push against the limited ideals of inclusion and stood in solidarity with those left behind as the past of new, affirmative gay identities: those who lived, quite literally, outside the walls of liberal institutions, on the streets of the seedy city. The possibilities and contradictions of a politics of the street provide an invaluable context for analyzing the tricky place of antinormativity in critiques of liberalism, especially as they have been staged in rapidly changing U.S. cities.[163]

The Street and/as Vanguard

Although the Central City area activists campaigning against poverty and policing conceptualized sexual marginality as a limit to equal opportunity in the city, they did not necessarily see outsiderness as a viable status from which to organize.[164] They most highly valued top-down structures or the assimilation of community members into extant models. It was the everyday lives of sexual and gender nonconformers who continued to exchange sex for money or who pursued illicit pleasures that posed the most direct challenges to the rationality of representative liberal politics—those who were often outside of and even abrasive to formal organization. One group that tried to produce contexts for the organic ideas and cultural expressions of those who lived on the dominant culture's most sharp-edged margins was named Vanguard. Vanguard organized young people of the Tenderloin's streets—in particular those identified as hustlers and hair fairies, who exchanged sex for money and/or adopted unconventional gender roles—and the group emphasized the problems of police violence, exploitation, and discrimination as core issues. Vanguard was founded with the assistance of Glide, and the organization interfaced with the antipoverty project; many of its members learned about the group through youth dances organized by the church, and Glide provided physical spaces for youth to hang out in and hold meetings.[165]

Despite these overlaps in sponsorship, Vanguard diverged from the aesthetics and ethos of the homophile movement. The organization adopted a militant countercultural politics of social freedom that it publicized through dramatic actions and their zine-like publication.[166] In one issue from late 1966, the group reprinted a press release to showcase one such action: "Tonight a 'clean sweep' will be made on Market Street, not by the police, but by the street people who are often the object of police harassment. The drug addicts, pill heads, teenage hustlers, lesbians, and homosexuals who make San Francisco's 'Meat Rack' their home." The accompanying photo featured a group of young people ready to sweep Market Street—the main artery between the north and south parts of the Central City—holding signs that read: "All Trash Is before the Broom" (fig. 1.3).[167]

Vanguard sought to demonstrate that the police targeting of social outcasts was intimately tied to the city's real estate economy. In a flier the group declared: "We protest police harassment of youth in the area when the big time speculators seem to work openly and receive *no attention*." The end of a list of demands read: "We demand justice and immediate corrections of the fact that most of the money made in the area is made by the exploitation of youth by so-called normal adults who make a fast buck off situations everyone calls degenerate, perverted and sick."[168] Vanguard regularly assailed those who would partake of Tenderloin services while ignoring the needs of those who provided them, and the group theorized that economic speculation was aided by the devaluation of a neighborhood associated with a criminalized economy whose participants were marked as abnormal and disposable; this argument also exposed how it was possible to make a profit by increasing others' vulnerability to violence.

Although not fully incorporated in it, Vanguard overlapped with the EOC program. An early president of Vanguard, Jean-Paul Marat—who took as his pseudonym the name of the French Revolution's fiery advocate for the poor, the sansculottes—served as an area aide at the Center City Multi-Service Center. The inaugural issue of Vanguard's magazine was dedicated to the conditions of the Central City and included an article called "Exploitation," in which Marat described how redevelopment was having an adverse impact on the Central City and showed that its youth were among the worst victims.[169] Longtime Central City organizer Mark Forrester also included an essay titled "Central City: Profile of Despair": "Perhaps the big blast in all this is that in general, the outcasts of the Central City tend to hurt no one but themselves. The others manage through perseverance, dedication, faith, solidarity, and selfmanship to hurt almost everyone else that they touch: the Negro, the queers, the outcasts, all that their sanctimonious religion tramples on, all that their green greases up for quick sale."[170] But unlike the majority of the EOC leadership, Vanguard's members—in publications and participation in local politics, such as the contentious police community relations meetings—declared their explicit solidarity with the burgeoning radical sexual subculture and Black Power movement. While many homophile activists were careful to protect their reputations, *Vanguard* published

FIGURE 1.3 Clean Sweep Action, *Vanguard* (COURTESY OF THE GAY, LESBIAN, BISEXUAL, TRANSGENDER HISTORICAL SOCIETY)

pieces that speculated about police investments in the drug trade, included sexually explicit drawings, and declared a "race war" in which "the Negro and the Gay are fighting for the same exact thing: FREEDOM."[171]

Yet despite the rabble-rousing of Vanguard's members, their ideals none-theless mostly matched those of the leaders of the Central City target area: both groups turned to a "like race" model for understanding marginalized identity and social movements, and both adopted a psychologized interpretation of inequality and sought participation and integration for their members. Although Vanguard named itself as allied with a wide variety of the most marginalized of people, its actual membership was somewhat limited.

Stryker analyzes Vanguard in the context of pre-Stonewall trans politics, noting the organization's strong support and inclusion of those of gender variant and trans experience. The centerpiece of Stryker's film *Screaming Queens* is an uprising at Compton's Cafeteria in the Tenderloin, a place where Vanguard had staged a boycott and picket complaining of ill treatment.[172] Yet the film also shows that Vanguard did not speak to everyone; as one interviewee explains, many members of Vanguard were middle-class white radicals whose opposition to a staid homosexual movement did not always translate into the building of a coalition of the Tenderloin's most far outsiders.[173]

Although Vanguard advocated for a mix of people who lived long and hard on the streets, from drug users to sex workers, a key piece of the organization's identity was to mark the group as apart from the dominant and staid homophile movement. Distinguishing himself and his comrades from the closeted middle-class men who he felt filled the ranks of homophile organizations, Marat described Vanguard as comprised of "the other 1% of the homosexuals in the country." He continued: "We are the hustlers. . . . We are the people with long hair. . . . We are the young homosexuals."[174] Ultimately, Vanguard had an unstable stance, sometimes valuing those prideful of new sexual minority identities; sometimes advocating for economic opportunity as a solution to situational homosexuality, drug use, or thievery; and sometimes seeking alternatives for those who refused or failed to abide by either position. Ultimately, it is clear that Vanguard's members—actual or imagined—were not always amenable to the terms set forth by Glide and other proponents of equal opportunity, including Vanguard's own leaders, and that was a cause of tension in the group. Doug Patrick, a later president of Vanguard, complained in an article about the "boos and heckling" at one of the police community relations meetings from "so-called adults and the T.L.'s [Tenderloin's] children . . . who acted in an irresponsible manner." He concluded his piece by asking, "Are you a member of the Great Society?"[175] Another writer commented that the participants simply "went home and vomited."[176]

When Vanguard dissolved soon thereafter, some of the group's former members announced they were moving to Los Angeles, while others promoted a new project at Glide called the Street Prophets.[177] The latter announcement came with the reminder: "We have no confidence in an eternity of the Street Prophets, nor for any of its successors in the Tenderloin in the foreseeable future. Even as they organize, they decay. They factionalize & die. The complexities of structure rip apart the brotherhood. The drags and the hustlers have an innate dislike for superstructure. They do not seek another staid conformity."[178] Indeed, some members of Vanguard were distinguished from homophile activists not only by their rejection of gender and sexual respectability and by their exclusion from the formal economy, but also by their refusal to participate in normative political culture and its institutions. This included their unwillingness to adopt new, stable sexual identities and War on Poverty uplift protocols, as well as their rejection of dominant social movement forms. These aspects of outsiderness were often described by those inside and outside Vanguard as self-imposed, cultural, and intractable, and they put such individuals alongside other members of the poor who failed to follow the demand of the War of Poverty that the downtrodden govern themselves. In other words, they refused to receive the encouragement of the state to practice self-restraint through community self-help and thus highlighted many of the contradictions of liberal social programs.

But it would be shortsighted to idealize Vanguard. To repeat, the organization included middle-class whites whose rejection of participation was not always due to lack of opportunity, and the group's leaders and members alike often advocated for the same goals as the EOC, albeit in different form. No doubt, to create *queer* political alternatives is no small task; historical models of critiquing liberalism often sustain an investment in normativity based in the family or secular rationality or reduce all identity-based oppression to mere symptoms of other forces. In addition, Vanguard's call to expand the terms of inclusion or to stand outside them—be that in the form of unconventional sex/gender or the advocacy of alternative terms for productivity and value—often maintained the primacy of atomized individualism. This again highlights some of the conflicts in defining radicalism in LGBT movements: as militancy, antinormativity, or a critique of a market economy. Furthermore, it is also true that a wide variety of political strategies are complicit in those paradigms that they denounce. Liberalism's core tenets allow for its critique, and the logics of competing political systems in the West can overlap as much as they diverge—especially when it comes to the question of agency.[179] One example is the concept of self-determination, a common ideal of radical critics of the War on Poverty; as Denise Ferreira da Silva argues, it is based on the fantasy of a sovereign subject, an ideal itself vested in racial subordination.[180] Critiques of normativity are complicated as they, too, are often conceived in the limited terms of free choice and autonomy. Vanguard's call for freedom—from economic exploitation or from social norms—thus could sidestep its own investments in a self-realization outlined by structures of race, gender, nation, and labor. All that noted, Vanguard's vision was unique, and the fact that the group stood near to forms of outsiderness and refusal that were not always legible within these terms is significant.

Frances Fox Piven and Richard Cloward argue that federal antipoverty programs were, at the end of the day, a way of controlling 1960s social disorder and imposing a managerial structure that would shape the poor's political trajectory.[181] The authors value political actions that are often described as "inchoate." [182] They show that supposedly disorganized forms of resistance, such as riots or rent payment delinquency, linked social movement actors and inspired federal responses, even if such resistance was later compromised by the terms of reform. One possible example in San Francisco was the riot at Compton's Cafeteria. But one might also consider those who refused to adopt new identities provided to them by social movements—and also by the medical establishment and the federal government—as they continued to turn tricks, do drugs, and live outside the law. Even more important, one cannot assume these to be only expressions of individualized alienation or lack of agency, rather than alternate modes of defiance expressed in or outside of formal organizations.

In short time, the Castro would gain prominence as San Francisco's gay neighborhood, but it would not replace the Tenderloin or other parts of the Central City so much as it would mark the fact that certain forms of homosexuality were no longer associated with urban disorder. In other words, the ideas of deviance and criminality that were ascribed to the deep poverty of so-called red light districts and skid rows of the city were not assumed to have a relationship to the new gay culture that was taking form.[183] As I showed earlier, organizations like SIR would categorically dismiss such connections, and support for activities against police violence would continue to dwindle in favor of other reform-oriented initiatives. And even a growing cohort of gay liberationists would see the places and people of the Tenderloin as self-destructive or self-denying, stuck in the past of new militant performances of pride.

Conclusion

In the report opening this chapter, the activist Tom Ramsay differentiated between the individualistic concerns of homosexuals, addicts, and immigrants and the more group-based problems of the rest of the poor. Ramsay was wrong. Part of what makes the limited campaigns of the Central City so compelling was how the politics of sexual and social normativity were stitched right into the cloth of broad campaigns for economic redistribution. Unlike the language of visibility, which would become so popular in the later gay movement, themes of state violence and the encroachments of redevelopment provided useful ways to think about how regimes of sexual normalization were linked to other forms of exploitation and subjugation. This was a politics of neighborhood, to be sure, but one that did not lock identities into bounded areas. Instead, it announced that the places where people live and work and play—on land that loses and accrues market value—constitute the sites in which uneven power is most manifestly staged.[184] Thus the War on Poverty's "maximum feasible participation" provided at least a slim possibility for bottom-up visions. But in conforming to the terms of the good, self-regulating citizen, homophile and other activists clamped down on alternative visions. The organizations profiled in this chapter saw reforms as key to responsible citizenship, but the scarce resources and alarmist fears of the War on Poverty's federal officials limited even those modest possibilities. Moreover, homophile and other Central City efforts at collaboration often rested on analogous and sometimes competitive analyses of race and sexuality that limited the possibilities of coalition with, in particular, San Francisco's active African American leadership. This was made worse by white activists who subscribed to racist stereotypes about homosexual identity and thus were unable to recognize lesbians and gay men of color in their midst. As a result, the model of gayness as an autonomous (white) interest group continued to gather currency, and the optimism of multi-issue politics became only a rhetorical trace.

Yet acknowledging that these activist struggles were shaped as much by the inequality of San Francisco geography as by the rejections of those deemed normal shows that they stand as an exception in both U.S. homophile and urban history. More to the point, in these campaigns marginalization was not restricted to the so-called closeted experiences of homosexuals but was explained as lack of access to equal opportunity for all those outside social norms—including *hotel loners*, *prostitutes*, and *pill poppers*. Yet insofar as many of those it sought to serve did not find the narrow requirements for inclusion achievable or appealing—or did not have access to new affirmative marginal identities that might qualify them for such liberal benefits (transsexual did not yet have that status, and sex worker would emerge only many years later)—the promises remained elusive. This tug of war between the street youth and the respectable adult, between the criminal and the homosexual, would result in two pieces of broken rope by the 1970s.[185]

Hence, this history is important to the book's look at the evolution in the 1970s and 1980s of what would become a dominant model of antiviolence activism in the city. As I noted earlier, the homophile movement's lack of a documented response to individual street violence is striking. This would change in the 1970s: the issue of street violence would then take center stage in many political organizations, and activists would continue to expand the terms of threat (for example, including language) while parsing its explanation (to "homophobia"). Yet the long history of state and structural violence experienced by a diversity of queer people that organizations like Citizens

Alert and Vanguard and other Central City activists sought to highlight challenges the assumption that sexual politics must always be only one of recognition. This interpretation requires a distillation of sexual oppression from other forms of social inequality and a limited understanding of sexuality itself; it suggests that sexuality becomes salient only when other social structures, such as race, gender, and class, are suspended.[186] This approach to identity is, in part, what has entangled so much of the subsequent LGBT movement in the web of single-issue politics. It has also contributed to the understanding of vulnerability to violence as a vested component of LGBT identities, despite its resolutely uneven impact.

CHAPTER 2

BUTTERFLIES, WHISTLES, AND FISTS

Safe Streets Patrols and Militant Gay Liberalism in the 1970s

"A New 'Polk Street' Comes Alive," declared *Vector* in its July 1971 issue announcing the "welcome mats" out on Castro Street.[1] Yet this clearly was not the Polk Street that ran through the Tenderloin, lined with seedy bars, discreet meeting places, and sites of explicit sex trades (fig. 2.1). Rather, the short article extolled the area's antiques shops and boutiques that featured chic new styles; recommended a stop by the baths after dinner; and photographed its fit blonde model visiting a pet grooming shop, florist, and laundry. The article concluded that by 1971, 30 percent of local businesses were run by gay men, demonstrating the neighborhood's rapid growth. In fact, the first Castro-based realtor to advertise in *Vector*, then one of San Francisco's main gay magazines, had done so as early as 1965, and by the start of the 1970s the Castro neighborhood had firmly established its gay identity.[2] As the 1970s advanced, gay activists' concerns about police violence and entrapment in the Tenderloin continued and became a central issue for the growing number of nightclubs in the South of Market area. But within the gay-settled Castro—and along its boundary with the Mission District and in the nearby Western Addition neighborhood—fears about a different kind of violence also began to brew, fears that would firmly take hold in activists' imaginations by the end of the decade.[3]

Before the 1970s, gay activists' worries about antigay street violence were rarely articulated in public forums.[4] It was not until the start of that decade that activists began to design formal, collective response strategies to violence perpetrated by people

FIGURE 2.1 "A New 'Polk Street' Comes Alive: Strolling Castro Street," *Vector* magazine, July 1971 (COURTESY OF THE GAY, LESBIAN, BISEXUAL, TRANSGENDER HISTORICAL SOCIETY)

other than the police. The most popular solutions sought were street patrols. Approaches varied by neighborhood and one's political stance, ranging from analyses that emphasized a changing urban land market to those that highlighted the risky consequences of newfound visibility. This chapter tracks the emergence of safe streets patrols in San Francisco and New York throughout the 1970s and shows how these efforts shaped what are now common ideas of antigay violence and place-based lesbian and gay communities. I look at how a concern with safety merged with the goal of visibility and increasingly fit liberal gay politics into the broader forces of a city whose land market was ripe for new investment opportunities. During these years, approaches to economic development were joined by a shift in crime contro. strategies that saw 1960s models of community-based solutions to structural inequality, including violence, replaced by citizen patrols and other solutions that treated crime as an act of rational opportunity and called for protected neighborhoods. These changes shaped gay political organizing, a dynamic enabled, in part, by the public uptake—and merging—of urban and gay-affirmative social science.

Gay safe streets patrols popped up and almost as quickly disappeared across San Francisco and New York during the 1970s. A priest and his following of mostly young gay men and trans women carried shotguns in San Francisco's Tenderloin, gay men calling themselves butterflies blew whistles among pastel Victorians in the Castro, and guardian leathermen relied on the threat of hypermasculinity in New York's Chelsea and San Francisco's South of Market. All were short-lived, and many were more stunts or promises than efforts at sustained vigilance; nonetheless, they were a crucial part of the political landscape during the understudied years after the height of gay liberation and before AIDS activism. In addition, the status of these campaigns as militant publicity was central to their strategy: they advertised violence as a problem at the same time that they declared a spatial concentration of gay solidarity, and they celebrated the rejection of privacy as an act of radical transgression.

The legacy of 1970s safe streets activists would prove lasting, as patrols provided some of the earliest members of and models for what would become a national antiviolence movement by the 1980s. Those approaches that had a future were identity-affirmative efforts launched in the name of safe space reclamation. By the end of the 1970s, popular solutions to violence would increasingly call for urban policies such as street cleanups and heightened policing that, a decade earlier, had placed so-called sexual outcasts at odds with redevelopment and law and order, and would instead recast them as the very insurance of spatial visibility. Although this was not a goal of many early activists, who in general remained ambivalent about police protection, in both popular and social movement contexts gay vulnerability nonetheless slowly became, in effect and for the first time, the experience of being a crime victim. In outlining solutions, the independent imperatives of gay safety, gay identity, and gay neighborhood began to coalesce.

This chapter begins with an assessment of what is identified as the gay liberation era, from 1969 to 1972, in New York and San Francisco. It focuses on those organizations that might be understood as precursors to what would become militant gay liberalism—a nonapologetic, visibility-oriented approach to gay-centered left-liberal political reforms. Perspectives on vio-

, and neighborhood provide key measures for marking these
(At the start of the next chapter, the book returns to this pe-
s political visions that provided counterinterpretations in order
e critiques of policing and gentrification featured in that chap-
ving this review of the years around 1970, the chapter explores
three sa.. streets patrols from the mid-1970s: the Lavender Panthers in San
Francisco's Tenderloin, Butterfly Brigade in that city's Castro, and Society
to Make America Safe for Homosexuals in New York's Chelsea. I focus in on
a few themes—performative militancy, the definitions of threat, and the
promises of liberal psychology—that I analyze in the context of changing
urban policing and economic development regimes. In sum, this chapter
argues that these are the years in which militant gay liberalism began to assume hegemonic form and that at its center were issues of violence, safety,
and neighborhood. Moreover, I show how this set of concerns focused attention on dynamics that would be progressively diagnosed as *homophobia*.

Gay Liberation: Period and Politics

Many historians and popular sources identify the period of the mid- to late
1970s, when the first gay safe streets patrols were founded, as a time by
which both gay liberation and the homophile movement had faded from
prominence.[5] As a result, this period is mostly absent from LGBT movement
history, save for the attention paid to some select organizations and individuals, such as the late gay San Francisco Supervisor Harvey Milk. The movement returns in the 1980s with the growth of a national civil rights model
and radical HIV/AIDS-related activism. This telling discounts the continua-
tion and birth of a wide range of radical LGBT mobilizations throughout the
1970s, even as it acknowledges the tremendous momentum of radicalism
that condensed around the start of that decade. The dominant narrative
also marks the end of one civil rights model—with the demise of the homophile movement by the early 1970s—and the birth of another in the 1980s,
without analyzing the links between them. Thus it is necessary to review
some of the contentious developments that occurred in the years strad-
dling 1970 in New York and San Francisco, when gay liberation is said to
have quickly supplanted homophile politics and then just as rapidly receded
from view. To do so, a loose periodization is called for, one that strains at the
normative temporal brackets for gay liberation that puts the Stonewall riots
as the point of origin in the summer of 1969 and puts the end at the folding
of the New York Gay Liberation Front (GLF) in 1972.

LGBT activists were involved in political organizing that sought to shake
the status quo for years prior to Stonewall. Individuals challenged staid

homophile organizations while working with those who abraded the norm and were actively involved in leftist, counterculture, feminist, and black and Third World liberation struggles throughout the 1960s. In addition to organizations like Vanguard that refused dominant social mores or homophile activists who sought to widely distribute the promises of uplift, there are numerous other examples that blur the normative time lines of gay radicalism. For example, José Sarria and Guy Strait founded the bar-based League for Civil Education in San Francisco in 1961. Well-known as a drag performer, Sarria ran for city supervisor that year, and the league sponsored campaigns against police abuse and for voter registration; Strait continued to run newspapers that were unapologetic in assailing homophile and police complicity, including challenges to members of Mattachine. In April 1969 Leo Laurence, who had briefly served as editor of *Vector*, the publication of the Society for Individual Rights, penned a fiery article in which he called homophile leaders on the West Coast, including the society's members, "timid . . . with enormous ego-trips, middle class bigotry and racism," who are "afraid to become militant, afraid to put personal conviction behind their hypocritical mouthings that Gay-Is-Good." He went on to lambast the Tavern Guild, the gay bar association, as racist for refusing at one point to work with the police watchdog group Citizens Alert.[6] After being forced to leave *Vector*, Laurence cofounded the Committee for Homosexual Freedom, which blended elements of left radicalism and militancy with exuberant gay pride. A flier distributed by the committee in late 1969 featured not only the oft-repeated "Gay Is Good" following "Black Is Beautiful," but also another aphoristic allegiance: "No Vietnamese Ever Called Me a Queer." The text of the flier linked police brutality in the United States with the violence of the war in Vietnam.[7] The committee was quite active in 1969, both prior to and during the time of the Stonewall riots, working with the East Bay Gay Liberation Theatre and the Sexual Freedom League.[8]

Pre-Stonewall militancy was also alive in New York; by 1969, its homophile organizations included members such as Jim Fouratt, Craig Rodwell, and Randy Wicker (and collaborations with D.C. activist Frank Kameny), all of whom pushed daily for increased militancy if not always a stronger leftist critique.[9] On both coasts, the Daughters of Bilitis adopted a mix of political stances that flouted more norms than they honored. And individual activists cultivated radical sexual critiques, sometimes in other, unlikely social movements. All of these efforts—plus an even longer legacy of informal resistance, like other spontaneous bar revolts—made the moment ripe for a consolidated liberation vision. In other words, Stonewall is best seen not as a single point of origin, but as a spark flung from a smoldering movement. In fact, the Stonewall riots were not even mentioned in the San

Francisco–based *Vector* until four months after they happened, when a small note was published indicating that they had received a lot of press in New York.[10]

Before the fires of Stonewall had cooled, the GLF was founded in New York. In less than a year, there were branches in San Francisco, Berkeley, Los Angeles, Chicago, Philadelphia, and Austin, as well as on college campuses nationwide.[11] The branches were united on a few key points: social reform and cultural assimilation were limited; gay liberation must be tied to the liberation of women, people of color, and decolonizing nations (the name itself was another retooling of the rhetoric of analogy and alliance, based on the National Liberation Front of South Vietnam); and oppression was an issue of structural power, linked at once to the institutions of capitalism, patriarchy, white supremacy, and imperialism. Some suggest that this analysis was simplistic and utopic; the historian Terence Kissack calls it "not . . . very sophisticated" and "sometimes clumsy" for its vague and functionalist claims that gay oppression emerges from the matrix of "the system."[12] In many ways this is true; the GLF often favored the crafting of sharp rhetoric over the drudgery of practical strategy. Yet, as Kissack points out, this characterization is a not uncommon description of radical movements, and gay liberationists did consistently return to at least one issue that linked different parts of the movement together. Although efforts were made in various documents to connect the oppression of gays to that of women through the rigid function of the family or to that of people of color through discrimination, the most effective umbrella category was structural violence, and how the judicial system, military, and police functioned as overarching institutions of social control. As had been the case in the founding of Citizens Alert in 1965, the point that most linked gay politics to the struggles of other marginalized communities was that of state violence—in particular, police brutality.

In the GLF's coalition work with the Black Panthers, for example, resistance to the police was a key meeting point. One of the New York GLF's earliest actions was to support the imprisoned Panther 21;[13] and GLF members also attended the 1970 Black Panther Revolutionary People's Constitutional Convention, in which challenges to state power were leading agenda items.[14] New York GLF activists were central participants in a series of actions against the entrapment of gay men and the policing of sex trades in Greenwich Village and Times Square. In some of these collaborations, gay liberationists discussed policing as an example of how capitalism, patriarchy, and racism conspired to restrict bodily autonomy; such an analysis was a top priority of the statement produced by gay activists at the Revolutionary People's Constitutional Convention, in which members of the New York

GLF spin-off, Third World Gay Revolution, played a key leadership role.[15] But the Chicago Gay Liberation's contribution to the convention well summarizes another common concern among many liberationists of that era:

> Our most immediate oppressors are the pigs. We are beaten, entrapped, enticed, raided, taunted, arrested and jailed. In jail we are jeered at, gang-raped, beaten and killed, with full encouragement and participation by the pigs. Every homosexual lives in fear of the pigs, except that we are beginning to fight back! The reasons are not that the pigs are just prejudiced (which they are) or that they "over-react," but that they are given silent approval by the power structure for their violence against us. Since our *lives* are defined as illegal, immoral, and unnatural, there is no reason why the pigs shouldn't harass us—and they are never punished for it.[16]

The writers of the manifesto tried not to conflate the activities of individual officers with the more systemic problem of policing; instead, policing is understood to be the very expression of uneven power. Yet planted in this quote are the seeds of an analysis that would eventually unravel violence as an easy point of unity between gay and other liberation movements. In discussing prison violence, the authors suggest two kinds of threat, one from the general population of those incarcerated, and the other from the police. Although they implicate the tacit encouragement of prisoner-on-prisoner violence by the police and prison guards in their broader critique, they leave the fact and function of interpersonal violence unclear.

Carl Wittman begins to elaborate one explanation for interpersonal anti-gay violence in his widely distributed and highly influential 1970 "A Gay Manifesto," written about San Francisco.[17] The first entry in the section on "oppression" is, in fact, about physical attacks, which Wittman defines as inclusive of police and prison violence. Yet his initial example of the threat of physical violence is as follows: "'Punks,' often of minority groups who look around for someone under them socially, feel encouraged to beat up on 'queens,' and cops look the other way. That used to be called lynching." This slippage from police violence to street violence is telling. The ideas that antigay violence is disproportionately committed by people of color and that it is expressive of other forms of inequality are early hints of what would emerge as a key aspect of the new gay rights activism. Although the police gesture of "looking away" figures this violence as a form of state oppression (and suggests the basis for his dubious comparison to lynching), Wittman's response to the symptom that is homophobia is to be wary of coalitions. He suggests alliances with women, hippies, street people, and homophile groups, but—notwithstanding that he acknowledges the existence of lesbians and gay men of color—he goes on to diagnose as "tenuous" any relationship with black liberationists (because of their "understand-able" "uptightness and supermasculinity") and Chicanos (because of "the traditional pattern of Mexicans beating up 'queers'"). He also warns against "White radicals and ideologues," calling both capitalism and socialism anti-gay at their roots. Wittman writes: "The bulk of our work has to be among ourselves."[18]

The fact that this isolationist analysis emerged in the context of an essay about the limits of the new "gay ghetto" is important. Wittman explains that "San Francisco is a refugee camp for homosexuals" and that "ghettos breed exploitation" by landlords, the Mafia, police, and small business own-ers. He concludes that "to be a free territory, we must govern ourselves, set up our own institutions, defend ourselves, and use our own energies to improve our lives." At the core of improving lives is "to come out every-where."[19] In later years, Wittman would extend this analysis to a discussion of places outside the city through his involvement in the publication RFD, which described itself as "a magazine for country faggots."[20]

The emphasis on isolationism was not uniform among gay and other sex/gender liberationists; as I show in the next chapter, organizations like Third World Gay Revolution and Street Transvestite Action Revolutionaries defined the limitations of separatism and were at the forefront of struggles against policing. Furthermore, many gay liberationists considered them-selves allied with a Third World Left, and a class analysis that was concerned with racism and advocated for land claims based on self-determination for non-U.S., indigenous, and other "internal colonial" subjects.[21] But in extend-ing this position, many white gay male activists, in particular, moved to con-stitute gay politics as a sort of national liberation movement, naming gay neighborhoods and rural areas as liberation zones. One of the most striking examples is from 1970, when GLF activists from Los Angeles and North-ern California sought to establish a gay town in Alpine County, California. Emily Hobson shows how rife with contradictions the Alpine Liberation Front (ALF) was, as activists like Charles Thorpe compared ALF to the Ameri-can Indian Movement even as ALF members called themselves pioneers and held the project up as a pedagogical example for people of color-based move-ments. The effort failed as an organized vision and was dismissed by other radical activists as counterrevolutionary.[22]

Nonetheless, many of ALF's tenets—including its faith in claims for place and its use of racial metaphors—would remain popular among a majority of white gay activists in rural and urban locales. These included collectives, such as the one at Magdalen Farm in Wolf Creek, Oregon, which helped to organize the 1976 "Faggots and Class Struggle" conference, which later led to the birth of the Radical Faeries.[23] The flattening of national liberation struggles recast for gay liberation purposes not only included the reclamation of gay neighborhoods from the Mafia and the police and so-called pioneering on rural lands, but it also had visibility as a top priority. Furthermore, this stance of alliance with the Third World Left, however contradictory, also shaped gay liberationists' interpretation of the *uses* of violence. ALF member Charles Thorpe was also a San Francisco State University student activist and a member of the Committee for Homosexual Freedom. In a speech he gave at the National GLF Student Conference in August 1970, he turned to Frantz Fanon's work to argue that revolutionary consciousness is wrought out of the dialectic of violence, concluding: "If violence shall oppress us so shall it liberate."[24]

But not all gay activists were happy with the multi-issue thrust of an anti-imperialist stance. A concern with maintaining an explicit, gay-only focus was behind the founding of the Gay Activists Alliance (GAA) when its members broke away from the GLF in New York at the start of the 1970s, citing the need to focus on a more gay-centric agenda, pursue winnable social reforms, and look for positive publicity.[25] GLF members who were in solidarity with broader liberation politics were criticized by GAA founders for subordinating the concerns of gays to the struggles of "others" (even as the former position also tended to default to a focus on white gay men). Frequently made in such general terms, this complaint was nonetheless often a thinly veiled expression of opposition to working in solidarity with Black Power and Third World liberation campaigns, especially support of Cuba.[26] This sentiment fed into popular conceptions of antigay violence that slid between presumptions about the demographics of those who were violent and assertions of white gay masculinity and that, in general, individualized the problem. For example, the GAA increasingly understood the problem of police brutality less in terms of institutionalized state violence and more as a crisis of officers in need of reform, an analysis that also affirmed the power of individual masculinity to repair itself. Although by 1972 the GLF had folded in New York—the GAA would last in some form until the 1980s—the tension between these positions would play out throughout the rest of the 1970s. Indeed, GLF- and GAA-identified and/or -styled organizations would sustain throughout that decade in both New York and San Francisco, and debates between these groups were often framed by issues of race, gender, and class—and focused on contested ideas about gay protection and territory.[27] The split in San Francisco between the GAA and the GLF echoed many of these themes albeit with a decided twist that I describe later in the chapter.

In marking the supposed end of the gay liberation era, it is important to note that—although it is generally agreed that the political climate changed after 1972—any comprehensive effort to describe the aftermath is a real challenge. In sum, during the 1970s groups of various scales pushed a shift in organizing that would establish the dominance of a more reform-based, single-issue-oriented national movement by the early 1980s, even as the end of the decade also saw the growth of small, radical organizations that would multiply for years to come. Some of this was due to the growth of party politics oriented toward lesbians and gay men, as shown by the founding of the Alice B. Toklas Democratic Club in San Francisco and national policy organizations like the National Gay (and Lesbian) Task Force, first based in New York. It was also influenced by the rise of organizations challenging the antigay bias of professional fields, such as the Gay Academic Union and Identity House—a gay psychotherapy center—both in New York. The result was that by the start of the 1980s, there would be a constituency of lesbian and gay professionals dedicated to the ideological and economic support of a national movement for liberal reforms.

A final lasting influence of the early 1970s was the direct action strategy known as zaps. Zaps were loud, visible protests directed at specific individuals or institutions; the GAA, for example, directed zaps against New York City Council Majority Leader Thomas Cuite and Mayor John Lindsay. Protests were often costumed and choreographed; in one, the activist Marty Robinson dressed as a duck and led twenty others to protest the head of a private investigation agency who had claimed that he could find homosexuals because "if one looks like a duck, walks like a duck, associates only with ducks, and quacks like a duck, he probably is a duck."[28] The activist Mark Segal of the Philadelphia organization the Gay Raiders handcuffed himself to a railing at a taping of The Tonight Show and also disrupted a CBS news broadcast anchored by Walter Cronkite.[29] Individual organizations may have differed in their analyses of the issues at stake, but in general, zaps were always at least somewhat theatrical. Drama had long been a feature of political protest in a variety of movements, especially in acts involving civil disobedience—and almost all activism hopes to court public attention—yet these actions were unique for the ways in which they narrowed the focus on their targets so as to maximize notice and adopted a distinctly campy flair. This brand of publicity also shared much with the language of visibility, as each were increasingly understood as ends unto themselves.

Ray Broshears and the Lavender Panthers

High on the list of San Francisco activists best known for their love of drama and publicity was Raymond Broshears. Rumored to have been, at various times, an informant for the Federal Bureau of Investigation, undercover police officer, militant leftist, Republican, pedophile, publicity machine, mental patient, and ex-Baptist, and to have been involved in assassinations both successful (John F. Kennedy) and not (Lyndon B. Johnson and Gerald Ford), Broshears was a man generally regarded with suspicion within a variety of circles.[30] He had moved to San Francisco in the mid-1960s and was ordained in the Universal Life Church and later the Orthodox Episcopal Church of God.[31] Based in the Tenderloin, Broshears was a fellow traveler of Vanguard, and he moved among—and, just as often, against—Central City–based and other lesbian, gay, and trans activists. Broshears always wore his clerical collar, and he ministered to the socially marginalized—especially youth and the elderly, single men, sex workers, and the gender nonconforming, who referred to him as Brother Ray and supported his often combative outbursts at meetings as well as his efforts to grab the rally microphone. Otherwise, he seemed to have been pretty uniformly disliked by gay politicos; as Community Relations Police Officer Elliott Blackstone—who continued to monitor police relations with LGBT people in the Tenderloin well into the 1970s—is rumored to have once said, "if Broshears was killed they'd need the Civic Auditorium to hold the suspects."[32]

Perhaps because of a personality and a political stance deemed unstable by many, Broshears's role in the gay political landscape of San Francisco has not received much recognition. The main exception is the historian Susan Stryker, whose discovery of the uprising at Compton's Cafeteria was sparked by a narrative provided by Broshears. Nonetheless, he is a key figure in San Francisco LGBT history. He founded San Francisco's Gay Activists Alliance and one of the first pride celebrations, was regularly featured in the local press, and initiated the first nationally documented (if not the first existing) gay safe streets patrol, the Lavender Panthers.[33] And although this book focuses on group actions rather than biographies of specific individuals, it is hard to differentiate between the two in the case of Broshears's participation. This is due in part to his strong personality, but it is also an unsurprising feature of a strategy of performative publicity. The singularity of Broshears distills some of the ideals, such as the power of individualism and representativeness, at the core of political models based on militant visibility.

Broshears was active in San Francisco in the 1960s as a collaborator with Vanguard; he assumed a kind of prominence in 1971 when he led San Francisco's GAA in breaking away from the GLF.[34] The founding of the new group attracted local publicity about its decision to exclude heterosexuals; otherwise, the division looked like that in New York, with the GAA declaring it would focus on "gay issues."[35] But unlike the New York GAA, which considered the more middle-class Greenwich Village rather than Times Square to be its prime home territory, the San Francisco GAA was located in the heart of the Tenderloin and not the emerging gay neighborhood of the Castro.[36] Also in contrast to the New York GAA, which had a contested relationship with the trans activist organization Street Transvestite Action Revolutionaries, the San Francisco GAA established a formal if fleeting relationship with the California Advancement for Transsexuals Society, even sharing members.[37]

Bishop Michael-Francis Itkin, then of the Evangelical Catholic Communion, served as the first GAA president, with Broshears as the group's spokesman. Itkin was another controversial figure of that era, and he was involved in politics in New York, San Francisco, and Los Angeles. Broshears and Itkin were both in what was not an uncommon mold for gay activists in the 1970s: those associated with sex radical subcultures, including leather and sex work, who were also spiritually oriented and often members of small, offbeat religious groups—some of which they themselves founded—that combined a wide variety of traditions, including paganism. Most strongly influenced by a New Age thinking dedicated to embodiment and self-help as well as the charismatic movement and spirit-filled evangelicalism, both of which grew in popularity during the 1960s and 1970s, these groups often explained eroticism and social resistance as spiritual exercises. And they reached out to segments of the poor who fell between the cracks of progressive churches and leftist movements, such as those who would be stigmatized as "mentally disturbed" or seemed to have chosen life on the streets.[38] Itkin wrote: "Take a moment to talk to adolescent runaways, youth without homes, street people, Black people, Latin and Indian Americans, the aged, the handicapped, draft resisters, demonstrators for peace, and revolutionaries who rightly feel that the institutional church has betrayed the revolutionary message of the Gospel . . . which is an outrageous shout of Love and Joy!"[39]

Sometimes anarchistic and more often motley in their political affiliations, figures such as Broshears and Itkin played active roles in homophile, gay liberation, and other activist scenes. For example, Itkin was among those who disrupted the 1970 American Psychiatric Association meeting, demanding that homosexuality no longer be designated a mental illness. As a result, these activists cannot be simply dismissed as eccentrics, especially insofar as they were among the few people who sought to include the broadest categories of outsiders within their fold. Furthermore, they did so with virtually no intention of normative rehabilitation or assimilation, and—like many of their followers—they were stigmatized for their mix-and-match gender presentations, appearance in both leather and religious garb, and refusal to adopt many of the conventions of political rationality and interpersonal propriety. Indeed, both men reportedly cultivated a kind of charisma that at once repelled and enthralled. This was not only a trait of personality; their religious beliefs magnetized many of their followers but put them at odds with other urban outreach churches and radical gay activists who also spoke to the poor and saw social change as a religious responsibility.[40]

Furthermore, despite a wide welcome, the San Francisco GAA had clear enemies: they officially "purged" "Trotskyites" (namely, members of the Socialist Workers Party) while also publishing a list of homosexual "oppressors" that was topped by the gay magazines the *Advocate* and *In Unity* (of the gay Metropolitan Community Church), and also included the Alan Stanford Modeling Group, Dial-a-Model, and the San Francisco Police Department, among many more. Broshears is reported to have tried to keep lesbians from speaking at the first pride parade.[41] And on more than one occasion GAA members crashed homophile events, shouting "fascist pigs."[42] Granted, the exclusion of Socialist Workers Party members was by no means unusual among leftist or liberal organizations during that time, nor was a liberationist rejection of gay organizations dedicated to assimilation. But Broshears's alliances were far from consistent and could shift in an instant. At other times, the GAA touted good relationships with homophile organizations, gay businesses, and the police. Broshears even kept a letter of commendation from Officer Blackstone.[43] But Broshears also declared: "For any Gay person to work with the SFPD at a time like this, when they are using the Gay as the election year scapegoat, would be the same as a Jewish person helping the American Nazi Party down in Pacifica," and the GAA undertook numerous actions challenging police harassment and nonresponse to antigay violence.[44]

In 1973 the GAA would sharpen its focus on violence by forming the Lavender Panthers (originally described as the Purple Panther Division of street people), which sought to address the problem of antigay and antitrans violence by patrolling the Central City areas of the Tenderloin and South of Market with sawed-off pool cues and shotguns, and the group's membership was based in those active in street economies.[45] The announcement of the Panthers' founding spread around the nation; reports surfaced in *Time, Rolling Stone*, and newspapers as far away as Texas, and the group was featured in the pages of the *San Francisco Examiner*.[46] The press photo of the group's announcement featured Broshears sitting in the center with a clerical collar, cross, pool cue, and shotgun, flanked by two more feminine-presenting people (called drag queens by the *San Francisco Examiner*), one mod and one hippie, holding a revolver and another shotgun (fig. 2.2).

By their choice of name and press photo—which resembled the now iconic portrait of Bobby Seale and Huey Newton—the Lavender Panthers

"LAVENDER PANTHERS" WOODY AND FINIS FLANK REV. RAY BROSHEARS
Patrol armaments will include guns and sawed-off pool cue displayed at press conference
—Examiner photo by Bob Bryan

Gay Vigilantes to Fight Back

FIGURE 2.2 Lavender Panthers, *San Francisco Examiner*, July 7, 1973

presumably sought to pay homage to the Black Panthers across the Bay, in Oakland. This is also suggested by the logo used—the same roaring panther, although lavender. But I am unaware of the existence of any practical alliance between the Lavender Panthers and the Black Panthers.[47] Moreover, the patrols that the Black Panthers started in 1966 were primarily to watch for police abuses, and the later Seniors Against a Fearful Environment program organized free transport and escorts to serve the elderly rather than try to catch their attackers.[48] The Lavender Panthers' focus, in contrast, was on the problem of so-called punks. Although the supposed perpetrators of violence were rarely explicitly racially identified by the group, according to *Rolling Stone*, they were primarily Chicanos, and, as reported in the magazine *Coast*, included many who were black and some who were Chinese.[49] As Broshears reported in his newspaper the *Gay Crusader* (and repeated in *Time*), he had founded the Lavender Panthers after he was attacked by teenagers, whom he described as causing havoc in the neighborhood with firecrackers. According to Broshears, when the teenagers discovered he had called the police, they beat him.[50] The same issue of the *Gay Crusader* reported on two other attacks on gay and/or trans people—one on a neighborhood resident

FIGURE 2.3 *Gay Crusader*, August–September 1973 (COURTESY OF THE GAY, LESBIAN, BISEXUAL, TRANSGENDER HISTORICAL SOCIETY)

named Jimmy Lorton (also identified as Sally) by "gangland mugging" and another on two gay sex workers by the police (fig. 2.3).[51]

Broshears saw the police as at once nonresponsive and the source of unchecked brutality. He called for faster response times, but alongside the articles cited above, the *Gay Crusader* also included a cartoon in which two men from the "'responsible' gay leadership" watch a beating of two others, one by the vice squad and the other by a random mugger. The wry caption reads: "If only we had more police on the streets, we could all feel so much safer." Notwithstanding this critique, the solution the Lavender Panthers chose still might best be described, as it was by local papers, as vigilante vengeance.[52] As Broshears explained to *Time*, "We didn't even ask questions. . . . We just took out our pool cues and started flailing ass."[53] The *Examiner* conducted an informal poll that suggested that the people of the Tenderloin appreciated the Panthers; nonetheless, gay organizations joined with Frank Fitch, then president of the Society for Individual Rights, to denounce the Panthers as a mere publicity stunt.[54] Although this was no doubt the move of a more conservative organization eager to court police support, the fact of Broshears's isolation from most other gay groups, including other liberationist ones, is worth noting.

The Lavender Panthers and the GAA advocated revolution but eschewed socialism and did not avow anarchism; instead, the organizations put forth an analysis of an underclass produced from the nexus of sexual and gender marginalization and poverty. (In one article Broshears was quoted describing those who identified with the Panthers as "the very poor, the crippled, the transients, ones who have been in prison, those who have really been shat upon."[55]) Nonetheless, the GAA had been formed in the name of a focus on gay issues, in opposition to multi-issue organizing. In addition, Broshears spouted a somewhat unexpected cultural moralism, given his sympathetic portrayal of the most marginal. He despised drug use and pornography, and he selected drug dealers as one target of the Lavender Panthers and also "purged" them alongside "deadwood," "talkers/informers" and those "who did not subscribe to the six points of the Manifesto of Gay Liberation."[56] A later article presumably written by Broshears blasted "trash gays" as "have-nots" who violently attack the "haves" and comprise a destructive "under-world" based in thievery and drugs.[57] Granted, Broshears's ire was reserved for those whom he felt ensnared the most marginal into what he considered a culture of dependency and exploitation. Accordingly, he wrote articles claiming there was a connection between the Central Intelligence Agency and the drug trade, and he made many complaints to the city about strip clubs and the aforementioned modeling agencies.[58] Ultimately, Broshears and his organizations manifested an idiosyncratic mix of libertarianism, anarchism, New Age and charismatic religious ideology, and sex radicalism. But the question remains as to how Broshears managed to become one of the most visible members of San Francisco gay liberation at the start of the decade and then was so quickly shunted from view.

The most common theory held by fellow activists is that Broshears was an agitator for the Federal Bureau of Investigation. Broshears either eschewed or spoiled many of the kinds of alliances between gay organizations and others that the bureau's Counter Intelligence Program was most aimed at disrupting, including black freedom struggles, socialist groups, and women's liberation.[59] Broshears had had a contentious relationship with the Bureau since he had testified against David Ferrie, naming him a conspirator in the Kennedy assassination; also, Broshears's own convictions for corrupting minors—most likely an antigay charge—may have left him compromised.[60] Many people were also surprised to learn that Broshears was cited by *San Francisco Chronicle* columnist Herb Caen as a friend of Oliver Sipple, who is credited with knocking away the arm of Sara Jane Moore, President Gerald Ford's would-be assassin.[61]

A more likely explanation has to do with the politics of publicity: in the still relatively embryonic gay political climate of the early 1970s, the spectacle that Broshears and his crew presented certainly made good media copy. The absence of evidence demonstrating that Broshears's actions were typically sustained after he held an initial press conference at least suggests that publicity itself was a central part of his strategy, one that he may have tried to model on the Black Panthers' own vexed relationship with media coverage.[62] Broshears's success was also arguably due in no small measure to political geography. His projects were not the only gay liberation visions in town; Emmaus House and the Committee for Homosexual Freedom, GLF-Berkeley, campus organizations, and various rap groups were also in full swing. But the most active centers of gay liberation were close to the ground zero of—and often collaborated with—California's New Left, black radical, and lesbian-feminist scene across the San Francisco Bay in the cities of Berkeley and Oakland. Broshears's GAA and Lavender Panthers fell into the overlapping areas of—and gaps between—three countervailing forces in San Francisco: a dominant, albeit declining, homophile movement in the Tenderloin that ministered to the city's nonnormative poor but also maintained a gay-focused and reform-based agenda; a growing gay neighborhood in the Castro that was modeled in many ways in opposition to the deviances associated with the Tenderloin; and a counterculture that embraced nonconformity but was often heterosexual or uninterested in political organization. Broshears's identification with the Tenderloin's broad matrix of marginality and his rejection of assimilation—combined with his rhetorical support of the primacy of gay identity and the need for social transformation—placed him between San Francisco's homophile groups, church and city programs, and counterculture. His religiosity, however atypical, also set him outside the constellation of many groups on the left, as did his advocacy for those whom many dismissed as the so-called lumpen proletariat. His sense of affinity with the Black Panthers—who also named the *lumpen* as part of their cohort and rejected what they considered to be the empty promises of city reformism—makes sense; Broshears's advocacy of the explicitly sexual (and, in particular, homosexual)—as well as the suggested racial antagonisms behind Broshears's patrolling—nonetheless set them far apart.

In keeping with his support of the urban poor, Broshears and his comrades organized many Tenderloin protests against hotel development and related antiloitering sweeps and housing evictions. Working with the Neighborhood Legal Assistance Foundation, they filed a court case against the San Francisco Police Department alleging that the police targeted gay and street people for loitering as a way to remove them from the neighborhood while the San Francisco Board considered an area redevelopment proposal.[63] This action was evocative of the "Clean Sweep" protests by Vanguard six years earlier, when that group proclaimed, "All trash is before the broom." Yet unlike many other radicals of the time, Broshears insisted that his project was, first and foremost, one of gay and religious organizing—as opposed to the more common forms of multi-issue left internationalism—and he felt antipathy toward many of those with whom he might have collaborated. As a result, he failed to capture many activists' imaginations by showing that a wide range of nonnormative identities and social arrangements were subject to social exploitation and control in the city. Like the homophile and other Central City activists some years earlier, Broshears ultimately did not provide a clear analysis of how gay identity per se constituted a position of structural social inequality staged at the level of neighborhood. The Lavender Panthers' inclusion of trans women and the gender nonconforming did differ from other activist visions that cast gender nonnormativity as an unintended negative consequence of social rejection, and the Panthers did not adopt a reparative or aspirational model for sexual or gender identities. In addition, although the hybrid religiosity of Broshears and his fellow travelers included a selective asceticism that disparaged drug use and prostitution and advocated for self-help solutions that were, like liberal reform efforts, indebted to popular psychology, the activists did not necessarily model productivity, propriety, or participation. Furthermore, this religious approach cultivated a hierarchal leadership that valued transformation through faith in a leader—who in this case was at least somewhat motivated by a strong sense of his own personal marginalization. In a city in which a democratic and reform-oriented homophile movement had long predominated, Broshears's outrageousness and his authoritarian conduct meant that it was easy for others to dismiss his example. And activism related to neighborhood inequality that was based on the violence of policing linked to redevelopment would be increasingly supplanted by gay calls for territory. But the Lavender Panthers' strategy of focused publicity would prove lasting. Patrols effectively declared that street violence was a problem and that neighborhood protection would be the ground on which security would be won.

The Lavender Panthers dissolved in 1974 after opposition to their activities grew; the media may have also lost interest in the group. Many of its members were supposedly committed to building a new group called the People's Guard.[64] Broshears and his publications and organizations stayed on the scene throughout the 1970s, earning the ire of many radical- and reform-oriented gay activists. He appears to have focused much of his energy on two groups—the Old Folks Defense League and its Helping Hands Services—which provided advocacy and support to the Tenderloin's elderly and fought for, among other things, the protections of rent control; Broshears also founded the Teddy Roosevelt Republican Club during this time.[65] Yet unlike in the early years, Broshears's activities stayed on the margins of gay politics, as other groups formed. Once the spearhead of the gay pride festival in San Francisco, he had been ousted from its leadership by the following year. Broshears would still attempt actions of small numbers of people and large promotional efforts, but the press no longer framed his fringe activities as models of San Francisco gay radicalism. Otherwise, for the most part by 1975 his star had faded. At the end of that decade, Broshears called for the resurrection of the Lavender Panthers, but nobody seemed to hear; he died in relative obscurity in 1982.[66]

Bay Area Gay Liberation, Gay Action, and the Rise of the Butterfly Brigade

Just as the Lavender Panthers were dissolving, a new organization was conceived to unite gay politics with a broad network on the left, particularly the labor movement. Founded at the start of 1975 in part by the labor organizer Howard Wallace and Claude Wynne, a former youth member of the New York GAA, Bay Area Gay Liberation (BAGL) would be involved in some of the most successful political campaigns of the 1970s, including the Coors Beer boycott and the defeat of the Briggs Initiative that sought to outlaw lesbian and gay schoolteachers. In the year of its founding, BAGL put forth a radical gay agenda based on a broad, multi-issue critique of capitalism and the state but aimed at targeted reforms that were meant to maximize the group's chances of attaining winnable goals.[67] BAGL's stance on policing reflected this position. Members of the Gay Community Defense Committee advertised what would be the founding meeting of BAGL in conjunction with a citywide campaign for police accountability: "We understand police all too well—BY THEIR DEEDS! From the racist zebra dragnet to the Chinatown payoffs to the failure to investigate widespread reports of brutality against Chicanos and Latinos in the Mission to police infiltration of progressive organizations to the 'clean up' of pornography and prostitution in the Tenderloin to the crackdown on gays and shakedown of gay businesses—BEHAVIOR, NOT WORDS, TELLS THE STORY!"[68] The police problem was understood to be multifaceted and endemic, yet open to reform.

In the fall of 1976, after a year of increasing debate, BAGL split into two discrete organizations, due to by-then familiar rifts over adopting a broad-based leftist versus gay-focused agenda.[69] The more left-identified Progressive Caucus continued affiliation with BAGL, pursuing coalition work on issues as varied as support of farmworkers and solidarity with the Chilean resistance to military dictator Augusto Pinochet.[70] The group's members argued that a struggle unilaterally focused on gay oppression would only assist "white middle class men" and that "gay people's problems cannot be solved by reacting to the symptoms of anti-gay prejudice, but must attack the system at the root . . . : Imperialism."[71] The spin-off organization, Gay Action, had a different aim in mind. The second item in its statement of purpose proclaimed: "We support the right of self-defense. We will resist violent attacks against individuals in our community."[72] In December 1976 Gay Action initiated what would be its biggest project: the Richard Heakin Memorial Butterfly Brigade. The patrol was named after a gay man who had been murdered by high-school students in Tucson, Arizona; the openly antigay judge in the case limited their sentences to probation. Outraged activists took this as a reflection of resurgent national antigay sentiment, spearheaded by the vitriolic proclamations of Anita Bryant, a celebrity whose antigay crusades had garnered attention across the country. Gay Action decided it was necessary to develop a local response, and the group chose a location that was considered the ground zero of both community and risk: the Castro.[73]

By the mid-1970s the Castro had established itself as the locus of gay residential, commercial, and social concentration and was featured in articles— such as the one in *Vector* discussed at the opening of this chapter—as the place where gay life could be fully realized. This idea is also supported by the sociologist Manuel Castells's famous study that measured business and bar locations alongside residential populations in the 1970s Castro. His indicators of residency are based on gay-identified informants who had worked as pollsters for gay candidates, voter registration data on multiple-male households, gay-identified businesses and bars, and the concentration of votes for Harvey Milk, the 1975 gay candidate for city supervisor.[74] Thus for many men who voted, identified as gay, socialized in gay-identified places, and did not live with family members, the Castro was a place they called home.[75]

The members of the Butterfly Brigade were a mixed bunch, although they were almost exclusively white gay men.[76] Randy Alfred was a well-known gay journalist who was news editor of the *San Francisco Sentinel*. Hank Wilson and Ron Lanza had both been founders of the Gay Teachers Coalition, which would later be involved in the fight against the Briggs Initiative. Assunta Femia was a Radical Faerie who had gone to prison for antiwar protesting, and Ben Gardiner was an actor, activist, and local character.[77] Ali Marrero was one of the few women and people of color in the group, and the only woman of color. Marrero was also active in lesbian feminist organizing in the nearby East Bay cities of Oakland and Berkeley; she later remembered that she first came to the Butterfly Brigade in large part because she used to hang out in the Castro on her motorcycle.[78] Although the protections offered by the Butterfly Brigade extended to women, its membership—and the demographics of the Castro's street life at the time—was dominated by men.

Not all of the Butterfly Brigade's members did—or could afford to—live in the Castro. Nonetheless, it functioned as an important place of symbolic identification, and the patrollers' actions marked its hubs and borders. Every weekend patrollers would meet around 10:00 PM on the corner of Castro and 18th Streets (the center of the area's commercial strip), near the "control center"—a converted bakery delivery truck that they would park in an always available (since it was illegal) spot in front of a fire hydrant. The truck was occupied, in keeping with an unspoken agreement with the police that it would be moved if an officer requested. In two shifts, groups of activists would take up positions on designated street corners, including in a popular cruising park, near a public transportation hub, and in other spots considered most central to gay nightlife. Armed with whistles, index cards, pens, and walkie-talkies, they were supposed to respond to any incidents and to record the license plate numbers of cars whose passengers shouted antigay epithets (or threatened worse), and to blow their whistles loudly if any threat came up close. Once they collected information, they looked up license plate numbers and sent letters to the cars' owners. The letters carefully recorded "conduct" and included slurs spoken and aggressive gestures (indeed, the majority of incidents recorded on the forms or index cards were of verbal threats or antigay epithets and harassment).[79] The index cards noted even more details, including, on occasion, the race of attackers, in particular when they were people of color.[80] The fact that race was usually not indicated suggests that the patrollers assumed that the race of most potential attackers was white (a common default, especially in majority white contexts), or that members of the Brigade considered race irrelevant. Years later, many former members of the patrol remembered the primary threats to be young white men from San Francisco suburbs. They also recalled the limits posed by the group's status as mostly white; as Alfred described, this was a feature of gay life in the Castro, but he also acknowledged that "we tried to be more inclusive but trying isn't becoming more inclusive, necessarily, and some of the reasons probably had to do with structural issues."[81]

Although the group received a few irate letters back, the campaign continued without real complaint and petered out after a year or so. In spite of activist burnout, the Butterfly Brigade believed that the project had been a success and that the rare confrontation with violence signaled to potential attackers that people in the Castro were not to be messed with. The whistle strategy became the enduring legacy of the patrol, borrowed from the feminist antirape movement and combined with general anticrime guidelines.[82] Wilson estimated that over 30,000 whistles were distributed in an ongoing, widespread campaign to furnish them as a welcome to new gay arrivals to San Francisco and, by doing to, to forge a symbolic marker of community

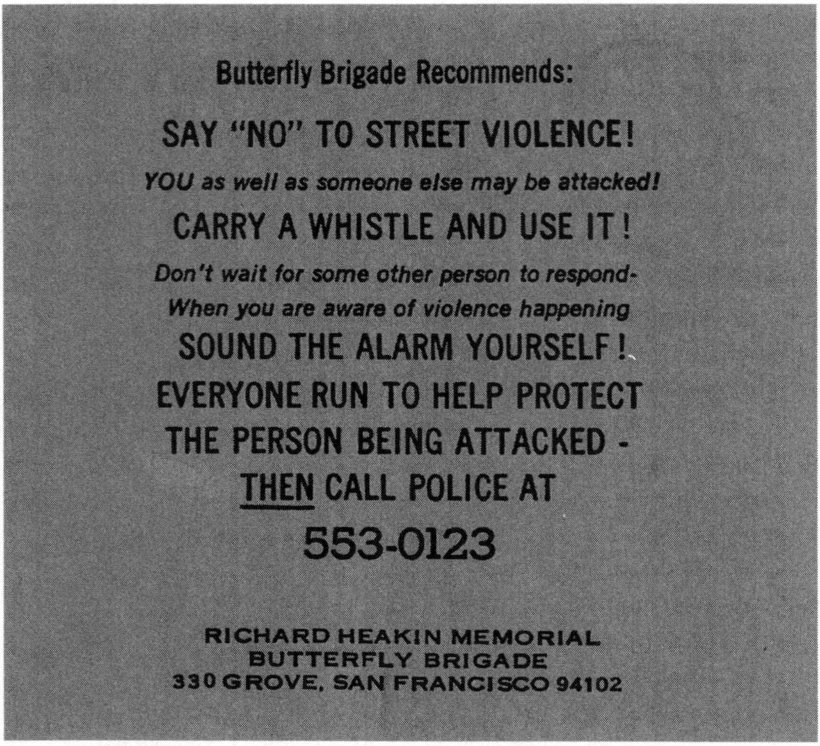

Butterfly Brigade Recommends:

SAY "NO" TO STREET VIOLENCE!

YOU as well as someone else may be attacked!

CARRY A WHISTLE AND USE IT!

Don't wait for some other person to respond-
When you are aware of violence happening

SOUND THE ALARM YOURSELF!
EVERYONE RUN TO HELP PROTECT
THE PERSON BEING ATTACKED -
THEN CALL POLICE AT

553-0123

RICHARD HEAKIN MEMORIAL
BUTTERFLY BRIGADE
330 GROVE, SAN FRANCISCO 94102

FIGURE 2.4 Butterfly Brigade card (COURTESY OF THE GAY, LESBIAN, BISEXUAL, TRANSGENDER HISTORICAL SOCIETY)

(fig. 2.4). The whistle campaign was also intended to push gay men to invest in each other. Wilson said: "We were all taking care of each other, and that was a conscious thing," and "part of our intention was to change the psychology of that community, of our community, so that people would help each other."[83] Many of the activists involved in the Butterfly Brigade held onto moving memories of successful whistle-blowing moments, in which windows were flung open, gay men came running, and attackers had no place to hide. Gardiner recalled a night a few months after the patrol had begun, when many Brigaders were taken off the beat to attend a fund-raiser: "And so we went in the [Castro] theater and we said: OK, whatever happens, happens. We came out and there had been an incident. The community had reacted perfectly. And the cops came. All of the whistles blew. . . . We thought, wow, we have accomplished our goal."[84]

Although the Butterfly Brigade did not work with the police directly, they collaborated informally, even after the *San Francisco Examiner* published an inflammatory piece calling the Butterfly Brigade a "semi-vigilante"

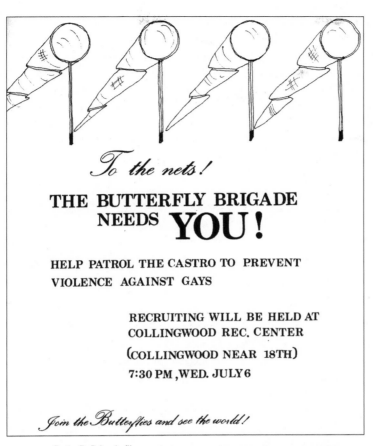

To the nets!

THE BUTTERFLY BRIGADE
NEEDS YOU!

HELP PATROL THE CASTRO TO PREVENT
VIOLENCE AGAINST GAYS

RECRUITING WILL BE HELD AT
COLLINGWOOD REC. CENTER
(COLLINGWOOD NEAR 18TH)
7:30 PM ,WED. JULY 6

Join the Butterflies and see the world!

FIGURE 2.5 Butterfly Brigade flier (COURTESY OF THE GAY, LESBIAN, BISEXUAL, TRANSGENDER HISTORICAL SOCIETY)

group.[85] Yet far from Broshears's promises of swift justice with the fist, the Butterfly Brigade was committed to being peaceful, with the goal of restraining attackers until the police—summoned by a chorus of whistles—arrived on the scene (fig. 2.5). Many gay San Franciscans responded proudly to the brigade. In *The Mayor of Castro Street*, Randy Shilts declared: "The fact that a virile gay community was taking care of its own problems startled the city's establishment, which could barely deal with homosexuals of the Judy Garland vintage."[86] As the masculinism of Shilts's comment suggests, a desire for order arguably linked, rather than separated, the Brigade and the police. This was despite the facts that members of the Butterfly Brigade did avow a commitment to feminism and that the flair and even anarchistic style of the patrollers—who marched in the annual Gay Pride parade carrying large butterfly nets and sometimes had to be discouraged from walking off shifts with tricks they had picked up—was counter to the top-down structure of formal policing.[87] Indeed, although most of the sissy-identified gay men stayed within BAGL after Gay Action's split, some, such as Radical Faerie Assunta Femia, stayed in both organizations and struggled with ambivalent feelings about policing. In the 1970s very few gay activists—regardless of their formal political position—fully trusted the police even as their primary concerns varied from naming police violence to police harassment to police inattention.[88]

Although those remaining in BAGL maintained a more hardline opposition to the police writ large, the members of the Butterfly Brigade argued that it was important to demand police protection as part of a critique of unchecked state power. As Wilson remembered, the Brigade was dedicated to "process" and "critique," and its primary goal was to forge a community-based response as an alternative to the ineffective state model. Wilson explained that this was why they did not wear uniforms (which would have been too "militaristic") and that their purpose was self-determination: "we didn't want to give the community an illusion that someone was taking care of us. We wanted everyone in the community to feel like they were on patrol, all the time, looking out for everybody else."[89] Yet the fact that the Butterfly Brigade hoped to inspire action on the part of the police is crucial to understanding the broader—and lasting—implications of the group's analysis of urban violence and gay community. Individual members of the patrol were active in the push for a police reform campaign that would increase the number of lesbian and gay officers and institutionalize sensitivity training. This was not only to stem police violence but also to make officers aware of the simultaneously general and specific needs of gay victims. Indeed, these would be the primary demands of antiviolence organizations that followed on the heels of the Butterfly Brigade.

The argument for increased policing arose from activists' faith in a theoretically neutral third party, but it also stemmed from the widespread conviction that antigay violence was produced by the very phenomenon of an openly gay population. According to Shilts: "Attacks came with the neighborhood's national prominence."[90] There was a distinct sense that the gay community was caught in a vicious circle: new rights led to more visibility, which produced more backlash—which, in turn, led to the need to find new ways to protect rights. Visibility was often equated with coming out and its attendant risks and possibilities. One extension of this concept was the assumption that lesbians and gay men were forced to manage their risk of violence through the decision of whether or not to disclose their identity or to pass as straight, and that either decision would have its benefits and limits.[91] In his study of the Castro, Manuel Castells described this dynamic: "A typical gay around the Castro may be characterized as having short hair and a moustache, and dressing in a T-shirt, jeans, and leather jacket. This 'code' serves to increase visibility and communication amongst gays as well as helping to identify intruders and potential attackers."[92] That said, the popularity of a supposed gay look was also considered troublesome by activists, especially among those who had begun to argue that dress and comportment that were gender nonconforming might increase one's risk of being a target. This was linked to commonplace complaints about an emerging "clone" culture of athletic white men in mustaches and Levis.[93] Cultural activism hoped to undermine stereotypes, and thus many activists avoided the assumption that one could *spot* homosexuality. In this way, visibility was understood to be most realized via representation or abstraction; in other words, visibility simply functioned as shorthand for an increased presence in the public sphere, from media coverage to electoral power to neighborhood life. Neighborhoods came to be seen as an expressive demonstration of gay identity and thus the collective asset most in need of protection.

The idea that increased visibility led to increased violence worked in tandem with different estimates about who was the most likely to commit antigay violence. To repeat, members of the Butterfly Brigade later described attackers as mostly young white men in their late teens and early twenties from a variety of areas, mostly the suburbs or outlying parts of San Francisco.[94] Despite the fact that the members of the Brigade did not necessarily trade in racial stereotypes about violence and antigay threat, they were well aware of a general concern held by white middle-class gay men that lower-income neighborhoods with a majority of residents of color near the Castro—including the Latino Mission District to the east and the African-American Western Addition to the north—might be perceived as a threat.[95] Marrero described her decision to become involved as also linked to her concerns that "young Latino men were being blamed for antigay violence in the Castro."[96] It was her strong connection to and trust in Butterfly Brigade members Lanza and Wilson that made her hope for more effective collaborations between organizations of mostly white gay men and those of Latinos, in general.

But a viewpoint that valued commonality over difference could not be described as widespread, and accusations became heated when in 1977 Robert Hillsborough, a white gay man, was killed on his way to his home in the Mission after a night out on the town. The contentious Ray Broshears is rumored to have called a march on the Mission; others, including those associated with the Butterfly Brigade, discouraged people from following Broshears and the media from paying him any mind.[97] But in the ensuing years, public concern about antigay sentiment in neighborhoods like the Mission would grow and would be tied to discussions of gentrification in which white gay men played a markedly visible role; the narratives told overwhelmingly cast gay people as white and local residents of color as homophobic. That was far from the only explanation for such events—for example, in her famous essay "Thinking Sex," Gayle Rubin noted that in San Francisco developers were the main driver of a real estate industry that excluded, among others, low-income gays. Nonetheless, Rubin's conclusion was a popular one: that "competition for low-cost housing has exacerbated both racism and homophobia, and is one source of the epidemic of street violence against homosexuals."[98]

Debates about gay participation in gentrification and its relationship to antigay violence are described in detail in the next chapter, but here it is useful to explore some of the broader contexts in which the model of safe streets patrols developed. Many gay activists and Castro denizens considered it to be common knowledge that signs of threat such as aggressive language and gestures led to violence, and that increased visibility increased violence. Yet these correlations, like assumptions as to who tends to be most violent, reflect various strains of social science scholarship in the 1960s through 1970s that were being taken up in public policy and popular commentary. Often working toward different ends, such studies included research on the causes of disorder, violence, and hate as well as practical blueprints for local solutions. Although ostensibly independent, they overlapped in a few key understandings. As I elaborate later, one common theme was that urban violence and homophobia were symptoms of other forms of social inequality. Another shared interpretation was that self-monitoring communities were best equipped to recognize threat, and that signs of threat (visual and otherwise) often signaled violence to come. By the end of the decade, the merging of these formulas would guide the shift from grassroots patrolling to evidence gathering, as later evinced by the formalized antiviolence movement's collection of surveys and personal testimonials.

A variety of initiatives for putting a stop to violence adopted these perspectives, including the 1967 President's Commission on Law Enforcement and the Administration of Justice and the 1968 National Advisory Commission on Civil Disorders. In 1968 the Omnibus Crime Control and Safe Streets Act emphasized participatory solutions by identifying a community policing model for addressing urban crime. Advocating the role of residents in neighborhood watch efforts, these solutions were seen by many on the left—including activists who had been involved in organizations like Citizens Alert during those years—as viable alternatives to top-down policing strategies such as the growth of Special Weapons and Tactics units (San

Francisco's Tactical Division was formed in 1967) and the subsequent law-and-order ideologies of Johnson's successor in the White House, Richard Nixon. By the mid-1970s, such programs were common in middle-class neighborhoods gripped by fears of crime and committed to community identity—not unlike the Castro—and they ultimately linked the work of the police with that of residents and business owners. Indeed, the Tavern Guild provided economic support to the Butterfly Brigade, and the Golden Gate Business Association supported watch efforts that would follow in the wake of the patrol.[99]

The sociologist David Garland interprets community policing programs as efforts to involve citizens in the process of policing themselves. In later years, such alliances became foundational to a new wave of policy philosophy about crime that Garland dubs the "criminologies of everyday life."[100] This approach advocates civilian participation in the management of "criminogenic" situations, which include factors such as victim conduct and criminal opportunity.[101] Such theories take crime as a given and thus emphasize the calculation of risk and prevention. Simply put, they manage victims and environments deemed vulnerable. Among the early proponents of this line of thinking were James Q. Wilson and George L. Kelling, who in 1982 developed the infamous "broken windows" theory of crime control that sees all signs of disorderly life in a neighborhood as encouragements to criminal behavior. As Garland shows, this analysis would be enabled by rational choice theories that discounted the need for social intervention and advocated increasing penalties as a deterrent. The latter policy would become a key goal of the gay antiviolence activism that followed in the wake of the Butterfly Brigade, when rational choice theory began to dominate criminology in the 1980s. Community policing, though, is a policy that tends to appeal across the political board. Thus in the mid-1970s, the informal data-gathering activities of the Brigade, which recorded not only actual violent crime but also *signs* that violence *might* follow, paralleled the development of Wilson and Kelling's argument, even if for divergent ideological ends. In other words, both the Brigade and "broken windows" proponents were on the lookout for strangers versus regulars, and called for familiar on-the-beat cops.[102]

To understand how the representation of threat was increasingly equated with the power of violence itself, it is important to examine the relationship between the Butterfly Brigade and one of the group's avowed primary influences, the feminist antirape movement. This link was assumed most salient with those aspects of antirape activism focused in the public sphere—in the realms of representation, the street, and the law. A prime example during the late 1970s was when feminists began "Take Back the Night" marches to reclaim city streets from violent attack. One of the most famous was held in 1978, when more than 3,000 women, many attending a conference sponsored by Women against Violence in Pornography and Media, walked through San Francisco's North Beach district.[103] This was the third consecutive year that the group had organized rallies down San Francisco's main pornography strip, Broadway. Although many gay safe streets activists cite the tactical use of whistles and street patrols as the most prominent links between early gay and feminist antiviolence movements, also important is the shared interpretation of certain acts as simultaneously directives to and realizations of violence. Pornography and antigay epithets, in the absence of actual attacks, were treated as injuries unto themselves, with the threat of violence both promised and assumed manifest.[104]

The organizers of the 1978 San Francisco march through North Beach not only considered the threat to be pornography but also the city, as did New York feminist antipornography activists who hosted tours of Times Square in the 1970s.[105] By merging the fight against pornography with that against street violence, activists identified the city as one place in which the violent promise of pornography was fulfilled. In the case of the Women against Violence in Pornography and Media campaigns, merging the fight against pornography with that against unsafe streets cast the *signs* of the seedy city as sinister. The preface to the book *Take Back the Night*—edited by Laura Lederer, a member of the group—reads: "We live in cities like the tame pheasants who are hand-raised and then turned loose for hunters to shoot, an activity called sport."[106] Pornography and city streets are formally different, but they both attest to the tenuous power of visual iconography. During the early years of the "Take Back the Night" movement, Kelling published his first essay on his 1970s fieldwork on neighborhoods' "quality of life."[107] As explained earlier, his approach treats signs of disorder (from broken windows to loitering to strangers) as symptomatic imperatives that, in the long run, operate not unlike pornography. Put another way, signs of urban disorder, like pornographic images, are understood to act as directives to commit violent crimes. When quality-of-life theory became manifest in urban policy many years later, these visual (and audible) signs—that is, young people sitting on stoops with open drinks or talking loudly late at night—were considered, as was pornography, violence unto themselves.[108] This is a telling reversal of Del Martin's police beat columns (see chapter 1) that considered police entrapment of homosexuals to be continuous with the anti-obscenity regulations applied to theaters that screened pornography.

One of the first places where Kelling's theories would be translated into policy years later was Greenwich Village, where quality-of-life violations were often interpreted as particularly threatening to the neighborhood's gay community. For this reason, it is important to note the significance of paying attention to the language of antigay threat, including epithets, and to recording details such as the automobile makes of attackers. Although Butterfly Brigade members collected this information so as to track down those whom they had already identified as perpetrators, the use of general descriptive information in outlining those marked as criminals was returning in significance as explicit policy during this period. (It had previously been a long-standing if not always avowed feature of anticrime policy.[109]) For example, racial profiling was first instituted by the Drug Enforcement Agency during the late 1970s, and it depended on signs connoting race and class. One outcome would be that certain visual, auditory, and other cultural features were treated as not only linked to people labeled violent or criminal, but were increasingly understood as inherently violent themselves. In later years, these claims—that cruising cars, youth hanging around, or loud talking were threatening or violent acts—functioned to defy research that challenged the claim that violence or crime was increasing and became a reason to demand that new studies be done.[110]

Members of the Butterfly Brigade indicated that the group ended after a short time because there was simply no longer a need for it. People were using whistles, and violence was decreasing. Ambitious plans to bring the patrol to other neighborhoods, like Polk Street in the Tenderloin, were deemed unfeasible.[111] And by 1978 property values in the Castro were escalating, and a wider mix of gay and lesbian residents were seeking homes in more affordable places like the Mission and Western Addition. BAGL released a warning: "Speculators Get out of Our Neighborhood!"[112] The group argued that gay people were being used by speculators to "bust" neighborhoods by moving white gays in and families of color out. BAGL continued to support a San Francisco Housing Coalition campaign for a municipal antispeculation tax, and members of BAGL's Progressive Caucus and Gay Action were part of the long-standing fight against the eviction of Filipino and Chinese tenants of the International Hotel.[113] Although the Butterfly Brigade had not been formed for the project of claiming new territories per se, others would use the model of citizen participation and call for police responsiveness in order to make areas more amenable to higher-paying tenants, and they often capitalized on racial tensions.

From Police Action to the Leatherman Stroll: Patrolling in New York

In 1976, the same year the Butterfly Brigade was founded, a new organization was formed in New York, just north of Greenwich Village in Chelsea. The Society to Make America Safe for Homosexuals (SMASH) was formed by a small group of new gay residents of the gentrifying neighborhood.

A mixed-use area with light-to-moderate industry, small businesses, and residences adjacent to a nearby waterfront economy, Chelsea was home to a decreasing number of working-class whites and poor and working-class Puerto Ricans and African Americans, many of whom lived in the postwar public housing units in the neighborhood. As was happening throughout New York, the departure and displacement of racially diverse working-class communities from dilapidated housing stock was followed by an influx of middle- and upper-income whites who refurbished homes and businesses. The area was also home to the majority of New York's gay leather and S/M bars, courtesy of its emptying industrial spaces and proximity to the popular public sex spot of the piers along the West Side.

According to its founders, SMASH was developed to stop a spike in antigay violence perpetrated by the neighborhood's teenage boys.[114] Gay residents claimed that young men and boys from the neighborhood had been targeting so-called macho gay men as a way to assert their own masculinity and that the police turned a blind eye. In response, SMASH decided to send out patrols as decoys, so that they could prove to attackers the power of gay masculinity. They also hoped that by rousing and documenting antigay violence, they might elicit a formal police response. Like other patrols of the era, visibility was to be realized in physical space and involved making threats visible as well. At least one former member, Michael Shernoff, explicitly identified the group as "vigilante."[115] Like Broshears's earlier patrol, SMASH's was identified as publicity; the founders even called it a "smoke and mirrors" operation, in which the distribution of a press release ranked among the most significant aspects of their actions.[116] (The press release not only announced SMASH as a new organization in Chelsea but declared its presence in neighborhoods ranging from the East Village to Central Park West and Brooklyn Heights; it appears, though, that only Chelsea was patrolled.) Their ultimate goals were an increase in police presence and a neighborhood wide recognition that antigay violence was unacceptable.

Unlike the Butterfly Brigade, which emerged directly out of political organizing, SMASH was a small group of about seven people, some of whom had been involved in gay politics and others of whom were self-identified gay businessmen, artists, or professionals more active in gay professional and cultural organizations. Like Wilson and Lanza from the Butterfly Brigade, Shernoff was a former teacher; he later became a well-known psychologist and writer focusing on gay issues. The main founder of the group, Louis Weingarden, was a composer who was later involved in a New York City Human Rights Commission challenge to HIV/AIDS discrimination and harassment by landlords.[117] Like the Butterfly Brigade, SMASH members were a majority, and perhaps exclusively, white. In this mix of features, SMASH might be considered a hybrid between its contemporary, the Butterfly Brigade, and other organizations of patrolling leathermen in San Francisco's South of Market that would appear a few years later, such as the Surveillance Squad and the Gay Guards.[118] The latter organizations were self-identified as neighborhood anticrime projects rather than gay safe streets patrols. Although they expressed concern about antigay violence, they were vehement that they were there to protect both gay and straight and often clarified that they were not collaborating with local gay organizations.

What is most compelling about SMASH, though, is the status of psychology in the organization. At least one member was a professional psychologist, and the group's public interpretation of the causes of violence appealed largely to psychological causation. For example, cofounders Larry Durham and Louis Weingarden gave a television interview in which they argued that the young men from the neighborhood were eager to prove their own masculinity, which Weingarden claimed had been damaged by the fact that "half of their fathers were out of work." Due to the economic disinvestment in urban manufacturing and services of the 1970s, Durham argued, youth did not have access to employment or youth services and instead were "hanging out" all day long. According to Weingarden, these young men were not interested in battery for the purposes of theft or in the cause of antigay prejudice only; rather, their violence was a "testing ground" for an insecure masculine identity and a way to take out the frustrations of social inequality. The hypermasculinity of gay leathermen served as an ideal target.[119] Although as far as I am aware the members of SMASH never publicly addressed the racial identities of the young people involved, they sometimes used coded language to suggest that the attackers were Puerto Rican or African American, indicating, for example, that threats came from west of 8th Avenue, where most of the public housing—whose residents were significantly Puerto Rican or African American—was located.[120]

The focus on low-income youth of color was particularly curious, given the events of the summer of 1976. That June a fifteen-year-old boy from Greenwich Village stabbed a fellow Villager to death. Allegedly linked to violent gang activity, the incident received much attention since the killer was middle-class, an honor student, and most likely white.[121] Just after the creation of SMASH, in September 1976, there was a murder in Washington Square Park. In this case, the victim was of Dominican descent and the attackers were presumed to be white Italians. The *Villager*, a local newspaper, included numerous pieces featuring residents who described the perpetrators as the real victims and declared that if the police would "do their job" to get "undesirables" out of "our parks" none of this would have happened.[122] Residents even went so far as to organize a rally, in which they held signs

reading "Don't Punish Our Kids for Trying to Do Your Job."[123] These sentiments typified a highly racialized public discourse of social conflict among
white working-class New Yorkers during the late 1960s and 1970s, which
identified white ethnic communities as the victims of the larger social and
economic changes involved in the period's so-called urban crisis.[124]

Despite a context in which violence was often associated with white youth
in the middle-class Greenwich Village, the members of SMASH continued to
patrol areas that were largely home to low-income people of color. The view
of the neighborhood's public housing as a source of violence continued even
as the patrol sought a well-publicized truce with Greenwich Village youth.[125]
The prevalence of this understanding of race, poverty, and violence must be
analyzed in light of the public discussion of this nexus in the 1970s. Wilson
and Kelling's "broken windows" research built on the growing backlash to
liberal social science research that had been commissioned by the Johnson
administration a decade earlier. Although the studies most associated with
the racial liberalism of the War on Poverty had at least named the structural
roots of violence and crime in spite of focusing on their cultural and psychological dynamics, new research used many of those same logics to call for
individual responsibility rather than publicly funded social programs.

Key was the continuous influence of those ideas typified by *The Negro
Family: The Case for National Action* (the Moynihan Report) from over ten
years prior. The "culture of poverty"–type thesis at the center of the report
had been roundly criticized after its release. For example, Lee Rainwater and
William L. Yancey published an edited volume whose contributors argued
that low-income communities of color were far from pathological and that
the economic and political causes of poverty must be at the analytic fore.[126]
Yet the racialized paradigm of a cycle of poverty retained currency across political positions as it associated poverty with undesirable behaviors, rather
than asking why certain acts were stigmatized or questioning the predictive instrumentalism of the social-scientific method from which it came.
For liberals concerned about the dismantling of social programs, solutions
based on individual participation and improved psychological health would
continue to appeal, as would rhetorical metaphors combining the roots of
sexual nonconformity and racial alienation. Although it would be put to different programmatic ends, a model that correlated racialized poverty with
violence and other antisocial behaviors would persist.

During the late 1960s, when the culture of poverty thesis was most
widely popularized, another line of research had begun to develop that was
also deeply rooted in the psychological explanations for social inequality
endemic to postwar liberalism: the study of *homophobia*, a term that first
appeared in Kenneth Smith's "Homophobia: A Tentative Personality Profile"

and George Weinberg's *Society and the Healthy Homosexual*, both published by 1972.[127] As Daniel Wickberg contends, the concept of homophobia did not have much popular currency until the 1980s; nonetheless, it was quite familiar to gay psychologists in the 1970s.[128] Many of these psychologists were activists; as members of the Gay Activists Alliance and Mattachine Society, they advocated for the removal of homosexuality as a mental illness from the American Psychiatric Association's *Diagnostic and Statistical Manual of Mental Disorders* while forging new community-based alternative mental health services (a possible affiliate of SMASH was reported to be an early member of the gay psychology association called Identity House[129]). The Mattachine Society organized a public event with Weinberg in the early 1970s, and his book was reviewed in numerous gay magazines.[130] Weinberg had himself even published pieces about homophobia in the gay press, including an article about the "homophobic scale" produced by Smith; he also wrote about gay activism.[131]

Weinberg's and Smith's writings presented homophobia as a measurable set of negative attitudes rooted in a pathological fear of lesbians and gay men.[132] Although Weinberg's work targeted the therapeutic profession and neither source named poor people or people of color as uniquely homophobic, persistent ideas about the supposed problems of the black urban poor provided a key context for analyzing the popular uptake of new psychological research on the roots of antigay sentiment. Here it is important to remember at whom the Moynihan Report directed its most fierce indictment: female-headed households, which allegedly had a negative impact on normative masculinity and male self-esteem. Weinberg's work, which circulated among activists, presented a psychodynamic analysis that understood homophobia to be rooted in insecure masculinity and an unstable sense of self that could find expression in violent behavior. As a result, in activists' imagination, homophobia and a racialized culture of poverty might be understood to share the same origins. For many white and middle-class reform-based activists who saw ending poverty as unfeasible, this correlation translated into a growing fear of the poor and people of color despite calls for social services.[133]

Although this was by no means a uniform assumption of lesbian and gay activists, it echoed the thoughts of gay liberationists like Carl Wittman, who—in his 1970 "A Gay Manifesto"—had diagnosed as "tenuous" coalitions with African Americans and Chicanos because of a homophobia that was assumed at once to be "cultural" and "understandable."[134] These assumptions minimized the experiences of LGBT-identified people of color as well as antigay sentiments among white people. Furthermore, in addition to theorizing about the roots of interactional homophobia, new gay-affirmative psychology asserted that a public gay identity was correlated with high self-esteem. Weinberg was among the first to theorize what he called "internalized homophobia" (itself evocative of racial liberals' persistent diagnosis of black "self-hate").[135] Thus, women and men who engaged in same-sex relations but did not identify with lesbian or gay—identities that were increasingly seen as the privileged forms of homosexuality—were often presumed to be suffering from an intractable but self-imposed low self-esteem.

Conclusion

Such ideas about the causal dynamics of identity, violence, and neighborhood would, over time, influence the trajectory of antiviolence activism and determine how the public perceived homophobia. Although SMASH existed for only a couple of months, many of its members joined a new neighborhood organization, the Chelsea Gay Association. The group was the first block association organized under the banner of sexual identity, and from it the Chelsea Anti-Crime Task Force—later the New York Anti-Violence Project—emerged.[136] Although few activists in the groups profiled here named neighbors who were low income and of color as representing a primary threat or posed crime as a singular category of analysis, the convergence of dominant understandings about violence, poverty, and homophobia and an emerging model of community policing amenable to the juridical amelioration of violence and homophobia would inevitably shape how these efforts were received and replicated. The result would be a set of generalizations that, in the following years, would assume the status of common sense in popular discourse: visibility begets violence, people of color and those of low income are uniquely homophobic, and antigay violence should be considered first and foremost a crime.

These correlations would also inform subsequent academic narratives of the period. For example, in *Erotic City: Sexual Revolutions and the Making of Modern San Francisco*, Josh Sides dedicates a chapter to "Taking Back the Streets of San Francisco."[137] Sides describes the response to antigay violence during the 1970s as a struggle between straight Latinos and white gays in the Mission and Castro, and between straight African Americans and white gays in the Fillmore in the Western Addition. Although Sides notes that homophobia alone is an inadequate measure to assess these dynamics, his conclusion—that "non-Latino gays—themselves victims of a unique brand of homophobia—were discouraged from moving where they pleased, from exercising the same democratic rights that politically active Latinos demanded for themselves"—is an example of the limits behind the assumptions that marginalized sexual identity parallels or operates apart from racial segregation in the urban land market.[138] Furthermore, Sides considers this history alongside campaigns against pornography, yet in his account, homophobic Latinos in the "provincial world of San Francisco's ethnic neighborhoods" act parallel to City Hall and feminists who attack "smut" and also fall on the same side as Hollywood's representations of antisex vigilantes.[139] But the antisex zoning restrictions inaugurated during these years—or even the zeitgeist that sensationalized as it demonized sexual underworlds—were part and parcel of a transformation of U.S. cities that would not benefit poor and working-class Latinos and African Americans, and instead would stigmatize them by using the very terms of sex, intimacy, and kinship.[140]

This history makes explicit how the idea of homophobia can be a racial project.[141] This is not to say that violence against gay men (of color or white) was not fueled by homophobia; of course, it often was. But the names used for this violence and the remedies proposed for it would, especially in the years following, draw on very narrow modes of interpreting sexual stigma and the regulation of sex/gender roles. In other words, the sins of the city were understood by those in power to be manifested not only by the supposedly perverse sexual mores of homosexuality, but also by the failed normative gender roles, family structures, and sociality associated with racialized poverty. The ongoing patterns of reinvestment in central cities would call for neighborhood cleanups that concentrated on the removal of low-income people of color—including those of LGBT identity—while naming white, middle-class gay men as beacons of the future.

This dynamic would be dubbed gay gentrification by many, and it would intensify after the heyday of groups like the Butterfly Brigade and SMASH. And despite the fact that activists initially called for gay-responsive policing in the increasingly middle-class Castro and Chelsea, new residents would demand policing in areas undergoing the early stages of gentrification—namely, disinvestment and displacement. As the antiviolence movement grew and formalized, emphasis would expand from the protection of designated gay spaces to include the qualification of threats beyond neighborhood borders, yet definitions of victims and intent were predicted on the ideas about geography described here. These changes would be linked to the success of gay activist calls for increased visibility; the performative militancy of gay liberation had put lesbians and gay men into a media spotlight that activists used to focus attention on the problem of violence and the power of neighborhood. Their determined and unapologetic demands for representative government and its responsive administration combined many of the tactics of a range of protests in the 1960s and 1970s with the exuberant flair of gay pride. The election of San Francisco Supervisor Harvey Milk in 1977 was a prime example of a political campaign that resembled in many ways the homophile movement's emphasis on gay rights but dispensed with its respectable appearances in terms of modest and gender-conventional dress and a more subdued (if also determined) approach. Furthermore, this militancy tended to distill sex/gender transgression to highlight those privileged by gay liberalism's unmarked racial and gendered terms: based in visibility, outside families of origin, and within the dominant forms of public recognition.

The motley mix of goals and tactics that would characterize this mode of militant gay liberalism was not unfamiliar to a variety of social movements in the 1970s, including those of the propertied and those who sought to restrict sexual and gender-based rights: the 1970s tax revolts in California and the anti-abortion movement that followed the 1973 Supreme Court decision in *Roe v. Wade* are but two examples. To make this last point is not to make all gay and property rights parallel. In fact, Isaac Martin argues that the 1970s tax revolts were initially motivated by small homeowners seeking protection from the market rather than a uniform expression of conservative business interests.[142] But the point is to highlight the complex ways in which radical tactics and liberal goals were expressed in the same terms during this period. Nonetheless, this was not an uncontested process, and other ideas about violence and neighborhood were in play. New organizations took as their mission to challenge the call for safer streets via police protection; in doing so, they linked police violence to patterns of gentrification and placed the protection of white gay people at its contested center. Forged by activists on the left, many of them lesbian feminists and of color, these arguments would highlight the contradictions inherent to this model of militant gay liberalism. These activists would argue that gay rights claims based on state protection and neighborhood ownership must be understood alongside the economic retrenchment that characterized the late 1970s and early 1980s, and they called for alternate activist visions.

CHAPTER 3

"COUNT THE CONTRADICTIONS"

*Challenges to Gay Gentrification at
the Start of the Reagan Era*

When the world isn't all wrong or right
And the truth isn't clear at first sight
And you don't know who you ought to fight—
That's contradictions!
—"That's Contradictions!," from "Count the Contradictions,"
by Lesbians Against Police Violence

On January 21, 1979, as they left Amelia's—a lesbian bar in San Francisco's Mission District—Sue Davis and Shirley Wilson were harassed and detained by the police, who then charged them with disorderly conduct. Soon after, Davis and Wilson were contacted by the organizations Wages Due Lesbians and Lesbian School Workers.[1] In less than three weeks, a meeting was called to discuss their case at the Women's Building, a community space then newly relocated in the Mission. Over a hundred women attended. The discussion focused on what solutions should be sought, from the establishment of what would later become the city's Office of Citizen Complaints to an increase in lesbian officers to a more systematic challenge to policing.[2] Among adherents to the last position, Lesbians Against Police Violence (LAPV) was born (fig. 3.1).[3]

Lesbian School Workers, which had called the mass meeting, had emerged out of the struggle against Proposition 6, also known as the Briggs Initiative. Sponsored by California State Senator John Briggs in 1978, the initiative sought to ban lesbians and gay men, and their supporters, from teaching in the public schools. For many

FIGURE 3.1 Lesbians Against Police Violence flier (COURTESY OF THE GAY, LESBIAN, BISEXUAL, TRANSGENDER HISTORICAL SOCIETY)

of the women who would join LAPV, the 1978 election had cut both ways, resulting in the defeat of Proposition 6 but the passage of Proposition 7, another contested item on that year's ballot. Proposition 7 cemented the reinstatement of California's death penalty, and it was also supported by Briggs. The consciousness that lesbian and gay empowerment could happen alongside currents of disenfranchisement—and the fact that this was not a concern shared by all lesbian and gay activists—was at the core of LAPV and its campaigns that would follow. As a former member, Maggie Jochild, later described the 1978 election, "We lost in equal number. And I felt this huge gulf between me and the men, you know, *the boys*. Who were just thrilled. I had my roommates, my collective, and I had other people by that time, but there was still this sense of alienation. And they didn't—the boys suddenly were like, 'Well, our job is done. We're done.' And we didn't feel done."[4]

Ronald Reagan, formerly governor of California and soon to announce his run for president, publicly opposed Proposition 6 but supported Proposition 7. A few months earlier, Reagan had also pushed for the passage of Proposition 13, which decreased property taxes.[5] After Reagan's election as president in 1980, the differences between gay-focused and multi-issue political strategies would grow. Antigay violence continued to be a concern of gay activists, who presented the rising influence of the Religious Right as the cause of a spike in antigay bashing, and by the early 1980s, antiviolence organizations would be established on a local and national scale.[6] But although the formal LGBT antiviolence movement would focus on the establishment of police sensitivity programs and, later, hate crime laws, a wave of other lesbian and gay activists took on what would become known as Reaganomics.[7] These activists argued that the coalition of interests in the Religious and New Right not only represented a moralistic assault on sexual freedom but also stood for a regime of law and order and economic retrenchment that would cut stark lines of inequality not easily reduced to sexual identity alone. And they believed that the growing apparatus of state punishment, in the form of new crime control strategies and the restructuring of urban neighborhoods, provided particular opportunities for lesbian and gay activists to pursue multi-issue political organizing.

Organizations like LAPV and the Alliance Against Women's Oppression (a multiracial offshoot of the Third World Women's Alliance) in San Francisco; Dykes Against Racism Everywhere (DARE) and the Coalition Against Racism, Anti-Semitism, Sexism, and Heterosexism in New York; and Black and White Men Together (BWMT) in both cities, among other groups, organized systematic attacks on Reagan's policies as they crafted critiques of a dominant gay political agenda that they felt presented too limited a vision.[8] They pursued campaigns against Reagan's proposed 1981 Family Protection Act, attacks on women's reproductive rights, prison expansion, and police violence; they participated in the movement against apartheid in South Africa and the resurgence of the Ku Klux Klan in the United States; and they called for house worker unionization and an end to white gay racism. In sum, these activists understood the parallel reduction of public services, expansion of the criminal justice system, and barricading of family and neighborhood alongside a growing lesbian and gay rights movement to be key contradictions inherent to liberalism—contradictions that hinged on the interlocking of sexual, racial, economic, and gender-based subjugation.[9]

Although few groups outside of the growing antiviolence movement put anti-LGBT street violence at the top of their agendas, a range of radical organizations worked to dislodge the main anchor of increasingly mainstreamed antiviolence ideologies: the quest for gay responsive policing in designated neighborhoods. They also showed how certain lesbian and gay people were harmed rather than benefited by gentrification. Moreover, they refused the discourse of protection as they sought safety outside traditional measures, often rejecting the empirical studies and institutional demands that marked gay liberal reform as well as many heteronormative leftist alternatives. In doing so, they demonstrated that identification with the state risked making a call for violence while seeking a wide variety of lesbian and gay rights claims, even as many of these activists also maintained that demands on the state be a key political strategy.

This chapter focuses on activist critiques of gay participation in gentrification as they turned on the question of violence, both state- and street-based, during the late 1970s and early 1980s. I provide a look at the activities of three organizations: the Third World Gay Coalition (TWGC), LAPV, and DARE, all of which were active around 1980. These groups presaged the impacts of a new economic and spatial order, and they modeled innovative responses based on leftist critique and an embrace of everyday life. All of the organizations featured were majority lesbian, two exclusively; all prioritized antiracism, one was a group of all people of color. These groups' analyses were parts of an array of activisms that strayed from the data-centered approaches that increasingly characterized militant gay liberalism and its logic of visibility, and they provide an important interpretive perspective on the dynamics of gentrification. Indeed, this chapter puts the intellectual work of these groups into direct conversation with the scholarly literature about that period. Consistent with the book's focus, these examples are drawn from New York and San Francisco. Yet I approach these areas beyond bounded core neighborhoods, looking to the East Bay outside San Francisco and to boroughs other than Manhattan in New York, areas where many people of color, women, and radical activists (and, of course, those who were all three) not only found community but also affordable housing.

But the chapter first provides a review of lesbian, gay, and trans organizations from the 1970s that focused on issues of race, gender, and class. I also take a quick look at a group outside my geographic focus: the Combahee River Collective, a black feminist organization in Boston, Massachusetts, active from 1974 to 1980. Although the mainstream LGBT antiviolence movement had its roots in New York and San Francisco, this cannot be said of alternate visions. It is impossible to map in that same way the converging influence of a variety of feminisms and racial justice movements, an outcome in part of the ambivalence many of these activists had toward— and their unequal access to—the land market and public social programs.

The Combahee River Collective developed foundational analyses that would be taken up by small organizations across the country even as these arguments would be ignored by most mainstream movement trajectories. Thus in order to understand the history of the LGBT antiviolence movement's consolidation—as well as the concerns of its critics—one must consider this genealogy. Nonetheless, the chapter otherwise sticks to New York and San Francisco, noting that the stronghold of lesbian and gay antiviolence organizing that was linked to neighborhood protection did, in turn, influence the actions of those who ultimately challenged such a strategy.

Gay Liberation: Period and Politics, Take Two

Chapter 2 described some of the contested issues central to gay liberation politics at the start of the 1970s and demonstrated how they shaped activists' ideas about violence and neighborhood in the following years. Nonetheless, the scene I have thus far painted does not represent the full terrain of politics and purpose, especially in the years following 1972. The unfolding of the 1970s saw the elaboration of ideological differences that reflected divergent positions across aspects of identity, such as race and gender, and among those who were increasingly out as lesbian and gay members of Marxist-Leninist and Maoist parties. On the most basic level, this is reflected by the fact that many of the most militant at Stonewall were also active in Black Power, Third World liberation, radical feminist, and New Left politics or shared the no-holds-barred ethos of street youth.[10] Considered this way, using Stonewall as a marker is not only arbitrary because of the kinds of radical activism that preceded it in places all across the country, but also because it cleaves Stonewall from other social movements of the period. Karla Jay explains in her political memoir, *Tales of the Lavender Menace*:

> [The events that night] were made possible by the passion of activists who had gained expertise in the women's movement, the civil rights struggle, student uprisings across the country, the antiwar movement, and socialist or communist groups. Stonewall happened because Rosa Parks had refused to give up her seat to a white man and lived to tell the tale, and because Martin Luther King, Jr., had walked peacefully down many southern streets and been assassinated for his efforts. The Stonewall uprising was not so spontaneous after all; it arose out of the courage and vision of participants in other movements.[11]

Despite substantial differences, the majority of the members of both the Gay Liberation Front and Gay Activists Alliance in New York were gay white men, and many reported the groups as unwelcoming, tokenistic, or even hostile to other people. Thus new organizations were born: lesbians joined with those alienated by the mainstream feminist movement to found Radicalesbians; Sylvia Rivera, Bubbles Rose Lee/Marie, and Marsha P. Johnson were three of the first members of Street Transvestite Action Revolutionaries (STAR), which focused on trans politics alongside the needs of street youth and did not stigmatize survival strategies; the Third World Gay Caucus was an effort of radical people of color inside the Gay Liberation Front, which later spun off as the autonomous Third World Gay Revolution (TWGR); Bob Kohler, who remained a mainstay of Greenwich Village gay politics for decades, was among the core members of the social activities–oriented Aquarius cell of the front; Marxist-Leninists began Red Butterfly; Lee Brewster initiated the Queens Liberation Front in the name of so-called drags; Gay Youth organized young people excluded from the bar culture; and Transsexuals and Transvestites brought together those so identified to craft activist and other plans.[12] These were joined in subsequent years by groups, such as the Black Lesbian Caucus of the Gay Activists Alliance (whose members later founded Salsa Soul Sisters, Third World Wimmin, Inc.) or El Comité Homosexual Latinoamericano, who organized campaigns and social outings among varied arrangements of lesbians and gay men of color.[13]

Similar developments unfolded in the San Francisco Bay Area: Third World Gay People broke from the Gay Liberation Front in Berkeley; and the Gay American Indians, Gay Latino Alliance, Third World Gay Caucus, Black Gay Caucus, and Asian American Feminists were among the many organizations that paid primary attention to the analyses and experiences of lesbians and/or gay men of color.[14] The National Transsexual Counseling Unit was founded in 1969 and worked with the smaller groups COG (which stood for either or both Conversion Our Goal or Change: Our Goal) and the California Advancement for Transsexuals Society; these organizations also collaborated with the projects of Ray Broshears. Also during these years, a series of Third World lesbian and gay conferences were held, including one in Oakland, California, in 1976. In 1979 the first National March on Washington for Lesbian and Gay Rights was held simultaneously with the first National Third World Lesbian and Gay Conference, which numerous New York and San Francisco activists attended.[15] Although these groups pursued different and sometimes contradictory goals, they represented many trajectories that would not be taken up by mainstream lesbian and gay organizations.

A prime example of a divergent goal was that of gay place-based self-determination. TWGR, for instance, emphasized control over one's own body and destiny rather than the establishment of separate territories. Its sixteen-point plan for liberation was based on the Black Panthers' ten-point program of 1966 and included a strong rhetorical indictment of the judicial system.[16] As Abram Lewis argues in his study of multi-issue organizing and coalition work by the Gay Liberation Front, TWGR's influence helped usher in an emphasis on antiprison and police brutality activism among a mix of gay liberationists in the early 1970s.[17] Members of TWGR also emphasized the points that racial and sexual identities are not autonomous categories and that for many lesbians and gay men of color, gay separatism was neither appealing nor feasible. TWGR advocated coalitions with black and Third World liberation struggles and challenged white gay liberationists who claimed that such organizations were intractably antigay or who focused on the sexism of black men over that of white men.[18] And although TWGR described black and Latino antigay sentiment as, at least in part, a symptom of "masculinity-deprived Third World males," it did so in a way that attempted to sidestep—even as it somewhat replicated—the instrumentalism of liberal psychology. For example, in its statement "The Oppressed Shall Not Become the Oppressors," TWGR set concepts like "real man" and "masculinity" off in quotes, marking them as idealized and unattainable constructions.[19]

This approach to antigay sentiment was also echoed by the Black Panther Huey Newton's own public statement of solidarity with gay liberation: he noted that it is a "kind of psychology" that drives antigay violence as well as violence against women.[20] In addition to suggesting that an antigay response is at least somewhat rooted in insecurities born of oppression, Newton highlighted the ways in which American masculinity, in general, is premised on the fear of lost manhood. In this way, TWGR and Newton did not locate the origins of homosexuality in damaged psyches (as many liberals did) nor in the decadence of capitalism (as many leftists and nationalists did); neither did they advocate for rights-based or revolutionary curatives, arguing instead for bodily freedom and new coalitions. Although TWGR's emphasis differed from that of other liberation groups, it was by no means a solitary exception. STAR's writings also focused on the free, self-determining body. Finally, the assumption that sexual and gender nonnormativity were scorned by heterosexual black and Latino people was also routinely denied by activists who touted good relations with their family and other political comrades or who underlined the kinds of queer desires that structure heterosexuality in general.[21] In sum, issues of alliance, bodily integrity, and multiply marginalized experiences—and how each made separatism or land claims more or less desirable—would be key features of many future organizations of lesbian, gay, and trans people of color and multiracial groups dedicated to an antiracist vision.

Another concern of many of these campaigns was the systematic exclusion of lesbians, gay men, and trans people of color from not only hetero-sexual but also normative gay institutions, and the solutions they sought were as rooted in process as they were a demand for inclusion. The Black Gay Caucus of the San Francisco Bay Area said: "We want to provide an alternative to traditional white-oriented gay institutions. We want to share emotions and resolve problems through open dialogue."[22] One major target was the bar scene. Bars constituted the social core of many LGBT people's lives, but they also manifested rigid exclusions—from within and without—along race, gender, and class lines. Throughout the 1970s and into the 1980s, groups such as DARE in New York, the Gay Latino Alliance in San Francisco, and BWMT in cities across the country joined other organizations to challenge violent police attacks on some bars (in particular, those frequented by people of color and the gender nonconforming) and exclusionary practices in others (such as those that would "double card" or deny entrance to members of these targeted communities).[23] Activists would also take on normative gay culture's aesthetic and cultural rejections, especially those manifested by the white and masculine homogeneousness of the popular "clone" look.

Inclusion in formal institutions had never really been an option for some of these activists, and they choreographed strategies that were often less comprehensible to activists with stringent movement ideas. Organizations like STAR did innovative work to cast activities of daily life as alternative world making, especially for those whose lives were marked by stigmas beyond homosexuality and who also lacked access to material resources—such as street kids who turned tricks, or low-income trans people locked out of formal employment and social services. STAR was at the forefront of activism that addressed street-based sex trades in Times Square, and the group fought police abuse while providing informal housing and monetary and legal aid to each other. This was also the case for the Queens Liberation Front, which made great strides in the fight against antitransvestism laws.[24] Although many of these groups did participate in formal campaigns, they just as often rejected—and were rejected by—the majority of those radical-identified activists because (like many of the members of Raymond Bro-shears's crew) they refused the everyday affects and formal tenets of both revolutionary leftism and reformism. This could include embracing combativeness and aspirational wealth rather than proscriptive forms of inter-personal communication and antimaterialism, prioritizing immediate plea-sure over long-term progress, or cycling in and out of heterosexual worlds. They also promoted informal modes of collectivism that were counter not only to official forms of social service provision but also to pedagogical models of anarchism. In this way, they cultivated an approach that was at odds with the revolutionary versus reform divide that dominated the white and more gender-normative liberationist scene.

Considering different models for what counts as activism is also helpful for analyzing the significance of hobby- or arts-based organizations. These groups engaged themes like violence or neighborhood, yet since their activities centered around poetry, dances, sports, and pooled child care—to name but a few—they tended to be regarded by others as nonmovement commitments. Nonetheless, cultural productions and community discussions reconceived queer critique by bridging the divides between public and private, politics and culture, and by designing innovative forms of collective organization; *This Bridge Called My Back* and other publications done by Kitchen Table: Women of Color Press provide perfect examples of the mix of strategies showcased during this period, in particular by feminists of color.[25] Also significant during the 1970s was how many lesbian and gay members of socialist and communist parties and nonaffiliated activists identified with a leftist perspective drew on Marxist theories in order to explore the limits of the liberalism behind new lesbian and gay rights claims.[26] Examples include the Stonewall Coalition, in San Francisco, and the Lavender Left and Union of Lesbian and Gay Socialists, both in New York.[27] These groups took on common debates on the left—for example, about the benefits of cadre formations or the so-called national question—at the same time as they struggled with how to integrate issues of sexuality into the development of a political line. One of the key thinkers to whom many lesbian feminists turned was Mao Zedong, especially his writings on contradiction and self-criticism. Mao's take on contradiction highlighted particularity as a way to understand the precise challenges of any given struggle and became one way in which activists sought to balance what was being constituted (and denigrated) as identity politics with their anticapitalism. Self-criticism also became a mode of incorporating ideas of personal experience or standpoint into the process of political struggle.

A final key influence that emphasized an account of location was put forth by the Combahee River Collective. The collective was founded in Boston in 1974 by black feminists seeking to build a more radical group than the National Black Feminist Organization, which had started the year before.[28] Unlike its predecessors, the collective was explicitly supportive of lesbian issues—lesbians, in fact, constituted a majority of the group—and its analysis focused on the interlocking structures of racism, sexism, heterosexism, and class. Their affirmative politics was centered on the experiences of black women and pointedly addressed the racisms of white feminism and white lesbian separatism as well as the sexism of many expressions of black nationalism. The group also identified with socialism. In their 1977 manifesto "A Black Feminist Statement," the members wrote: "The most general statement of our politics at the present time would be that we are actively committed to struggling against racial, sexual, heterosexual, and class oppression and see as our particular task the development of integrated analysis and practice based upon the fact that the major systems of oppression are interlocking."[29] Contrary to a politics that might signal essentialism, the statement asserts that the group's "particular task" is a broad "analysis" and a coalitional "practice" that refuse singular and determinist understandings of identity: "As Black women we find any type of biological determinism a particularly dangerous and reactionary basis upon which to build a politic."[30] Their initial projects focused on labor, policing, and segregation.

In early 1979, the Combahee River Collective began a campaign addressing the murders of numerous black women in Boston. Minimized by the mainstream press, the murders were hailed by many as a reason for more policing or male protection, and the group sought other approaches to safety. One of their primary actions was to distribute a pamphlet titled "Six . . . 7 . . . 8 . . . Black Women: Why Did They Die?" (fig. 3.2).[31] The pamphlet asserts that the murders must be understood as antiblack and antiwoman, dynamics that cannot be simply added together or teased apart. The pamphlet is also significant in its declaration of what black women needed to do to organize for safety: "WE HAVE TO LEARN TO PROTECT OURSELVES." The pamphlet included a list of sixteen self-protection tips, only one of which—the twelfth—was calling 911. At the end was a poem by Ntozake Shange titled "with no immediate cause." The poem uses time as a measure of the violence women experience—the phrase "every 3 minutes, every 5 minutes, every 10 minutes" is repeated throughout. Yet, as Grace Kyungwon Hong has argued, the poem only appears to rest on empirical authority. The title makes that clear: "immediate cause" is what the authorities require in order for women to act in self-defense.[32]

The materials that the Combahee River Collective distributed markedly strayed from the two cornerstones of the movement to combat violence against women that were also shared by the emerging lesbian and gay antiviolence movement: it did not call for the primacy of state protection nor empirical enumeration. Like other radical feminist organizations inclusive of lesbians and committed to antiracism, like Women Against Prison, the collective sought alternative frameworks for understanding violence and power.[33] In other words, the collective did not see as a solution the effort to make identities visible through a tabulation of violence in the frame of crime-based state recognition. In addition, it refused to ascribe violence to a single causality, and it named political organizing along multiple lines of difference and socialism as ways to ensure something like safety. As the group's

ELEVEN
SIX BLACK WOMEN
8 7 WHY DID
THEY DIE?
—This pamphlet was prepared by the Combahee River Collective, a Boston Black Feminist Organization (c/o AASC, P.O. Box 1, Cambridge, MA 02139.) It was created for Third World women. If you are not a Third World woman, please read it and share it with Third World women.

FIGURE 3.2 Combahee River Collective pamphlet (COURTESY OF THE LESBIAN HERSTORY ARCHIVES, BARBARA SMITH COLLECTION)

mission was described in an issue of *Radical America* later that year: "it is women organizing together that will create the conditions in which women will be free of fear."[34] In other words, protection might be found in collective action. Although the Combahee River Collective had folded by 1980, their statement would be widely distributed in the leftist and feminist press: it was first published in the 1978 volume *Capitalist Patriarchy and the Case for Socialist Feminism*, edited by Zillah Eisenstein, and then in the 1979 and subsequent editions of the anthology *This Bridge Called My Back*. Discussions of the collective's campaigns and its antiviolence pamphlet were quoted or reproduced in numerous books, magazines, and other sources.[35] The writings done by members of the collective directly addressed movement actors, offering interpretive frames for crafting strategy, and were influential to a wide range of radical feminist antiviolence efforts. Nonetheless, the lessons of their activism would have an uneven influence on the lesbian and gay antiviolence movement that followed. Thus it is important to analyze when lesbian and gay activists did or did not take up the call for integrative critique, the challenge to state-based remedy, and the promise of collectivist—most often, socialist—solutions.[36]

Count the Contradictions: Police Violence and Lesbian Safety

In the late 1970s in San Francisco and New York, gentrification was a hotly debated topic in the mainstream and alternative press as well as among activists and academics. The British sociologist Ruth Glass first coined the term *gentrification* in 1964 when writing about the shift of some of London's neighborhoods from working- to middle-class. Commentators soon identified gentrification as a phenomenon happening in cities all across Europe and the United States. The concept of *gentrification*—as opposed to the related terms *revitalization* or *redevelopment*—quickly became associated with a critical analysis that emphasized the forced displacement of poor and working-class residents and businesses rather than celebrating a process of supposedly natural succession. Explanations for gentrification were most commonly found in the conditions of economic restructuring, focusing, during the 1970s, on the concentrated rise of a white-collar and service-sector economy (particularly, the finance, insurance, and real estate sector) and demise of manufacturing within the central city (even as scholars and activists also found precedents in other sociohistorical contexts). Yet those concerned about gentrification were by no means united in their understanding of its motives or motors, and they were divided in particular between analyses that emphasized the choices of housing consumers (renters and homeowners) and those focused on the role played by producers (real estate developers). Often omitted on both sides of the debate was the way race, gender, and sexual identity might figure in this process.

In San Francisco the two neighborhoods central to this conversation were the Fillmore in the Western Addition, located north of the Castro, and the Mission, which abuts the Castro to the east. In New York, among the key areas were the edges of Chelsea, north of Greenwich Village, the Lower East Side (especially the section renamed the East Village), and the neighborhoods across the East River that had been dubbed by some Brownstone Brooklyn.[37] Despite the piecemeal benefits of public funds at the end of the 1960s, decades of urban renewal, suburbanization, and sustained capital disinvestment had left these neighborhoods with high levels of poverty, dilapidated housing, and inadequate social services. Reports of police misconduct there were rampant.

The dynamics of racial segregation and capital flight also meant that these places were home to many low-income people of color: African Americans in the Fillmore; Latinos in the Mission; Puerto Ricans and African Americans alongside dwindling white ethnic communities in Chelsea, the Lower East Side, and Brooklyn. Soon, white gay men would be among the most visible, if far from the only, new investors in these areas, purchasing depreciated houses for renovation.[38] A growing number of gay and lesbian renters—some of whom felt pushed out by rapidly rising prices in the Castro or Greenwich Village, others of whom sought community outside of what they felt to be homogenous gay and inhospitable heterosexual cultures—also began moving into communal apartments. Although new residents included people of color and of working-class background, the businesses and cultural institutions that appeared to serve new lesbian and gay communities heightened the visibility of the middle-class white people who often owned them.

In a short time, gay residents in gentrifying areas began to report violence, and the scene became increasingly polarized between new gay residents and long-term neighborhood members. Popular narratives tended to cast gay interests as white (and white interests as gay), and people of color as straight. Those who crossed these divides were more often than not maligned or ignored. For example, in the 1977 elections for supervisor of San Francisco's District 6, which included the Mission, the Gay Latino Alliance was criticized by many white gay constituents when the group, citing white gay stereotypes about Latino masculinity and the importance of maintaining the Mission's status as a family neighborhood, sponsored Gary Borvice, a candidate who was favored by most Latino organizations but by very few gay groups.[39] Comments such as those made by Rafael Cedillos, a coordinator of the La Raza Information Center in the Mission, exemplified the kinds of responses that many white gay residents took to be indictments of gayness writ large, despite any qualifications: "We are not saying (members of) the gay community are speculators period. They're also being victimized. But gays are a major part of the influx of white-collar professional types."[40]

As these debates were captured in the press, the most common story told—in the broadest of strokes—involved white gay men moving into neighborhoods primarily inhabited by low-income people of color, where existing residents would meet the newcomers with violence. In some cases, white gay men would be cast as all upper-income and profit-driven, and the violence they encountered would be presented as an economic response of the poor—deemed either justified or pathological. In other characterizations, the gay men were of various classes and their whiteness asserted by default; in these cases, their status as outsiders from middle-class propriety and family-centered economies gave them nowhere else to go, and the risk of violence was simply one price they had to pay. In both scenarios, residents of color were represented as overwhelmingly antigay. In 1980 the late-night news program *Tomorrow with Tom Snyder*, on NBC, included a segment that featured all of these characters: a white gay developer in the Fillmore who announced that those who could not afford to live in San Francisco should just leave, white gays and lesbians teaching each other self-defense, and Latino men bemoaning the encroachment of homosexuality as they drove—as depicted in the news piece—low riders that the viewer was to find equally noisome. Downplayed (or, more often, ignored) in these representations were lesbians and gay men of color and, to a lesser degree, white lesbians. Trans people—so central to debates about places like the Tenderloin—were completely absent from these narratives.[41]

Certainly some lesbians and gay men of color, white lesbians, and trans people were among the residents who were moving into gentrifying territories, either as homeowners or as so-called exiles from heteronormative culture. This was an assertion sometimes made by gay developers to justify new investment opportunities, as well as by gay activists and residents who hewed to the we-have-no-other-option scenario. It was often combined with a tacit acknowledgment that lesbian, gay, and trans people might be silently suffering among those displaced by gentrification.[42] But also significant were the facts that lesbians and gay men of color, white lesbians, and trans people could often be found dispersed across urban regions rather than in designated neighborhoods and that they were decidedly rare among developers—considered by many the real motors of gentrification. Nonetheless, three key questions remained: What particular benefits attached to some lesbian and gay residents that would enable them to prevail in these neighborhoods, despite the threats of violence that they apparently faced? Were these protections shared with LGBT people who were threatened with the loss of their homes? And how might LGBT people concerned about speculation tied to gay developers position themselves? These issues were ignored by most popular commentators and activists; instead, they would be taken up by groups such as the TWGC, LAPV, and DARE, who distinguished their stance from the prevailing approach to both violence and gentrification. The groups did this by developing an understanding of gay participation in gentrification as inclusive of, but not restricted to, either real estate consumption or development. In addition, they posed violence—as racism and poverty, police brutality, and a criminal category—as gentrification's enabler. By paying attention to the operation of race, gender, and sexual identity, these groups produced analyses that not only transformed activism but that also provide important theoretical perspectives on still-ongoing debates about the phenomenon since dubbed gay gentrification.

The TWGC was based in the Pacific Center for Human Growth, which was founded in Berkeley in 1973 and sponsored a mix of lesbian and gay activist and social groups and therapy services.[43] The membership of the TWGC was mixed in gender and of people of color, but the majority of members were black lesbians. They had come to the group from a variety of political paths. For example, one key member, Helen Keller (who now uses the name Lenn Keller) had made her way to lesbian activism through a route that included participating as a teenager in protests against the Vietnam War and in radical black activism against redevelopment in Harlem. (Specifically, Keller had been among the handful of young people organized by the Harlem Community Coalition, who—during the same month as Stonewall—squatted on the construction site of the future Adam Clayton Powell State Office Building on 125th Street in New York's Harlem, dubbing it "Reclamation Site No. 1."[44]) Keller moved to San Francisco in 1975 and became a musician during the next decade and a well-known photographer and filmmaker in the 1980s and 1990s.[45] Many of the members of the TWGC were artists and social workers, and their activities varied from sponsored community events and forums to the production of a resource guide for lesbians and gay men of color. The TWGC was a part of the East Bay Action Coalition against the Briggs Initiative, which sponsored a coalition-building event at the Black Panthers' Oakland Community Learning Center.

One of the most public actions that the TWGC took was in response to the media frenzy about gay participation in gentrification. In 1979 the group applied for money from the Third World Fund in San Francisco to broker conversations between gay and black communities—understanding each as inclusive of the other, yet exclusive in popular rhetoric—regarding the contested gentrification of the Fillmore in the Western Addition.[46] The Third World Fund, which was associated with the Glide Memorial Church in the nearby Tenderloin, had spoken out against gay speculation, publishing a piece in its newsletter at the end of 1978 assailing white gay men for forcing families of color out. The TWGC hoped to provide a space for exchange that would challenge gay white men who ignored the ways in which they benefited from race- and class-stratified urban markets, but that would also encourage residents of color and antigentrification activists in the neighborhood to recognize the problem of antigay bias.[47]

In a public statement, the TWGC described the dual problems of the displacement of "third world people" as well as violence against gays and concluded: "The larger factors behind these events—housing shortages, discriminatory loan practices, unemployment among minority youth, and the failure of schools to provide young people with demystifying information about sexuality—should be receiving the attention of both communities."[48] The TWGC hoped to build a speakers' bureau whose members would highlight analyses of structural issues so as to show how a lack of resources—educational or economic—limited the possibilities of equitable community growth. Furthermore, the group acknowledged the increase in violence but considered it less as antigay crime (or as a product of the so-called culture of poverty) and more as a result of the broad conditions of "fear" that "[was] being played on to create conflict between third world and gay people," adding that "these problems should be considered a crisis that threatens the whole movement for nonviolent social change in the Bay Area."[49] The group continued: "We believe the most effective means for social change is the interaction of people on a community-wide scale through organizing. What is missing now is the voice of those people who are third world *and* gay."[50] In other words, like the Combahee River Collective's claim that black feminism, and not policing, would be the route to safety, TWGC activists shifted the terms of violence away from individual actions and to a call for collective social movement, analyzing fear less as a reactive symptom of inequality than as a tool of political division.

Without explanation, the TWGC was denied funding by the Third World Fund. In response, the group began a pressure campaign, writing to the media and gathering support. In an open letter to the Third World Fund published in the lesbian newspaper *Plexus*, Keller explained that without the active participation of groups like the TWGC, the debate would be presented in overly stark terms that would risk being inflammatory—including the Third World Fund's own editorializing—and further set gays as white against people of color as straight. She wrote: "We believe it is time to call on all community organizations, Third World and gay, to take responsibility for the racism and homophobia within their communities, and to take a step forward towards understanding the forces in society that foster false and demoralizing divisions between gay and non-gay, Third World and white."[51] The TWGC gained support for its proposal from a large number of public figures and activists, including Democratic State Representative Ron Dellums; Ericka Huggins, director of the Black Panther–founded Oakland Community School; the well-known Latina lesbian feminist activist Luz Guerra; and the prominent psychologist and black lesbian feminist activist E. Kitch Childs.[52] The funding never came through, and the situation in the Fillmore continued to worsen. In August 1980, the white publisher of the gay newspaper the *San Francisco Sentinel*, Charles Lee Morris, claimed that black youths associated with a "revolutionary" and "terrorist" group had attempted to kidnap him, delivering a "communiqué" that the paper said "blamed gays for displacing blacks in the City and accused gays of participating in the genocide against blacks." Morris concluded: "There is no doubt this group of nuts has declared war on gays."[53] In response, the editor of the newsletter for the San Francisco branch of the organization BWMT bemoaned the lack of substantive engagement by San Francisco's gay and black "leaders."[54]

Although individual activists with the TWGC would continue to participate in public opposition, their formal plans ultimately fizzled. Despite the fact that this particular campaign was so short-lived, the group provided a clear contribution to popular debates on what was increasingly being called *gay gentrification*. Most important was their elaboration of a public position that was uncompromising in its indictment of white gay speculation and homophobia. Never in their statements did TWGC members justify investments in the market as gay identity claims, but neither did they see an identification with gayness and its nonnormative domestic structures to be only that of one racialized (white) or class formation. Moreover, in meetings and other exchanges the group emphasized gendered forms of labor and the restricted access to capital and space experienced by women, especially lesbians of color (Keller herself was a single mother with a young child at the time), by noting the benefits of place-based communities for pooling resources and other forms of shared support. And the group explicitly called for antiprofit, prosexuality political solidarities.

The TWGC's perspective on gay participation in gentrification provides an important corrective to the academic model first delineated during those same years. The sociologist Manuel Castells's 1983 study of the Castro was the first major look at gay gentrification, which Castells described as an expression of "territorialization" essential to gay men. He suggested that the settlement of the Castro during the 1960s and 1970s was not gentrification in the sense of forced displacement, but a positive expression of political liberation enabled by white working-class suburbanization, and the benefits to gay men of the growth of white-collar and service-sector jobs in the city.[55] The TWGC's example demonstrates that although the growth of the Castro may have involved minimal displacement, that did not make white gay territorialism value neutral. The group also showed that gay community should not be equated with white male land claims, as it critiqued gay developers' use of the term *community* to prime the market for speculation rather than help distribute resources equitably. Recognizing that many lesbian and gay renters and tourist consumers of the neighborhood might assist in this process, the TWGC rejected the assertion of any gay neighborhood identity that did not put race or class alliances at the center and that cultivated affinities between gay landowners and renters, rather than among renters or diverse neighborhood users.

The TWGC's analysis also underscored the limitation of gay liberal politics guided by even the most abstracted goals of protection when staged within a free-market economy. As Jeffrey Escoffier puts it, "organizing to create protection for all lesbians and gay men across the board has reinforced a sense of community; at the same time, the gay market, like markets in general, tends to segment the gay and lesbian community by income, by class, by race and by gender."[56] Escoffier offers this observation following a discussion of what he calls the "territorial economy" stage of lesbian and gay economic history (in Europe and the United States), in which lesbians' and gay men's efforts to provide for themselves the "public goods" denied to them constituted a form of group "protection."[57] Escoffier puts this in general terms, referring to the range of community-based institutions and businesses that arose in the period; indeed, in the Fillmore, new gay bars and other businesses were seen by many gays as a sort of safety network. Organizations like the TWGC refused to pay the price of this protection, demanding instead that lesbians and gay men realign their affinities against accumulation.

LESBIANS AGAINST POLICE VIOLENCE

The TWGC highlighted the ways in which white land speculators sought to buffer critique through gay identification, while Fillmore neighborhood organizers relied on antigay tropes. The TWGC called for a broad-based left analysis critical of white supremacy, sexual normalization, and a polarized politics of fear. Central to the group's concern was not only protection in its broadest (yet also the narrowest) terms—as rights, or in the market—but also the tricky acknowledgment of the fact that lesbians and gay men did experience violence, yet calls for more police did not seem to be the best solution. This final concern was at the core of another organization active in the Mission District just as the TWGC's campaign was waning: LAPV. LAPV showed the specific effect that white working- and middle-class lesbians might have on gentrification: the call for heightened policing in response to street harassment and a fear of violence.

As in the Fillmore, gay participation in gentrification in the Mission was garnering attention.[58] New white gay residents had begun purchasing and renovating property, and reports of violence supposedly committed by Latino residents were mounting. Also visible was a large community of new lesbian and gay renters, many of them white: people who were not buying properties but who were changing the cultural landscape of the neighborhood and sometimes also paying higher rents than long-standing tenants. All of LAPV's members identified as lesbians or bisexual; the majority of the organization's members were also white, and many identified themselves as Jewish and/or working-class. Most had come to the group through feminist and Third World Left solidarity activism. Pamela David, a member who was originally from Chicago, described her own path as influenced by multiple political trajectories, which had included time at the Highlander Research and Education Center:

> So, there I am [at Highlander], at the birth of the modern civil rights movement, I get introduced to the women's movement, to the Redstockings Manifesto, by a group of ex-nuns living in Appalachia doing work around strip-mining. For me, the issues have never been . . . single-issue. I've always appreciated the kind of roots . . . in the civil rights movement and antiwar movement, in particular, in shaping my politics. Like a lot of other folks who got involved in early lesbian and gay organizing, most of our roots were in the women's movement, and we were already lefties, of one sort or another.[59]

Many members of LAPV were active in organizations opposed to the two Briggs propositions, such as Lesbian School Workers and the Bay Area Coalition against the Briggs Initiative. David and member Lois Helmbold were also involved in the movement for establishing women's studies programs in colleges and universities in Northern California; Helmbold was then a graduate student in history at Stanford University. Maggie Jochild, quoted at the start of this chapter, had arrived in San Francisco from Texas, where she had been active in lesbian feminist politics on and off campus at North Texas State University and in the city of Austin. Joan Annsfire had moved to California from Cleveland, Ohio, in 1973. She arrived in San Francisco in 1975 and held a series of low-wage jobs in the city, including working at a wind chime factory, as she moved between different social and political lesbian scenes.[60]

Police violence, as it affected lesbians (the case of Sue Davis and Shirley Wilson being one high-profile example) and as it was manifested in response to lesbians' calls for protection, was the issue that many white lesbians thought might place their political struggles within the context of a broad-based antiracist left. Members of LAPV argued that the threat of police violence was shared, yet experienced most strongly by people of color. They also pointed out that a lack of resources pit (white) lesbians and (heterosexual) people of color against each other, in search of limited housing, community services, and a sense of neighborhood belonging. The solution, the group's members argued, was to educate fellow white lesbians about their place in

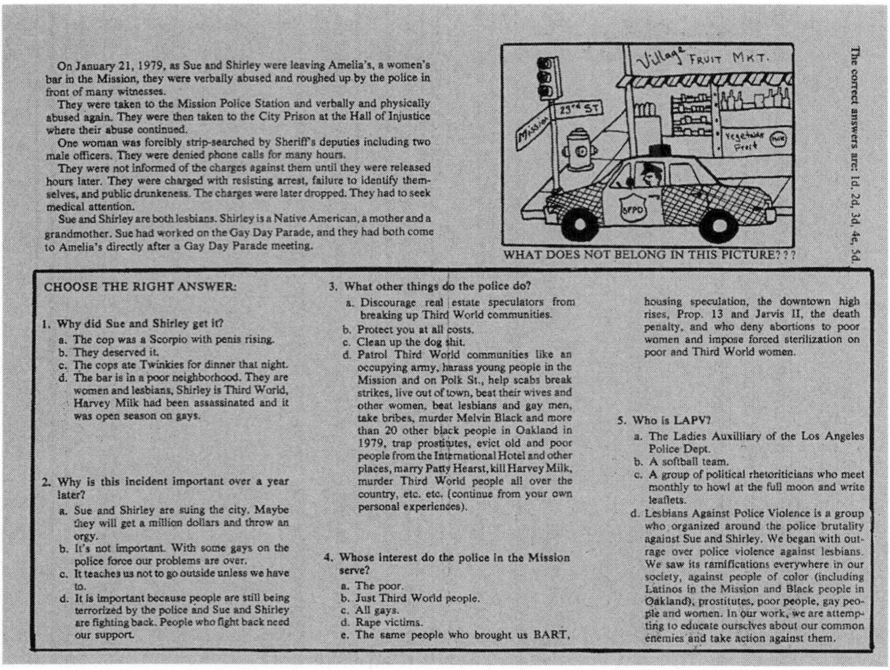

On January 21, 1979, as Sue and Shirley were leaving Amelia's, a women's bar in the Mission, they were verbally abused and roughed up by the police in front of many witnesses.

They were taken to the Mission Police Station and verbally and physically abused again. They were then taken to the City Prison at the Hall of Injustice where their abuse continued.

One woman was forcibly strip-searched by Sheriff's deputies including two male officers. They were denied phone calls for many hours.

They were not informed of the charges against them until they were released hours later. They were charged with resisting arrest, failure to identify themselves, and public drunkeness. The charges were later dropped. They had to seek medical attention.

Sue and Shirley are both lesbians. Shirley is a Native American, a mother and a grandmother. Sue had worked on the Gay Day Parade, and they had both come to Amelia's directly after a Gay Day Parade meeting.

WHAT DOES NOT BELONG IN THIS PICTURE???

The correct answers are: 1d, 2d, 3d, 4e, 5d.

CHOOSE THE RIGHT ANSWER:

1. Why did Sue and Shirley get it?
   a. The cop was a Scorpio with penis rising.
   b. They deserved it.
   c. The cops ate Twinkies for dinner that night.
   d. The bar is in a poor neighborhood. They are women and lesbians, Shirley is Third World, Harvey Milk had been assassinated and it was open season on gays.

2. Why is this incident important over a year later?
   a. Sue and Shirley are suing the city. Maybe they will get a million dollars and throw an orgy.
   b. It's not important. With some gays on the police force our problems are over.
   c. It teaches us not to go outside unless we have to.
   d. It is important because people are still being terrorized by the police and Sue and Shirley are fighting back. People who fight back need our support.

3. What other things do the police do?
   a. Discourage real estate speculators from breaking up Third World communities.
   b. Protect you at all costs.
   c. Clean up the dog shit.
   d. Patrol Third World communities like an occupying army, harass young people in the Mission and on Polk St., help scabs break strikes, live out of town, beat their wives and other women, beat lesbians and gay men, take bribes, murder Melvin Black and more than 20 other black people in Oakland in 1979, trap prostitutes, evict old and poor people from the International Hotel and other places, marry Patty Hearst, kill Harvey Milk, murder Third World people all over the country, etc. etc. (continue from your own personal experiences).

4. Whose interest do the police in the Mission serve?
   a. The poor.
   b. Just Third World people.
   c. All gays.
   d. Rape victims.
   e. The same people who brought us BART, housing speculation, the downtown high rises, Prop. 13 and Jarvis II, the death penalty, and who deny abortions to poor women and impose forced sterilization on poor and Third World women.

5. Who is LAPV?
   a. The Ladies Auxilliary of the Los Angeles Police Dept.
   b. A softball team.
   c. A group of political rhetoriticians who meet monthly to howl at the full moon and write leaflets.
   d. Lesbians Against Police Violence is a group who organized around the police brutality against Sue and Shirley. We began with outrage over police violence against lesbians. We saw its ramifications everywhere in our society, against people of color (including Latinos in the Mission and Black people in Oakland), prostitutes, poor people, gay people and women. In our work, we are attempting to educate ourselves about our common enemies and take action against them.

FIGURE 3.3 Lesbians Against Police Violence flier (COURTESY OF THE GAY, LESBIAN, BISEXUAL, TRANSGENDER HISTORICAL SOCIETY)

neighborhoods like the Mission and to reach out across racial and sexual identity divides. They did so through a variety of mediums—including cultural productions such as cartoons, parodic multiple-choice exams, and on-the-street performances as well as direct action strategies—all of which were inflected with humor (fig. 3.3). Their main approach was performing creative skits in public venues such as community centers, bars, and rallies.[61]

The most elaborate skit performed by LAPV was "Count the Contradictions," which was set up as a game show with two contestants: Miss Deborah Dyke and Mr. Joe On-the-Beat (OTB), a police officer.[62] In the opening scene, the Moderator explains that the two lead characters will view a series of dramatic scenarios, and their task is to "count the contradictions." The next scene takes place at the home of two "dykes" living in the Mission. Although the dykes are not racially identified, the demographics of LAPV and the narrative that unfolds point to them as white. One shares confused feelings about the catcalls and antilesbian slurs she has encountered on the way home. In between sips of herbal tea, the two continue to talk. Their conversation turns to another incident that day, in which one of them observed the police beating Latino men in the neighborhood while white lesbians were left alone. To the tune of "Charlie Brown" (popularized by the Coasters in 1959), she sings:

Well, there were all these low riders
Driving through the Mission, low and slow
Racist cops get nasty when resistance starts to show
Illegal searches, roundups too
Early curfew, and they're not through
Kids are being busted, just you watch and see
WHY IS EVERYBODY ALWAYS PICKING ON ME? [Chorus]
Who is that trigger-happy bunch? WHO?
Kills only acting on a hunch YEAH?
Full of corruption and deceit
It's THE COPS, THE PIGS, THE HEAT!

The scene ends with a revelation that police violence is selectively used against lesbians and people of color—in particular, lesbians of color—and that the unevenness of law enforcement is one way that the state keeps people apart. The two women wonder aloud whether they can challenge the police, and they turn to the audience and ask: "Can we?!!!" Following the chorus (the refrain that opened this chapter), the two contestants provide their analyses of what the audience has just observed. Joe OTB declares that the "kids" in the neighborhood need to stop hanging out and harassing "girls," and that "law and order" is the solution. Deborah Dyke sees a situation rife with contradiction, and to the tune of the Beatles' song "Things We Said Today" she sings:

You think you are safe here
But it's just not true
Others are in danger
Soon it could be you
Remember the White Riot, Elephant Walk and Peg's Place too
These things we remember
And it's nothing new.[63]

Citing key examples of police violence against lesbians and gay men in San Francisco, the song also includes an indictment of John Briggs and Ronald Reagan and closes with the phrase: "Some victories we've accomplished, but our struggle's far from through."

The scene that follows builds on the theme that (white) lesbians and (heterosexual) people of color are being pitted against each other by the interests of the state and capital. A real estate agent with Landshark Realty posts a sign: "All Flats Are Rented." Outside his offices, a "Mrs. Martinez" encounters "Dyke," to whom she vents her frustration that no realtor wants to rent to a Latina woman with children. Dyke replies that unmarried women with limited incomes are also not popular tenants. Their conversation is interrupted when a gay man, "Fag," walks up and complains that there are no affordable apartments, and Dyke snaps, "I'm surprised you didn't put in a bid to buy the place. What's the matter, did you run out of houses in the Fillmore?" The gay man explains he is only a waiter, evicted by a gay landlord. To the tune of "Wouldn't It Be Loverly," each character describes their ideal home: Mrs. Martinez longs for a nearby laundromat, store, decent school, and bus stop; Dyke for sunlight, space, and a short walk to the "Wimmin's Building"; Fag for good bars, a yard, and a place where "I can show I'm queer." As they sing, the realtor arrives with Nelson Exxon the Third, who purchases the property as part of his "Plan" to evict the poor, build a commuter rail, and "renovate with folks RICH WHITE AND STRAIGHT." In the wrap-up scene, Deborah Dyke and the other Dyke grab the microphone and, backed by the full cast, sing to the tune of "You Can Get It If You Really Want," by Jimmy Cliff:

> Those in power keep us apart
> To end isolation we must start
> To talk to each other, find a common goal
> Fight each other's battles, we can take control
>
> We can change it if we really want
> We can change it if we really want
> We can change it if we really want
> But we must try
> Try and try, try and try
> And we'll succeed at last!

LAPV's members hoped to realize this goal of solidarity through a series of political support actions on behalf of lesbians and people of color. Their primary undertaking was to monitor police violence in the Mission.[64] Like the statement from the TWGC, this act was a public gesture intended to underscore LAPV's interpretation of what violence was at stake. The group's members wanted to declare that they stood alongside other liberation movements against police power and in search of a socialist ideal. They also sought to develop this position through collective study; two of the books read by members were *Strictly Ghetto Property: The Story of Los Siete de la Raza*, by Marjorie Heins, about the trial of seven Latino men accused of murdering a police officer in 1969 that became a focal point for radical solidarity activism in San Francisco; and *The Iron Fist and the Velvet Glove: An Analysis of the U.S. Police*, a Marxist critique written by members of the Berkeley-based Center for Research on Criminal Justice, which features a comprehensive history of the police, private security, and military technology and concludes with a list of organizations, primary documents, and bibliographies useful for building a grassroots movement.[65]

A further reflection of this stance is LAPV's emphasis on "contradiction" that is informed by a Marxist analysis. LAPV's own use was arguably influenced—as were many U.S.-based leftist and lesbian organizations during that period—by a loose interpretation of Mao's thought. In the case of Mao's analysis, contradictions were understood not only as the primary antagonism between proletariat and bourgeoisie but also as including secondary contradictions that highlighted the unevenness within social formations and thus might account better for identity-based political frameworks.[66] In appropriating Maoism—sometimes directly, but more often in "subterranean" fashion (and far from its original contexts)[67]—organizations like LAPV sought to challenge the exclusion of culture and identity in leftist politics and of class within gay liberalism, while also focusing on anti-imperialist and antiracist struggles and a feminist valuation of experience and self-awareness.[68]

It is also important to note that in crafting the language of solidarity and alliance, LAPV's analysis nonetheless sometimes replicated the popular diagnosis of gay gentrification. Although activists flipped what had become a familiar script about the violence faced by gay communities, they risked reinforcing the assumptions that gays were white and people of color were straight. Often these assumptions were simply rhetorical; the use of the terms *lesbians* and *people of color* together was not unique to LAPV and does not mean that each group should be taken as being exclusive of the other—even though this tendency can end up suggesting a parallel juxtaposition of *white* and *straight*.[69] LAPV did consistently acknowledge the struggles of lesbian and gay people of color; in their skits, members explicitly named lesbians of color as the most marginalized. But this marginalization was sometimes cast as an extreme example of what lesbians as a generalized category experienced, and the organization's formulation of *lesbian* hewed rather closely to a specific subculture of (mostly) white lesbian life. In turn, and less frequently, LAPV described lesbians of color as the recipients of a specialized racism. This additive or symptomatic understanding of identity was reflective of those leftist analyses that treat racism and sexism as primarily the on-the-ground weapons of class warfare. It was also a feature of many white antiracist groups active in San Francisco, such as the African People's Solidarity Committee (a white solidarity group affiliated with the African People's Socialist Party), in which some LAPV members were also involved.

These approaches could ultimately treat individual accountability about racism as political discipline. In other words, racism functioned as a barrier to revolutionary consciousness, and antiracist exercises were considered to be self-improvement in part. This was evident in two of LAPV's skits: "What Makes Racism So Difficult to Talk about Anyway?" and "Non-Confrontation of Racism in a Group of White Women That Claim to Be Anti-Racist," both of which revolved around how white members might make and respond to accusations of racism. These plays are also important to consider in the context of LAPV's commitment to the practice of "criticism/self-criticism" (often referred to as crit/self-crit), which was popular among many leftist and lesbian organizations during these years.[70] Crit/self-crit was influenced by a Marxist model, yet ideas about the connection between the transformation of the self and the group could sound not unlike the kinds of liberal ideals that leftist critiques sought to displace.[71] All that said, LAPV was unusual among majority white lesbian organizations for its hard-nosed and consistent attention to racism inside and outside the group; furthermore, the vexed dynamics of how to balance white self-accountability with a commitment to multiracial movements was a topic that many members continued to keep as high priority in their activism following the life of the group.[72]

LAPV's confusion about how to sort the relationship between racial, gender, and sexual identity within the spaces of the city reflects a common feature of activist and academic debates about gay participation in gentrification since the 1980s. Lesbians are largely omitted from Castells's analysis since, in his view, they tend to be more interested in "their own rich, inner world" and "thus they are 'placeless.'"[73] LAPV's "Count the Contradictions" follows this perspective to a degree but suggests a much less essentialist distinction between the gendered affective and social desires for "sunlight," "space," and "short walks" held by Dyke, and Fag's desire for visibility and territory—"bars," "a yard," and a place to "show I'm queer." Tamar Rothenberg challenges Castells in her study of the gentrification of Brooklyn's Park Slope; she argues that lesbians do assert a need for physical space and feel conflicted about their participation in gentrification. Rothenberg traces the growth of lesbian Park Slope from the 1970s through 1990, and concludes by exploring the relationship between lesbian collective identity and the so-called new middle classes that then were increasingly associated with the gentrification of the postindustrial city.[74]

Castells's and Rothenberg's arguments are part of a conversation about gentrification since the early 1980s that has highlighted the fact that the demands resulting from the growth of social justice movements since the 1960s, along with other social changes, have informed a desire for central city housing linked not only to economic investment but also to social benefits such as independence and proximity to friends and leisure—a desire experienced by both new middle-class renters and first-time homeowners. Writing of this dynamic in 1984, the geographer Damaris Rose suggested that such individuals were not typical profit-seeking members of the gentrifying class, and that the interests of college-educated single mothers, middle-class lesbians and gay men, and young single women—who occupy a gendered and often ignored role in the work of social reproduction, in particular—can be closer to those of displaced residents than to those of profit-seekers. Rose describes them as "marginal gentrifiers."[75]

This was one of the key questions addressed by LAPV: do working- and middle-class white lesbians occupy a "contradictory class location" in the gentrification process?[76] Although the members of LAPV concurred that the growth of lesbian communities in the city did not automatically place them on the side of capital, especially since few if any of them were property owners, they did usefully highlight how a turn to policing might flip the balance. Although they stopped short of fully outlining how white supremacy, gendered power, and sexual normativity might delimit the social positions of a wide variety of actors within the processes central to gentrification, they were keenly aware of the key role played by the politics of state punishment.

DYKES AGAINST RACISM EVERYWHERE

Concern about the broad operation of gentrification was at the ideological core, if not always at the top of the agenda, of another organization active during these years, far across the country in New York City. DARE was also including the issue of gentrification in its organizing, doing so by critiquing private property, white supremacy, patriarchy, and police power as part of a call for new social movements. DARE had been formed by women involved in the protests against the killing of labor activists and Communist Workers Party members by the Ku Klux Klan and American Nazi Party in Greensboro, North Carolina, in 1979.[77] The group was racially mixed and most of its members identified themselves as socialist. They wanted to make a more assertive place for lesbians in leftist organizing and to push lesbian and gay politics to address issues that might not seem obviously lesbian or gay, while focusing on the importance of antiracism. DARE's members came from a variety of activist backgrounds, especially related to reproductive rights and racial justice. Many lived in collective homes in Brooklyn, but their activism took on issues that played out across the city, including in gentrifying neighborhoods in Manhattan, such as the Lower East Side. Joan Gibbs was one of the group's founders; at the time she worked at Liberation News Service and was active in black radical, lesbian and gay liberation, labor, women's, and prisoners' rights movements. She described the position of DARE many years later this way: "We had more of a Gay Liberation Front perspective, as opposed to what later came to be. And so we wanted to share that perspective. . . . A revolution was in the offering, if not around the corner, in the distant future. And so we were trying . . . to bring people to that perspective. Understanding, as I understand, the central barrier to building a multinational left movement in this country is racism."[78]

DARE pursued this goal from multiple directions: the group's members demonstrated against the exclusion of black women from a lesbian bar called Bacall's; organized panels about the resurgence of the Klan in conjunction with activists such as Frances Beale, founder of the Third World Women's Alliance but then representing the National Anti-Racist Organizing Committee; screened films and sponsored discussions about apartheid in South Africa; coordinated petition drives on behalf of the re-authorization of the Voting Rights Act; and called for an antiracist critique to join gay rage in response to the 1980 movie *Cruising*.[79] In particular, DARE homed in on the problem of punitive state powers and the limits of police protection in relation to lesbian and gay communities. The group organized a forum for pride week called "The Lesbian Community and the Police" that analyzed the police's function, history, and connection to the organized right, and members ended the evening by questioning whether the police might ever help women who have been raped. They invited fellow activists to "Hiss with Us!" against a police sergeant slotted to speak at the lesbian and gay pride march. They declared: "Police forces were founded to protect private property, not people, and the people who face the brutality of the police most often are Third World people."[80] And DARE was an active member of the Anti-Police Abuse Coalition that addressed, among many examples, the police attacks on a black gay bar, Blues, as well as the death of Michael Stewart, a young black graffiti artist, while in police custody.[81] One of the group's fliers against police brutality featured an image of women in protest, with the lead sign held in opposition to gentrification (fig. 3.4).

The members of DARE were also intellectual critics and creative workers. For example, Gibbs was a founding member of a journal called *Azalea* that featured writings by lesbians of color, some of whom were members of DARE, and Elly Bulkin was a well-known poet and critic who cofounded the lesbian publication *Conditions*.[82] Gibbs also collaborated with fellow DARE member Sara Bennett to edit *Top Ranking: A Collection of Articles on Racism and Classism in the Lesbian Community*. *Top Ranking* was published in 1980 and is anchored by a lengthy essay coauthored by Gibbs and Bennett titled "Racism and Classism in the Lesbian Community: Towards the Building of a Radical Autonomous Lesbian Movement."[83] The essay is a sharp polemic

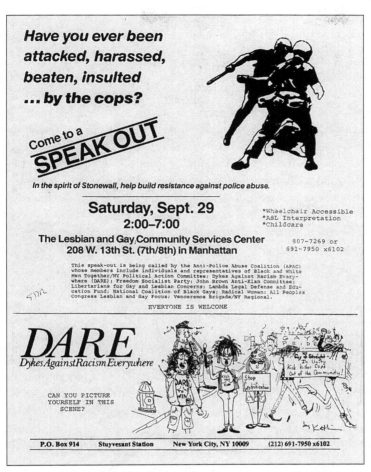

FIGURE 3.4 Dykes Against Racism Everywhere flier (COURTESY OF THE LESBIAN HERSTORY ARCHIVES, DYKES AGAINST RACISM EVERYWHERE ORGANIZATIONAL FILES)

on the status of colonialism, racism, and imperialism in lesbian politics, and the core of the essay is an ambitious summary of the history of racism in the "U.S." from 1492 on. (Throughout the volume, "U.S." and "Americans" are usually set off in quotation marks.) The history of racism that Gibbs and Bennett write outlines the taking of land from, and genocide of, indigenous peoples; the centrality of slave labor to capital accumulation; the free market as empire expansionism; the unearned wages accrued with white identification; and the gender and sexual roles that prescribe lesbian domestic and workplace opportunities. Throughout, the spatialized sorting of social categories and violent enforcement of norms exist in a symbiotic relationship with economic exploitation.

Although the essay is written as a collaboration between Gibbs, who is black, and Bennett, who is white, a section of it is penned by Gibbs alone, who focuses on the limits of land acquisition for lesbian and gay liberation movements:

> Coming from a working class background, I've always had to work or hustle to survive. As a child, growing up in the South and later, after I moved North, I learned that I would never be free until I was free from the oppression that I faced as a Black person. . . . When [lesbian] separatists talk about moving to the country and buying land, I know that I can't and don't want to do that—isolate myself from Black women, men and children. Why would I, a Black woman, even be interested in buying land in the first place, when Third World people, Black, Native and Hispanic peoples—within the current borders of the U.S. are fighting for liberation, for land?[84]

In line with the Combahee River Collective (whom the essay later cites), Gibbs expresses frustration with white lesbian separatism as well as a commitment to stand in solidarity with black men, women, and children; she also suggests that land ownership is itself premised on exploitation. By naming the "current borders of the U.S.," Gibbs denaturalizes the U.S. settler state, naming it as colonial power. Yet in asserting land as among the goals of liberation while naming the displaced as a wide variety of peoples of color, Gibbs calls for a broad-based movement not to condemn all spatial claims, but to challenge how the expansion of capitalism and empire privatize land.[85] To do so, she, along with Bennett (as the essay continues), show how the commodification of land pairs investment in one place with dispossession elsewhere without dismissing—or embracing—all forms of territorial self-determination.[86] In this way, Gibbs and Bennett put forth a critique that focuses on a structural and global analysis of capital rather than a perspective based on local consumption patterns, at the same time as they acknowledge the complex set of identifications and desires that motivate and differentially position people in addition to class status. When applied to the issue of gentrification, this position places the history of white supremacy, gender roles, and sexual normativity within an analysis of the production of gentrified housing and considers the impacts of disinvestment alongside those of selective reinvestment.

Rose's discussion of "marginal gentrifiers," mentioned above, was developed in part as a response to a Marxist explanation that does not account for the social dynamics that produce and reproduce gentrifiers; a position she describes as typified by the ideas of Neil Smith.[87] Smith favors an approach that focuses on the production of gentrified housing to one that emphasizes the activities of housing consumers; for him, the prime forces behind gentrification are cycles of capital accumulation on a global scale, not a place-specific process of local interests. Smith counters claims of a "back-to-the-city" movement of people with an emphasis on the return of capital to the inner city after sustained devalorization. Here the impacts on the local scale include the differentiation of land uses and populations, as well as the variable valorization and devalorization of the built environment. According to Smith, then, an analysis of gentrification involves both an understanding of the local function of ground rent and the multiply scaled dynamics of uneven development.[88]

Gibbs and Bennett's analysis of lesbian politics was unique in the way that they kept issues of sexism and heterosexism central while maintaining a focus on racial capitalism. This was also the case for DARE, which treated the liberal state as a racial formation. The group's members saw their task as to challenge a left that operationalized racism and relied on rigid gender roles and sexual normativity; in this way, DARE did not dismiss identity as only the politics of consumption. This position was elaborated in DARE's direct action strategies that focused on how the aiding of gentrification by policing was an emblematic example of how lesbian and gay politics could be complicit with capital accumulation, rather than indict lesbian and gay desires for neighborhood writ large.

In its introductory brochure, DARE's first statement read: "We think it is important that lesbian and gay male issues not be seen as in opposition to the struggles of Third World communities, particularly considering questions currently being discussed within the lesbian and gay male communities such as police violence vs. police 'protection,' and increasing gentrification in Third World neighborhoods (often by white lesbians and gay males)."[89] The group pointed to the facts that demands for increased policing aided gentrification and that racial and sexual identity can work together to either increase or reduce one's opportunity to benefit. In other words, DARE constructed sexual marginalization in the city as in tandem with—not parallel with or counter to—racial and economic inequality, and the group emphasized the ways in which white middle-class lesbians and gay men acted according to their racial and class self-interest. In particular, DARE detailed examples of wealthy gay residents targeting low-income lesbians and gay men of color for neighborhood cleanups that heightened police violence against all people of color.

In this way, despite sometimes rhetorically separating "lesbian and gay" from "Third World," DARE did not erect a distinction between gays and lesbians as implicitly white and middle-class, on the one hand, and those displaced by gentrification as straight, on the other hand. Nor did the group adopt a formula that associated low-income people with violence or gay people's desires for place-based communities as the primary contradiction. Indeed, DARE instead highlighted the vulnerability of some lesbian and gay people to gentrification alongside the operations of capitalism. Around 1980 DARE joined the Sedition Ensemble's Lower East Side antigentrification festival because, as the group's members explained, "many of us have already lost our apartments to sky-rocketing rents and have suddenly found ourselves homeless. Often we have had to double up with friends or family or leave our neighborhoods entirely and relocate in unfamiliar areas outside the city. Needless to say, as lesbians and gay males we are not always welcome, and the threat of anti-lesbian/anti-gay violence is heaped on top of the racist and/or economic oppression those of us most affected by gentrification already face."[90]

Members of DARE, like many other lesbian and gay activists, sometimes treated violence as a symptom of other social problems and called for visibility as a part of the solution; indeed, publicity was, in many ways, as central to the strategies of DARE, the TWGC, and LAPV as it was to the patrols highlighted earlier. Nonetheless, the approaches of these organizations diverged from those of the patrols in significant ways: they tended to abstract violent actors and indict precise political formations (such as the right) and called for recognition from leftist movements rather than focusing on the particular institutions of liberal inclusion. In other words, while safe streets patrols tended to fold generalized references to police violence into a focused critique of street violence (that is, naming actors of interpersonal violence as the problem that the police tacitly authorize), groups like DARE, the TWGC, and LAPV did the reverse, seeing generalized individual violence as part of a problem of state violence (that is, an environment of police abuse is made worse by the absence of safety in the places where people might seek it). Their solution lay in challenges not only to individual sentiments, then, but to state and market forces, while they also asked white and middle-class lesbians and gay men to think hard about what role they played in either exacerbating (e.g., by calling for police protection) or—just as important—failing to challenge the situation (e.g., by not joining collective social movements). Their chief goal was to build a radical movement.

Rather than interpret lesbian and gay claims to neighborhood group unity as misguided or the threat of antigay violence as imaginary, they affirmed that the stigmatization of nonnormative sexuality and gender marginalization could have a geographic and material dimension. DARE, like the TWGC and LAPV, did not deny the sense of security and pleasure lesbians and gay men felt living among each other, explaining, as in the example above, that the risks of displacement included increased vulnerability to hostile neighbors or families. Their concern instead was how lesbians and gay men could work at the intersections of sexual, racial, gender, and economic justice. Although they sometimes spoke in the language of common interests in a way that might suggest they assumed lesbians (in particular, and as a generalized category) could occupy a kind of contradictory location between classes or racial identities, their agendas ultimately focused on the project of solidarity across difference with those whom they understood to be most exploited in a given situation. This is a position in line with the "heterotopic mode of comparison" diagnosed by Grace Kyungwon Hong and Roderick Ferguson as characteristic of women of color feminism during this period.[91]

Specifically, activists considered the ways in which gender and sexuality shape one's residential patterns within extant structures of racial discrimination and segregation and gender and class stratification. In the context of gentrification, this activist model demonstrated how nonpropertied lesbians could benefit from the forms of protection and pooled resources afforded by the concentration of other lesbian households and services, especially given the gendered aspects of labor and limited access to a real estate market. But it also showed that insofar as the set of practices often grouped under the label of *lesbian* crossed other categories of distinction (and manifested its own exclusions), only some lesbians would be able to quite literally capitalize on that shared identity. The result would be the eventual eviction of not only the wide range of people, including lesbians, already living in low-income neighborhoods, but also those newer lesbian residents who did not have the means to buy or to pay escalating rents and who would, too, be among those displaced. To activists from DARE, the TWGC, and LAPV, this was not a contradiction of lesbian identity per se but of the dual tendencies toward equalization and differentiation central to capitalism. The challenge, then, was how those who claimed a lesbian identity might undermine others' efforts to mobilize the unpropertied for profit.

This perspective is in line with the geographer Lawrence Knopp's case study of the gentrification of the Marigny neighborhood of New Orleans in the 1970s. After discussing the role of new gay speculators and residents, he concludes: "In terms of how theories of urban land markets work, this suggests that the class interests of certain actors (e.g., speculators) can be facilitated and legitimated by forming cross-cultural and cross-class *alliances* with certain groups of consumers (in this case, a diverse community of gay men, including relatively poorly paid service-sector workers from New Orleans' French Quarter). The stigmatization and segregation of these groups can thus be turned to the short-term advantage of both producers and consumers of housing."[92] The alliance of gay speculators and lower-income lesbians and gay men increased the desirability of the area for investment even as that meant that those same lower-income lesbians and gay men later could no longer afford to live in these neighborhoods. Knopp thus shows how gay collective actions can be mobilized as part of the production of gentrified housing rather than only being an expression of cumulative consumer demand, even as gay experience is not of a singular class formation. Rose's analysis of "marginal gentrifiers" concludes with a call for a new form of politics that might link differentially situated actors in gentrification, especially those who are at once implicated in and made vulnerable by it.[93] Although Smith agrees that more research is warranted on the role played by certain residents during the early stages of gentrification, his response to Rose—that the category of people she describes as "marginal" are, in fact, marginal to gentrification and that class is not so vague—highlights that certain coalitions may risk clouding clarity about the commodification of urban space and whose interests are at stake.[94] The organizations profiled in this chapter extended both of these leading academic arguments further. They suggested that rather than looking for commonality or focusing only on class formation, activists might align, contingently, across differences as they directed their aim on the means by which subjects become fixed in space.

"DARE to Struggle, DARE to Win"

It is important to note that these organizations were not alone;[95] in San Francisco, the Prairie Fire Organizing Committee (a multisited group founded following the publication of *Prairie Fire: The Politics of Revolutionary Anti-Imperalism* by the Weather Underground) released a statement linking white gay calls for police protection with gentrification, and members of the Gay Latino Alliance also spoke out about this process.[96] The socialist Stonewall Coalition put critiques of housing privatization and the nuclear family at the top of its agenda and included indictments of gentrification.[97] Years later, in San Francisco's Tenderloin, radical therapists responded to the conjoined regulation of mental health and residence in public service provision by forming Dykes and Faggots Organized to Defeat Institutionalized Liberalism (best known as DAFODIL), and groups such as Women Against Prison continued to combat the use of psychiatry as a tool of violent punishment, especially in the imprisonment of lesbians of color.[98] The aforementioned Coalition against Racism, Anti-Semitism, Sexism, and Heterosexism (a.k.a. CRASH) and the Anti-Police Abuse Coalition in New York also pursued these issues, as did the Alliance Against Women's Oppression in the Bay Area.[99]

Although many of these organizations were short-lived and their campaigns against gentrification brief, they highlight the central role place and protection played in radical critiques of lesbian and gay politics that took form in the context of neoliberalism and law and order. All across the United States, lesbian and gay activist interventions named the operation of violence in restructuring cities as a key site and metaphor. For example, Cherríe Moraga's preface to the 1981 *This Bridge Called My Back* opens with a meditation on racial segregation, suburbanization, and criminalization.[100] Hong shows that Moraga's narrative outlines the political economy of the late 1970s city and, by extension, its contradictions.[101] It is the uneven threats of violence across the city of Boston—against Julie, a black lesbian, and against an anonymous fourteen-year-old black youth—that inspires Moraga to ask exactly what a "lesbian revolution" has to do with it.[102] Here, visibility is presented as not only affirmative; it is, as Hong puts it, the "hypervisibility" of the black youth that promises his vulnerability.[103]

By the early 1980s the number of organizations representing LGBT people of color had exploded, and there was also a vibrant mix of multiracial LGBT groups on the left. A total assessment of these organizations could fill volumes, although it would be quite challenging to keep pace with each group's rapid starts, finishes, and changes. But part of what united these disparate organizations was their embrace of identity and culture, together with their sustained critique of capitalism. Yet since many groups envisioned their politics within aesthetic forms or everyday practices and included issues that were not so easily identified as lesbian or gay, they have been largely cast outside of the history of left and LGBT movements. One prime example is Gente, an early 1970s, Oakland-based, softball team of players who identified themselves as Third World and lesbian. Ali Marrero, a member of Gente (who had also been involved with the Butterfly Brigade), described the group as including women who were African American, Latina, Native American, Asian American, and of mixed race identity. Marrero's family was originally from Puerto Rico; raised in California, she lived in Puerto Rico after high school before moving to New York and then back to California.

Gente also included the black lesbian poet Pat Parker, and it was the basis of an offshoot music group called the Gospeliers, which included the musician Linda Tillery. Gente raised money for the defense of Joan Little, a black woman in North Carolina charged with murdering a prison guard who had attempted to rape her. Members of Gente traveled to North Carolina to provide in-person support to what became a large and diverse social movement.[104] Formed as a political and women-of-color-based alternative to the sports teams sponsored by white bar owners, Gente members also understood themselves to be organized for group protection. But instead of focusing solely on antilesbian threats found on the street, the group also highlighted the real and symbolic violence practiced by many white lesbians and gay men. Marrero later explained: "We were being seen by the white bar owners who were also lesbian as rowdy, rabble rousers, a gang. . . . For me, when we talk about a history of violence, just in the words and in the racism that was involved against our little group of about maybe fifteen or twenty women, was really intense."[105]

The members of Gente noted not only the threats of violence that they faced as lesbians of color, but also how quickly others would invert that formula so as to constitute lesbians of color as the source of violence. This move was enabled by the absence of lesbians of color in the still emerging homophobia discourse that ascribed violence to men of color and imagined lesbian and gay vulnerability as white. It was also exacerbated by the dynamics of gentrification described here. Gente interpreted this dynamic in temporal terms; an article about the organization in the newspaper the *Tide* (fig. 3.5) described (presented as subtitles within the piece) how lesbians of color were perceived as "invisible if we're alone, violent if we're together" and noted that for white people, "the Third World past is safer than the Third World future." (Although the *Tide* interview was held with the entire softball team, the interviewer, identified as sudi mae, clarified that "they preferred that we not single out any sisters by name. They work and think as a team. This is their collective statement."[106]) Like all of the organizations profiled here, Gente members took this as a call for action. The newspaper quoted the team as saying: "I don't see it as a utopian world. I see it as a really long process and a continual struggle. Anytime we stop struggling, we're gonna be sitting just like fat cats do in Washington. We just can't sit."[107]

Like many feminist organizations in the 1970s and 1980s, Gente moved between activities often described by others as political versus social. DARE, for example, frequently paired with the lesbian group Salsa Soul Sisters in organizing potlucks, dances, films, lectures, and open discussions. Both groups worked on more than one occasion with the Committee for the Visibility of the Other Black Woman, which sponsored a conference on community survival skills in New York in 1982.[108] The move between a direct action against police violence and a hot and happening dance, or picking up one's kid at child care, was considered more continuous and complementary than disjunctive. This was based in the popular argument that the personal was political, but it was also a recognition of the unique challenges and responsibilities that came with gendered labor or limited access to the public sphere, as well as the pleasures and possibilities of alternative kinship forms. Similarly, small publications would mix and match the materials they featured. The San Francisco–based *Black Lesbian Newsletter* of the early 1980s—to which Lenn Keller contributed—included articles about Reaganism and calls for a "Black Lesbian Front" alongside poems and clas-

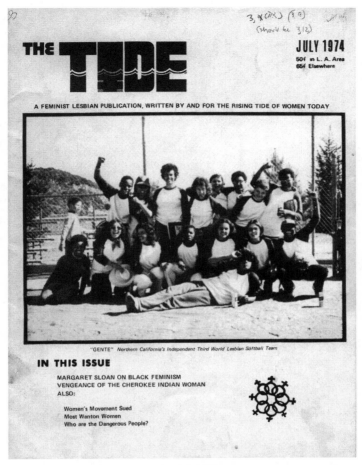

THE TIDE

JULY 1974
50¢ in L. A. Area
65¢ Elsewhere

A FEMINIST LESBIAN PUBLICATION, WRITTEN BY AND FOR THE RISING TIDE OF WOMEN TODAY

"GENTE" *Northern California's Independent Third World Lesbian Softball Team*

IN THIS ISSUE

MARGARET SLOAN ON BLACK FEMINISM
VENGEANCE OF THE CHEROKEE INDIAN WOMAN
ALSO:

Women's Movement Sued
Most Wanton Women
Who are the Dangerous People?

FIGURE 3.5 Gente on the cover of the *Tide*, July 1974 (COURTESY OF THE LESBIAN HERSTORY ARCHIVES, PERIODICALS COLLECTION)

sified ads for services and dating.[109] The February–March 1984 issue of the publication, renamed ONYX: *Black Lesbian Newsletter*, featured a stunning illustration of black women protecting each other as they fight back against a horse-mounted, club-wielding white police officer (fig. 3.6). Presenting the women in rich and expressive detail, the image literally whites out the officer and places him on the cover's margin.

Azalea, cofounded by DARE member Joan Gibbs along with Robin Christian and Linda Brown, not only included essays and poems but also political treatises in unconventional forms.[110] For example, in "Foundations: Why the Cultural is the Political: Validity, Purpose to Womyn who are working for

political and societal change thru cultural levels," Linda J. Brown spoke out against the ways in which her work as an artist was treated as a literal *"after"* to political events *"rather* than be defined in a political context from the beginning."[111] She concluded: *"i don't have definitions or solutions that are phonetically correct—or intellectual in the context of 'correct' wording or rhetorical allegiances. the view i've presented is inclusive, but most singular views are."*[112] Brown not only called for innovative forms of political expression, but she also succinctly dispensed with dismissive takes on the particularity of experience.

Although many scholars and activists have cast cultural activities in opposition to social movements in the history of the left, this perspective is upended by a close look at actual organizational activities. The legacy of the groups featured here is that of a social movement, albeit one of a hard-to-pin-down agglomeration of small, fleeting, and local collectives. Sharing key analyses and praxes, they would develop a sustained critique of models that were being presented on national stages and would shape decades of activism that followed. Based instead in networks between movements and neighborhoods, these activists elaborated an epistemology in line with their conditions of possibility: one that found a force in culture and experience and that embraced, highlighted, and manifested the contradictions of "community."[113] This is in line with Anne Enke's approach to second-wave feminism, which she discusses through a history of place-based activities rather than official political identifications. She demonstrates "how diverse people generated social positions and identities in the process of inhabiting public spaces already built around exclusions and privileged access," and thereby accounts for the transformative and theoretical work of the quotidian.[114]

It would be misleading not to note that this history included both wide gaps and divisions and conflicts—political and personal. LAPV and the TWGC addressed overlapping issues and neighborhoods but shared neither members nor campaigns, and the era's emphasis on the personal as political could create deep schisms that left permanent scars.[115] In addition, just as many men from the 1970s patrols later died young due to AIDS, lesbians of color and/or working-class background associated with these groups often died prematurely or struggled with addiction or lived more economically precarious lives than their white and/or wealthier comrades. Yet their visions resonate with a range of radical political struggles that have existed at the margins of normative social movement history and that teach us not only about activist strategy but also about how to understand the political economy of space.[116]

Conclusion

The safe streets patrols described in the last chapter were one example of how publicity about violence linked to new political values of public self-identification and visibility could become a way to mark areas as gay territories. The fact that many gay activists in places like the Castro did not explicitly target low-income people of color did not mean that the model of patrolling and naming threat, especially as it would be taken up at the neighborhood's most contested edges, might not work to this effect. In turn, although lesbian and gay antigentrification activists considered the detrimental role that the presence of white and/or middle-class lesbians and gay men might play in making prime neighborhoods ripe for speculation, their focus was on building a broad-based, antiracist, feminist, socialist movement rather than advocating for the power of use values turned into consumer choices. LAPV demonstrates this dynamic well in the second song of "Count the Contradictions," in which the characters compare the different use values a Latina (heterosexual) mother, a white (childless) lesbian, and a white gay man might ascribe to "home" in the context of rapidly increasing exchange values, from school proximity to backyards to gay bars.[117]

Yet despite these activist developments, many organizations were stymied by the difficulty of defining the relationship between marginalized sexual and racial identities when it came to urban space. According to their meeting minutes and skits, the majority of LAPV's members saw themselves as working-class and thus less different from their Mission neighbors than other new white residents were. They also understood that as women they had less access to private property than did white gay men. But it is also arguable that their whiteness functioned as a form of added value to housing and neighborhoods that helped make them attractive to speculators. This was one of the key themes taken up by groups like DARE: how might white supremacy stratify the experiences of lesbian and gay people in the urban land market? Moreover, as LAPV, the TWGC, and DARE demonstrated, these dynamics need not happen only via the most recognized mechanisms of gentrification—be that historic preservation, professional opportunity, or election wins—but could also manifest in an activist call for police protection.

None of the actions outlined in this chapter led to the kind of institutionalization that would follow on the heels of gay safe streets patrols when they were succeeded just a few years later by a formal antiviolence movement. But rather than narrate this period in the same way others have described the gay liberation era—as a spark that was extinguished before it had a chance to become a full-fledged flame—it is more useful to recognize that many radical organizations were inheritors of earlier and existing networks that shared aims as they adopted different forms, and even as they were upstaged by a national movement that was taking form. Common in these approaches were three primary desires: to highlight the contradictions of liberalism, to assert the particularity of experience, and to counter the simultaneous totalizing and individualizing ethos of data-driven claims. Furthermore, they demonstrated that grassroots activism that lies far outside the orbit usually associated with property ownership or commercial culture—and might even be considered to be in opposition to them—can be implicated in the dynamics by which neighborhoods are claimed. By doing so without denying the vulnerability of LGBT people or the desire for self-identified community, these activists asserted a queer alternative to the model of militant gay liberalism that would continue to gain momentum for years to come.

CHAPTER 4

VISIBILITY AND VICTIMIZATION

*Hate Crime Laws and the Geography
of Punishment, 1980s and 1990s*

CASTRO YOU ARE:

AS DIVERSE AS THE CITY THAT SURROUNDS YOU . . .

YOU ARE: THIRD WORLD

YOU ARE: LEATHER

YOU ARE: WHITE

YOU ARE: POOR

YOU ARE: WEALTHY

YOU ARE: VISITORS

YOU ARE: RESIDENTS

YOU ARE: ASIAN

YOU ARE: LESBIAN

YOU ARE: OLD

YOU ARE: YOUNG

YOU ARE: MERCHANTS

YOU ARE: REVOLUTIONARIES

YOU ARE: MIDDLE CLASS

AND YOU ARE ALL POTENTIAL VICTIMS

—Community United Against Violence flier

The idea that the ever-present risk of victimization is intrinsic to
gay experience became common within gay subcultures during the
1980s and 1990s. This was not a totally new concept; as the preced-
ing chapters demonstrate, the fear of some kind of violence—be
it by the state or in the street—had occupied activists for decades.
Nonetheless, activists increasingly thought the threat of violence

unified diverse individuals as they adopted shared, public gay and lesbian identities. Moreover, as the above quote taken from a flier distributed by the San Francisco organization called Community United Against Violence (CUAV) attests, neighborhood was increasingly effective shorthand for gay community. In places like the Castro, political stance (for example, "revolutionaries") and sexual style (such as "leather") supposedly joined race, class, and age as categories that all failed to mitigate the equalizing violence that was considered the risk of a visible gay identity.

Far from an unfamiliar formulation, fighting the threat of violence was also central to many feminist activists, and during this time they too were gaining attention on a national stage (even as small, more radical organizations continued their work with less publicity on the ground). In the case of both the national feminist and lesbian and gay antiviolence movements, activists dedicated to ending violence found promise in empirical evidence and the rule of law, documenting rates of violence and using this information to demand legal recognition and remedies. On a local level, feminist and lesbian and gay antiviolence organizations often shared members and supported each other's actions. Yet this was not always the case on the national scale. Many of the key figures of the lesbian and gay antiviolence movement were gay men, and gender was not initially treated as a category that might separate gay men and lesbians.[1] The move to include antitransgender violence would not be formalized until the 1990s, and the inclusion of transgender people would remain contested.[2] Instead, mainstream lesbian and gay and feminist movements traveled on parallel yet separate paths. Both movements grappled with debates about the role of the state in combating violence. Each negotiated charges of racism, as majority white movements that were slow and sometimes resistant to including or working in coalition with people of color. Each tried to balance the provision of social services with grassroots activism and to better understand their relationship to crime victims, in general. Both movements also experienced tension between the ethos of local organizing and the visions of national movement building, as well as between the legacies of 1960s radicalism and the pressures of immediate reforms.[3] Because of these commonalties, antiviolence activism as a generalized concept and model continues to be most associated with feminist and LGBT organizing, despite its appearance in other political formations.

Notwithstanding their areas of overlap, the mainstream feminist and LGBT antiviolence movements have, in fact, mostly remained separate, at least on a national scale, as organizations have pursued different long-term policy goals.[4] One cause of the gap between the two has been the LGBT antiviolence movement's demand that sexual orientation and, later, gender identity join race, religion, and national origin as protected categories under hate crime laws—laws that document or punish crimes motivated by prejudicial bias—a group from which gender was initially excluded. In prioritizing this goal, the national lesbian and gay antiviolence movement sought to form a coalition with the primary advocate for hate crime laws during the 1980s, the Anti-Defamation League (ADL) of the Jewish service and rights organization B'nai B'rith, as well as with the ADL's partners in the crime victims' rights movement.[5] In fact, that movement emerged on the legislative scene at the very same moment as hate crime law advocacy did: the first "victims' bill of rights" was passed in Wisconsin in 1980.[6]

The 1964 federal civil rights law and modifications to it in the years immediately afterward are considered by many a kind of early hate crime legislation. Considered this way, hate crime laws have always included race, and the mobilization against hate violence is narrated as an extension of the civil rights movement. Nonetheless—or, perhaps, because of this—few major organizations focused on the rights of people of color have been at the forefront of campaigns for the formalization and expansion of both local and federal hate crime laws. Civil rights organizations such as the NAACP, the NAACP Legal Defense Fund, and the Puerto Rican Legal Defense Fund have a long history of activism against violence and have supported efforts to pass hate crime laws. But the civil rights organizations most centrally involved in these campaigns, such as the National Institute against Prejudice and Violence, the Center for Democratic Renewal, and the Southern Poverty Law Center, have been those dedicated to tracking hate-motivated violence done by organized hate groups. The Center for Democratic Renewal, founded in 1979 by civil rights activists as the National Anti-Klan Network, provided support and training to local antiracism campaigns before it closed in 2008. The Southern Poverty Law Center has a long legacy of pursuing legal precedents in civil rights activism. However, the primary work of these groups in relation to hate crime law advocacy has been monitoring hate groups. The leading actor in the movement for hate crime legislation has been the ADL, which has had uneven relationships with many African American, Arab American, and Muslim civil rights groups over the ADL's accusations of anti-Semitism and ongoing debates about Zionism and Israeli state policy.

By contrast, campaigns to pass hate crime laws have been at the top of the agendas of the largest LGBT rights organizations, such as the Human Rights Campaign and the National Gay and Lesbian Task Force, as they fought for lesbian and gay people to be included for protection under proposed laws at the same time as they campaigned for their passage. But the disjuncture between LGBT activism against violence and that based on race and gender is not only due to divergent national policy aims and perceived constituencies. It is also attributable to different understandings of the roots of, and remedy for, misogynist, racist, and anti-LGBT violence. The national LGBT antiviolence movement's focus on visibility as both problem and solution has been distinctive. Furthermore, the notions that visibility causes violence and that making violence visible is the first step toward ending it have been responsible for an understanding of gay victimization with a distinctly spatial character. This has been supported by the ADL's model hate crime legislation, which puts considerable emphasis on places and properties that are representative of victimized identities and that advocates for penalty enhancement as a solution. It is also amenable to an empirically oriented hate crime law movement dedicated to the tracking and criminalization of bias. The consequence of these strategies has been a narrowing of the categories of discriminatory violence and victimization, despite efforts to expand them.

This chapter begins with a short review of the founding of the formal lesbian and gay antiviolence movement in San Francisco and New York with the local groups CUAV and the Chelsea Gay Association (CGA). I then mark the movement's rise to national prominence with the establishment of the (Anti-)Violence Project of the National Gay (and Lesbian) Task Force (NGLTF).[7] Next, I provide a quick overview of the history of hate crime laws. I then trace a history of NGLTF-led advocacy for LGB(T)-inclusive hate crime laws, paying particular attention to two issues. First, I look at the significance of the dual assumption that the increased visibility of LGBT people leads to increased violence against them and that the empirical documentation and publicity of violence are central to ensuring its prevention. Second, I analyze how an activist emphasis on documentation shifted to a call for penalty enhancement, and I explore what types of coalitions made this possible. Throughout, I consider the spatial implications of these issues. At the end of the chapter, I look at how these ideas were taken back up by local neighborhood-based responses to violence, most particularly by the safe streets patrols that spun off of Queer Nation chapters during the 1990s.

Local to National Movements

CUAV and the CGA, the two organizations most credited as having begun formal LGBT antiviolence work, each had links to the Butterfly Brigade and the Society to Make America Safe for Homosexuals in San Francisco and New York, respectively.[8] Members of the Butterfly Brigade, which had dissolved soon after its establishment, continued informally to distribute whistles, and by 1979 they were among those who had begun to meet as part of a new, all-volunteer organization: CUAV.[9] In New York, many members of the Society to Make America Safe for Homosexuals also belonged to the neighborhood-based CGA, which was dedicated to providing social and support services to new gay residents of Chelsea. In the late 1970s the CGA began sponsoring a series of meetings with the local police precinct and advertised whistle distribution inspired by CUAV.[10] By the early 1980s both CUAV and the CGA had phone lines where people could call in to report assaults and to seek legal and emotional assistance. Both groups had also incorporated as nonprofit agencies. In 1981 the City and County of San Francisco contracted with CUAV to provide services for victims of hate crimes.[11] In 1983 the volunteer hotline and victim support project of the CGA was incorporated as the New York City Gay and Lesbian Anti-Violence Project (AVP).[12] Yet in order to receive money from the New York State Crime Victims Board, the group also had to incorporate a separate entity called the Chelsea Anti-Crime Task Force, omitting the words *gay* and *lesbian*.[13]

Despite this exclusion, antiviolence activists often acknowledge this to have been among the first large-scale lesbian and gay activist projects to receive governmental and foundation funding on both coasts. David Wertheimer notes that the first gay rights organizations that foundations like the Joyce Metz-Gilmore Foundation and the Open Society Institute funded were antiviolence ones.[14] The Fund for Human Dignity of the National Gay Task Force (NGTF) was the first gay organization to receive tax-exempt status in 1977. Although the fund was not dedicated to antiviolence organizing, the first major grant from a corporation that it received was $10,000 from AT&T in 1985 to support Crisisline, the AIDS information and antiviolence hotline that the NGTF had developed in 1982.[15] In 1991, the NGLTF would receive its biggest grant to date from the Public Welfare Foundation for the Anti-Violence Project, which would also be the foundation's first lesbian and gay issue grant.[16]

In the early 1980s CUAV and AVP overlapped in their emphasis on providing victims' services, including court support and emergency hotlines. CUAV also dedicated energy for a short time to ongoing street patrols that reported incidents to car owners (extending the Butterfly Brigade's tactics) and collaborated with organizations such as the Mission neighborhood's Centro de Cambio to provide for an on-the-street community presence.[17] Although street patrols only lasted through the early years of the 1980s, CUAV activists maintained a strong commitment to whistle distribution and developed a safety monitoring program for large public events like the annual Pride Parade. In addition, soon after their founding, CUAV and AVP built education-oriented prevention programs, such as speakers' bureaus, whose members visited schools. Another shared strategy was to collect statistics on antigay violence, especially as each group's client base grew, and AVP and CUAV both pressured the local police to record antigay incidents. In February 1980 CUAV suggested to the San Francisco Police Department that police add a "check box" to record antigay assaults. (Activists affiliated with the CGA in New York pursued a similar campaign in 1981.[18]) The San Francisco chief of police, Cornelius Murphy, replied that this was not an option for the department's computer system and that it risked invading the privacy of victims and making assumptions about perpetrators' motives.[19] Instead, the police adopted a new policy in which officers were directed to include in the narrative description of an incident whether or not it may have been "gay-related."[20] In a letter to CUAV, Murphy wrote that a failure to record assaults as antigay did not adversely affect the allocation of resources to the problem of assaults against lesbians and gay men. He explained: "The location of every assault, regardless of motivation, is recorded and these figures are utilized to determine the allocation of the resources of the patrol division. The department is interested in each assault, regardless of the motive of the assailant or the sexual orientation of the victim. The fact that crime in a particular area is higher than another will result in a concentration of police efforts."[21] In this response, the police assumed what had been suggested by CUAV's initial focus on the Castro District and Polk Street area of the Tenderloin: antigay violence was correlated with gay neighborhood identity.[22] Although the police in New York and San Francisco would not institute formal tracking systems for antigay crime until the late 1980s, and although both CUAV and AVP would expand their geographic reach, the association of motive and place would remain an undercurrent of documentation efforts.

Documentation continued to be a major part of the work of AVP and CUAV, yet it was systematized and developed into a transferable model under the auspices of the Violence Project (later renamed the Anti-Violence Project) of the NGTF, later known as the NGLTF. The NGTF was founded in New York City in 1973 by former members of the Gay Activists Alliance who were seeking to build a national organization dedicated to policy reform.[23] In 1982 the director of the NGTF Fund for Human Dignity, Virginia Apuzzo, along with Lucia Valeska, then NGTF executive director, began the Violence Project; Kevin Berrill was soon hired as its director.[24] The project was described as the "first *national* campaign to research, document, publicize and combat anti-gay violence in all its aspects and wherever it takes place." A booklet outlining its plans stated: "NGTF's Violence Project is a cooperative effort with local anti-violence groups—e.g., San Francisco's Community United Against Violence and New York's Chelsea Gay Association—that have pioneered in mobilizing effective community response to this problem. Their accumulated expertise needs to be shared so that other organizations can quickly duplicate existing, successful programs: anti-violence hotlines, trial monitoring groups, self-defense classes, street patrols, survivor-support groups, police-gay liaisons and sensitivity training, and others."[25] The Violence Project focused on collecting data from local antiviolence projects, news reports, and NGTF's national hotline, Crisisline. This information was to be supplemented by in-depth interviews with callers and information on questionnaires compared with control groups of both gay and straight people. After that, the plan was to publish the results and "how-to" guides—from how to establish a local antiviolence project to how to pursue legal cases, as well as how to use the data to "facilitate efforts to make local police more sensitive to gay issues and responsive to gay needs."[26] The production and dissemination of annual reports on anti-gay violence, victimization, and defamation became the cornerstone of the Anti-Violence Project and remains one of the most central components of all national organizing efforts on this issue.

By taking nationwide toll-free calls while sponsoring the development of local documentation efforts and training activists in data collection, the NGTF hoped to paint a comprehensive picture of antigay violence as sweeping the United States. Crisisline was also to give referrals to local organizations and "in some instances [to] provide limited referral information about A.I.D.S. hotlines and clinics."[27] Yet in its first three months of operation, the vast majority of calls were not about street violence, but requests for information about AIDS. The disease was a new threat to gay populations, and public health agencies had provided little information about it. Thus it is probably not very surprising that the majority of the 791 calls received between October and December of 1982 were about AIDS, while only 22 calls reported violence.[28] Although organizers debated the cause of this discrepancy— attributing it to victims' fears of pursuing legal measures, the bad publicity internal strife had caused the NGTF, and the unbalanced coverage that a Phil Donahue television show on AIDS had provided—they maintained that Crisisline should be committed to tracking violence.[29] By the following year the number of violence reports had jumped to "epidemic" proportions, a change that was explained as a "backlash" to AIDS.[30]

Throughout the 1980s and 1990s, the (Anti-)Violence Project also prioritized police relations, focusing on the recruitment of gay officers and the development of sensitivity training programs. The head of the project, Kevin Berrill, testified at a federal hearing on November 28, 1983, about police misconduct, collaborating with racial justice activists—including James Credle of Black and White Men Together in New York, who spoke of the campaign against the police raid on the black gay bar, Blues.[31] Citing reports from Crisisline and an NGTF-sponsored study from the previous summer, the NGTF also submitted formal recommendations to the House of Representatives' Criminal Justice Subcommittee, chaired by Representative John Conyers, a Democrat from Michigan. These recommendations included an end to sexual orientation discrimination in the hiring of law enforcement officers, mandatory sensitivity training for them, institutionalized contact between officers and members of the lesbian and gay community, and the passage of a federal law to secure the civil rights of gay and lesbian people.[32] The Violence Project also pushed for the establishment of civilian review boards, noting the disproportionate amount of police violence against people of color, and began a project to fight hate in schools and on college campuses.[33] Additionally, during this time, the NGTF developed closer ties with the National Organization for Victim Assistance as well as with the U.S. Justice Department's victim assistance programs (and the organization would move its main office to Washington, D.C., in 1985).[34] These alliances would prove crucial in the following years, when the Anti-Violence Project would develop a focus on advocacy for hate crime laws that included sexual orientation as a category and took the lead of a national lobby called the Hate Crimes Bill Coalition.

Defining Hate Crime

Although the concept of violence motivated by hate has been invoked to describe acts with varied historical roots, the concept of *hate crime* (also referred to as *bias crime*) was developed in conjunction with legislative efforts to designate it as a specific criminal category, much of it fueled by the ADL's development of model legislation in the early 1980s. According to the legal scholars James Jacobs and Kimberly Potter, hate did not exist as a category of crime prior to the Hate Crime Statistics Act, which was introduced by Representatives Conyers; Barbara Kennelly, a Democrat from Connecticut; and Mario Biaggi, a Democrat from New York in 1985 and passed by Congress in 1990. The term was quickly taken up by newspapers: Jacobs and Potter note that in 1985 there were 11 citations of the term; in 1990, 511; and in 1993, over 1,000. In 1991 the *Guide to Legal Periodicals* created *bias crime* as a new subject heading.[35] The sociologists Valerie Jenness and Ryken Grattet describe hate crime as a new "policy domain" that came into being through the ideas and work of collective actors, including "politicians, experts, agency officials, and interest groups." According to the authors, most important among these were social movement organizations, in particular civil rights (broadly conceived) and victims' rights movements.[36]

Hate crime is an umbrella term that is best defined as "unlawful, violent, destructive, or threatening conduct in which the perpetrator is motivated by prejudice toward the victim's putative social group."[37] As such, hate crimes are distinguished from acts that are lawful. Although some have sought to rhetorically broaden the category to include historical state-sanctioned prejudicial acts—for example, the expropriation of indigenous people's lands justified by the ideology of manifest destiny, the state-sanctioned lynching of African Americans, and the internment by the United States of Japanese Americans during World War II—doing so would downplay its status as a category for state-administered condemnation.[38] In addition, hate crimes can be committed regardless of the position of a given group vis-à-vis broad structures of social power. In fact, the affirmation that antiwhite bias-motivated crime can be a hate crime was central to the 1995 Supreme Court ruling in *Wisconsin v. Mitchell* that upheld the constitutionality of hate crime penalty enhancements in a case in which a young African American man had been convicted of inciting an antiwhite bias assault.[39] It is also important to note that hate crimes often involve *hate speech*, another category hotly contested during the 1980s and 1990s; indeed, language is a key way in which motive is ascertained. Nonetheless, hate speech falls under hate crime law when it is invoked in the process of an activity that is already criminal, such as assault, trespassing, vandalism, or harassment; this is a separate issue from the debates about the power of hate speech to function as legally unprotected "fighting words."[40]

Two features of the Hate Crime Statistics Act are worth highlighting: first, the act is considered the first federal statute to have been passed that explicitly recognized lesbian, gay, and bisexual people (and it was reported as the first time lesbian and gay activists attended a presidential bill signing, with President George H. W. Bush in 1990); second, starting in 1993, the Federal Bureau of Investigation began releasing annual uniform crime reports in line with the act's guidelines.[41] From 1985 to 1990, the years between the introduction and the adoption of the act, numerous states instituted their own hate crime laws. Some followed the example of the federal act, requiring that records be kept of crimes (including homicide, assault, robbery, burglary, theft, arson, vandalism, trespass, and threat) that were designated as motivated by bias based on race, religion, sexual orientation, and ethnicity. Other states included only some of the designated categories—for example excluding sexual orientation—or included others such as disability, age, or gender. Some local statutes required increased penalties for those convicted of hate crimes rather than emphasizing documentation. A handful also included, for example, provisions that mandate police training or criminalize the wearing of masks or hoods while interfering in others' civil rights.[42] Many states followed the guidelines for hate crime laws developed and promoted by the ADL. Its model legislation, first drafted in 1981, drew attention to institutional vandalism; provided for penalty enhancements and the opportunity for civil action; called for state-sponsored documentation and law enforcement training; and, after much debate, included sexual orientation and gender in addition to race, color, religion, and national origin. Through the work of the ADL, these features not only appeared in local statutes, but they also became national activists' goals for federal policy that exceeded the documentation focus of the Hate Crime Statistics Act. Thus the next stage of advocacy focused on penalty enhancement, pursued in conjunction with the victims' rights movement. In fact, the California Victims' Bill of Rights, promoted as a model for all crime victims in the early 1980s, focused on restitution, safe schools, and truth in evidence, while also providing for some sentencing enhancements.[43]

The 1994 Violent Crime Control and Law Enforcement Act—more commonly known as President Bill Clinton's controversial law-and-order "Crime Bill"—included the Hate Crimes Sentencing Enhancement Act, which raised offenses by three levels if it was found that, for crimes on federal property (including state parks), "the defendant intentionally selected any victim or any property as the object of the offense because of the actual or perceived race, color, religion, national origin, ethnicity, gender, disability, or sexual orientation of any person."[44] The act also established the definition of *hate crime* used in subsequent federal laws. Another section of the Crime Bill was the Violence Against Women Act, which called for training for police and prosecutors and funding for domestic violence and rape crisis centers. It also provided a civil rights remedy that allowed for punitive and compensatory damage awards for gender-motivated crimes; this provision was later deemed unconstitutional.[45]

Two years later, in 1996, Congress passed the Church Arson Prevention Act, which made it easier to prosecute and punish people for crimes committed against houses of worship. The 1998 Hate Crimes Prevention Act was first introduced in 1997 by Senator Edward Kennedy, a Democrat from Massachusetts; it was updated in 2001 by the Local Law Enforcement Enhancement Act and later renamed the Local Law Enforcement Hate Crimes Prevention Act and then the Matthew Shepard and James Byrd Jr. Hate Crimes Prevention Act in 2009. Under consideration by Congress throughout the 2000s, these bills died in the House or the Senate, sometimes under the threat of executive veto, as they were modified and attached to or stripped from multiple Department of Defense authorization bills. It was not until 2005 that any measure proposed the inclusion of transgender as a protected category (in the form of "gender identity"). On October 28, 2009, the Matthew Shepard and James Byrd Jr. Hate Crimes Prevention Act was signed into law by President Barack Obama.

Although not initially dedicated to something called "hate crime," Title 18, Section 245 of the U.S. Code, enacted as part of the 1968 Civil Rights Act, had focused on bias-motivated violations of federally protected activities. Arguing that federal civil rights protection was narrow, the Hate Crimes Preventation Acts first proposed in 1997 and passed in 2009 expanded the protected categories of race, color, religion, and national origin to include sexual orientation, gender, gender identity, and disability. It also targeted all violent hate crimes, not just those that interfere with federally protected rights, such as voting. And it added gender and gender identity to the Hate Crime Statistics Act and modified that law's data collection section to trace information about crimes done by and against youth.

In the early years of advocacy, some of those critical of hate crime laws but supportive of lesbian and gay rights opposed the bills for creating *hate crime* as an autonomous and new category of criminalization, rather than expanding the terms of civil rights inclusion.[46] I discuss this position later. But the perspective that most caught the media's attention was that of those who rejected the category of *hate crime* by arguing the reverse: that the bill worked to include sexual orientation for civil rights protection, and thus implicitly sanctioned homosexuality. Senator Jesse Helms, a Republican from North Carolina, was most associated with the latter viewpoint; he also opposed the Hate Crime Statistics Act on the same grounds. Thus much of the energy that NGLTF activists put into advocacy for hate crime laws was in arguing for the inclusion of lesbian and gay sexual orientations as valid, marginalized identities, and not on the merits of the laws as a tool against violence. Those sympathetic to lesbian and gay identity often affirmed hate crime laws as a strategy to seek civil rights protections for lesbians and gay men in a piecemeal fashion, following the defeat of the Equality Act of 1974—sponsored by Representative Bella Abzug, a Democrat from New York—that looked to expand federal civil rights protections to include sex, marital status, and sexual orientation. In its place, bills such as the Employment Non-Discrimination Act (ENDA) and the Hate Crimes Prevention Acts were proposed.[47]

Another point of contestation was the repeated suggestion made by some legislators that the bill should include a death penalty provision, which would permit the sentences of those convicted of hate crimes to be enhanced to include execution. In its first recommendation, this provision was opposed by many civil rights organizations, including the NGLTF and the NAACP Legal Defense Fund. Nonetheless, the gay rights group the Human Rights Campaign initially did not challenge its inclusion or the exclusion of gender identity, although they later opposed both. One of the most outspoken national organizations to take a position against penalty enhancement was the Quaker American Friends Service Committee. The committee's LGBT Rights and Recognition Program, then led by Kay Whitlock, published numerous public letters and policy statements opposing punitive, state-based solutions to hate crime.[48] The national organization INCITE! Women of Color against Violence also issued a statement opposing criminal justice–based solutions to violence.[49] Throughout the first decade of the twenty-first century, activists highlighted the racism of the U.S. judicial system, demonstrating how hate crime laws call for protection from violence deemed illegitimate while expanding the state's own use of violence. The fact that the hate crime acts were attached to Department of Defense authorization bills further cemented this association. As Chandan Reddy describes the eventual passage of the act in 2009, it functioned to authorize the largest defense budget in history for an administration that was expanding its global military actions. Reddy shows "freedom with violence" to be the condition of possibility for the liberal state, and he outlines how the LGBT civil rights project is, literally, amended to both U.S. racial globalism and capitalism.[50]

LGBT/queer racial justice advocates' call for community-based and restorative justice solutions were echoed by numerous local activist projects, such as—in later years—the Safe OUTside the System Collective of the Brooklyn-based Audre Lorde Project and a reconfigured CUAV in San Francisco.[51] However, the majority of critics of hate crime laws have not presented a racist and punitive state as their primary concern. Jacobs and Potter do note that "insufficient or unduly lenient criminal law is not a problem that afflicts the United States." Nonetheless, their ultimate criticism of hate crime laws is that they uphold "identity politics" based in "victimization" and criminalize free speech.[52] Their argument is a popular one among civil libertarian opponents of hate crime and speech laws on the left and right. Other scholars, such as Judith Butler, demonstrate that language may be able to "act," but that "does not necessarily mean that it does what it says."[53] Unlike the civil libertarian perspective, such analyses provide a stance that is critical of legal regulation, but they do not target the objects of hate as the main problem. Similarly, the position that hate crime laws redress group injury has not only been countered by those who argue that group injury is a thing of the past or that claims of injury are fueled by a *ressentiment* that substitutes concern with individual harms for a broader critique, but also by those that highlight the limited ways in which vulnerable groups are defined.[54] These other critics point out, among many arguments, that in some states white people have been named as the single largest group of victims of racially motivated hate crime, pointing to the *Wisconsin v. Mitchell* decision.[55]

The argument that motive is not transparent has also been made by those underscoring the multiplicity, rather than the irrelevance, of identity or other social categories. For example, in her interviews with individuals convicted of antigay violence, the criminologist Karen Franklin found that antigay sentiment sometimes functioned as a vector for class-based anger.[56] Kimberlé Crenshaw argues that "the problem with identity politics is not that it fails to transcend difference, . . . but rather the opposite—that it frequently conflates or ignores intragroup differences." She criticizes the use of a gender-only lens to analyze the problem of violence against women because it fails to show how race, gender, and class affect the broader political implications, and variety of victims, of violence.[57]

Despite these arguments about the structural and situational complexity of violence, the shape of hate crime laws followed the dominant model developed by the ADL. The ADL's model legislation—which made hate speech a central target and penalty enhancement its key solution—remained at the core of social movement agitation for the local and federal hate crime statutes that were proposed over these years. As I indicated, though, sexual orientation was not always included in the ADL's proposed policy, nor was it initially on the agendas of other leading advocates for hate crime laws, including those in the crime victims' rights movement.[58] The shift in the 1980s came about as a result of sustained activism by the NGLTF's (Anti-) Violence Project, and that activism succeeded by demonstrating that antigay violence had reached what they described as "epidemic" proportions.[59] To make its case, the NGLTF needed to provide a generalized understanding of motive and an acceptable form of proof; these were made available by local antiviolence projects that started in San Francisco and New York and proliferated nationwide. First was the argument that increased visibility caused increased violence; second was the evidence provided by documentation. Once the NGLTF had made the case that hate crime laws should include lesbians and gay men as protected categories, the group moved to ensure that the laws would pass.

Visible Violence: Documenting Hate

The following lengthy quote comes from one of the Violence Project's first publications explaining the problem of antigay violence:

> Violence against gay people is nothing new. Harassment and attacks against us because of our sexual orientation are a long-standing aspect of society's homophobia. However, the number of reported incidents is increasing at an alarming rate. The dramatic rise in anti-gay violence has not yet been documented *nationally*, but many of us reading this page

can testify to the fact that it is pervasive because we—or gay people we know—have been its victims.

As long as gay people were alone, closeted, and mired in self-hate, they did not pose a serious challenge to heterosexual power and privilege. Internalizing society's vicious judgments against us, we acted as our own "fifth column," staying "in our place," living narrow, hidden lives on society's fringe, and doing our best to avoid the more savage forms of our oppression—including physical violence. Only as we came out and identified ourselves and each other were we able to overcome the lies we had been told, find self-respect, and join with other gay people as friends, lovers, and in community. Being visible is essential for any kind of positive gay identity in a heterosexist society, but visibility also poses problems. For, in coming out to each other we have also come out to those who hate us and want to harm us. As growing numbers of us . . . choose to live openly as lesbians and gay men, the number of those who want to bludgeon us back into the closet also grows. Those who choose to remain "closeted" are not exempt from homophobic violence. When they resort to covert means of finding partners, they are sometimes blackmailed, robbed, assaulted and even murdered.[60]

This extract combines many of the key assumptions that fueled the campaigns that followed: violence is an intrinsic feature of gay life, experiential knowledge of violence is supported by research, refusal of a gay identity is self-hating and politically damaging, and "coming out" increases violent risks but is necessary. As this book has thus far asserted, violence is unevenly experienced by different lesbians, gay men, transgender people, and other sexual and gender non-normative or nonconforming peoples, and the choice to identify oneself with certain categories does not provide a neat formula for acceptance or rejection. In addition, the idea that homophobia is something that one *knows* has been a prevalent form of affective political claims since the 1970s that can be a powerful means to ignore the presence of other expressions of abusive power. This narrow vision is further tightened by a dominant discourse of coming out that demeans strategies of silence and privacy as always homophobic and self-hating.[61] Furthermore, these dynamics have a spatial dimension, as the politics of visibility and self-identification is correlated with efforts to claim physical space; visibility as an abstraction of a generalized public sphere is, typically and quite literally, grounded in gay neighborhood. For example, in describing the conditions leading up to the founding of the antiviolence movement, David Wertheimer, the former director of the New York AVP, writes: "Antigay and antilesbian violence were quietly accepted as the price tag for even marginal visibility in the earliest gay ghettos. Bashings and bar raids were considered the inevitable response to the sexual-minority community's most modest attempts at self-expression."[62]

Although hate crime laws appear to resist this correlation—they address crimes linked to acts, not to places—the modes of measuring visibility and motive often turn on geography. In his statement on behalf of the passage of the Hate Crime Statistics Act, Gregory Herek, then chair of the Committee on Lesbian and Gay Concerns of the American Psychological Association, suggested that along with demographic information—gender, race and ethnicity, and age—about victims and perpetrators, the first data to be recorded should include location, setting, and neighborhood qualities.[63] Antiviolence activists' strategies further reinforced this sentiment. In May 1983 the Violence Project sent letters to Manhattan gay bars, "selected [for their] popularity and geographical location," in order to survey patrons' experiences of violence and to suggest modes of protection.[64] Fliers, such as the one from CUAV excerpted at the start of this chapter, often addressed gay populations in gay-identified neighborhoods. There were exceptions, such as when New York activists sponsored a "five borough" action throughout New York City in the early 1990s.[65] Yet the notion that gay enclaves were a kind of ground zero for violence and needed to be protected was dominant.

Although this logic reflects common sense—there are more gay institutions in these than in other neighborhoods—it risked downplaying certain places and types of violence. For example, a memo from someone at the Gay and Lesbian Community Action Council of Minneapolis addressed to the Anti-Violence Project in 1991 made this clear: "I have had several cases where the victim was of color. The most striking involve transvestite/transexual [*sic*] black men/women. These cases involved police abuse. It appears that our fine police force is often out looking for people they believe are hookers and these folks get picked up a lot. One case involved a black transexual who wanted to visit her boyfriend in prison and was given the run around and restricted quite severely. This particular case is well known and *probably not appropriate for your report*" (emphasis added).[66] This is not to say that the NGLTF would have agreed that this case was not appropriate—and the organization in Minneapolis did go on to report it as police abuse—but the concern as to its fit demonstrates how naturalized the assumption had become that antigay violence was primarily a street crime directed at gay-identified individuals in designated neighborhoods. As the Dallas Anti-Violence Project wrote in an open letter to business owners and residents of the gay neighborhood of Oak Lawn, "The goal of the Anti-Violence Project is to get criminals out of our neighborhoods. By documenting incidents of crime in our neighborhood we hope to have the documentation necessary to demand additional police protection for one of the highest crime per capita neighborhoods in the City."[67]

The conflation of neighborhood crime and antigay violence shaped the NGLTF's national campaign, but it would be shortsighted to assert that this reflected a directed political vision. To repeat, early national lesbian and gay antiviolence activism was dedicated to expanding proposed hate crime laws to include sexual orientation as the first form of federal legislation passed in the name of lesbian and gay rights, and not to discussing the legislation's applications. (Although activists debated these issues, they tended to be internal rather than public or policy-based concerns.) Thus, lesbian and gay activists addressed those already leading the hate crime law movement, such as hate violence watchdog groups and crime victims' rights advocates. When, in time, LGBT activists became agenda setters themselves, they retained the same community of affiliation. For example, in 1987 the NGTLF helped found the Hate Crimes Bill Coalition, which included the American Civil Liberties Union, the American Jewish Congress, ADL, People for the American Way, and the Lutheran Council, as well as supporters from the victims' rights movement and law enforcement agencies.[68] Throughout the 1980s and 1990s, representatives of the Anti-Violence Project participated in the annual conferences of the National Organization for Victim Assistance (and the director of the project briefly joined its board) and met with representatives of the National Criminal Justice Association, Police Foundation, Prosecuting Attorney's Research Council, American Bar Association, and National Association of Public Interest Lawyers, among other groups.[69]

These efforts at collaboration were joined by the collection of social science research and expert testimony on the problems of violence. In 1985 the NGTF submitted a survey to the U.S. Commission on Civil Rights that had been endorsed by the liberal criminologist Marvin Wolfgang.[70] Wolfgang is best known for his "subculture of violence" theory; in line with the culture of poverty formulation, it argues that violent values are a common, culturally adaptive feature of African American communities.[71] Wolfgang was also a leader in statistical approaches to criminology, and he espoused the argument that a disproportionate amount of juvenile crime was done by "chronic offenders."[72] In 1986 Wolfgang testified to the Subcommittee on Criminal Justice of the House Judiciary Committee about the lack of, and need for, research on antigay violence: "Much remains to be learned about the full scope of the problem: We know little about anti-gay homicide. We know little about the perpetrators of anti-gay crimes and their motivations for victimizing lesbian and gay people. We know little about anti-gay violence against the young, or against members of racial minorities or individuals who live in rural areas. I recommend governmental research support on these topics."[73]

Wolfgang's call to expand the frame of inquiry aligned with the remedy many assumed would be found via a commitment to further study. But in the immediate absence of gay-specific research, activists drew on the approaches to violence and neighborhood that were already common in that era, which included the lasting influence of researchers like Wolfgang and the growing popularity of rational choice criminology typified by criminologists like Charles Murray, James Q. Wilson, and George L. Kelling that called for neighborhood "citizen" solutions.[74] The Anti-Violence Project collected reports about such research along with studies from local gay antiviolence initiatives; taken together, these materials reflected an inconsistent sense of what gay bashing was and named perpetrators alternately as suburban white teenage boys guided by normative masculinity and low-income black teenagers expressing economic resentment. This collection of explanations reflects the contradictions in the activism of the 1970s; by the mid-1980s the assumptions at the core of these conflicting ideas had become common knowledge. NGLTF activists were aware that the terms of economic crime, antigay sentiment, and violence could overlap, but since the bulk of activists' energy was dedicated to the inclusion of sexual orientation in hate crime legislation, the broader contexts of antigay violence rarely received in-depth analysis as activists called for neighborhood block organizations and various policing models.

Moreover, as was the case in the field of criminology more generally, the antiviolence movement's own conception of evidence increasingly narrowed as the language of legislation shifted from mandating the collection of *information* to that of more systematized *data*. In essence adopting the recommendations of early activists that antigay violence should have a "check box" in crime reports, the possibility of collecting narrative information that might highlight the complexity of violence was increasingly written out. This was by no means the intention of many activists; for example, Berrill, the director of the project, had emphasized to Crisisline workers the importance of the narrative sections of reports. Nonetheless, it would shape the course of advocacy for hate crime laws to come.[75]

The result was that by the time the Hate Crime Statistics Act had passed at the start of the 1990s, neighborhood crime and antigay violence were being treated virtually interchangeably. For example, early in that decade, the NGLTF Policy Institute released a guide called "Personal and Community Safety." It discussed the benefits of whistle campaigns, "defined by geography rather than identity." It continued: "In Boston, for example, all people—regardless of sexual orientation—who are living in particular neighborhoods or blocks are encouraged to carry whistles."[76] Despite the fact that this argument represented an effort to build across constituencies, when such campaigns were forged in middle-class or gentrifying neighborhoods, they risked asserting a feeling of community within a very small group of lesbians and gay men and middle-class residents and business owners. Although NGTLF activists clearly understood that hate violence emerged from a broad social context—Berrill was on the vanguard of antiviolence education and often collaborated with racial justice advocates—on-the-ground strategies still tended to treat targeted identities as discrete from one another. In addition, causal explanations based on economic alienation risked being detached from structural analyses of unequal power. For instance, in a speech Berrill drafted for a 1988 conference dedicated to crime victims' assistance in Colorado, he explained: "You may wonder where does the hate of hate crimes come from? The Justice Department study explains that it is the result of increased competition from minorities, increased visibility of gay people, ethnic neighborhood transition, and a perceived decrease in government efforts to prevent discrimination. I would add that hate crimes come from the devaluing and demeaning of certain groups in our society, a process that is expressed and perpetuated by the way we use certain words."[77] Although it is important to note that this was a draft of a speech for a conference about crime victims, and thus its language was aimed at a broad and, most likely, politically conservative audience, it is worth analyzing how the quote ultimately compartmentalizes motive while leveling injuries across groups. Here "minorities," "gay people," and "ethnic neighborhoods" function as discrete social phenomena that are linked through a concern with being "valued." This explanation also allows for understandings of crime and violence rooted in notions of rational choice from which the violence of the state is exempt. Thus, the third item on the list—"ethnic neighborhood transition"—is the most confusing: is the meaning the violence of displacement under gentrification or the vigilantist violence of those who challenge efforts to end racial segregation? These dynamics are not distinguished.

In *Sexuality and the Politics of Violence*, the British legal scholar Leslie Moran and the sociologist Beverley Skeggs show how "property talk" can be a central feature of how lesbians and gay men speak of safety.[78] Moran and Skeggs based their book on interviews with lesbians and gay men in the "gay Village" of Manchester, England, in the 1990s. The authors found that the language of property overlapped with that of propriety, and that the possessive language of neighborhood ownership often was a vehicle for describing a desire for order. As such, "property talk" also becomes a mode of inclusion and exclusion, by which strangers are regulated by the laws governing crime and social order. Thus those criminalized and considered to produce disorder are subjected to a range of exclusionary regimes. Central to these dynamics is the visibility of both LGBT people and of anti-LGBT crime. Moran and Skeggs argue that one of the key claims of those advocates of antiviolence surveys in Britain—that antigay violence is underreported—is premised on the idea that antigay violence is visible only when lesbians and gay men see their "safety management" to be within the realm of crime control.[79] This sentiment is well captured in the May 6, 1989, meeting minutes of the strategic planning group of the NGLTF, when someone summarized the history of the organization as a "shift from government out of our lives to government saving our lives to government affirming our lives."[80]

In the United States, the concern that visibility could cause violence was almost exactly mirrored by the claim that the visibility of violence was central to its eradication. One discussion of the topic in the organization was summarized as follows: "Anti-gay violence was invisible to the larger society, and yet very visible to those of us surviving this brutality within the community. The [Anti-Violence] Project was born out of the recognition that hate violence is the most brutal manifestation of homophobia. And that the first step to combating injustice was to render that injustice visible."[81] Thus, within the dominant rhetoric of lesbian and gay antiviolence politics, hate violence against gay people must be considered, first and foremost, as a crime. In turn, violence that is not made visible risks not being considered either antigay or a crime. Moran and Skeggs describe the call for punitive hate crime laws this way: "The demand for law, we want to suggest, is a demand for violence, albeit a particular form of violence: legitimate violence, good violence . . . in and through the state institutions of criminal justice."[82] The shift in the mid-1990s in the U.S. antiviolence movement from demands for documentation (as in the Hate Crime Statistics Act) to demands for enhanced punishment must therefore be seen as part of the logic of visibility. This is well captured in a draft "talking point" written in response to the claim that jails are overflowing and higher sentences will only make that worse—"Well, the people who attacked us are undersentenced."[83] The ability to quantify injuries and make them visible within the criminal justice apparatus provides the very terms by which justice is measured. By 1992, the Anti-Violence Project would be issuing annual reports that would compensate in density of data for what they often lacked in visualizing detail (fig. 4.1). Indeed, over the next years the organization's annual reports would seek to bring *visibility* through the stark representation of exhaustive enumeration and would become the antiviolence movement's most lasting influence. Although the NGLTF's Anti-Violence Project eventually ceased for-

FIGURE 4.1 NGLTF 1992 Antiviolence report (COURTESY OF DIVISION OF RARE AND MANUSCRIPT COLLECTIONS, CORNELL UNIVERSITY LIBRARY)

mal operations, the National Coalition of Anti-Violence Programs, based in New York, today carries on the commitment to documentation.

In 1992 Berrill collaborated with Gregory Herek to edit *Hate Crimes: Confronting Violence against Lesbians and Gay Men*. The book is the first comprehensive approach to the issue, and it includes statistical and psychological studies of violence and an overview of the movement's founding. In their introduction, the editors note limitations of the book—that it is focused on the United States and "more on Whites than people of color, more on men than women, and more on middle-class adults than on the poor, the elderly, and youth."[84] Although the editors recognized this exclusion to be a problem endemic to the field, it is more than an issue of omission. Instead, the tendency to link generalized street crime and social disorder with the problem of antigay violence defined the parameters of what counted as violence against lesbians and gays—and even what counted as lesbian and gay people—in very concrete ways. The person in Minneapolis who assumed that police violence against trans women of color did not belong in the report is a perfect example. Again, I am not suggesting that activists associated with the NGLTF would have agreed with this exclusion, or that they did not recognize the racialized core of criminalization in American society. In fact, individuals such as Berrill often went out of their way to emphasize the heightened vulnerability of people of color to crime.[85] Nonetheless, even this approach tended to sustain the category of antigay violence as individualized crime, rather than examine the racial, sexual, and gendered construction of crime categories or the broad operations of power that propel and define violence.

The emphasis on individual rather than structural violence also worked counter to two key arguments made by advocates of hate crime legislation: that hate crime laws would be a sort of back door to civil rights recognition; and that hate violence is an attack on the group, rather than the individual. Lesbian and gay activists outside the antiviolence movement sometimes declared their frustration with the fact that so much more enthusiasm was generated over a crime bill than a civil rights bill, regardless of the success of either legislation.[86] Furthermore, even the NGLTF played down the civil rights component when lobbying.[87] The assumption that hate crime laws would address group injury was asserted in numerous ways, but most strongly through analogy; the NGLTF reports painted a picture of antigay violence as "terrorism,"[88] a "guerrilla war,"[89] and a "rising tide"[90] that placed a "community . . . under siege,"[91] and they did so by comparing street violence to AIDS, gay people to Jewish people and African Americans, and state violence to individual violence. Some of these comparisons must be analyzed in the context of the NGLTF's central collaboration with the ADL, which was building support against the first Intifada during the late 1980s. Informally invoking the ways in which marginalized sexual and religious identity overlapped, NGLTF antiviolence advocates spoke out in alliance with the ADL; although they did not necessarily publicly support the ADL's Zionist stance, neither did they speak in opposition to it. Often implicit in these claims was the assumption that gay and Jewish people are linked by a sort of invisible difference as well as by their need for bounded territories.[92] This ideology also carried over into explanations of what counted as hate. In a training video the NGLTF used to reach out to police officers, an example of hate violence featured teenagers of color in public housing throwing rocks and stones at police officers. The idea that rock throwing by children at state officers constituted an example of hate violence must be seen in the context of the most visible representation of rock throwing during those years—by Palestinian youth against Israeli authorities. The video was made with the participation of the New York City office dedicated to lesbian and gay concerns and was sponsored by the ADL's William and Naomi Gorowitz Institute on Terrorism and Extremism;[93] at the time, the ADL was also organizing and funding a trip of New Jersey law enforcement officials to Israel to exchange training about policing strategies.[94]

The NGLTF's approach to hate crime was also influenced by the group's adoption of the ADL model legislation's focus on institutional vandalism. The ADL's model legislation was based on anti-Semitic violence, which is often expressed through attacks against the built environment—such as synagogues, cemeteries, and mortuaries. The model legislation also included "community centers" and applied not only to the buildings and structures of institutions, but also the "grounds adjacent to, and owned or rented by" these institutions— in other words, the areas in which they are located.[95] This response strategy was by no means restricted to the targeting of gay and Jewish people: black churches were also key sites of protection. But following the passage of an early yet restrictive statute against religious arson, the Hate Crimes Bill Coalition emphasized that institutional vandalism was still important for inclusion in the Hate Crime Statistics Act, and they pointed to this as a concern of the ADL and the NGLTF in particular.[96] Unlike the category people of color, which was assumed to always already manifest visibility, the definition of people by religion or sexuality was more often made relationally—in neighborhoods, among social groups, or in connection with property.

All that said, the connection between the NGLTF and the ADL hardly happened quickly, and it was only after years of pressure by lesbian and gay activists that the ADL agreed to include sexual orientation in its model hate crime legislation. Also, the organizations didn't always see eye to eye. For example, in the early 1990s, and after some debate, the NGLTF opposed the first Gulf War.[97] The ADL, on the other hand, was beginning a campaign on college campuses charging that antiwar activism—as well as a new investment in what the group described as "political correctness," "diversity," "multiculturalism," and "ethnic studies"—were fomenting anti-Semitism, especially among students of color.[98] (Years earlier the ADL had been involved in a fight with the NAACP over the ADL's criticism of the National Education Association's claim that the Ku Klux Klan was "not an aberration" and that racism in the United States was "entrenched."[99]) Nonetheless, the ADL and NGLTF's close collaboration and shared leading role in the hate crime law movement is worth noting; in these kinds of coalitional contexts, organizations often share and learn from each other's ideologies. The result is to stitch many of these seemingly disparate stances together.

The Return of Street Patrols

The blurry line between crime and antigay violence increasingly defined the parameters of local organizing in the 1990s, as hate crime laws gained visibility on the national stage and the problem of antigay violence continued to grab media attention. By extension, the distinction between anticrime neighborhood associations and gay organizations also became less clear during these years, when a second wave of gay safe streets patrols emerged across the country in cities such as Seattle, Boston, Chicago, Philadelphia, San Francisco, and New York.[100] The San Francisco Street Patrol—founded by members of the 1990s activist group Queer Nation—was active in the Castro. (It was begun by members of the Queer Nation affinity group Defend Our Rights in the Streets/Super Queers United against Savage Heterosexism [DORIS SQUASH].) In New York, the Christopher Street Patrol was founded by residents and business owners—both gay and straight—and was separate from the New York Pink Panthers, another Queer Nation invention. Although the Christopher Street Patrol focused on the street after which it was named, the Pink Panthers walked all of Greenwich Village, as well as nearby neighborhoods. The Pink Panthers were targeted by MGM Studios for copyright infringement but remained popular nonetheless, and groups were also founded in other cities.[101]

Famous for their cultural propaganda, often delivered via bright stickers, one of Queer Nation's best-known slogans of the era was "Queers Bash Back" (and "Gays Bash Back"), a theme that became a hallmark of many, although not all, street patrols.[102] In their essay "Queer Nationality," Lauren Berlant and Elizabeth Freeman analyze the cultural work of Queer Nation and the Pink Panthers, arguing for their critical recasting of nationalist sensibilities based in violence and injury. Berlant and Freeman explain that the phrase "Bash Back" "announces that the locus of gay oppression has shifted from the legal to the extralegal arena, and from national-juridical to ordinary everyday forms."[103] Although absolutely right—in the case of San Francisco, this shift also depended on an appropriation of (and identification with) national-juridical modes of *redress*. The San Francisco Street Patrol's logo was a modified Gadsden flag, with its coiled snake and phrase "Don't Tread on Me" emerging from a pink triangle.[104] The first flag of the U.S. Navy and a key emblem of the American Revolution that was taken up by Minutemen militia, the insignia is today most associated with patriotic, independent militarism. But although the original Gadsden flag warned the British government away, the San Francisco Street Patrol used it to call out support for defeating gay bashers on the street, and they supported the bolstering of state penalties.

In addition to T-shirts with the patrol's logo, members wore fuchsia berets, referencing the Guardian Angels with whom the San Francisco Street Patrol collaborated. At the time, the Guardian Angels were a hotly contested anticrime street patrol, whose members—wearing red berets—walked first through New York and then through other cities to combat what they described as the "constant victimization of ordinary people by the street punks who have taken over the streets of our cities."[105] Although considered by many to be vigilantes, the Guardian Angels gained the support of New York City Mayor Rudolph Giuliani in the 1990s.[106] Giuliani and Curtis Sliwa, founder of the Guardian Angels, shared a conservative populism, with a focus on neighborhood control by the owners of local businesses and homes and law-and-order responses to street crime.[107] In particular, both men advocated quality-of-life policing that targeted nonviolent offenses such as drug dealing and prostitution as a way to limit urban disorder and crime.

In response to criticisms for their collaboration with the Guardian Angels, members of the San Francisco Street Patrol clarified that they would not interfere in nonviolent criminal activity and further explained: "All the GA's [Guardian Angels] that we have come in contact with have been unfailingly supportive and queer-positive. No one has tried to indoctrinate us into the GA political agenda. To the best of our knowledge, there is no GA political agenda, nor is there a GA social agenda, except that they are opposed to crime."[108] This response reflects the Street Patrol's understanding—like that of the dominant movement for hate crime laws—that the primary status of antigay violence is a crime (a national-juridical category), and the organization's relations with law enforcement officials supported this perspective. In their newsletters there were cheeky references to flirting with police officers,[109] and to the importance of hate crime legislation.[110] They also included tips on self-defense, photographs of patrollers in action, recruitment information, art, and other forms of organization propaganda (fig. 4.2). At one meeting that the newsletter reported on, members proposed that the police establish a kiosk in the Castro for faster response time and sketched out a system for the exchange of information on suspected perpetrators (called "mutants" by the Street Patrol), such as license plate numbers and names of repeat offenders.[111]

The Street Patrol also made recommendations that pushed the limits of the law, not by challenging criminalization but by asking for its expansion. Among a set of safety tips titled "Walking on the Wild Side: A Few Handy Hints on How to Avoid Getting Your Ass Kicked by Crazed Heterosexist Slime," a member of the group identified as Adam Z suggested:

FIGURE 4.2 *Street Patrol Newsletter*, May 1991 (COURTESY OF THE GAY, LESBIAN, BISEXUAL, TRANSGENDER HISTORICAL SOCIETY)

Don't be afraid to call the police. If somebody is following you around, or seems to be interested in something other than fun, call the cops straight away. While it's true that the police can't arrest someone just for acting creepy, they will be glad to harass someone if you spice up your complaint some. Instead of, "There's a hetero guy walking around Collingwood Park and looking at people funny" (oh, yeah, we'll send out a squad car *right away*, pal), try something like, "This guy threatened me with a switch-blade." This sort of thing perks up the attention of the law enforcement community like a charm, and if they don't find anyone with a knife at the scene, well, at least there's a bunch of cops running around to scare off the potential basher. Be sure to describe the suspect in minute detail. The cops will take a detailed report much more seriously.[112]

In addition to proposing draconian policing, the above suggestion rests on an assumption that the nature of the threat is evident and shared. Later in the list of tips, threats are described as groups of teenagers, cars crammed with people, "hets" outside of gay bars, and young men drinking beer on street corners. Since the gay night life of the Castro certainly included gay teenagers and beer drinkers, and socializing in the free spaces of cars and street corners is common among many people, the advice given by the Street Patrol resembles the vague categories by which neighborhood "insiders" and "outsiders" have been identified in middle-class and upper-income neighborhoods. The following description of a Street Patrol event captures it well: "We first noticed them hanging out by the 7–11 at 18th and Noe earlier in the evening. . . . They were in a big, beat-up blue '68 Chevy and a decorated, mid '70s GMC van. They looked like gang members, wearing fur-lined hooded jackets even though it was a hot night."[113] This is not to say that there were not groups of people looking to assault lesbians and gay men, but the sentiment expressed can be understood only as part of a commitment to a notion of neighborhood belonging in line with Moran and Skeggs's concept of "property talk." In another article, a street patrol coordinator described the problem of antigay violence as one in which people "come into *our* neighborhood to beat us up—for fun."[114] Perhaps for this reason, the New York–based Christopher Street Patrol met with the San Francisco Street Patrol to discuss strategy and consider building a national network, despite the fact that the former was a resident and business association, unaffiliated with activist groups like Queer Nation.[115] The proposed network never materialized.[116]

Although the New York–based Pink Panthers defined themselves in contrast to the Christopher Street Patrol—for example, the Pink Panthers did not have a formal collaboration with the Guardian Angels—their strategies nonetheless overlapped with those of the San Francisco Street Patrol. The Pink Panthers addressed citywide violence but were committed to neighborhood. They also stood behind the slogan "Remember: Lesbians and Gays Bash Back."[117] In the *Village Voice*, the journalist Alisa Solomon described a night spent on the Panther beat: "I have little doubt that an August night I spent with the Pink Panthers—a gay and lesbian street patrol modeled on the Guardian Angels—would have ended violently if anyone had been packing a piece." The night she wrote about—which included a group of thirty white gay men and lesbians chasing two black men accused of molesting a woman as a white bystander shouted racial epithets—ultimately amounted to "a violent free-for-all of bias." Turning to a feminist critique of violence, Solomon remarked that such arguments all too often fall on unhearing gay ears.[118] For the street patrols, their violence was cast as a militant response to the violence of others; the masculinism of violence was purportedly undercut by the campy presentation of femininity deployed by many members of the patrols.[119] Needless to say, this argument about gender simply reinforces notions that femininity is artifice and masculinity the stuff of substance, with the former working at the service of the latter.

Although the Christopher Street Patrol's strategies were, for the most part, the same as those of Queer Nation's spinoff patrols, the tone of the former group was different, particularly in its lack of colorful and creative fliers and campy humor. Furthermore, the Christopher Street Patrol took a decidedly unstable position concerning what kinds of crimes constituted a threat, as well as what types of solidarity would be in its members' best interests. The group's allies ranged from anticrime organizations to the formal lesbian and gay antiviolence movement, and they variously targeted or deemphasized problems like violence, drinking, and even honking.[120] For example, in 1990 the gay magazine *OutWeek* reported that the Christopher Street Patrol, "according to Merchants Association President Michael Mirisola, will concentrate on inhibiting violent crime, including gay-bashing and drug sales, and will not interfere with 'public drinking, rowdiness and noisemaking,' which he characterized as long-standing neighborhood traditions."[121] One year later, the patrol released "A Report to Our Neighbors," describing the group's top commitments as being to "*improve the quality of life* by deterring crime[s] — particularly those which are caused by drug sales and use" and "preserve the special nature of Christopher Street and stop gay-bashing."[122] Although drug use is omitted in the first description, it is aligned with the violence of drug sales in the second and distinguished from public drinking; this is not surprising, given the response to crack cocaine use in 1990. What is significant is the characterization of the neighborhood as a place of "rowdiness" in the first quote and gayness in the latter. It is unclear if the two overlap.

This ambiguity is clearly displayed in a flier that the Christopher Street Patrol distributed in collaboration with AVP, the Mayor's Office of Lesbian and Gay Affairs, and a group of tenant and business associations. Titled "Christopher St. Is a Special Place: Let's Work Together to Keep It That Way," it declares that "MANY THINGS ARE TOLERATED, *BUT THESE ARE NOT*," and it continues with a list of unacceptable behaviors:

1) Violence of any kind, however small or personal, including harassing or hassling people who are trying to walk down the street

2) Drug dealing and drug use
3) Other crime of any kind (including shoplifting)
4) Drinking by minors/selling of alcohol to minors .
5) Illegal parking
6) Noise that bothers other people, especially after 10 pm (includes boom boxes that can be heard more than 50 feet away)
7) Urinating on streets/buildings (or any other ruining of some one else's property)
8) Blocking public access (like to Path Station, other doorways)

It concludes: "*You are welcome on Christopher Street to be who you are and to have a good time.* BUT YOU ARE NOT WELCOME TO BREAK THE LAW, TAKE AWAY THE RIGHTS OF OTHERS, OR OTHERWISE ACT IN DISRESPECT OF THE NEIGHBORHOOD AND OTHER PEOPLE. THESE ARE BASIC LAWS/RULES OF PUBLIC SAFETY AND HUMAN DECENCY. HAVE FUN, BUT *PLEASE RESPECT THE NEIGHBORHOOD AND ALL OF OUR/YOUR FRIENDS AND NEIGHBORS.* THANK YOU!"[123] Here the category of violence expands to include "violence of any kind, however small or personal." And despite opening with a recognition of the importance of Stonewall, the flier removes gayness as a targeted or protected category.

Conclusion

As I have argued, to cast so-called *bashers* as *criminals* is correct yet narrow, especially insofar as it suggests the reverse: that those deemed *criminals* are the *bashers*. Indeed, ideologies of criminality directly shaped patrol members' notions of among whom and where antigay threat was to be found—a dynamic familiar to the hate crimes movement as well. Middle-class, majority-white gay enclaves like New York's Greenwich Village and San Francisco's Castro were places where the *criminal* was easily substituted for those outside the area's residential demographics. In this way, these patrols found easy alliance with anticrime activism defined by claims to neighborhood rather than sexual identity.[124] In the case of the San Francisco Street Patrol, for whom potential bashers were most often named as "hets" from "outside" the neighborhood, "us" over "here" versus "them" over "there" became "queer" versus "straight." In her reading of the Queer Nation manifesto "I Hate Straights," the political scientist Cathy Cohen shows how this stance can conflate the heterosexual with the heteronormative and ignore unequal access to power among both heterosexuals and homosexuals. Cohen shows that race, class, and gender status are intrinsic to how sexual subjects are situated and "either enhance or mute the marginalization of queers, on the one hand, and the power of heterosexuals, on the other."[125] The majority of the members of street patrols in both cities were white, and Adam Z's suggestion of trumped-up and vague descriptions of potential bashers all too clearly evokes the dynamics of racial profiling well established in U.S. cities by the 1990s. Furthermore, such hyperbolic recommendations must also be seen as part of the theatrics for which Queer Nation became so well known, rather than as a singular anomaly; patrols relied heavily on the power of suggestion. Like the advocates of the patrols of the 1970s, which focused on the power of publicity as visibility, and the mainstream antiviolence movement's own contention that both abstracted and embodied visibility were the routes to safety, San Francisco Street Patrol members were sure that their very presence contributed to the decline in reported attacks in the area.[126]

Berlant and Freeman echo the argument that the protection the Panthers provided was largely symbolic, the possibility of violence promised by counterpublicity. They write: "In this way, the slogan [Bash Back] turns the bodies of the Pink Panthers into a psychic counterthreat, expanding their protective shield beyond the confines of their physical 'beat.' Perhaps the most assertive 'bashing' that the uniformed bodies of the Pink Panthers deliver is mnemonic. Their spectacular presence counters heterosexual culture's will not to recognize its own intense need to reign in a sexually pure environment."[127] This is true, especially the reminders that the thematization of the presence of outsiders can highlight structures by which they are excluded, and that the Panthers rarely did use physical violence. Nonetheless, the boundaries of sexual purity in city space have not only been drawn along the lines of queerness as it is used here. The mnemonic provided by the Panthers is also one of racial segregation, which has long relied on ideas of sexual purity and the threat of state punishment. The performative power of the Panthers signals that it is a specific mode of queerness and structure of injury's recognition that define the gay neighborhood's borders. Those who are not legible within certain racialized modes of sexual or gender identification or who are vulnerable to forms of violence that are not restricted to the so-called crime of the street risk being the objects of an activist call for violence in the pursuit of safety.

This is the local manifestation of the national antiviolence movement's hate crime strategy. Moreover, this vision also has its own national(ist) dimensions, insofar as Queer Nation had chapters across the country and given its very name. Lisa Duggan describes Queer Nation's "militant nationalism" as part of its commitment to publicity and direct action, while challenging liberalism's core tenet of privacy. But as Duggan further elaborates in discussing Queer Nation's "outing" strategies, this approach also depended on a liberal ethos that treats group membership as bounded in identity and uniform in interests.[128] In this way, Queer Nation–styled projects can be seen as an extension of the militant gay liberalism I described earlier, given that both challenge some of the privacy-oriented aspects of homophile-era gay liberalism at the same time as they advocate state-centered solutions.

By the 1990s the antiviolence movement had succeeded in producing a shared investment in the goals of gay safety, achieved through anticrime strategies, and visibility, aided in large part through the protection of gay-identified neighborhoods. Furthermore, the two sides of each equation had become sutured to each other—gay safety to visibility and anticrime strategies to gay neighborhood protection. Thus, the special character of gay neighborhoods had become just as defined by anticrime measures as it was by those who made it gay; and the idealized category of *gay* would—like violence determined by crime categories—condense. In fact, during the 1990s and into the 2000s, the Christopher Street Patrol's targets tightened their focus on LGBT/queer youth and transgender women, both of color, whom they accused of being the primary perpetrators of quality-of-life violations. Residents and business groups would draw on the idea of the "special character" of Christopher Street and Greenwich Village as one opposed to the "neighborhood tradition" of "public drinking, rowdiness, and noisemaking" that they increasingly deemed "violent." For this, they would not only turn to some of the strategies and common-sense lessons of the LGBT antiviolence movement, but they would also draw on the legacies of progressive, community-centered urban-planning mechanisms. Although they would find opponents in new queer activist groups, they would also find support among lesbian- and gay-identified elected officials, and they would not encounter opposition from city agencies or from national groups organized in the name of LGBT protection. The idea that LGBT safety would come through neighborhood-based crime control strategies had become so commonplace that the target of Greenwich Village residents' neighborhood protection efforts would be the very people who most face the kinds of interpersonal, state-sponsored, and structural violence that the LGBT movement had been founded to fight.[129]

CHAPTER 5

"CANARIES OF THE CREATIVE AGE"

Queer Critiques of Risk and Real Estate
in the Twenty-First Century

Muggings and purse-snatching on Bedford Street! Neighbors attacked and beaten by a group of kids (some as young as 14), again on Bedford Street! A man slashed on Christopher Street while his wife was robbed! Drug dealings on Perry Street! Pizza deliveryman jumped and robbed on Barrow Street. Prostitution from Greenwich Street to Greenwich Avenue! Shopping bags pushed out of the arms of older residents on Christopher Street! The list of offenses goes on and on.

What have been the Village's greatest assets—*its acceptance and diversity*—have become its greatest liabilities.

—Dave Poster and Elaine Goldman, "Gay Youth Gone Wild," *Villager*, **2005**

The epigraph to this chapter quotes the words of Dave Poster and Elaine Goldman—identified as presidents of the Christopher Street Patrol Association and Christopher Street Block and Merchants Association, respectively—and was published in 2005 by the local Greenwich Village paper, the *Villager*. Poster and Goldman's dystopic vision of Greenwich Village extends the fearfulness of the Christopher Street Patrol of a decade earlier. But it replaces the risk of gay vulnerability with the "liabilities" of "acceptance and diversity." Although patrols had long argued that gay visibility carried the risk of violence, the residents-based Christopher Street Patrol of the early twenty-first century contended that it is tolerance that placed Greenwich Village at risk. In addition to patrolling the streets armed with walkie-talkies with the support of the Guardian Angels, during the early 2000s the Christopher Street

Patrol strengthened its collaborations with business owners and residents, the latter of whom reportedly also adopted eggs as weapons.[1]

The introduction to this book opened with one such event from May 2002, the rally "Take Back Our Streets" outside the Stonewall Inn. This action was but one of many taken in the streets, churches, and public institutions of the neighborhood. With LGBT youth and transgender adult women of color as their primary targets, and the piers along the Hudson River on the west side of the neighborhood identified as ground zero, residents complained that their neighborhood had been taken over by outsiders whose threatening activities promised to bring down the so-called quality of life of the neighborhood. The primary stages for their accusations were the monthly hearings of the local community board and police precinct community council, city-sponsored mechanisms for neighborhood-based decision making. Overwhelmingly, residents and business owners demanded more policing and changes in land use policy under the auspices of securing safety. The key tools they hoped to wield were the retention of a curfew at the neighborhood's waterfront, as well as the heightened enforcement of former Mayor Rudolph Giuliani's quality-of-life policies that target offenses such as public drinking, noise, and loitering.[2] Access to public space and quality-of-life regulations thus became the focal point for political response, and counteractivists representing nonresident LGBT youth of color attended community board hearings and police precinct community councils demanding that they too should be eligible to give input and that their safety was also at stake.

The Christopher Street Patrol gained supporters among residents, officials, and some lesbian and gay activists despite the fact that the group's position appears contradicted by what was then popular policy wisdom on the beneficial effects of the social tolerance associated with gay populations.[3] The Gay Index, based in the research of demographer Gary Gates, was, by the start of the 2000s, a measure celebrated by city agencies from Washington, D.C., to Oakland, California, because it was highly touted as predictive of the regional success of high-tech industries.[4] This argument had been publicized by the urbanist and policy consultant Richard Florida, who contended that a concentration of gay men—and, to a lesser degree, lesbians—reflects a region's social "tolerance," which he considered to be a draw factor for the creative class of workers at the center of the (then) "new economy."[5] In this formulation, gay space is, thus, an index of economic competitiveness in a global marketplace for business location. This understanding of gay space is just one held by Gay Index proponents; another is that gay people tend to live in neighborhoods with dilapidated housing stock and high crime rates. As Gates explains: "It could be that gay and lesbian people are less risk averse. They've already taken the risk of coming out of the closet, so it could be that they're willing to take more risk in other dimensions of their lives as well."[6] But what are the risks associated with these areas—physical violence or speculative investment? For many, housing location is not based in choice, and same-sex activity is not correlated with being out as gay. Can those deemed to be *at risk*—an epidemiological category that often includes those who are young and poor, or who are homeless, or who do not identify as gay when practicing same-sex sex—bank (quite literally) on these same risks?

The "canaries of the creative age" to which the title of this chapter refers, are, according to Gates and Florida, gay populations whose survival in urban regions is cast as an indicator of the "last frontier" of social tolerance and diversity and the promise of a successful economy.[7] Although for Florida acceptance of gays represents the far reaches of tolerance and diversity, his curious definition of the latter is absent of people of color. As Florida observes when describing the Composite Diversity Index of which the Gay Index is a part (together with the Melting Pot Index and the Bohemian Index), "the diversity picture does not include African-Americans and other nonwhites." He continues: "My research identifies a troubling negative statistical correlation between concentrations of high-tech firms and the percentage of the nonwhite population."[8] Thus the vision of the Christopher Street Patrol, which primarily targets people of color in Greenwich Village, is not counter to the ideals of popular urban planning after all. As the saying goes, birds of a feather flock together, and some "canaries" are understood to be guarantors of demise. The complaints made by residents demonstrate the contradictions of contemporary urban politics, in which one can celebrate diversity and cast tolerance as a new investment strategy at the same time as one assails those very features by naming the acceptance of people of color, transgender women, and people of low income as "liabilities" of a neighborhood best known for its gay populations and bohemianism.[9]

These are the contradictions at the core of neoliberalism. Since the 1970s, many of the central terms put forth by postwar urban reformers have been promoted by neoliberal city programs through a deft reworking of the ideals of community, participation, and safety in the service of initiatives set to dismantle Keynesian-influenced New Deal and Great Society programs in favor of those guided by distilled free market values.[10] Neoliberalism has reshaped U.S. cities like New York and San Francisco in ways that foster hypersegregation and exploitation: the privatization of public services, corporate tax breaks, attacks on tenant protections, the expiration of mandates for low- and middle-income housing, public subsidies for private market-value construction, and the mass expansion of security forces are but a few of its policies. The skyrocketing values of real estate in urban cores means that almost all new claims to these neighborhoods are property investments and acts of racial dispossession. Indeed, the profits and punishments of these policies have been doled out along stark racial and class lines, and it is this very disproportionate impact that neoliberalism, as a set of ideological imperatives, has worked hard to elide.[11] Yet the approach to identity and economy taken by the liberalism associated with earlier political and economic orders, such as that of the Great Society, is part of this historical trajectory. The focus on the individualized psychology of prejudice, the ideal of blindness to difference, and the goal of equality were part and parcel of the postwar liberal consensus outlined by Gunnar Myrdal that would set the stage for discussions about inequality that followed. As Jodi Melamed argues, ideas of "race as culture," the individually reparative rather than structurally transformative features of antiracism, and the devaluation of economic justice took form in postwar racial liberalism but continued to evolve in what she dubs the emergence of "neoliberal multiculturalism."[12] Thus, in today's cities, marginalized identities can function as markers of cultural value (as in the commodity known as lifestyle) but cannot be considered as vectors of exploitation.[13]

The ways in which the concepts of *identity* and *economy* are stitched together and cleaved apart has influenced the landscape not only of everyday urban life but also of activist response. To return to the War on Poverty of the 1960s, workers in antipoverty programs, like civil rights activists, did not have a single vision, and they pursued campaigns to make economic justice a part of rights claims and to call for reforms even as they pursued systemic change. They often highlighted the entwined functions of racism and economic exploitation, and—as shown in the case study in chapter 1— tried to connect the enforcement of sexual norms with economic development plans. Nonetheless, 1960s liberal programs were also based on individualistic critiques that, in the case of lesbian and gay politics, would by the 1970s bolster a concept like *homophobia*—a manifestation of liberalism's psychologizing ethos—even in campaigns that might make modest redistributive demands.

Since then, as mainstream LGBT activism has homed in on the project of inclusion, it has simultaneously maintained an analytic separation of sexual and gender normativity from racism and political economy via the use of metaphor and the advocacy of privatization and criminalization. In the case of LGBT antiviolence politics, concerns about personal safety well demonstrate the continuities between postwar liberalism and neoliberalism, as well as their striking differences. For example, hate crime laws seek legal redress for individual injuries so as to assert group rights, but the same laws support the rapid expansion of the punitive security state. Community policing involves collaborations between governmental programs and local communities and are today most informed by approaches based in the risk calculations of rational choice theory. This is also the case with gay neighborhoods, which are at once claimed as spatial expressions of minority rights and as consumer demands that have promoted the growth of niche markets for retail and realty.[14]

This has meant that as public welfare programs and civil liberties are dismantled, those on the left have diverged in their opinions of how activists' energy should be distributed between halting rollbacks and forging new alternatives. Furthermore, these contradictions have sometimes been manifested in a focus on individualized injury among activists otherwise committed to broad-based change. Even more often, these contradictions have fostered narrow left-liberal urban politics that insist that culture, desire, and identity are irrelevant. This chapter highlights these debates as they played out in Greenwich Village, demonstrating how liberal neighborhood reforms were used to exclude those whom they were once imagined to serve. I then consider one group's queer critique of the neoliberal city, showing how they recoded dominant stories of LGBT and queer vulnerability to violence and the need for safe space in the city by at once refusing and turning to the participatory ideals of declining public institutions.

Community Planning and the "Special Character" of Greenwich Village

In order to understand these conflicts, it is crucial to first outline the mode of governance that has served as the primary stage for these struggles in Greenwich Village—New York City community boards—as well as the emergence of activist opposition. Community boards are made up of individuals who live or work in a given neighborhood. The boards serve many purposes, from fielding complaints to processing permit applications, but chief among their responsibilities is to provide input on land use, zoning, and other planning issues.[15] The development of community boards in the 1960s was in part in response to the calls for participation in local government common to that era. Greenwich Village played a key role in the demand to include residents in the New York City planning process, most famously in the challenges made by the neighborhood activist Jane Jacobs to development plans in the 1950s and 1960s. In 1961 Jacobs published *The Death and Life of Great American Cities*, in which she railed against the heavy hand of planners, lambasting urbanisms based on instrumentalist notions of place, efficiency ethics, and a disregard for the "ballet" of urban street life.[16] Jacobs called, instead, for urban design that promoted street culture:

dense, low-level housing and mixed-use zoning. She argued that the most effective way to fight urban disorder was through internal mechanisms, claiming that the "eyes on the street" of neighbors and "public characters" are more important than state programs.[17] According to her, by locating services, workplaces, and homes together one could create communities that celebrated rather than feared density and heterogeneity. Jacobs's critics often called her utopian, arguing that the ideals she had drawn from her middle-class Greenwich Village were not applicable for areas in deep poverty. Indeed, her views on the city have found both critics and advocates from across the political spectrum.[18] For example, Marc Stein argues that in Jacobs's description of the "pervert park," "sexual perversion functions . . . as a symptom, source, and sign of urban disorder."[19] As a result, among Jacobs's admirers the application of her vision can vary widely, from the family-friendly planned towns of the new urbanism to the public sex spots extolled by Samuel Delany.[20] Regardless, Jacobs's activities also have indelibly marked Greenwich Village as an area imbued with a populist disdain for top-down municipal planning.

Despite Jacobs's celebrated calls for reform, actual community-initiated plans were not given official standing in New York until 1989.[21] Yet a series of developments worth noting paved the way, starting in 1961—the same year that *The Death and Life of Great American Cities* was published. That was when the city passed its first modification of the 1916 resolution that had established zoning.[22] The 1961 revision set maximum population densities and separated three primary categories of zoned use: residential, commercial, and manufacturing.[23] Although use-based zoning has worked as a safeguard against unchecked market forces, it also exacerbated the racial and class segregation of the city, as places of employment were separated from those of residence, lower-value uses were banned to the periphery, and use laws limited the growth of manufacturing jobs and affordable housing.[24] In 1963 a revision to the city charter set up community planning boards to provide neighborhood input into municipal decisions about zoning and land use; by 1969, the City Council had created paid positions on community boards.[25] In the 1970s, as the federal government canceled Great Society–era programs, New York strove to strengthen community boards: the adoption of the Uniform Land Use Review Procedure empowered residents by mandating community board reviews; later, the modification of Section 197-a of the city charter allowed community boards to sponsor their own plans (now referred to as "197-a plans").[26] In low-income neighborhoods, community-initiated plans implemented since the late 1980s have been used to fight the negative impacts of privatization via demands that the city maintain an industrial base, require that new development guarantee local employment, build affordable housing, or prevent the disproportionate placement of environmental toxins in low-income neighborhoods.[27]

In 1990 Greenwich Village Community Board 2 (CB2) submitted a 197-a plan, "The Special Greenwich Village Hudson River District," which focused on protecting the area's meat market and printing industries; cultivating the graphic arts industry; preserving the views of and access to the waterfront; maintaining the low-rise scale of the area; securing its tourist base; and providing low-income housing for seniors and people with disabilities, including those with AIDS. This plan was withdrawn due to administrative obstacles and pressure from the real estate industry.[28] In 1992 the Department of City Planning released a Comprehensive Waterfront Plan. In response to residents' concerns, the Manhattan section focused on natural preservation, public access, and the protection of a working waterfront, while also allowing for some new development.[29] At the same time, the Hudson River Park Conservancy of the Empire State Development Corporation began, with the sponsorship of the City and the State of New York, to redevelop the west side of Manhattan's waterfront, from Battery Park City to 59th Street (inclusive of Greenwich Village's piers).[30] Using public and private funds, the goal of the park was to prioritize public access to the waterfront while nominally safeguarding the land from the market, prohibiting "any new buildings on parkland that have no relation to the water or the park experience—such as office or residential buildings or hotels."[31] In 1998 Governor George Pataki signed the Hudson River Park Act, which created the Hudson River Park Trust (HRPT).[32] In HRPT's vision, the Greenwich Village section was to focus on the development of the neighborhood's Pier 40 from a parking and storage facility into a recreational space with retail uses and the city's flower market. Other piers were to be renovated to maintain public access to them. These were not new private developments per se, which were prohibited by waterfront rezoning in the comprehensive plan, yet they were sure to increase the value of neighboring residential zones.

HRPT framed its "concept plan" as a part of the uniqueness of Greenwich Village: "Design of the Greenwich Village waterfront must meet the needs of many different constituencies while respecting the community's desire for passive open space, broad vistas of the Hudson river, and a link to the historic past of this waterfront."[33] This is significant because it recognizes waterfront users other than just the residential "community" and acknowledges that the piers have a historical value. Although this might seem to suggest that HRPT understood the area to be a public gathering space for a variety of recreational users, one might argue that it was a way for HRPT to suggest that commercial developers might count as nonresidential "constituencies." CB2 opposed many of the city-supported plans for the waterfront, rejecting commercial uses in the hope of maintaining open space.[34] The board members insisted that the majority of piers be reserved for "passive recreation," and they were committed to keeping parking.[35] Throughout the process, CB2 tended to refer to the waterfront in the possessive—as ours.[36] HRPT began renovations on the Greenwich Village waterfront in 1999, closing off most public access for reconstruction and instituting an interim curfew.[37] The immediate effect was to drastically limit the public's access to the piers.

LGBT people from inside and outside the neighborhood were among those most affected by the closure. In addition to Greenwich Village's status as a symbolic place of LGBT and bohemian life since the early twentieth century, the piers have their own queer history. In the years of abandonment brought by deindustrialization, their status as informal public gathering places had grown. In the 1960s and 1970s, the piers were popular spots for public and commercial sex between men (many, but by no means all, white). In the 1980s, increasing numbers of people of color began to socialize in the area, many of whom had been pushed out of Washington Square Park in the neighborhood's core following the "cleanup" of the park discussed in chapter 2. During this time, the local sex work economy was also restructured, and transgender women who usually worked closer to Times Square often joined the Greenwich Village scene. Free to enter and accessible by public transportation, the area also became a central gathering place for youth and people of low income. The life on the piers was featured in a range of mainstream and subcultural representations during this time, including the gay S/M world of the film *Cruising* (1980); the cult classic *Times Square* (1980), in which the piers are home to two runaway girls (whose queer desires are forged in rejection of the redevelopment of Times Square);[38] the ball scene of the 1980s, highlighted by the documentary *Paris Is Burning* (1990);[39] and the makeshift homes of gay and straight men and transgender women living in New York City sanitation trucks in the documentaries *The Salt Mines* (1990) and *The Transformation* (1995).[40]

By 2000 the demographic characteristics of the piers' social users had significantly diverged from those of the neighborhood's residential population, the latter of which was 75 percent white, with only 5.2 percent of residents receiving public assistance, Supplemental Security Income, or Medicaid.[41] Although the long-standing antidevelopment stance of CB2—against commercial uses counter to the character of the neighborhood—would persist, from the 1990s into the 2000s the activities of nonresidential users also were cast as highly undesirable and as a municipal imposition. Although residents continued to use CB2 to register opposition to New York University's expansionism, the spread of condominiums, and the rescinding of rent control, some also opposed social service agencies and businesses that served primarily LGBT people of color. For example, the Neutral Zone, a drop-in center for youth, was initially located at the end of Christopher Street, not far from the piers. The center operated a late night social space and provided counseling, health, and cultural programs. By 1995 residents had successfully campaigned for its closure; they also succeeded in having street outreach vans removed soon afterward.[42] As the years passed, many gay bars whose clientele was mostly black and Latino were also driven out because of residents' complaints and real estate market forces.[43]

Initiated by a small group of residents, the campaign against nonresidents was not uniformly considered that of a renegade group, and the campaigners received the support of Aubrey Lees, a lawyer who was then head of CB2 and who has also served as president of the Lesbian and Gay Law Association of Greater New York and vice president of the Stonewall Democratic Club. Residents' actions were also not immediately opposed by LGBT or public space activists, probably because Greenwich Village residents' demands have been linked in public discourse to a progay, anti–private development sentiment in line with the neighborhood's historic resistance to top-down planning.[44] Since proposals such as HRPT's acknowledged users other than residents in part to make room for developers, residential opposition to nonresidents could be characterized as populist opposition to imposed city policy. This is well demonstrated by the two examples that open this book: the 2002 "Take Back Our Streets" rally and the campaign against the expansion of PATH train entrances into Greenwich Village. The anti-PATH Christopher Street Preservation Alliance cited, along with traffic concerns, the threat that overdevelopment posed to the integrity of the Stonewall Inn.[45] (In fact, historic preservation, a classic tool of gentrification, actually has been used to counter speculative growth in the area.[46]) Thus the special neighborhood character to be preserved is one that indexes a populist and lesbian and gay history, neither of which is imagined to include its more contemporary queer users.[47] As HRPT began to fence off the piers for construction and to set a curfew, LGBT people who hung out there faced a dilemma: residents were dedicated to keeping them out of the residential parts of Greenwich Village, but the public spaces of the piers simply no longer existed. Residents' demand for the heightened enforcement of antiloitering laws literally kept people moving, with nowhere to go except out of the neighborhood or into jail. And despite insistence by the city and residents that the renovation would be temporary, few piergoers believed that they would be a part of the area's future.

That's FIERCE!

In short time, a contingent of staunch adversaries to the redevelopment of the waterfront appeared on the scene. In March 2000 a group of mostly queer youth of color banded together to form Fabulous Independent Educated Radicals for Community Empowerment (FIERCE), and they began to challenge the increase in policing and disappearance of public space on the piers.[48] The first members of FIERCE had met in the late 1990s through a series of political education workshops sponsored by a youth social service organization, Project Reach; most of them were queer high-school students of color who lived in New York's outer boroughs. This included Bran Fenner and Krystal Portalatin, who would later serve on FIERCE's staff and as directors of the organization. They were joined by Jesse Ehrensaft-Hawley, a queer white man originally from California who had had summer internships at Project Reach while he was a student at Oberlin College and who joined the staff after graduation; he would become FIERCE's first director.

In 1996, grassroots racial justice organizations in the city had begun the New York City Coalition Against Police Brutality (CAPB). One member group was the Audre Lorde Project (ALP) in Brooklyn, which had been founded in 1994 by members of Advocates for Gay Men of Color. ALP developed a Working Group on Police Violence, which played a central role in CAPB. As part of CAPB, ALP would help organize People's Justice 2000, a campaign mobilizing around two high profile cases of police violence in New York—the police assault of Abner Louima in 1997 and murder of Amadou Diallo in 1999[49]—as part of a call to end police violence citywide; they would also help build the national network Racial Justice 911. ALP identified its primary constituency as lesbian, gay, bisexual, two-spirit, and transgender people of color (ALP now uses the term *trans* instead of *transgender* and includes the gender nonconforming), and the Working Group on Police Violence had located the Greenwich Village piers as one emblematic place where LGBT people of color in New York faced sustained forms of state violence.[50] Some members of FIERCE were involved in ALP and participated in these coalition actions.

In addition to ALP, CAPB also included the Malcolm X Grassroots Movement, National Congress for Puerto Rican Rights (now the Justice Committee), and CAAAV: Organizing Asian Communities. Although CAPB kept sexual and gender identity on the political agenda, this was not always the case for other formations against police brutality in the city. In addition, the members of FIERCE were eager to found an organization that kept the concerns of youth primary, especially those of the piers. Fenner later explained: "With all the groups doing prison abolition work and work against police brutality, there was an entire section of the city that was missing. And we were all the pier kids in one way or another. And we were noticing different trends [there], like mass police presence and brutality in general and harassment of trans women in particular. And so that's why we started."[51]

As FIERCE began to coalesce, its members searched for an office. In the meanwhile, the Neutral Zone, which had been evicted from Christopher Street, had added "New" to its name and moved north to Chelsea. The New Neutral Zone was beyond the borders of Greenwich Village, but it was near the waterfront, and a number of the youth it served identified as "pier kids"—young people who socialized at the piers, many of whom were marginally housed or lacked supportive services in their home neighborhoods. Ehrensaft-Hawley began working for the New Neutral Zone, and soon afterward FIERCE found an office for itself in the same building. As some members were still in high school and others had gone away to college (both Fenner and Portalatin began college at the State University of New York at Purchase), Ehrensaft-Hawley became the group's director. Among the organizations with which FIERCE initially collaborated was New York PoliceWatch, a project of the Ella Baker Center for Human Rights in Oakland. The center had been founded in 1996 by members of Bay Area PoliceWatch, a hotline run by the activist Van Jones; the center was also a part of Racial Justice 911. Its focus was on police brutality, with an emphasis on youth, and among its projects was TransAction, a collaboration with San Francisco's Community United Against Violence.[52] FIERCE sought the center's financial sponsorship since, as a fledging group, it lacked nonprofit status of its own; as a result, New York PoliceWatch joined FIERCE in its new office.

FIERCE built its membership within pier youth culture as well as among young people associated with youth agencies. In New York's political and economic geography, this meant that the initial staff and targeted base membership were largely low-income and working-class young people of color. Ehrensaft-Hawley's status as a middle-class white queer man and the organization's close relationship to youth services would be the topic of internal and external dialogue, sometimes vexed—the organization's mission sought to foster leadership abilities among its core constituency and to challenge the limited terms of state programs. The directorship of Ehrensaft-Hawley, as well as the dramatic scenes of Greenwich Village conflict, also made FIERCE a popular topic for media coverage and attracted a great deal of interest from an array of college students, activists, researchers, and other allied individuals. This meant that although FIERCE maintained an emphasis on Greenwich Village and a commitment to racial, sexual, gender, and economic justice, the identity and purpose of the organization would be a topic of self-conscious engagement and change.

All of these facets of FIERCE's founding are key, for they locate the organization in tight relation to youth social service programs and squarely in a national network of grassroots organizing against police violence. FIERCE was just one of many groups founded in the 1990s and 2000s with the goals of racial, economic, sexual, and gender justice as they fought against the dismantling of social programs, expansion of the penal system, and privatization of public space. These groups often emerged in affinity with social movements other than the dominant LGBT one; in line with earlier models like Dykes against Racism Everywhere, organizations like FIERCE, ALP, and the Sylvia Rivera Law Project (founded in 2002), sought to challenge the exclusion of queer and trans issues in racial justice politics and of race, sexuality, and trans/gender issues in other forms of leftist movement building across the city. Furthermore, although these groups took on the problem of violence outside of the mainstream LGBT antiviolence movement, they did not dispense with an antiviolence rubric altogether. Many organizations joined with groups like INCITE! Women of Color against Violence to put critiques of state violence (including hate crime laws) into the center of antiviolence visions. Thus, organizations like FIERCE extended the kinds of critiques put forth by earlier anti-racist LGBT activists and were also parts of a network of local efforts that provide a different model for national movement building than the centralized one adopted by organizations like the National Gay and Lesbian Task Force. Although the examples cited here were based in New York and the San Francisco Bay Area, over the years they forged collaborations across the country, including with groups such as Southerners on New Ground, which had been part of a long-standing alternative antiviolence trajectory.[53]

At the start of the new decade, FIERCE initiated a campaign to redefine who could make claims to Greenwich Village and to push back against anti-crime policies, naming the vulnerability of LGBT/queer young people to street and state violence. The group did so by refashioning the terms of community, safety, and participation and challenging the administration of community boards that residents used to restrict access. Years later, many members would call the campaign a success, as FIERCE gained the right to participate in decision making and to propose use and design visions for the area. What these wins mean for the future of violence and so-called disorderly queer life in New York is still to be seen. The remainder of this chapter highlights FIERCE's strategies—from cultural productions to rallies—and it unfolds thematically along a loose timeline from its first years right up to the present day.

FIERCE began with the primary argument that nonresidents should have a claim to the neighborhood due to the historical significance of Greenwich Village for LGBT people far beyond the neighborhood's borders as well as the role the area plays in the lives of those rejected by their families or neighborhoods of origin and those with limited access to LGBT social services. These ideas were first circulated in FIERCE's 2001 video documentary *Fenced Out!*, made in conjunction with the New Neutral Zone and the collective Paper Tiger Television. Developed out of a series of workshops, FIERCE built its early membership through participation in the video's production. Fenner later explained that making *Fenced Out!* was among the most effective activities that FIERCE undertook to involve regular pier-goers in the organization, and Portalatin described how the documentary was also shaped by a creative survey and outreach approach she and others drafted for pier-goers.[54] In FIERCE's first years it screened the documentary at meetings, with community groups, and in schools to build a base of support and the documentary functioned as a clear counterargument to residents' contentions that nonresidential queer youth had no claims to the neighborhood.

Fenced Out! traces the history of the waterfront through interviews and archival footage, from gay men who used the piers for sex during the 1970s, to homeless transgender women who created makeshift houses there during the 1980s, to LGBT people of color who have socialized on the piers ever since. This history is narrated neither as a positive progression nor as a dejected dissolution; the slow emergence of a dynamic queer of color culture on the piers is joined by increased police presence, so that the community is threatened to be undone as soon as it has formed. Bob Kohler, a former Gay Liberation Front member, and Sylvia Rivera, a cofounder of Street Transvestite Action Revolutionaries, explain in the documentary that it was only when the piers were transformed into a social gathering place for people of color, rather than an anonymous sex spot, that residents began to complain. That view is echoed by the famed vogue choreographer Willi Ninja, who notes that the ball scene moved to the piers because there were fewer police there than in Washington Square Park.[55] Earlier uses are described as free yet exclusive and now lost (such as public sex cultures stratified by race and class) or inclusive and gone but not necessarily something idealized (such as informal survival economies). For example, archival images of mostly white men having open sex on the piers is accompanied by an interview with Regina Shavers, a black lesbian activist with the Griot Circle, who responds to a question about whether there were public spaces for lesbians of color in her youth with, "No—that's a joke, right?" She explains that public space and civil rights were restricted for black lesbians during her adolescence, as was the case for all black people.

The process of creating the video and crafting a historical narrative are made explicit in the video itself, as it combines first-person voice-overs about the project with scenes of the filmmakers interviewing other people and each other. Throughout *Fenced Out!*, references are made to the past, present, and future. For example, although the reconstruction of the piers is to be temporary, FIERCE members are clear that they do not imagine themselves included in its future. In a later interview, Portalatin described the intense feeling of attachment people had for the piers and observed that when the area was blocked off, they had "this sense of loss and mourning. . . . What's happening? Why is this fence going up? When is it going to come down? When can we go back?"[56] The answers were nowhere to be found. The idea that this is a repeating process is also noted by the video's closing dedication to Marsha P. Johnson of Street Transvestite Action Revolutionaries (who was found dead near the piers in 1992), which celebrates her fight for the piers "past and present." And in another scene, Sylvia Rivera takes the filmmakers on a tour of where, when homeless, she had lived on the piers. The image shifts to footage from fifteen years earlier, and in an almost perfectly matched contemporary voice-over she narrates a walk through her former home that is no longer there. The result is to conjure up a place in which every gain is met by a loss, little gets better, the past warrants no nostalgia, and the future is for others.

This approach to time evokes the kind of future in the present described by José Esteban Muñoz that rejects both liberal optimism and totalizing negation in favor of that which is simply "not yet." Muñoz's argument is based in a reading of Amiri Baraka's *The Toilet*, in which Baraka describes a final, tender gesture within a brutal scene of antigay violence that—although not redemptive—suggests the idealistic view that in endurance there might be something more. Muñoz writes: "The queer futurity that I am describing is not an end but an opening or horizon. Queer utopia is a modality of critique that speaks to quotidian gestures as laden with potentiality."[57] Similarly, *Fenced Out!* depicts a present in which young people leave the violence of home for Greenwich Village, where they then face the violence of police and others; yet rather than presenting the piers as a place of salvation or abjection, the documentary shows everyday activities at the piers, like dancing, kissing, smoking, dressing up, sleeping, playing music, or taking care of one's children. Joan Nestle, a white lesbian activist and author, explains in the video: "We lived with violence, but we lived."

The focus on the history and violence of the piers poses an alternative lens on the temporal relations central to the spatial commodification of the area.[58] Poverty is named as the price tag of the privatization of the piers, which, in turn, is shown as part and parcel of the cycle of abandonment and reinvestment that exists throughout the city. This is illustrated through a series of oppositions: HRPT's pier development is contrasted with the limited funds devoted to services for homeless LGBT youth, and scenes of police demands that youth stop loitering and "keep walking" are accompanied by an officer's explanation that "the local community here has been complaining about the littering and noise." Power is figured as the ability to claim permanence in place while moving forward, rather than existing in a contingent present—dynamics that take form in an uneven geography of profit and punishment. The activist Malkia Cyril explains in the video: "All displacement is, is moving people from one part of the city to another part of the city. It's not like they disappear. If they're moved from here, the only place to move them to is the jail."[59]

Residents opposed to the nightlife on the piers cast their concerns in similar terms to those used by FIERCE, but with starkly different analyses of its causes or solutions. They tended to cite the uneven distribution of acceptance and services that sent people to Greenwich Village and also named the area's historical significance as a draw factor, but their conclusion was that this left Greenwich Village disproportionately burdened by failed state responsibilities. Their solution was to increase the criminalization of what they considered to be undesirable activities and to decrease the accessibility of public space and social services, thus providing disincentives that would force people to leave. This was despite the fact that the police were by no means reluctant to use quality-of-life regulations in the area. In fact, the neighborhood's police precinct, located a few blocks from the piers, had hosted the city's first quality-of-life pilot program in 1994 and, in the years immediately after, issued more quality-of-life summonses than all the precincts in the rest of Manhattan combined.[60] Despite this, by late 2001 and early 2002 City Council Member Christine C. Quinn and Assemblyperson Deborah J. Glick had each issued requests to the New York Police Department and Police Commissioner Raymond Kelly for additional police forces in the area.[61] Glick also asked for mounted horse patrols to provide a "visible and commanding presence" to counteract "an unprecedented spike in illicit and illegal activities that threaten [residents'] safe1y [sic] and impinge on their rights as citizens."[62] Also during that time, CB2 adopted a resolution worth quoting in its entirety:

> *Whereas* parts of our district, but especially northwest Greenwich Village, for decades have been the site of street prostitution and attendant loitering, vandalism, public urination and, sometimes public sex and

Whereas changes in the character of the Times Square district (which was the predominant "sex-for-sale" locale in Manhattan South) has brought increased street prostitution in certain areas of Community Board #2 (CB #2) and a change in demographics have increased the residential population of these areas and

Whereas these changes have resulted in an increased nuisance with more residents than ever here feeling personally menaced and made unsafe by unwholesome and illegal behavior occurring in their midst and

Whereas police action to alleviate the problem has so far been inconclusive resulting merely in the rotation of activity from one site to another within the overall area and whereas such action and neighborhood watches have, sometimes, unwittingly led to the abuse of the law-abiding members of the lesbian, gay, bisexual and transgender community in the area and

Whereas scores of residents individually and as signers of an organized petition have made known their demands for greater police enforcement against street prostitution and

Whereas our district is a magnet for lesbian, gay, bisexual and transgender youth (LGBTY) who perceive our area as a safe haven for the exploration [of] their identities and

Whereas CB #2, in its concern for the condition of such youth, supports the work of social service organizations who minister to LGBTY here but also recognizes with alarm the dangers of drug addition, FHV/AID [*sic*] infection and homelessness which beset such youth and lead them, as a matter of survival, to become street prostitutes and

Whereas CB #2, in its desire for intelligent, sensitive but firm action to alleviate the problem of street prostitution, approvingly notes that the Midtown Community Court (MTCC) may now include our catchment with respect to arrests for prostitution and

Whereas the MTCC (which adjudicates nuisance crimes to which the traditional justice establishment gives low priority) may mete out jail time, it may instead sentence defendants to constructive participation in programs of therapy and community service and

Whereas the MTCC encourages police to give serious attention to "quality of life" crimes by providing tools and resources to police in fighting such behaviors and, by providing a venue for the serious treatment of such crimes, dispels police frustration at the traditional pointlessness of such arrests and

Whereas, in making its determinations, the MTCC actively considers the interests of neighborhoods and utilizes the testimony of local residents affected by crime and

Whereas, although the ultimate answer to the problem of street prostitution may require changes in the law (to be dealt with by a separate CB #2 resolution), CB #2 supports the efforts of police, court and community in alleviating the problem of street prostitution in our catchment,

Therefore be it resolved that Community Board #2 (Manhattan) supports ongoing work by our Sixth Police Precinct and the Midtown Community Court to alleviate the problem of street prostitution here and urges them to meet to coordinate their efforts to this end and, paramount, include in all such meetings local block associations and any other members of the community who may wish to participate and [also] representative of the social service providers who reach out to our lesbian, gay, bisexual and transgender youth populations.[63]

Here prostitution is named as cause and outcome, the source of both undesirable activities and residents' attendant discomfort—but also the result of the alienating conditions that draw LGBT youth of color to the neighborhood. The only solution to this closed circuit is that of expanded criminalization, or a zero-tolerance policy for those regulations already existing. This position functions as a "not in my backyard" response to undesirable municipal services insofar as the problem is described as locational, due both to the expanding residential uses of once industrial areas and to the lack of accessible places for LGBT youth. The residents' strategy is to naturalize the push and pull factors of a market-based approach to urban regional development and migration and to use governmental disincentives in the form of heightened criminalization and privatization. (This is strikingly similar to Arizona's proposed solution for unauthorized migration: legislation based on the logic of "attrition through enforcement."[64])

At the start of the following year, the *New York Times* published a piece featuring explicit indictments of the neighborhood's "transvestites" and youth by Lees, the head of CB2, and Jessica Berk, the founder of the neighborhood anticrime group Residents in Distress.[65] At this point the accusations of residents had reached a feverish pitch, but they were matched by the growing momentum of FIERCE, which continued to use *Fenced Out!* to reach out to pier-goers, activists, and sympathetic residents. These dynamics culminated in a large community board hearing dedicated to quality-of-life issues held on February 12, 2002, at the neighborhood's main hospital, St. Vincent's.[66] Speakers included representatives from FIERCE and Residents in Distress as well as from the neighborhood's LGBT Community Center's youth drop-in program, Metropolitan Gender Network, Bleecker Street Merchants and Residents Association, CB2's public safety committee, Sixth Precinct Community Council, and Manhattan District Attorney's Office. Lees led the meeting, which was also attended by Councilperson Quinn, Police Commissioner Kelly, and officers from the Sixth Precinct. Fox News was also present.

The themes that night would be repeated in community board hearings for years to come: Greenwich Village was unduly burdened with undesirable city services, and existing crime control was insufficient. Residents bemoaned the lack of police responsiveness to quality-of-life crimes (complaining that "on the Upper East Side police would care" and that the police "lack visibility") and the absence of deterrents ("Why aren't judges giving out maximum sentences [for prostitution convictions]?").[67] They offered to assist the police, saying, for example, "I'm not here to criticize. . . . How can we help out the Sixth [Precinct] in combating these crimes?" Occasionally, some residents gave perspectives that emphasized the radical history of the neighborhood: "Not everyone hanging out on the street is breaking the law. This is where Stonewall began." Youth organized by FIERCE joined in, complaining to the police: "Where are you when gay people get beat up?" In the latter half of the meeting, Kevin Fitzgerald, deputy inspector of the Sixth Precinct, announced the West Village Initiative, which had been approved the day before. The initiative increased the number of uniformed officers on duty late at night and early in the morning as well as bolstering the Vice Enforcement Division, challenging panhandling, increasing homeless outreach, and "cracking down" on public urination and other quality-of-life violations. Once implemented, the West Village Initiative added twenty-three officers to the local force, and a "zero tolerance corridor" was established from Washington Square Park to the piers.[68] During the meeting, Fitzgerald mostly ignored comments from young people and deferred to residents. For example, in response to a question about racial profiling posed by a young Latino/a masculine-presenting person, Fitzgerald explained by means of what might be interpreted as a direct address, "If you fit the description, they're not harassing you."[69] Activists and youth repeatedly attempted to shift the discussion, asking about job creation and services and contending that "incarceration was no solution."[70] These suggestions were scoffed at by residents and dismissed by the police as beyond their jurisdiction.

In the years following this hearing, FIERCE activists and residents came head to head at innumerable Community Board 2 and Sixth Police Precinct Community Council sessions, often repeating the above debates again and again. Residents' complaints continued to be explicitly hostile to youth of color, complaining about the "BBQ people" (BBQ is a restaurant chain that has a large African American clientele),[71] "gang members,"[72] "Bloods and Crips,"[73] "kids of ethnic origins" and those who are "a part of the hip-hop crowd" carrying "Snapple bottles [with alcohol]" giving "gang signals" and "harassing females."[74] These were joined by proposals for a "four strikes" law, which would convert a fourth quality-of-life offence into a felony, and for a Trespass Affidavit Program involving the installation of cameras.[75] The routine announcement by police attending meetings that crime was down was met by demands for even more policing.[76] Years later, in August 2004, the West Village Initiative was joined by Operation West Side, focusing on drug sales and prostitution in the westernmost sections of Greenwich Village, along the waterfront.

On the surface, both FIERCE and the residents appear to have assumed that Greenwich Village is a safe space for queer youth. For residents, the assertion that the neighborhood is a haven for LGBT youth allowed them to acknowledge antigay sentiment while deflecting the accusation that they were homophobic. Furthermore, both groups understood Greenwich Village to be as much a magnet for, as it was a safe retreat from, violence. In their testimony and resolutions, residents portrayed youth as drawn to Greenwich Village but then caught up in drugs, prostitution, and violent behavior. This dynamic transformed the threat of violence from something faced by youth to something faced by residents. Residents' responses were to organize crackdowns on drugs and prostitution and to rhetorically call for supportive services in *other* neighborhoods. In turn, the members of FIERCE argued for Greenwich Village's importance as an escape from violence that nonetheless promised other forms of threat: being LGBT and a young person of color in the neighborhood marks one as a target of the violence of the police, resident vigilantism, and individualized anti-LGBT threat at the same time as it offers the protection of history and community. But FIERCE did not see a solution in policing. The group not only refused the strategies of residents but also rejected the LGBT antiviolence movement's focus on LGBT-responsive policing. FIERCE's members recognized that the dynamics in the neighborhood were inherently contradictory, and—as Fenner explained—"safety" is not something one can "guarantee" or barricade.[77]

In addition, as this book has argued, danger is not something that can be produced or avoided by simply being made visible. The parallels between residents' and activists' otherwise divergent perspectives do not so much reveal the latter's latent liberal assumptions as they highlight the insufficiency of arguments that extract the recognition provided by empirical knowledge or models of psychosocial causation from the matrices in which they are conceived. In other words, the fact of violence and the root of alienation are not irrelevant, but their revelations do not provide resolution.

Furthermore, the neighborhoods and families from which youth came— some of them nearby, others much farther away—sustained difficult relationships with sexual and gender nonnormativity that are not captured in the binary terms of acceptance versus rejection. Contrary to political visions that see homophobia as the problem of rural, suburban, or peripheral urban locations or of neighborhoods containing a majority of people of color, FIERCE sited LGBT rejection within the institutions of family and privatization, including gay enclaves.[78] One transgender woman associated with FIERCE explained: "Everyday I talk to my mother, just like all my mother's daughters. These are things a lot of people take for granted, but to me they are blessings. Many young people are homeless because their parents didn't want gay kids around. Just like you don't want gay kids on your block."[79] FIERCE activists tended to frame homophobia less as an individual sentiment than as a mechanism of exclusion, which can produce, for example, homelessness.[80]

FIERCE thus avoided the tendency of mainstream LGBT politics to define areas outside gay enclaves as "not LGBT"—a tendency that makes places like Greenwich Village into a unique commodity while failing to include other areas as central to queer politics. This was important because the assumption of the primacy of gay neighborhoods is what enabled gay residents to make claims about their own safety and to scoff when nonresidents described the area as unsafe. This happened when CB2 members suggested that the pier culture be moved toward Chelsea, and youth explained that they did not feel comfortable there. In a letter to a local paper, one resident wrote: "Chelsea is the gay capital of Manhattan. A gay person saying they feel unsafe in this district is akin to a Mormon saying he feels unsafe in Utah."[81] Yet it is exactly this response that explains why entry into gay neighborhoods is so difficult for those who do not match the racial, class, and gender demographic characteristics of the residents.

The tenuousness of safety for LGBT youth of color was made devastatingly clear on May 11, 2003, when a young African American lesbian named Sakia Gunn was murdered in Newark, New Jersey, after returning home from a night out in Greenwich Village.[82] FIERCE held a memorial service two months later that stressed the piers' role as a "safe space"; residents, in turn, repeated their claims that places such as Newark needed to provide services for their own residents. Surprisingly little attention was paid to the murder by the New York Anti-Violence Project, which—at least initially—seemed to see it as a New Jersey issue. In Newark, it became the grounds for new political mobilizing led by local African American activists against antigay violence and for the development of an LGBT center; Amiri and Amina Baraka, whose own daughter had just been murdered for reasons understood to include homophobia, participated in the mobilizing.[83] The claims of FIERCE activists that Greenwich Village is both a safe and unsafe space for LGBT youth not only worked to defuse residents' arguments that

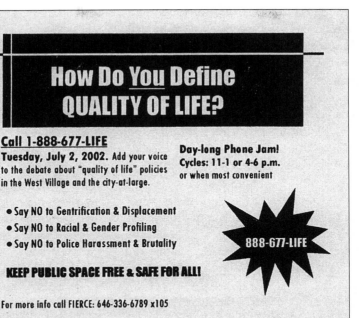

FIGURE 5.1 FIERCE flier

nonresident LGBT youth, by their very presence, constituted a threat but also demonstrated the inadequacy of a discourse of safety for describing vulnerability even as they continued to use those terms themselves.

Another action sponsored by FIERCE was a call-in to the city's quality-of-life hotline, asking people to report their own answer to the question: "How Do *You* Define QUALITY OF LIFE?" (fig. 5.1).[84] For FIERCE quality of life was measured not only in one's protection, but also in one's ability to participate in the kinds of everyday intimacy and shared care that exclusion from families or public services denied. Like Gente or the Third World Gay Coalition of previous years, FIERCE would show how the process of political organizing and the pleasures of everyday life might be the means by which they could "create the conditions," following the Combahee River Collective, to be "free of fear."[85] FIERCE would do so by continuing to return to the dominant terms of urbanism—both safety and participation—throughout its campaigns.

PARTICIPATION

A key issue of debate at various hearings was whether or not FIERCE members were eligible to give input. Few, if any, were residents of the area included within CB2, and FIERCE's offices were two blocks north of the community district's border. Youth attendees were usually denied the opportunity to speak. In addition to declaring youth contributions not "legitimate," residents often complained that the youth speakers "made no sense."[86] The anger of residents tended to be conspicuous, sometimes taking the form of adults yelling at young people to "shut up" or "sit down." The response of FIERCE activists was to continue to encourage young people to speak at hearings about the violence they had experienced, research they had done on the history of the neighborhood, and reasons why they were being ignored, among other topics. FIERCE's approach to speaking at hearings was aligned with the group's belief that all decisions, including what public stance it would take, should be made by those whom the group deemed were most directly affected by a given issue. The strategy of being led by those most adversely affected by what activists seek to challenge has been central to a variety of movements on the left, not only as a gesture of accountability but also as a means of building a solid base of support among those whose commitment is shaped by having the most at stake. Another key strategy in hearings was for youth activists to silently hold aloft signs with paired messages on each side, combining "We Are Worth More than Your Property Values" with "Where's Our Public Safety?"; "You Say 'Police Protection'" with "We Say 'Police Brutality'"; and "Whose Streets?" with "Our Streets Too!" The group's members also attached to neighborhood door handles cards that read: "Who Pays for Your Quality of Life? Queer youth of color, Trannies, sex workers and the homeless are being 'cleaned out' of the west village. But we are NOT trash!" (fig. 5.2). This was a sharp response to residents' claims that nonresidents were ejaculating on neighborhood doorknobs.[87] In addition, FIERCE created an alliance with the LGBT subcommittee of CB2 that was critical of citizen vigilantism and supportive of social services, if wary of unregulated public activity.[88]

The impact of FIERCE's speaking strategy was striking, for it would realign a cornerstone of progressive planning ideology—namely, participation. The persistent members of FIERCE attended community board hearings, signing up to speak as members of the public without ever agreeing to abide by the sanctioned terms for giving input. Even when their official participation was invited, for example by the sympathetic CB2 LGBT subcommittee, FIERCE members rarely followed through. As the issue gained more and more attention in the mainstream and alternative press, numerous university students and supportive political actors, including residents and business owners, approached the organization, eager to offer their official and approved voice. Rather than adopt speaking or decision-making roles, such allied players (including me) were assigned logistical tasks like administrative work and setting up for meetings (we also planned some allied actions).[89] Many of those inside and outside the organization greeted

FIGURE 5.2 FIERCE action card

this strategy with suspicion, as it seemed to rigidly prioritize experience and romanticize the position of youth. And to outsiders, in particular, it also appeared inefficient.[90] The approach did value the empowerment of a certain group of those most affected by policing in the area over those who had other specialized skills and access, including for doing surveys of the needs of youth on the pier, knowledge of municipal planning, the right to speak to the community board as a resident, or the means to sponsor a 197-a plan. The approach also prioritized youth over adults affected by the policy, who were in general less involved in the campaign. Instead, FIERCE members conducted their own survey of youth on the piers, remained resolute that they had a say in the process, and continued to attend hearings, putting forth a variety of planning proposals—none of which would be submitted to CB2 or the Department of City Planning for 197-a consideration.

But as the life of the waterfront changed, so did FIERCE's strategies. By 2003 Pier 45 had been renovated and reopened as open park space, and it resumed its use as a hangout for LGBT youth and other communities of color. The changes were not without problems, and FIERCE complained about harassment from the Hudson River Park Enforcement Patrol (PEP) officers who were monitoring loitering and gender-appropriate bathroom use (for whom the officers deemed acceptable *men* or *women*), as well as the continued aggressiveness of the Sixth Precinct officers.[91] Residents, in turn, claimed that the piers now drew even more so-called rowdies, and they worked with HRPT to put forth a proposal that would move the curfew up from 1 AM to 11 PM and install barricades to prevent people from leaving the area via Christopher Street to go to public transportation options. Another proposal suggested the renovation of Pier 54, located in a more commercial area but lacking electricity, so that young people would hang out and exit there. There was even a suggestion that PEP officers should carry firearms.[92]

For a series of community hearings in late 2005 and early 2006, FIERCE recruited hundreds of supporters to voice their opposition to these proposals, and the group advocated against barricades and for a 4 AM curfew, food vendors, and more toilets. It also highlighted the discriminatory intent of an official statement released by CB2's Committee on Waterfront, Parks, Recreation, and Open Space, which said: "Problems have arisen involving noise and also involving some rowdyism resulting from large crowds of young people, mostly lesbian, gay, bisexual, and transgender youth of African-American and Hispanic origin leaving Pier 45 at 1:00 AM on Friday and Saturday nights."[93] Although residents had sometimes hesitated to explicitly identify those they found threatening as being of color—opting instead for coded (and often quite bizarre) phrases such as "the Bloods and the Crips"—CB2 statements like this were clear about who was considered a problem by them. Retreating from the group's previous policy of limiting speakers to those "most directly affected," at this point FIERCE responded with supporters recruited from sympathetic residents, business owners, and staff members of social service agencies. These speakers argued that "a good night's sleep" is not a civil right, and that the problem "was not the people from the piers but from the middle class who have a sense of entitlement when they're drunk or drugged."[94] Coverage in the local and gay press was extensive.[95] The FIERCE challenge was successful: the proposal for an earlier curfew was dropped, and everyone agreed that after a trial period, the other options would be revisited.[96]

Although FIERCE staff members later attributed this success to more focused goals and the organization's maturation process as it sought to build an identity and a constituency, the victory also suggests that FIERCE's earlier approach was an effective strategy. Fenner describes the focus on leadership by youth of color as the result of a need to empower those young people of color who initially saw the participation of white allies to be necessary for success and to show other organizations that it was not limited by the identity of its first director, a white queer man. During this time, the organization had removed white allies from active positions (briefly creating the category of "satellites"), and Ehrensaft-Hawley prepared to step down. (Allies were later reintroduced, and Ehrensaft-Hawley continued to maintain a very close relationship with the organization.) Although this may provide one important piece of evidence of the increased confidence and skill set of FIERCE members, the strategy of focusing on those most directly affected also had the effect of asserting the importance of experience and identity in these debates. It drew out—as did CB2's official resolutions—residents' race-based claims. By rejecting young people's repeated declarations in meetings of their desire to participate, residents could not sidestep the issue of who they were treating as illegitimate. All the while, the insistence that the constituency of nonresidential pier users should be counted as city players became more of a reality.

In an article in the *Villager*, the reporter Lincoln Anderson quoted Rickke Mananzala—then campaign coordinator of FIERCE and later its director—talking to members of the group after a meeting that rejected the early curfew and proposal to move the pier scene north: "We just had a huge victory. We completely shot down the 13th St. Pier proposal. We completely shot down the 11 p.m. pier curfew proposal. *We will say that L.G.B.T. youth of color are policy makers.* We will win [a] 4 a.m. [curfew] with your support. To win we must love each other and protect each other! We have nothing to lose but our chains!"[97] FIERCE members often repeated the last two sentences, also inserting: "It is our duty to fight for our freedom. It is our duty to win." The attribution of the full phrase to the former Black Panther Assata Shakur aligns FIERCE with a radical liberation politics, but this quote also presents activism and kinship as the bases of the protection that the group's members sought. FIERCE's stubborn insistence that its members be recognized as neighborhood players was supported by their repeated presence, which functioned like the declarative sentences spoken and promised to be repeated again and again: "We will say that L.G.B.T. youth of color are policy makers."[98] The relentless repetition that they belonged in the neighborhood did result in their inclusion in later CB2 committees, as well as on other organizational and municipal boards. This, in turn, helped to buoy members' morale. Portalatin had left New York for some years after the organization's founding. When she returned, she was shocked to find that CB2 meetings were no longer only hostile gatherings and that FIERCE members, all youth of color, were leading the conversation. She remembered one meeting in which over 200 young people had turned out: "That, in itself, was huge and so helpful in establishing us in the community as a force to be reckoned with."[99]

FIERCE's effort to publicly assert the identities and experiences of those most directly affected by the closure and policing of the waterfront was not the only way in which the group demonstrated how culture and identity were at once traded and obfuscated in the neoliberal city. In addition to reworking concepts like safety and participation, FIERCE also shifted dominant understandings of value. It did so by not only emphasizing the use value of the neighborhood to low-income LGBT youth of color but also by demonstrating the exchange value that low-income LGBT youth of color produced for the neighborhood. Residents' desire to make their neighborhood a fortress appears on the surface to have been a direct expression of their class interests: a new park, more police, and fewer undesirable municipal services all help increase property values. As I have shown, these dynamics between homeowners and young people were neither new nor restricted to Greenwich Village. Street youth who were central to Stonewall also had a vexed relationship with residents and the police, and the attitude of "not in my backyard" about social services is common in middle-class neighborhoods. In this way, Greenwich Village residents' demands to the police joined a long and far-reaching legacy of white and middle-class neighborhood politics that collude with private interests in order to exclude others.[100]

But to say that residents of Greenwich Village acted solely out of their concern for property values as real estate investment is insufficient. As already indicated, CB2's own planning history had hoped to curb development and ensure the growth of subsidized housing for the elderly and people with AIDS. The latter group is presumably still growing, since the number of Medicaid recipients in the area included within CB2 has risen in the past years. Yet residents ended up turning to aspects of plans that they had opposed years earlier. For example, in 2005 residents—who had earlier asked the city that the waterfront be reserved for open use—invoked uniform park curfews as a way to drive certain recreational users of the park out. And an initial opposition to commercial services on the waterfront later gave way to the acceptance of vendors, so that visitors would not go into the neighborhood to buy food and drink. Finally, the promotion of family-oriented development and quality-of-life enforcement arguably aided real estate interests along the waterfront, even as CB2 supported zoning regulations that had blocked real estate development proposals for over the water itself. In other words, residents were not always acting in their own class interests: they were promoting policing and other conditions amenable to luxury development that would raise values for those who own their homes, but that would also put pressure on the majority of residents who rent.

(Here it is also important to acknowledge that residents were also not acting as a uniform body, which also accounts for their mixed interests.)

Greenwich Village, like most of New York City, is renter dominated. Around the start of the residents' campaign, 74.2 percent of them did not own their homes. Thus not all residents benefited from an escalating real estate market. In addition, according to the 2000 census, the median income in the waterfront region just south of Christopher Street was $125,295—well over double that of the two tracts comprising the neighborhood's residential core (which is also lower than that of the waterfront section just north of Christopher Street).[101] Although this might suggest that the primary players in this debate were homeowners, a common phenomenon in community board battles, participants at meetings often identified themselves as renters, and CB2 has a long history of advocating for rental protections. The contradictions of this phenomenon became quite clear when the Mitchell-Lama agreement that mandates subsidized rents for middle-income people expired for the West Village Houses, a complex located near Christopher Street and the waterfront.[102] The creation of the West Village Houses had been advised by Jane Jacobs, following her tenets of low-level, high-density development, and had been opposed by residents in the 1970s who feared that it would attract gay tenants.[103] The fact that after thirty years, residents of the West Village Houses—both gay and straight—were not visible players in defense of LGBT youth shows how race, in particular, is constitutive of people's sense of property.[104]

Participants at community board meetings included a mix of new and old renters and homeowners. Not all of them stood to gain from a rising tax base and inflated rental market; for some of them, property may be something other than their home. In other words, whiteness not only functioned as a kind of value added to real estate, but it was also a kind of property unto itself. The legal scholar Cheryl Harris has theorized whiteness as a type of "status property." She traces the history of the dynamics of race and property, and demonstrates that "property as conceived in the founding era included not only external objects and people's relationship to them, but also all of those human rights, liberties, powers, and immunities that are important for human well-being, including: freedom of expression, freedom of conscience, freedom of bodily harm, and free and equal opportunities to use personal faculties."[105] In other words, property can be more than just commodity object. Absent ownership of their homes, residents were seeking to protect through the law and the market their status as entitled white citizens. Here it is important to also remember Jeffrey Escoffier's argument about the 1970s and how protection was achieved through the market in a territory-based economy.[106] The protection of rights, viewed as public goods in the context of neighborhoods, reflects the forms of racial entitlements that were so distributed.

One slogan considered by activists for an early action in 2002 was "We don't bring down property value, we *are* property value." This was a different formulation than the more common claim they made: "We are worth more than your property values." The second argument reinforces the need to consider both use and exchange value, especially since the presence of low-income LGBT youth of color at the piers may be one of the few phenomena that actually stalls rampant development in the area, as public policies like restrictive zoning are repealed in favor of for-profit development. This is presumably why the HRPT did not initially turn to LGBT youth of color for input on design, and why it has supported businesses like the high-cost Chelsea Piers recreation facility. It is also significant that the phrase did not conclude with the common assertion "we *raise* property value," for that, although somewhat true historically, is not likely to be a real factor in recent years. By the start of that decade, Greenwich Village no longer boasted its edginess in the real estate market and, as I've shown, LGBT youth were not uniformly considered to be members of the gay neighborhood that might work as the draw factor that Florida described. Instead, since then, the neighborhood has been advertised for its proximity to Manhattan's two central business districts, plus its waterfront views and historic architecture.

The comment "we *are* property value" opens up much more, for it makes visible the process through which property values are constructed.[107] It shows that the presence of low-income LGBT youth of color in Greenwich Village was not the result of outsiders coming in to devalue the neighborhood—in part because Greenwich Village was already beyond that point in a value cycle.[108] In addition, it underscores the fact that development in an urban region is part of uneven development in a global economy, a process that gives properties in some parts of New York their high sale price. Neighborhoods have been stratified by race and class, and those with less access to public space, high levels of homelessness, and shelters inhospitable to sexual minority youth are a direct product of the flows of capital pushing the rezoning of former manufacturing areas and the distribution of tax abatements for elite condominium growth. The absence of jobs in poor neighborhoods is joined by the growth of criminalized informal economies (including sex work) and a concentration of low-wage service jobs near central business districts. Nonetheless, it is these very features—people hanging out in public spaces and finding alternate kinship networks, supporting themselves through sex work and other informal economies—that were and continue to be targeted by residents. Simply put, private property value requires poverty.

It is fitting that FIERCE would respond to the assault on both excep-

Featuring
performances &
testimony by:
Emanuel Xavier
Letta Neely
Leslie Feinberg
Imani Henry
Bob Kohler
Donald Yearwood
Jay Dee Melendez
Ian Sprattley
Lucia Gimeno
Justin Rosado
Erykah Ramdass
Zoraida Vazquez
Andre Lancaster
Kenyon Farrow
DJ Pran
DJ Ama
Corey Wiggins
Le'in
Jiggly
St. Thunder Kitten
St. Panama Prince
Elaine Matos
Jermain Green
Mariah Lopez
Marian Yalini
   Thambynayagam
Renita Martin
Robin
Ardis & Crew
Saje
Iman
performers from
   the House of Ninja,
& other singers, rappers, poets,
voguers & graffiti artists from the pier!

We are sick and tired of watching the
cops, big business, and wealthy
resident associations take over the
Village as part of the "quality of
life" campaign. We demand an end
to the curfew laws, misdimeanor
arrests, and physical violence that
target trans people, queer youth of
color, sex workers, and the
homeless.

**Reclaim!
Revolt!
Resist!**

FESTIVAL OF RESISTANCE
October 5th
Saturday from
Sheridan Square
7th Avenue & Christopher Street
FIERCE! (646) xxx-x789

This action is endorsed by:
Act Up, African Ancestral Lesbians United for Societal Change, Arise Magazine, Audre Lorde ..., Black Pride
NYC, CAAAV: Organizing Asian Communities, Critical Resistance, DRUM, ... Gay and Les... Dominican
Empowerment), GLOBE (Gays and Lesbians of Bushwick Empowered), G... ownsville You... cil Inc.,
GRIOT Circle, Harm Reduction Coalition, Homo Visiones, Housing Works, ...onal Action C... ws for Racial
and Economic Justice, The LGBT Center, Make the Road by Walking, Mak... rassroots Mov... National Youth
Advocacy Coalition, NYAGRA, People Of Color in Crisis, Picture the Home... rison Moratoriu... d (PMP),
Progressive Queers NYC, Reclaim the Streets, SACRD, Sage Queens, Sh... sider, Queer Ed... Justice
Network, Uprose, Urban Justice Center, Welfare Rights Initiative, The Ya-Y... ork, YOU (Youth ...zers United)

FIGURE 5.3 FIERCE flier

tional and quotidian modes of survival in the form of creative art actions
and street protests. In addition to counter-rallies for events sponsored by
Residents in Distress and the community board, FIERCE also organized or
cosponsored events as varied as a symbolic protest funeral for Sylvia Rivera
when she passed away, a vigil for LGBT victims of violence, and speak-outs.
One such rally was held on October 5, 2002, in response to the residents'
"Take Back Our Streets" action; FIERCE replied with "Reclaim! Revolt! Resist!
Festival of Resistance" (fig. 5.3). The event was divided into three parts: the
first was a rally in Christopher Park, featuring testimonials about violence
and belonging; the second was a march down Christopher Street, with participants shouting "Whose Streets? Our Streets!"; and the third was an open
microphone event across the street from the piers.

The organizers tried to re-create the things that young people had most liked about the piers prior to their enclosure for construction, and the event included spoken word, vogueing, music, a DJ, dancing, tables and chairs for playing cards, food, and some live graffiti writing. There were technical sna-fus, and—desperate for a new music source—two young men went into one of the few gay black bars left on the block, pleading for help. Despite the fact that bars and young people were the two primary targets of residents' criti-cism, age differences between youth and older bar-goers made cooperation difficult. But that day the bar owner dragged out an amplifier and speakers and carried them near the piers. Another bar owner allowed the event's orga-nizers to use his establishment's electricity source. The festivities continued with dancing, card games, and sandwiches, as well as poets and performers who addressed topics from police brutality to falling in love and having sex. People from the piers trickled over from across the street and hung out for hours. Although organizers had gotten a permit, the police shut the event down three hours early with the explanation that it was not a political rally.

FIERCE also sponsored smaller projects to present its ideas about a future for the neighborhood, such as speak-outs and ongoing peer-conducted sur-veys of pier-goers. Many of these were done under the auspices of the Edu-cation for Liberation Project, a political education program within FIERCE founded by Fenner. Participants received training in organizing skills and, at the time, worked on what came to be known as the "Save Our Space" cam-paign. In a regular workshop activity, participants drew up their visions of an ideal future for the waterfront. In one of the first ones completed, named a "Dream City," an after-hours club is connected to the post office, the theater district adjoins the welfare and Section Eight office, the airport is next to the bath house, and the 99-cent store is right outside the "LGBTST" (lesbian, gay, bisexual, two-spirit, transgender) center (fig. 5.4). The ultimate mixed-use design, this dream city is not founded on a model of a residential gay neigh-borhood. Rather, it pulls in and condenses an entire city, asserting that all space is queer space.[109] The vision is undoubtedly utopian, and the futuristic image of an airport in downtown Manhattan would be hailed by many as evidence that such kinds of cultural politics are not useful for campaigns for urban justice. Rather, these types of actions underscore the role of cultural and everyday practices in shaping the political economy of urban space.

The fact that the event with music, food, and cards was not read as a "po-litical" action is important not only in the face of police insistence, but also in response to the rigid assumptions of leftist and progressive urban reform-ism, in which intimate and cultural activities speak strictly to a politics of representation. This is despite the fact that these very activities—listening to music, dancing, eating, and playing cards—were directly regulated by

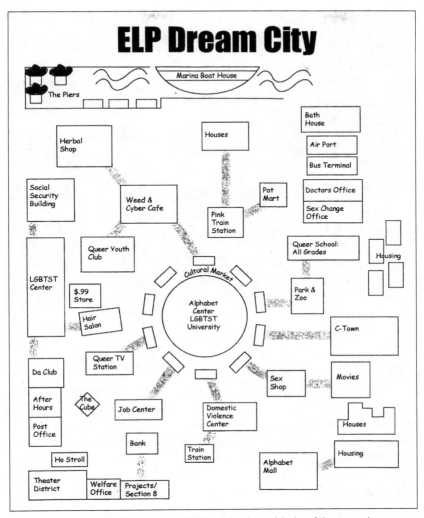

ELP Dream City

Marina Boat House

The Piers

Herbal Shop

Houses

Bath House

Air Port

Bus Terminal

Social Security Building

Weed & Cyber Cafe

Pot Mart

Doctors Office

Sex Change Office

Pink Train Station

Queer Youth Club

Queer School: All Grades

Housing

Cultural Market

LGBTST Center

$.99 Store

Hair Salon

Alphabet Center LGBTST University

Park & Zoo

C-Town

Queer TV Station

Da Club

Sex Shop

Movies

After Hours

The Cube

Job Center

Domestic Violence Center

Houses

Post Office

Bank

Train Station

Housing

Ho Stroll

Alphabet Mall

Theater District

Welfare Office

Projects/ Section 8

FIGURE 5.4 The Dream City Map, showing FIERCE members' reenvisioning of the geography of the piers. A copy of the map was provided at the graduation of an early Education for Liberation Project class.

quality-of-life policies. The argument that this event is not political requires looking at a single action without examining the campaign of which it is a part. It fails to see that the tenets of FIERCE's early activism—that low-income queer youth of color should be able to speak at hearings, that playing cards on a street corner is a political act, and that 99-cent stores (typically considered by urban planners to be a measure of "blight") belong in the center of a municipal plan—have all been part of a campaign, that, ten years after its founding, managed to get a sanctioned voice in a city-sponsored

FIGURE 5.5 FIERCE protest, 2004 (PHOTOGRAPH COURTESY OF EVA C. HAGEMAN)

community advisory board to make decisions about the piers that does not include just residents and business owners. During these years, FIERCE continued to plan actions that highlighted the connections between quality of life and racial profiling policies, and between the economic development of the area and the vulnerabilities of queer youth of color (fig. 5.5). But the community board and other city players increasingly integrated youth and their advocates into the conversation. In 2005, the New York City Human Resources Administration decided to ask the social service organization called The Door to conduct a massive study of gay youth in Greenwich Village.[110] By 2006 FIERCE had gained recognition as a neighborhood player, and its input was not only expected, but somewhat accommodated.

In recent years FIERCE has built a network of powerful allies, and among their joint projects have been various formal reports. Around 2007 HRPT put out a call for proposals for the redevelopment of Pier 40, and residents were included in HRPT's Pier 40 Working Group. In line with the community's history, they proposed alternatives to large-scale private development, including recreational space, art studios, and modest income-generating uses. In January 2008 FIERCE released its own proposal for Pier 40, completed in conjunction with an architecture firm, as well as the Urban Justice Center and students in a Columbia University public health class, that sought to fit LGBT issues into the Pier 40 Working Group's general vision. HRPT rejected the Working Group's proposals. In response, FIERCE released a white paper in March 2009 charging that HRPT had failed to live up to its obligation to ensure that there was sufficient public space on the piers, a view that FIERCE shared with CB2 members.[111] As of this writing, no final decisions about the development of the piers have been made. Although FIERCE still wages campaigns against quality-of-life policing, commercial development, and violence in the neighborhood, the group has already won its fight to be acknowledged as a community—in fact, a citywide—stakeholder: in September 2009 the group announced that it had been given a seat on HRPT's advisory council, and in that October a representative of FIERCE was named to the Mayor's Commission for LGBT and Questioning Runaway and Homeless Youth.[112] By no means does this guarantee that any of FIERCE's concrete proposals will be implemented—by 2012 HRPT was pushing to lift restrictions from the late 1990s on private waterfront development—but it does mean that FIERCE will probably be at least somewhat included in the process.

In *Barrio Dreams*, Arlene Dávila argues that culture can be mobilized both for and against private interests, and thus it is a crucial if often ignored factor in urban politics. *Barrio Dreams* includes a critique of the exclusive form of community boards and 197-a plans in New York, and it ends with a discussion of the "alternative logics" governing activist responses, including identity-based approaches that worked counter to pure profit motive. Dávila concludes: "There is a need to reevaluate, rather than deride and devalue, the validity of discourses of culture identity and community that are deployed by place-brokers and cultural activists."[113] Similarly, FIERCE's insistence on participation as based on one's use of the piers and status as most directly affected by policing and redevelopment proved an effective counternarrative to a community board's notion of participation based on residence. Far from a strategy based only on the primacy of experience, it was one that helped make explicit the ideal of a policy approach based on residence that makes its constitutive exclusions abstract. This alternative logic was, in turn, more than just a principled stance, but it provided the opportunity to transform neighborhood participation options. What might be considered activists' endurance did, in fact, lead to residents' retreat. It thus explains why, at a later date, the group more actively welcomed the involvement of political allies. This also shows that the strategies of identity politics are not as fixed as opponents see them. Furthermore, the fundamentally *queer* aspects of everyday sociality that include kinship and intimacy are shown be as responsible as other forces for making the piers what they were: a place of escape and speculative luxury investment, of abandoned manufacturing and informal sex economies, of chosen families and quality-of-life regulations.

Conclusion

In *The Trouble with Normal*, Michael Warner discusses the implementation in New York during the 1990s of public health codes that banned sex in commercial spaces and a new zoning law that restricted the siting of so-called adult establishments. He argues that the targeting of commercial and public sex has had deleterious effects on queer culture, in general, which itself had been made possible by these kinds of activities.[114] In the years since, the features of Greenwich Village life most targeted are no longer those forms of sex commerce. Youth are banned from the few sex establishments that remain, and, as I have shown, many of the young and low-income visitors to the area are discouraged from spending money in the neighborhood at all. In fact, on the waterfront, much of the informal economy has included prostitution, babysitting, and preparing for vogueing competitions, for example. These *queer*—as in neither heteronormative nor reducible to gay or lesbian—activities are now the primary objects of prohibition, or that most likely to be commercialized for the benefit of others (for example, the infamy of the film *Paris Is Burning*).[115]

Additionally, Warner cites the redevelopment of Times Square, vis-à-vis the use of Business Improvement Districts, and the administrative contradictions of the Uniform Land Use Review Procedure as two examples of city planning strategies that end up most benefiting private interests through a focus on the primacy of neighborhoods and residence. What is interesting here is that—unlike the creation of Business Improvement Districts, which were established to explicitly support private development—the initial implementation of the Uniform Land Use Review Procedure was part of early community planning efforts to keep private development in check, in particular on behalf of low-income residents. That Greenwich Villagers have used community boards to exclude low-income people of color further underscores the limits of the privatized ideals of residence and neighborhood that Warner sees at the core of dominant planning ideology. Restricted by the confines of municipal bureaucracy and shaped by a liberal understanding of urban problems as social symptoms best resolved though institutional remedy, community boards, especially in wealthy areas, can bolster the terms of exclusion they had sought to counteract. The limited access to, and the faith in the power of, the technologies of planning also have meant that the knowledge used comes from the same city-sponsored sources or is deployed by those with skills and disposable time. As a result, and as the core of the city has risen in value, community boards risk giving middle- and upper-income residents the opportunity to pursue exclusionary interests, despite an initial intention—and otherwise application—to empower low-income people. Furthermore, insofar as this specific campaign has been supported by renters as well as property owners, has targeted black and Latino bars and clubs, in particular, and has criminalized the public street life of queer youth of color, it is clear that the efforts of residents have rested on an affirmation of whiteness in LGBT neighborhoods and politics just as much as they have extended an ongoing assault in the name of normative, middle-class respectability.[116]

Thus it is crucial to come back to the Gay Index with which this chapter opened. Although by a variety of empirical measures Greenwich Village boasts a high concentration of gay households, the most vocal complainants at community board hearings were not uniformly gay.[117] In community meetings, Jessica Berk, the founder of Residents in Distress, described herself as a straight single woman, and Dave Poster, the head of the Christopher Street Patrol, never identified himself as gay. Yet Greenwich Village's reputation is as a gay enclave. This status has effectively cushioned these debates from mainstream critique. It has also given residents great leverage in their use of the concepts of risk and development—LGBT youth are at risk and thus a risk; luxury development is wrong, but poverty is a threat. It has also meant that the Village, famous for its populist refusal of top-down planning, allowed private interests to be rewarded through community empowerment—the very dynamic that community planning had sought to redress.

This has not only happened in Greenwich Village. During these same years, San Francisco's Castro was also the site of the targeting of LGBT youth, many of whom were of color, by white middle-class residents, many of whom were gay, in the name of their quality of life;[118] this dynamic was reprised with the introduction of the so-called sit/lie law that prohibits sitting or lying down on the sidewalk in that city.[119] A different remedy would involve urban and queer politics in the name of something other than safety since, as this book has tried to show, the strategy of mapping empirical measures of violence and acceptance—from hate crime statistics to Gay Index maps—has helped cement a relationship between a narrow notion of gay identity and privatized city space. It has also meant that the freedoms assumed to be afforded by gay concentration have been made possible through the very operations of violence that the consolidation of gay space was supposedly designed to prevent. As Martin Manalansan has shown in his study of the different kinds of violence in Greenwich Village's waterfront and in Jackson Heights—a multiethnic, multiclass enclave outside New York's core that is home to a large Latino and Asian American LGBT population—safety can never be reduced to the tolerance or refusal of same-sex sex per se, or to the simple fact of gay concentration.[120]

A more radical restructuring of space is in order, one that draws on the cultural and even the utopian understandings of the city put forth by organizations like FIERCE, but that—I would add—remains always wary of what is lost when one is on the side of the winners.[121] By the end of the first decade of the twenty-first century, FIERCE's successes had brought the organization national prominence and recognition by policymakers citywide. Its membership had grown, and its actions were well known among activists all across the country. Certain aspects of waterfront life had been preserved for LGBT and queer youth of color, including annual film showings on the piers and other social events. FIERCE produced trainings that were used as a model for other organizations, and, as of this writing, the group is gearing up to strengthen its campaign for a youth center on the piers that is open around the clock and to conduct its own safe streets patrols. It is unclear how CB2 will respond to either proposal.

It also remains to be seen, though, who would use such a youth center and whether it would accommodate those people on the piers who might be excluded by virtue of their status (for example, adult), practices (including sex work), identities (such as those that do not fit dominant social movement or service categories), or desires (for instance, not wanting to go inside). The membership of FIERCE has changed over the years, and although it remains an exclusively queer youth of color organization, it has, at times, included more college-educated members. In addition, they now more frequently collaborate with organizations and individuals who do not share the demographic characteristics of the group's members. Nonetheless, as the membership so quickly changes, so do these kinds of factors, and the issue of who is a part of FIERCE's constituency remains a topic of active conversation and is by no means fixed. Some features of FIERCE from its early years, such as countering the dominant logics of goal-driven strategies and improvement-based narratives, are now seen by its staff members as important but of the past, not only because the organization has matured but also because of the genuine pain that residents' blatant forms of rejection, exclusion, and attacks brought.[122] Movements need wins (as achieved goals are often called by activists). Nonetheless, wins can be fraught, especially when the world in which you find inclusion is not one that you want, or when the "winnable" becomes a goal unto itself. The importance of FIERCE's legacy is not only that it has brought issues of racial, economic, sexual, and gender justice together to demand a more equitable city, but also that in doing so, it recast the values of participatory democracy to include those queer qualities that are often dismissed as cultural, inefficient, or informal. How those features might be brought to bear in a continuous struggle remains to be seen.

CONCLUSION

During the 1970s, in neighborhoods like San Francisco's Castro and New York's Chelsea, the populations of self-identified gay residents grew, as did the areas' identities as gay enclaves representative of a new community taking form. On the surface, the reasons for this dynamic appear self-evident. But, as this book demonstrates, the process was far more complex. Neighborhoods like San Francisco's Tenderloin or New York's Times Square had long been home to same-sex practices and even residential concentration, but they did not join the Castro or Chelsea as gay havens to be protected. This was due in part to the growth of gay enclaves from places of residence to niche markets for retail and real estate, a transformation that was celebrated as a form of *visibility* that nonetheless was also assumed to increase one's vulnerability and thus to necessitate new strategies for securing safety. The decade saw the widespread disinvestment and selective reinvestment in U.S. cities. Scholars have debated what was the primary motor behind the gentrification of cities during this time, including the role played by white gay men. This book has shown that grassroots activism and its symbolic forms can be one part of the process by which neighborhoods are claimed, as well as the means to mobilize broad social movements counter to these dynamics.

Safe streets patrols were one example of how publicity about violence became a means by which areas were marked as gay territories. As the historian Martin Meeker shows, the growth of San Francisco as a gay region should not be understood only as a function of economic and social changes—such as those created by port cultures and events like the Gold Rush and World War II—that brought large numbers of single men and women together. He makes a convincing argument for the role of communication, specifically the publicity efforts of small lesbian and gay publications and organizations.[1] Similarly, this book demonstrates that the work of grassroots organizing can imprint ideas of urban neighborhoods in a broader gay imagination, in conjunction with economic shifts in the real estate market.

Since the 1970s, the political interests of mostly white middle-class gay men in establishing residential concentrations in central cities have fit into the larger flows of urban restructuring but have been understood locally as expressing new social and political demands. This is not to say these demands are all the same, or that they are responsible for one another. Rather, certain issues, such as violence, have served to connect—and even make indistinguishable—the property claims and rights claims of some lesbian and gay populations. This has been enabled in large part through the circulation of public knowledge about the supposedly causal links between poverty and violence, visibility and victimization, and empirical measure and social remedy that have been central to the shifting history of liberalism after World War II and the rise of neoliberal policy and ideology. Far from a cynical reading of LGBT activism, this understanding shows how the cultural tugs of economic restructuring can provide for profit in the name of community building.[2]

Central to this strategy was an assumption that community would be secured through visibility, including its attendant dynamic of coming out. Although coming out is most often understood in the form of verbal affirmation—"I am gay"—it also implies the terms of publicity in the public sphere, including neighborhood, and certain areas understood to be places of gay visibility were granted the same status of those of gay identity. In other words, public places associated with high or growing concentrations of gay residents and commerce were represented as the most risky and the most in need of protection. The thing to be protected was, by extension, a specific gay identity that reflected the race, gender, and class dynamics of the city itself. Thus a politics of self-determination was articulated in the terms of gay territory in which certain signs of gay identity—if not same-sex activity—were to be the markers of safe areas. In a real estate market that was economically and racially stratified, that meant that only some were privileged in gay space, and those who were limited by other social and economic restrictions were not. In contrast, activists who stood outside gay territories (literally or symbolically) effectively demonstrated not only that gay space—or, rather, *queer* space—might be everywhere, but also that it was the violence of policing or conflicts between renters and developers that carried the biggest threat, and they called for alternate forms of alliance. By focusing on the issue of violence, including that of the state and of private profit, these groups viewed the participation of LGBT communities in gentrification as including and exceeding real estate speculation.

These dynamics have, like capital, appeared in and retreated from major cities across the United States over the past fifty years.[3] At the same time, the growth of the LGBT movement on a national scale was led by an agenda that kept antiviolence at its fore. Although the initiative came from grassroots action, the institutionalization of antiviolence politics was greatly influenced by social-scientific studies and a growing call for empirical analysis. Surveys of violence provided the evidence for a newly consolidated lesbian and gay civil rights movement and enabled a formal coalition with the crime victims' rights movement. This combination helped shift emphasis from protecting designated gay spaces to qualifying threats, and in this process, new modes of understanding victims and intent were predicated on the very sense of urban geography that had been established just a few years before. Furthermore, as antigay violence assumed recognition as individualized crime, the broader contexts for understanding hate and violence became harder to address within activist forms. It is for these reasons that present-day debates about gay enclaves' quality of life are a key piece of LGBT antiviolence history, and, in turn, why the politics of protection—as property, as rights—fuel the changing forms of gay liberalism. Messy distinctions between crime and violence, safety and justice, underscore the flexibility of concepts such as risk and their centrality to the politics of development. Here risk is simultaneously the value of speculative capital (real estate) and the justification for crime control (so-called bad neighborhoods), the ever-present threat to gay autonomy (violence), and the symptom of irresponsibility (the designation "at risk"). Today, gay neighborhoods need not have a majority of gay residents in order to make a claim for their protection.

This formula is not only present in debates about urban development in the United States. International human rights advocates often invoke it when they describe lesbian, gay, or transgender identities as the solution to violent rejection elsewhere in the world.[4] Moreover, the language used to describe different orientations of sex/gender systems and their regulation outside the United States and Western Europe is also used to describe those inside U.S. borders yet outside certain privileged areas. Scholars and activists have unpacked this stance as it responds to the supposed homophobia of rural poverty and the assumptions of tolerance coded in the cultural maps of cities versus suburbs. Yet insofar as these dynamics also occur in discussions about low-income people of color within U.S. metropolitan regions, it demonstrates how the terms of domestic urban governance are also those of global empire. The continued travels of the culture of poverty thesis that provided the background for homophobia discourse in U.S. central cities is but one example. Indeed, claims about damaged masculinity, antisocial behavior, and cultural rigidity continue to support the stereotype that African Americans, certain migrant and religious populations, and poor whites are fundamentally *homophobic*. Far from a formulation only of the 1970s, these ideas continue to have traction.[5]

The ascription of threat happens despite the fact that this is also the logic that measures disproportionate sexual risk among racialized sexualities. One need only think of the creation and circulation of categories such as *men who have sex with men* to see how development narratives feature in the consolidation of at-risk designations.[6] These associations have been stitched together by a variety of postwar liberal and neoliberal social policies. In the 1960s, War on Poverty programs portrayed U.S. poverty as domestic underdevelopment, a stance that helped ground punitive demands for self-help in response to internationalist claims for self-determination.[7] In addition, the postwar emphasis on personality and the related tension between self-help and self-determination remained unresolved in the social movements that followed and gave birth to a contradictory politics of the individual who was at once a symptom of social inequality and an actor for social liberation. In the mainstream LGBT movement, this took the form of migration narratives, in which danger was found in so-called backwoods small towns, urban ghettos, and Third World nations, and safety existed in U.S. and Western European urban gay enclaves.[8] This argument has also captured nationalist rhetoric in these places about the risks presented by (and to) migrants who are described as having failed to shed "traditional" values.[9] These links make evident how much the wars on poverty, crime, drugs, and terror share, in spite of their differences, and why they have been staged on a world scale.[10] It also suggests that there is a reason to return to study those parts of the city—those described as vice districts and skid rows, in particular, but also spaces of migrancy—that once were at the center of the very development of these fields of study and programs of social control.[11]

All of these moves were enabled precisely because of a liberal emphasis on social symptoms, in which antigay sentiment was not a normative practice of the state as much as an unintended consequence of other forms of social inequality. Figuring homophobia as a social symptom allows gross generalizations about who its supposed practitioners are, while simultaneously providing the justification for state-sponsored punitive reformism (since racism and poverty are so often designated as beyond remedy). It also provides the opportunity for the conflation of social service with social movement. This has been made possible by the empiricist approach to social science research typified by the rational choice theory that propelled neo-

FIGURE CONC.1 FIERCE Protest, 2004 (PHOTOGRAPH COURTESY OF EVA C. HAGEMAN)

liberalism's ascendance—a strategy in contradiction with neither a liberal rights discourse nor a progressive psychology of the self.[12] Thus just as risk appears across the political spectrum, other terms of neoliberalism, such as *diversity* and *tolerance*, are also used to describe racially and economically homogeneous neighborhoods that are policed with a policy called zero tolerance. In sum, mainstream LGBT politics in the United States since the 1960s were built on the idea that community might be realized in bounded space. Gay enclaves were named, territorialized, and guarded, and they acquired valuable commodity status on the urban real estate market. This suggests a troubling link between the protective measures increasingly at the forefront of both dominant LGBT political movements and those development strategies that have transformed metropolitan regions so as to protect property values. Today, even as visible gay identities are more dispersed across space, the connections between gay protection, policing, and property continue to be salient in new geographies. Thus new activist visions have the challenge of developing movements without substituting the piecemeal services of prevention in promising the elusive protections of security.

But, as I have shown, this has been neither a singular nor a guaranteed path. Activists have pushed back at a variety of these approaches, highlighting the contradictions inherent to profit and the decidedly unstable status of safety. Yet even these strategies have struggled to account for how regimes of normalization might attempt to fix (meaning both remedy and lock) individuals not only within dominant systems of sexual or gender identification but also within alternatives that value precise idealizations of health, community, and inclusion. This is particularly important insofar as control and incorporation are approached through institutions of treatment as well as punishment that reach far into people's psychic and everyday worlds. Thus it is more important than ever to emphasize LGBT and queer interpretive activist modes that might not only seek affirmation— by the state or counter formations—but also learn from and act alongside those individuals against whom the mainstream LGBT movement has so systematically defined itself.[13]

EPILOGUE

In the spring of 2011, I received a last-minute announcement from the Washington, D.C., organization Gays and Lesbians Opposing Violence (GLOV) about a mayoral town hall meeting in which members of GLOV would testify about anti-LGBT hate crimes and police response in the District of Columbia. I have lived in D.C. since 2007, not far from where the hearing was to be held, so I decided to go.[1] There, members of GLOV and others spoke about antigay attacks in the city and demanded that the police increase their presence in gay areas, the Justice Department institute stiffer penalties for hate crimes, and local and federal agencies treat juveniles as adults in the case of hate crimes. In many ways the meeting reminded me of the police precinct councils that I had attended in New York during the first decade of this century, which also had featured enraged residents fearful for their safety and demanding crime-oriented solutions. As had been the case in New York, in D.C. the abstract figures of the resident in need of protection and the gay person vulnerable to violence were one and the same, embodied during that meeting as a majority of white, gender-normative, gay men.

But there were aspects of the meeting in D.C. that were distinctive from the situation in New York. Washington, D.C., is unique for a variety of reasons, not the least of which is its status as being under federal jurisdiction. It is also unusual in its extremes of wealth and poverty, and in the fact that until recently the majority of its residents have been African Americans, who also compose a significant number of federal and municipal government employees.[2] D.C. is also the U.S. city with the highest percentage of LGBT self-identified residents. As in Greenwich Village, and like the residents at the D.C. meeting, almost all of the top-ranking representatives of judicial agencies there to hear complaints were white. But almost all of the mid-level officials, police officers, and representatives of the mayor's office were black. And although there were a small number of individuals in the audience who spoke up and identified themselves as LGBT people of color and some who questioned the proposals put forth, no self-identified, organized activist voice spoke out to counter the calls for more police.

The meeting was held in a government building located in the northwest quadrant of the city, right outside the northeast edge of the historically gay Dupont Circle area and toward the end of the U Street Corridor, in the Shaw neighborhood. It is an area with great significance in the history of African American life in D.C.: long home to prominent black intellectuals, artists, and political leaders; the site of the riots in the city following the assassination of Martin Luther King Jr.; and part of D.C.'s vibrant nightlife and jazz club scene. It was also for many years the locus of black queer social life. The area underwent massive gentrification during the 1980s and 1990s. Although some working-class and middle-class black residents who have long lived in the neighborhood have managed to hold onto houses their families have owned for generations—or to stay in affordable apartments covered by the city's still existing (albeit weak) rent control laws—the majority of long-term residents had been displaced by the 2000s. And newer residents were overwhelmingly middle- and upper-income whites. By 2011 the neighborhood was arguably far gone in the cycle of disinvestment and reinvestment central to gentrification, and the early dynamics of the process were taking place farther north and east, in Columbia Heights and the rest of Shaw. Although Dupont and U Street have long been known as areas of varied yet segregated gay life, it is Columbia Heights and Shaw that today are touted as the hot spots for young white gay professionals, while black gay social worlds are spread out across the city (and the surrounding areas of Maryland and Virginia), with additional clubs located in southeast and northeast D.C.[3]

In many ways, this meeting summarized the history that I have told here. Today's GLOV is a resurrection of an organization first founded in the 1980s as an outgrowth of a 1978 group called Gays against Violence. The first GLOV collaborated with the National Gay and Lesbian Task Force's Anti-Violence Project; today's GLOV names its two primary partners as the Gay and Lesbian Liaison Unit of the Metropolitan Police Department and the D.C. regional office of the Anti-Defamation League.[4] The meeting I attended was held in the Frank D. Reeves Municipal Building at 14th and U Streets, which was built in the 1980s to spur economic development in the area.

The key neighborhoods that GLOV activists named as a problem were places like Columbia Heights and Shaw, and they presented the main trouble as coming from low-income youth of color; the primary solutions they sought were the enhanced enforcement and expansion of criminal penalties. They provided statistics to support their claims that the vast majority of hate violence in the city was antigay, and they gestured at the ambiguous line drawn between hate and economic crime not as a way to question their understanding of homophobia, but in order to unite residents and to profile likely "offenders." The organization has sponsored self-defense and police sensitivity trainings. And individual GLOV members used the language of racial metaphor, civil rights, and militancy as they demanded more resources from city agencies. Although GLOV has acknowledged the problem of antitrans violence in the city and has also spoken out on behalf of black victims of violence, including that committed by police officers, they have not vocally opposed the city's so-called prostitution-free zones that use quality-of-life ideals and target women of color, many of them trans, often in these same neighborhoods.[5]

This shows the extent to which the history I have told is by no means restricted to New York City or to San Francisco, nor that it is only one of the past. Similarly, in 2011 gay residents of Chicago's gay area of Boystown rallied for police crackdowns on youth of color whom they described as disruptive and violent, many of whom were LGBT or queer themselves. And LGBT youth of color who have organized formal or informal modes of self-defense—such as the group called Check It in D.C., or individual cases in cities like New York and Minneapolis—have been described more as a threat than a solution.[6] This story thus underscores the utter inadequacy of interpretations of and solutions to anti-LGBT violence that are based on criminalization and the policing of gentrifying neighborhoods in a city that has a rate of HIV infection that has been termed epidemic by the World Health Organization, but that also has legalized same-sex marriage; has seen the drastic loss of black middle-class residents, along with the largest ever gap between rich and poor; and saw the closing of what had been the country's oldest black gay bar, Nob Hill, in a neighborhood, Columbia Heights, now named as the best gay thing. It is also to lay open for further analysis a militant gay liberalism that stages the scene of conflict as between white entitled residents and black municipal managers in a city that has had among the most gay-inclusive laws for decades.[7] To cite Lesbians Against Police Violence: "Count the Contradictions!"

Finally, this meeting also highlighted for me the complicated dynamics of research and activism. I have debated how to position myself in relation to the variety of individuals and groups that I represent; in many ways writing this book has brought me further from rather than closer to these same social movements. As I have tried to suggest, incorporation is not only a process of explicit complicity; it is also one of fitting into the dominant terms of recognition. Similarly, although at once generalized yet narrow categories of gay and, increasingly, transgender have become disassociated with the racialized poverty of the city, the fight for justice is not only to be found in challenging or reshuffling these categorical distinctions but also in critically engaging the operation of these dynamics while acting in collective solidarity.

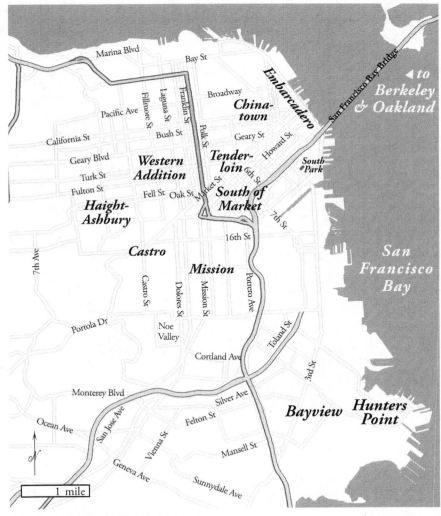

MAP 1 Map of San Francisco Neighborhoods (DESIGNED BY TIM STALLMANN)

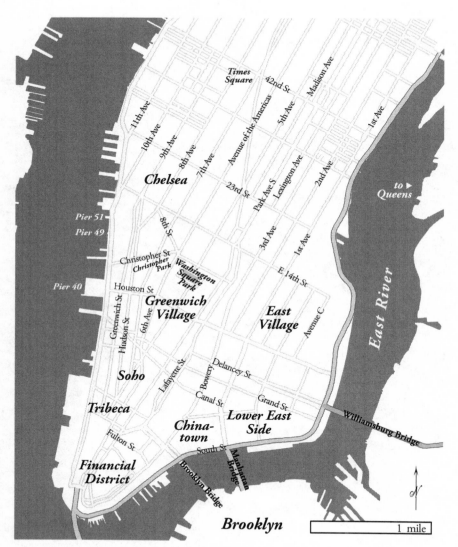

MAP 2 Map of New York City Neighborhoods (DESIGNED BY TIM STALLMANN)

NOTES

Introduction

1. Christopher Park is in the area also known as Sheridan Square; it is located in the triangle created by Christopher Street, West 4th Street, and Grove Street, just off 7th Avenue.

2. The Stonewall Inn was a popular gay bar in Greenwich Village during the 1960s. In the early morning of June 28, 1969, its patrons challenged a police raid—then a routine feature of gay bar life—and a series of riots ensued. Scholars and activists debate who was at the center of the uprisings, varying in their assessment of the participation of gay men, transgender people, street youth, and lesbians, as well as their calculations of how many were people of color. The elision of people of color, women, and the gender nonconforming from the story of Stonewall is often cited to support arguments that those at the center of the now mythical riot have been left out of the consolidation of a mainstream movement. For different versions of the riots, see Donn Teal, *The Gay Militants: How Gay Liberation Began in America, 1969–1971* (1971; New York: St. Martin's, 1995); Toby Marotta, *The Politics of Homosexuality* (Boston: Houghton Mifflin, 1981); John D'Emilio, *Sexual Politics, Sexual Communities: The Making of a Homosexual Minority in the United States, 1940–1970* (Chicago: University of Chicago Press, 1983); Martin Duberman, *Stonewall* (New York: Plume, 1993); David Carter, *Stonewall: The Riots that Sparked the Gay Revolution* (New York: St. Martin's, 2004). For discussions of the treatment of Stonewall as myth, see Scott Bravmann, *Queer Fictions of the Past: History, Culture, and Difference* (Cambridge: Cambridge University Press, 1997); John D'Emilio, "Stonewall: Myth and Meaning," in John D'Emilio, *The World Turned: Essays on Gay History, Politics, and Culture* (Durham: Duke University Press, 2002), 146–53; Elizabeth A. Armstrong and Susanna M. Crage, "Meaning and Memory: The Making of the Stonewall Myth," *American Sociological Review* 71, no. 7 (2006): 724–51.

3. This section is based on field notes I took at the event as well as media coverage. The rally has been also cited in publications about the activist group Fabulous Independent Educated Radicals for Community Empowerment, known as FIERCE (Justin Anton Rosado, "Corroding Our Quality of Life," in *That's Revolting! Queer Strategies for Resisting Assimilation*, ed. Mattilda Bernstein Sycamore [New York: Soft Scull, 2004], 299); youth organizing (Daniel Martinez HoSang, "Beyond Policy: Ideology, Race and the

Reimagining of Youth," in *Beyond Resistance! Youth Activism and Community Change*, ed. Shawn Ginwright, Pedro Noguera, and Julio Cammarota [New York: Routledge, 2006], 13); transgender identity (David Valentine, *Imagining Transgender: An Ethnography of a Category* [Durham: Duke University Press, 2007], 196–200); and young gay men of color in New York (Kai Wright, *Drifting toward Love: Black, Brown, Gay, and Coming of Age on the Streets of New York* [Boston: Beacon, 2008], 215).

4. For a history of quality-of-life policing in New York, see Tanya Erzen, "Turnstile Jumpers and Broken Windows: Policing Disorder in New York City," in *Zero Tolerance: Quality of Life and the New Police Brutality in New York City*, ed. Andrea McArdle and Tanya Erzen (New York: New York University Press, 2001), 19–49.

5. The West Village is part of the greater Greenwich Village neighborhood and most often defined as the area bounded by 6th Avenue to the east, the Hudson River to the west, 14th Street to the north, and Houston Street to the south.

6. "Notice of Public Hearing: Take Back Our Streets," City of New York, Community Board 2 Manhattan, undated document with fax stamp indicating that it was sent from Community Board 2's office on April 24, 2002. In author's possession; also on file at Community Board 2, New York.

7. Wendy Dixon, "Alice Certainly Doesn't Live Here," *Greenwich Village Block Association News*, Summer 2002, 3, http://www.gvba.org/PDFs/GVBANewspdfs/GVBANews _summer_02.pdf.

8. Albert Amateau, "Queer Youth and Residents Still at Odds on Park Use," *Villager*, December 14–20, 2005.

9. In this book, I use *lesbian, gay, bisexual, transgender*, and *queer* for those who so identify. Often, I use *nonnormative* or *nonconforming* to refer to those whose identities or practices place them outside of dominant categories of sexuality or gender but who may or may not identify as lesbian, gay, bisexual, and/or transgender (historically or in the present context). I use *queer* and *trans* and, more rarely, *sexual* or *gender minority*, for this same purpose. Relatedly, I use both *African American* and *black*. In general, I use *African American* to refer to U.S.-born people of African descent, and I use *black* to signal a broader category that is also more inclusive of new immigrant communities; nonetheless, since these two identities frequently overlap, I often use the two terms interchangeably. Similarly, I use *Puerto Rican* and *Latino*. Although *black* is not exclusive of these categories, nor they of each other, I often repeat terms for specificity. Thus, I repeat general categories that also intersect; for example, *women* and *people of color* or *lesbians* and *transgender people*. There are limits to generalization and to specificity: for example, the phrase *women and people of color* may seem to omit the recognition of women of color, but to add *women of color* to the list is not only redundant but enforces their exclusion from either category. Similarly, the phrase *lesbians and transgender women* may seem to ignore the fact that some lesbians are transgender women, but to specify *transgender lesbians* may stigmatize transgender women as a separate category of lesbian. In other words, combinations can naturalize exclusions even when done for the goal of inclusion. I aim for complexity and inclusivity while using the clearest language possible.

10. For a discussion of queer life on the piers, see Rosado, "Corroding Our Quality of Life"; Martin F. Manalansan IV, "Race, Violence, and Neoliberal Spatial Politics in the Global City," *Social Text* 23, nos. 3–4 (2005): 141–55. A history is also provided by the documentary *Fenced Out!* produced and directed by FIERCE, Paper Tiger Television, and the New Neutral Zone (2001). For a study of house ball culture in New York and its move from Washington Square Park to the piers, see Frank Leon Roberts, "'There's No

Place Like Home': A History of Butch Queens, Femme Queens, and House Ball Culture," *Wiretap*, June 6, 2007, http://wiretapmag.org/stories/43120/.

11. In both the 2000 and 2010 censuses, Newark was majority black (53.5 percent in 2000, 52.4 percent in 2010). Jersey City's single largest racial group was white (34.1 percent in 2000, 32.7 percent in 2010), but its combined black population (28.3 percent in 2000, 25.9 percent in 2010) and Hispanic/Latino of any race population (28.3 percent in 2000, 27.6 percent in 2010) together composed a majority.

12. Many residents joined the Greenwich Village Society for Historic Preservation to oppose a plan for a new PATH exit, citing its potential damage to the Stonewall Historic District—which surrounds the Stonewall bar and Christopher Park and was granted National Historic Landmark status in 1999. See the aptly titled article by Margery Reifler, "Village Alert—PATHology," *Greenwich Village Block Association News*, Summer 2002, 2, http://www.gvba.org/PDFs/GVBANewspdfs/GVBAnews_summer_02.pdf.

13. Quoted in Duncan Osborne, "Piers Fears Go Racial: With No Christopher Street Solution, Community Board Faults LGBT Youth of Color," *Gay City News*, March 9–15, 2006.

14. A small sample of articles from the first decade of the 2000s includes Osborne, "Piers Fears Go Racial"; Robert F. Worth, "Tolerance in Village Wears Thin," *New York Times*, January 19, 2001; Richard Goldstein, "Street Hassle: New Skool versus Old School in Greenwich Village," *Village Voice*, April 24–30, 2002; Mike Lavers, "Gay Youth Oppose Police in Village," *New York Blade*, October 22, 2004; Kristen Lombardi, "Gay and Loud: The New Battle over Queer Kids' Ruckus in Greenwich Village," *Village Voice*, March 14, 2006; Laurie Mittelmann, "Bagel Man Battles Hookers, but Needs a Hole Lot of Help," *Villager*, July 23–29, 2008.

15. Although this book does not explicitly trace the emergence and circulation of the term *safe space* since the 1960s, it attempts to mark some of its varied appearances.

16. One might also say that Stonewall took their money; Stonewall's open-door policy might be considered as much an act of Mafia-sponsored profiteering as one of benevolence. For the role of the Mafia at Stonewall, see Carter, *Stonewall*, esp. 80–84.

17. Carter, *Stonewall*; Duberman, *Stonewall*.

18. Quoted in Duberman, *Stonewall*, 207, and Carter, *Stonewall*, 196. Teal also reports gay and straight Villagers' complaints about "homosexual ruffians." In addition, he shows how this issue was taken up in other cities and by varied political sensibilities—for example, the Los Angeles Gay Liberation Front issued warnings in 1970 that "Residents Have the Right to Sleep and You Have the Right to Cruise! Cruise Early or on Business Streets!" as a way to avoid the vice squad (*The Gay Militants*, 185).

19. Terence Kissack, "Freaking Fag Revolutionaries: New York's Gay Liberation Front, 1969–1971," *Radical History Review* 62 (Spring 1995): 104–35.

20. Lincoln Anderson, "Potatoes to Pizza: Complaint-Plagued Bar Is No More," *Villager*, January 28–February 3, 2004. In a piece about its opening, Bar Nocetti is described as run by a network of Italian neighborhood residents who "transform[ed] what used to be a transvestite burlesque club into a place of their own" (Robin Raisfeld and Rob Patronite, "Village People . . . Later, Gator . . . Navigating Little Italy," *New York Magazine*, March 1, 2004, http://nymag.com/nymetro/food/openings/n_9918/).

21. See William Eskridge, *Gay Law: Challenging the Apartheid of the Closet* (Cambridge: Harvard University Press, 1999); Clare Sears, "Electric Brilliancy: Cross-Dressing Law and Freak Show Displays in Nineteenth-Century San Francisco," *Women Studies Quarterly* 36, nos. 3–4 (2008): 170–87. It bears repeating that this targeting was not evenly experienced across race, class, and gender lines. For example, George Chauncey

describes gay men's unequal vulnerability to policing in early twentieth-century New York City (*Gay New York: Gender, Urban Culture, and the Making of the Gay Male World, 1890–1940* [New York: Basic Books, 1994]).

22. That said, Stonewall was not the most popular bar for African American and Puerto Rican trans women who exchanged sex for money; that economic activity was centered in Times Square (Duberman, *Stonewall*, 181–83).

23. The most famous early case is that of Dale Jennings, who was arrested in 1952 for soliciting homosexual sex and then challenged these charges with the backing of the Mattachine Society. For a detailed analysis of this case, see Emily Hobson, "Policing Gay L.A.: Mapping Racial Divides in the Homophile Era, 1950–1967," in *The Rising Tide of Color: Race, Radicalism, and Repression on the Pacific Coast and Beyond*, ed. Moon-Ho Jung (Seattle: University of Washington Press, forthcoming). It is also discussed in D'Emilio, *Sexual Politics, Sexual Communities*, and Lillian Faderman and Stuart Timmons, *Gay L.A.: A History of Sexual Outlaws, Power Politics, and Lipstick Lesbians* (New York: Basic, 2006).

24. A recent example is the Crimes against Nature by Solicitation statute in New Orleans that had required those convicted of exchanging (only) oral and anal sex for money to register as sex offenders (see Joey Mogul, Andrea Ritchie, and Kay Whitlock, *Queer (In)Justice: The Criminalization of LGBT People in the United States* [Boston: Beacon, 2011], 157); it was later successfully challenged in court. For other examples, see Michael Warner, *The Trouble with Normal: Sex, Politics, and the Ethics of Queer Life* (New York: Free Press, 1999); Sylvia Rivera Law Project, "It's War in Here: A Report on the Treatment of Transgender and Intersex People in New York State Men's Prisons," 2007, http://srlp .org/files/warinhere.pdf; Sylvia Rivera Law Project, "Tips for Trans People Dealing with Cops," http://archive.srlp.org/node/382. Here it is worth noting that even legal gains can have limited benefits. For example, in 2003, the U.S. Supreme Court decision in *Lawrence v. Texas* (539 U.S. 558) overturned sodomy laws, essentially decriminalizing same-sex sexual activity. But as Teemu Ruskola and David Eng both argue, this decision emphasized the protection of privacy and still left many queer acts subject to regulation and disapprobation. See Teemu Ruskola, "Gay Rights versus Queer Theory," *Social Text* 23, nos. 3–4 (2005): 235–49; David L. Eng, *The Feeling of Kinship: Queer Liberalism and the Racialization of Intimacy* (Durham: Duke University Press, 2010).

25. Richard A. Cloward and Lloyd E. Ohlin, *Delinquency and Opportunity: A Theory of Delinquent Gangs* (New York: Free Press, 1960).

26. For a discussion of Mobilization for Youth and the War on Poverty, see Noel A. Cazenave, *Impossible Democracy: The Unlikely Success of the War on Poverty Community Action Programs* (Albany: State University of New York Press, 2007); Alyosha Goldstein, *Poverty in Common: The Politics of Community Action during the American Century* (Durham: Duke University Press, 2012).

27. See Erzen, "Turnstile Jumpers and Broken Windows"; Henry A. Giroux, "Racial Injustice and Disposable Youth in the Age of Zero Tolerance," *Qualitative Studies in Education* 16, no. 4 (2003): 553–65.

28. See Melinda Miceli, *Standing Out, Standing Together: The Social and Political Impact of Gay-Straight Alliances* (New York: Routledge, 2005); Sarah Mountz, "Revolving Doors: LGBTQ Youth at the Interface of the Child Welfare and Juvenile Justice Systems," *LGBTQ Policy Journal*, 2011, http://isites.harvard.edu/icb/icb.do?keyword=k78405&pageid=icb .page414421.

29. For a longer history of gay Greenwich Village, see Chauncey, *Gay New York*.

30. In 1995 the New York City Council approved a zoning amendment initiated by Giuliani that redefined and limited the siting of adult businesses. For an analysis of the

impacts of this amendment, see Warner, *The Trouble with Normal*; Samuel R. Delany, *Times Square Red, Times Square Blue* (New York: New York University Press, 1999); Dangerous Bedfellows Collective, *Policing Public Sex* (Boston: South End, 1996).

31. Patricia Leigh Brown, "Gay Enclaves Face Prospect of Being Passé," *New York Times*, October 30, 2007. The quote is from real estate broker Wes Freas. For an analysis of the decline of gay neighborhoods and the rise of "post-gay" identities, see Amin Ghaziani, "There Goes the Gayborhood?," *Contexts* 9, no. 3 (2010): 64–66.

32. The Rainbow Pilgrimage is described on the NYC.com website at http://www.nyc.com/visitor_guide/the_rainbow_pilgrimage.75900/editorial_review.aspx. Also see Sewell Chan, "Stonewall Uprising Given Role in Tourism Campaign," *New York Times*, April 7, 2009.

33. In *Imagining Transgender*, Valentine also notes that those opposing the 2002 Take Back Our Streets rally saw residents as "representative of a white, middle-class gay and lesbian elite" (196). Valentine argues that the activist response to residents—specifically, the call for "transgender inclusion" (199)—risked sidestepping other issues coded in residents' complaints, in particular race and class. Valentine cites this as an example of the limits of a discourse based in "inclusion" and "diversity," whether that is the claim of residents that they *are* inclusive and that they value diversity or the argument of activists demanding *more* inclusivity or diversity—because both approaches ultimately parse and contain identities rather than challenge social structures. I agree with Valentine's argument here, and much of the project of this book is to ask how the landscape of LGBT politics has come to be as he describes it. But, as Valentine notes, certain contexts can dilute complex arguments. I argue that a rally can be one such site, and that rallies are best analyzed as parts of ongoing campaigns. In the case of the 2002 rally, a variety of people showed up, many of whose signs and chants did narrow the field of critique. But for organizations such as FIERCE, this was just one event in an ongoing campaign against the privatization of space and criminalization, and not only a call for the inclusion of youth and transgender women of color in the West Village. That said, Valentine's observations—and my own example—point to the tricky ways in which liberal politics can treat identities as discrete and then fail to recognize other hierarchies of power in operation (195–203).

34. In the documentary *Fenced Out!* the late activist Sylvia Rivera recalls an era in which white gay men enjoyed public sex along the waterfront and "Christopher Street was their playground." She concludes: "For them to turn the tides around on the people of color and trans community now in the year 2001, thirty-two years after Stonewall . . . I find it completely unacceptable."

35. See David Boesel and Peter H. Rossi, eds., *Cities under Siege: An Anatomy of the Ghetto Riots, 1964–1968* (New York: Basic Books, 1971); John Mollenkopf, *The Contested City* (Princeton: Princeton University Press, 1983); Roger Friedland, *Power and Crisis in the City* (London: Schocken, 1983); Thomas Sugrue, *The Origins of the Urban Crisis: Race and Inequality in Postwar Detroit* (Princeton: Princeton University Press, 1996); George Lipsitz, *The Possessive Investment in Whiteness: How White People Profit from Identity Politics* (Philadelphia: Temple University Press, 1998); Rhonda Williams, *The Politics of Public Housing: Black Women's Struggles against Urban Inequality* (Oxford: Oxford University Press, 2004); Robert O. Self, *American Babylon: Race and the Struggle for Postwar Oakland* (Princeton: Princeton University Press, 2003); Christopher Rhomberg, *No There There: Race, Class, and Political Community in Oakland* (Berkeley: University of California Press, 2004); Kevin Mumford, *Newark: A History of Race, Rights, and Riots in America* (New York: New York University Press, 2007). On mobility rights in disability, see

Doris Zames Fleischer and Frieda Zames, *The Disability Rights Movement: From Charity to Confrontation* (Philadelphia: Temple University Press, 2001).

36. For a broad range of perspectives in addition to those cited above, see Thomas E. Cronin, Tania Z. Cronin, and Michael E. Milakovich, *U.S. v. Crime in the Streets* (Bloomington: Indiana University Press, 1981); Wesley Skogan, *Disorder and Decline: Crime and the Spiral of Decay in American Neighborhoods* (Berkeley: University of California Press, 1990); Elizabeth Wilson, *The Sphinx in the City: Urban Life, the Control of Disorder, and Women* (Berkeley: University of California Press, 1992); Elizabeth A. Stanko, "Women, Crime, and Fear," *Annals of the American Academy of Political and Social Science* 539 (May 1995): 46–58; Katherine Beckett, *Making Crime Pay: Law and Order in Contemporary American Politics* (New York: Oxford University Press, 1997); Elizabeth A. Stanko, "Victims R US: The Life History of 'Fear of Crime' and the Politicisation of Violence," in *Crime, Risk and Insecurity: Law and Order in Everyday Life and Political Discourse*, ed. Tim Hope and Richard Sparks (London: Routledge, 2000), 13–30; Michael Flamm, *Law and Order: Street Crime, Civil Unrest, and the Crisis of Liberalism in the 1960s* (New York: Columbia University Press, 2005).

37. But a few examples include D'Emilio, *Sexual Politics, Sexual Communities*; Faderman and Timmons, *Gay L.A.*; Elizabeth Lapovsky Kennedy and Madeline Davis, *Boots of Leather, Slippers of Gold: The History of a Lesbian Community* (New York: Penguin, 1994). Other examples are provided in later chapters.

38. See Gregory M. Herek and Kevin T. Berrill, eds., *Hate Crimes: Confronting Violence against Lesbians and Gay Men* (Newbury Park, CA: Sage, 1992); Valerie Jenness and Kendal Broad, *Hate Crimes: New Social Movements and the Politics of Violence* (New York: Aldine de Gruyter, 1997); David M. Wertheimer, "The Emergence of a Gay and Lesbian Antiviolence Movement," in *Creating Change: Sexuality, Public Policy, and Civil Rights*, ed. John D'Emilio, William B. Turner, and Urvashi Vaid (New York: St. Martin's, 2000), 261–79; Valerie Jenness and Ryken Grattet, *Making Hate a Crime: From Social Movement to Law Enforcement* (New York: Russell Sage Foundation, 2001).

39. New work in sociology has analyzed the strategies and ideologies of local and national LGBT movement building that includes antiviolence but does not focus on it. See Tina Fetner, *How the Religious Right Shaped Lesbian and Gay Activism* (Minneapolis: University of Minnesota Press, 2008); Jane Ward, *Respectably Queer: Diversity Culture in LGBT Activist Organizations* (Nashville, TN: Vanderbilt University Press, 2008); Amin Ghaziani, *The Dividends of Dissent: How Conflict and Culture Work in Lesbian and Gay Marches on Washington* (Chicago: University of Chicago Press, 2008); Deborah B. Gould, *Moving Politics: Emotion and ACT UP's Fight against AIDS* (Chicago: University of Chicago Press, 2009). An earlier example is Elizabeth A. Armstrong, *Forging Gay Identities: Organizing Sexuality in San Francisco, 1950–1994* (Chicago: University of Chicago Press, 2002).

40. For some excellent examples among many, see Judith Butler, *Excitable Speech: A Politics of the Performative* (New York: Routledge, 1997); Wendy Brown, *States of Injury: Power and Freedom in Late Modernity* (Princeton: Princeton University Press, 1995); Janet E. Halley and Wendy Brown, eds., *Left Legalism/Left Critique* (Durham: Duke University Press, 2002); Judith Butler, *Undoing Gender* (New York: Routledge, 2004); Siobhan B. Somerville, "Queer *Loving*," GLQ 11, no. 3 (2005): 355–70; Eng, *The Feeling of Kinship*; Chandan Reddy, *Freedom with Violence: Race, Sexuality, and the U.S. State* (Durham: Duke University Press, 2011). There is also a new generation of activist-oriented scholarship that has highlighted the complicities between LGBT social movements and law-and-order politics by critiquing the emphasis of present-day mainstream LGBT organizations on policy-based solutions rooted in inclusion. Examples include Ryan Conrad, ed.,

Against Equality: Queer Critiques of Gay Marriage, with an introduction by Yasmin Nair (Lewiston, ME: Against Equality Publishing Collective, 2010); Dean Spade, *Normal Life: Administrative Violence, Critical Trans Politics, and the Limits of the Law* (Brooklyn, NY: South End, 2011); Eric A. Stanley and Nat Smith, eds. *Captive Genders: Trans Embodiment and the Prison Industrial Complex* (Oakland, CA: AK, 2011); Mogul, Ritchie, and Whitlock, *Queer (In)Justice.*

41. On thick description, see Clifford Geertz, "Thick Description: Toward an Interpretive Theory of Culture," in Clifford Geertz, *The Interpretation of Cultures: Selected Essays* (New York: Basic Books, 1973), 3–32. For examples of scholarship that analyze the dynamics of sexuality, space, social movements, and violence in variable combinations, see John Howard, *Men Like That: A Southern Queer History* (Chicago: University of Chicago Press, 1999); Marc Stein, *City of Sisterly and Brotherly Loves: Lesbian and Gay Philadelphia* (Chicago: University of Chicago Press, 2000); Nayan Shah, *Contagious Divides: Epidemics and Race in San Francisco's Chinatown* (Berkeley: University of California Press, 2001); Ann Cvetkovich, *An Archive of Feelings: Trauma, Sexuality, and Lesbian Public Cultures* (Durham: Duke University Press, 2003); Manalansan, "Race, Violence, and Neoliberal Spatial Politics in the Global City"; Judith Halberstam, *In a Queer Time and Place: Transgender Bodies, Subcultural Lives* (New York: New York University Press, 2005); Robert McRuer, *Crip Theory: Cultural Signs of Queerness and Disability* (New York: New York University Press, 2006); Valentine, *Imagining Transgender*; Regina Kunzel, *Criminal Intimacy: Prison and the Uneven History of Modern American Sexuality* (Chicago: University of Chicago Press, 2008); Nayan Shah, *Stranger Intimacy: Contesting Race, Sexuality, and the Law in the North American West* (Berkeley: University of California Press, 2011).

42. David Harvey specifically discusses the decline of "embedded liberalism" after the 1970s in *A Brief History of Neoliberalism* (New York: Oxford University Press, 2007).

43. Here it is important to note that although neoliberalism casts itself as a pure free market, its realization depends on the state's participation in fostering the conditions for private profit. On the neoliberal city, see Jason Hackworth, *The Neoliberal City: Governance, Ideology, and Development in American Urbanism* (Ithaca: Cornell University Press, 2006); Neil Brenner and Nik Theodore, eds. *Spaces of Neoliberalism: Urban Restructuring in North America and Western Europe* (Malden, MA: Blackwell, 2003).

44. My use of the term *central city* can be confusing since it can refer to major cities within metropolitan regions or to central business districts or to what is often called the *inner city*; furthermore, the first chapter of this book is about a San Francisco area referred to as the Central City. I tend to avoid *inner city*, which carries a more derogatory connotation and does not adequately cover the range, and changing dynamics, of the areas I describe. Thus I use *central city* as my general term and use other language to specify a given area's features.

45. On the 1970s, see David Rothenberg, "Can Gays Save New York City?," *Christopher Street*, September 1977, 6–10, and Manuel Castells, "City and Culture: The San Francisco Experience," in Manuel Castells, *The City and the Grassroots: A Cross-Cultural Theory of Urban Social Movements* (Berkeley: University of California Press, 1983), 97–172. In the article "Can Gays Save New York City?" the author writes, "How many neighborhoods in Manhattan would be slums by now had gay singles and couples not moved in and helped maintain and upgrade them? A thriving Manhattan-based gay community has become necessary to New York City's survival" (9). The cover of the magazine that month features the title of the article above a photograph of two white gay men with mustaches, their arms encircling an image of lower Manhattan. On the late 1990s and early 2000s, see Richard Florida, *The Rise of the Creative Class, and How It's Transform-*

ing Work, Leisure, Community, and Everyday Life (New York: Basic Books, 2002). It is interesting to note that in the 1970s, researchers and popular commentators used the same terms that Florida would years later, highlighting the "creativity" of gay men as a positive factor in the new economy. See, for example, "Out & Around: Brownstoning," *Christopher Street*, August 1976, 3–5.

46. Following Jasbir Puar's writings on homonationalism, this is one example of how certain lesbian and gay subjects are constituted as life giving within dominant national cultures (*Terrorist Assemblages: Homonationalism in Queer Times* [Durham: Duke University Press, 2007]). Jin Haritaworn has recently elaborated on this connection in the essay "Colorful Bodies in the Multikulti Metropolis: Vitality, Victimology and Transgressive Citizenship in Berlin," in *Transgender Migrations: The Bodies, Borders, and Politics of Transition*, ed. Trystan Cotton (New York: Routledge, 2012), 11–31. Haritaworn's essay analyzes the travels of hate crime discourse within Europe via a case study of Berlin; also see Jin Haritaworn, "Queer Injuries: The Racial Politics of 'Homophobic Hate Crime' in Germany," *Social Justice* 37, no. 1 (2010–11): 69–87.

47. For a helpful analysis of the politics of sexuality and risk under neoliberal regimes, see Geeta Patel, "Risky Subjects: Insurance, Sexuality, and Capital," *Social Text* 24, no. 4 (2006): 25–65.

48. Halberstam, *In a Queer Time and Place*, 36.

49. Scott Herring, *Another Country: Queer Anti-Urbanism* (New York: New York University Press, 2010), 16.

50. On metronormativity and queer cosmopolitanism, see also Karen Tongson, *Relocations: Queer Suburban Imaginaries* (New York: New York University Press, 2011).

51. I want to note that two other people, Philip DeVine and Lisa Lambert, were murdered alongside Brandon Teena, a fact often obscured in the coverage and representation of the event.

52. For an early example of activist concern about rural violence, see National Gay Task Force Press Release, "Brydon Expressed NGTF Concern for Rural Gays at Conference in Sioux Falls, South Dakota," May 2, 1979, Box 36, Folder 118, National Gay and Lesbian Task Force Records (Collection 7301), Division of Rare and Manuscript Collections, Kroch Library, Cornell University.

53. For an analysis of the response to the murder of Matthew Shepard based on the politics of place, violence, and masculinity, see JoAnn Wypijewski, "A Boy's Life: For Matthew Shepard's Killers, What Does It Take to Pass as a Man?," *Harper's*, September 1999, 61–74.

54. Mary Gray examines the relationship between rural LGBT politics and national agendas in *Out in the Country: Youth, Media, and Queer Visibility in Rural America* (New York: New York University Press, 2009). For other analyses of rural, noncoastal, and/or small-city models of LGBT activism, also see Lisa Duggan, "What's Right with Utah," *Nation*, July 13, 2009, http://www.thenation.com/article/whats-right-utah; Mab Segrest, *Memoir of a Race Traitor* (Cambridge, MA: South End, 1994).

55. In a conversation, Mab Segrest helpfully reminded me that rural activism in the South during the 1980s and 1990s often merged anti-LGBT violence activism with movements against racist violence and thus led to different models. Organizations like Southerners on New Ground have often sidestepped the logics of the national LGBT movement. See also Segrest, *Memoir of a Race Traitor*.

56. Lisa Duggan, *The Twilight of Equality? Neoliberalism, Cultural Politics, and the Attack on Democracy* (Boston: Beacon, 2004). In a footnote to "Sex in Public" (n2), Lauren Berlant and Michael Warner defined heteronormativity as follows: "By heteronormativ-

ity we mean the institutions, structures of understanding, and practical orientations that make heterosexuality seem not only coherent—that is, organized as a sexuality—but also privileged. . . . It consists less of norms that could be summarized as a body of doctrine than of a sense of rightness produced in contradictory manifestations—often unconscious, immanent to practice or to institutions. . . . Because homosexuality can never have the invisible, tacit, society-founding rightness that heterosexuality has, it would not be possible to speak of 'homonormativity' in the same sense" (*Critical Inquiry* 24, no. 2 [1998]: 548). For Duggan, "the *new* homonormativity" is "a politics that does not contest dominant heteronormative assumptions and institutions, but upholds and sustains them, while promising the possibility of a demobilized gay constituency and a privatized, depoliticized gay culture anchored in domesticity and consumption" (*The Twilight of Equality?*, 50). There has been a proliferation of overlapping yet distinct terms to describe the imbrication of the LGBT/queer and neo/liberal. This includes the concept of "virtual equality" (Urvashi Vaid, *Virtual Equality: The Mainstreaming of Gay and Lesbian Liberation* [New York: Anchor, 1995]); the reference to a "virtual gay movement" (Michael Warner, "We're Queer, Remember?," *Advocate*, September 30, 1997, 7); the description of "selling out" (Alexandra Chasin, *Selling Out: The Gay and Lesbian Movement Goes to Market* [New York: St. Martin's, 2000]; the construction of a "Gay International" (Joseph Massad, *Desiring Arabs* [Chicago: University of Chicago Press, 2007]); the function of "gay imperialism" (Jin Haritaworn, with Tamsila Tauqir and Esra Erdem, "Gay Imperialism: Gender and Sexuality Discourse in the 'War on Terror,'" in *Out of Place*, ed. Adi Kuntsman and Esperanza Miyake [York, UK: Raw Nerve Books, 2008], 71–95); the theory of "queer white patriarchy" (Heidi J. Nast, "Queer Patriarchies, Queer Racisms, International," *Antipode* 34, no. 5 [2002]: 881); the variant uses of "queer liberalism" (Puar, *Terrorist Assemblages*; Eng, *The Feeling of Kinship*), and the concept of "homonationalism" (Puar, *Terrorist Assemblages*). Here it is worth noting that some of these terms signal a precise political ideology or program that might be adopted or dispensed with, while others (such as homonationalism) seek to emphasize a shared logic or condition of possibility. Finally, I want to highlight that one of Duggan's defining examples of homonormativity is drawn from the antiviolence movement: in 2001, the National Coalition of Anti-Violence Programs protested antigay graffiti on a bomb destined for Afghanistan without noting the violence promised by the bomb itself (46).

57. Kennedy and Davis, *Boots of Leather, Slippers of Gold*; Susan Stryker, *Transgender History* (Berkeley, CA: Seal, 2008). For additional examples of early acts of informal defiance, such as in Philadelphia, see Stein, *City of Sisterly and Brotherly Loves*; and Armstrong and Crage, "Meaning and Memory."

58. In *Fenced Out!* the late activist Regina Shavers summarized the approach she and fellow lesbians of color were forced to adopt in response to harassment and violence in the streets of New York during the 1950s and 1960s: "We kicked their fucking ass."

59. Julie Abraham, *Metropolitan Lovers: The Homosexuality of Cities* (Minneapolis: University of Minnesota Press, 2009). For other discussions of the *flâneur*, see Sally Munt, *Heroic Desire: Lesbian Identity and Cultural Space* (London: Cassell, 1998); Diane Chisholm, *Queer Constellations: Subcultural Space in the Wake of the City* (Minneapolis: University of Minnesota Press, 2005).

60. John D'Emilio, "Capitalism and Gay Identity," in *Powers of Desire: The Politics of Sexuality*, ed. Ann Snitow, Christine Stansell, and Sharon Thompson (New York: Monthly Review Press, 1983), 100–113.

61. Chauncey, *Gay New York*, 131.

62. Hazel V. Carby, "Policing the Black Woman's Body in an Urban Context," *Critical*

Inquiry 18, no. 4 (1992): 738–55; Roderick A. Ferguson, *Aberrations in Black: Toward a Queer of Color Critique* (Minneapolis: University of Minnesota Press, 2004); Kevin Mumford, *Interzones: Black/White Sex Districts in Chicago and New York in the Early Twentieth Century* (New York: Columbia University Press, 1997); Marlon B. Ross, *Manning the Race: Reforming Black Men in the Jim Crow Era* (New York: New York University Press, 2004).

63. Ferguson, *Aberrations in Black*, 41.

64. Siobhan B. Somerville, *Queering the Color Line: Race and the Invention of Homosexuality in American Culture* (Durham: Duke University Press, 2000).

65. Shane Vogel, *The Scene of Harlem Cabaret: Race, Sexuality, Performance* (Chicago: University of Chicago Press, 2009).

66. Shah, *Contagious Divides*, 31 ("true nature"), 78 ("perversions").

67. This policy was begun in response to the federal government's termination program that cut all economic support to sovereign Native lands (it was initiated in 1948, and formalized by 1952). A fascinating document of urban Native life right after this period can be found in the 1961 film *The Exiles* (directed by Kent Mackenzie). For an astute analysis of the film, see Laura Sachiko Fugikawa, "Domestic Containment: Japanese Americans, Native Americans, and the Cultural Politics of Relocation," PhD diss., University of Southern California, 2011.

68. These phenomena were often asserted through biological metaphors. The most famous example is Ernest Burgess's concentric circle map of the city, a key text of the ecological model of the early Chicago School. The map was first published in Robert E. Park and Ernest W. Burgess, *The City: Suggestions for the Investigation of Human Behavior in the Urban Environment* (1925) (Chicago: University of Chicago Press, 1967; repr. 1984), 51.

69. Margot Canaday, *The Straight State: Sexuality and Citizenship in Twentieth Century America* (Princeton: Princeton University Press, 2009), 3.

70. Cathy Cohen, "Deviance as Resistance: A New Research Agenda for the Study of Black Politics," *Du Bois Review* 1, no. 1 (2004): 27–45. Writing of black communities that have been labeled "deviant," Cohen responds to the work of Robin D. G. Kelley and James Scott to consider how "deviant choices that are repeated by groups or subgroups of people can create a space where normative myths of how the society is naturally structured are challenged in practices . . . and in speech" (38). Ultimately, though, Cohen argues for the importance of "intent" for the effective mobilization of such choices into new collective movements. Following a very different line of argument, Puar in *Terrorist Assemblages* critiques an approach to queerness based in an individualism that *chooses* "freedom from norms" (22); here she highlights the limits of a liberal conception of agency that undergirds the normative terms of "resistance" (23). Drawing on both Cohen and Puar, I am interested in the possibilities of deviancy that might not invest in the model of resistance critiqued by Puar, but that may still engage in the project of collective social movements as described by Cohen.

71. For a foundational critique of the racial politics of gay marriage activism that highlights how normativity has been cast as white and in opposition to black kinship relations, see Kenyon Farrow, "Is Gay Marriage Anti-Black?," 2004, http://kenyonfarrow .com/2005/06/14/is-gay-marriage-anti-black/.

72. These assumptions were popularized not only in policy but in the blurring between social scientific and popular writing. In *Criminal Intimacy*, Regina Kunzel shows how representations of prison sexuality in diverse textual sources contributed to broad cultural knowledge about race, poverty, and sexuality throughout the twentieth century.

73. On the concept of "spatial fix," see David Harvey, *Spaces of Capital: Towards a Critical Geography* (New York: Routledge, 2001) and "Globalization and the 'Spatial Fix,'"

Geographische Review 2 (2001): 23–30. In short, a spatial fix is an internal structure of repair (fix) for capitalist crises that grounds (fixes) capital in land. On the concept of "prison fix," see Ruth Wilson Gilmore, *Golden Gulag: Prisons, Surplus, Crisis, and Opposition in Globalizing California* (Berkeley: University of California Press, 2007).

74. Gilmore, *Golden Gulag*; Ruth Wilson Gilmore, "Globalization and U.S. Prison Growth: From Military Keynesianism to Post-Keynesian Militarism," *Race and Class* 40, nos. 2–3 (1998–99): 177–88. On gentrification, see Neil Smith, *The New Urban Frontier: Gentrification and the Revanchist City* (London: Routledge, 1996).

75. For a study of hate crime laws in Germany and how they target migrant populations, see Haritaworn, "Queer Injuries" and "Colorful Bodies in the Multikulti Metropolis." For another analysis of homonormativity in Europe, see Fatima El-Tayeb, *European Others: Queering Ethnicity in Postnational Europe* (Minneapolis: University of Minnesota Press, 2011). Also see Reddy, *Freedom with Violence*.

76. Mary Poovey, "Figures of Arithmetic, Figures of Speech: The Discourse of Statistics in the 1830s," in *Questions of Evidence: Proof, Practice, and Persuasion across the Disciplines*, ed. by James Chandler, Arnold I. Davidson, and Harry Harootunian (Chicago: University of Chicago Press, 1994), 420.

77. Self-determination itself can be a contradictory concept, moored to the logics of settler or imperial sovereignty. See Denise Ferreira da Silva, *Toward a Global Idea of Race* (Minneapolis: University of Minnesota Press, 2007).

78. José Esteban Muñoz, *Cruising Utopia: The Then and There of Queer Futurity* (New York: New York University Press, 2009).

79. See Self, *American Babylon*; Rhomberg, *No There There*; Eric Schneider, *Vampires, Dragons, and Egyptian Kings: Youth Gangs in Postwar New York* (Princeton: Princeton University Press, 1999).

80. For a history of LGBT activism in Los Angeles, see Faderman and Timmons, *Gay L.A.*; in Philadelphia, see Stein, *City of Sisterly and Brotherly Loves*; in Chicago, see Timothy Stewart-Winter, "Raids, Rights, and Rainbow Coalitions: Sexuality and Race in Chicago Politics, 1950–2000," PhD diss., University of Chicago, 2009; in Washington, D.C., see Kwame Holmes, "Chocolate to Rainbow City: The Dialectics of Black and Gay Community Formation in Postwar Washington, D.C., 1946–1978," PhD diss., University of Illinois at Urbana-Champaign, 2011. In many cities, activists made deft use of the media to critique policing. See Martin D. Meeker Jr., *Contacts Desired: Gay and Lesbian Communications and Community, 1940s–1970s* (Chicago: University of Chicago Press, 2006).

81. An uneven treatment of each city is manifested in this book. The first chapter looks primarily at San Francisco, reflecting the early emphasis on police violence among homophile activists there. Chapters 2 and 3 examine both cities, with a slight emphasis on the San Francisco area. Chapter 4 focuses on a national organization that began in New York and moved to Washington, D.C. The final chapter is on New York; the site of the only national organization dedicated to LGBT antiviolence activism and the ground zero of quality-of-life policing. I repeat that this book is not a movement history nor a comparative urban study, but a series of historical case studies with distinctly spatial features.

82. Lisa Lowe, *Immigrant Acts: On Asian American Cultural Politics* (Durham: Duke University Press, 1996).

83. For a brilliant analysis of second-wave feminism that is inclusive of the political work done by those not necessarily identified as feminist per se, see Anne Enke, *Finding the Movement: Sexuality, Contested Space, and Feminist Activism* (Durham: Duke University Press, 2007).

84. For a discussion of how announcing the limits of centering whiteness recenters

whiteness, see Andrea Smith, *Native Americans and the Christian Right: The Gendered Politics of Unlikely Alliances* (Durham: Duke University Press, 2008), xxvi–xxvii.

85. Tongson, *Relocations*, 50. The term *cultural style* is Tongson citing Chauncey, *Gay New York*.

86. Tongson, *Relocations*, 48.

87. In recent years the far rings of development in formerly rural areas have also faltered, while the middle places—often referred to as exurbs—have maintained more of the exclusive economic and racial characteristics formerly associated with suburbs. See Dolores Hayden, *Building Suburbia: Green Fields and Urban Growth, 1820–2000* (New York: Vintage, 2004).

88. With this use of *risk*, I hope to complement Tongson's critique of the turn to risk in queer studies by highlighting those queer subjects who are considered *risky* and thus are disavowed by or appropriated within dominant queer cultures.

89. In much the same way that this book does not extensively analyze the varied uses of the phrase *safe space*, it also does not trace the travels of the concept of *gay ghetto*. There is much to analyze here, from the use of *ghetto* as a term that is at once affirmative and derogatory, to the different (and often contradictory) understandings of forced containment behind the most popular modifications of that term (Jewish versus black versus gay). In addition, as Emily Hobson pointed out to me, the concept has been used to refer to aspects of gay life not necessarily staged on the neighborhood level: as a locked-in mind-set or forced set of cultural practices. For all of those reasons, I use *gay enclave* or *gay neighborhood* unless I am trying to point to a specific use of *gay ghetto*.

90. For speculation as to whether neighborhoods still are—and will remain—so prized among lesbians and gays, see Ghaziani, "There Goes the Gayborhood?" This book argues that even as gay neighborhoods decline in gay residence and business, the gay identity of many of these neighborhoods sustains and continues to work on behalf of anticrime efforts.

91. For an analysis of how teleology structures narratives of history and homosexuality, see Madhavi Menon, "Spurning Teleology in *Venus and Adonis*," GLQ 11, no. 4 (2005): 491–519; Heather Love, *Feeling Backward: Loss and the Politics of Queer History* (Cambridge: Harvard University Press, 2007). For other important work on sexuality and temporality, see Dana Luciano, *Arranging Grief: Sacred Time and the Body in Nineteenth Century America* (New York: New York University Press, 2007); Elizabeth Freeman, *Time Binds: Queer Temporalities, Queer Histories* (Durham: Duke University Press, 2010).

92. For an essay about some of the limits of narratives of improvement, see Kevin P. Murphy, "Gay Was Good: Progress, Homonormativity, and Oral History," in *Queer Twin Cities: Twin Cities GLBT Oral History Project*, ed. Kevin P. Murphy, Jennifer L. Pierce, and Larry Knopp (Minneapolis: University of Minnesota Press, 2010), 305–18.

93. Early and foundational work on this topic was done by Susan Stryker and appeared in Members of the Gay and Lesbian Historical Society of Northern California, "MTF Transgender Activism in the Tenderloin and Beyond, 1966–1975," GLQ 4, no. 2 (1998): 349–72; Stryker, *Transgender History*; and *Screaming Queens: The Riot at Compton's Cafeteria* (directed by Susan Stryker and Victor Silverman, 2005). Also see Kathleen Connell and Paul Gabriel, "The Power of Broken Hearts: The Origin and Evolution of the Folsom Street Fair," http://folsomstreetfair.org/history/. More recent scholarship includes Carter, *Stonewall*; Josh Sides, *Erotic City: Sexual Revolutions and the Making of Modern San Francisco* (New York: Oxford University Press, 2009); Jonathan Bell, "'To Strive for Economic and Social Justice': Welfare, Sexuality, and Liberal Politics in San Francisco in the 1960s," *Journal of Policy History* 22, no. 2 (2010): 192–225; Jonathan Bell,

California Crucible: The Forging of Modern American Liberalism (Philadelphia: University of Pennsylvania Press, 2012); and Martin D. Meeker Jr., "The Queerly Disadvantaged and the Making of San Francisco's War on Poverty, 1964–1967," *Pacific Historical Review* 81, no. 1 (2012): 21–59. On the organization Vanguard, see Stryker, *Transgender History*; *Screaming Queens*; Justin Suran, "Coming Out against the War: Antimilitarism and the Politicization of Homosexuality in the Era of Vietnam," *American Quarterly* 53, no. 3 (2001): 452–88; Jennifer Worley, "'Street Power' and the Claiming of Public Space: San Francisco's 'Vanguard' and Pre-Stonewall Queer Radicalism," in *Captive Genders: Trans Embodiment and the Prison Industrial Complex*, ed. Eric A. Stanley and Nat Smith (Oakland, CA: AK, 2011), 41–56; Betty Luther Hillman, "'The Most Profoundly Revolutionary Act a Homosexual Can Engage In': Drag and the Politics of Gender Presentation in the San Francisco Liberation Movement, 1964–1972," *Journal of the History of Sexuality* 20, no. 1 (January 2011): 153–81; and Joey Plaster, "Imagined Conversations and Activist Lineages: Public Histories of Queer Homeless Youth Organizing and the Policing of Public Space in San Francisco's Tenderloin, 1960s and Present," *Radical History Review* 113 (Spring 2012): 99–109.

94. Heather Love, *Feeling Backward*. My use of the terms *backward* and *shameful* are borrowed from Love, but what I describe here are not those who feel shame about their queerness or who are considered backward for their shame. Instead, I describe those who are named as shameful for expressing pride as they exclude others. Radical commentators often see such examples of activism as backward (that is, not progressive) and seek to shame such pride; although I tend to be in agreement, I am trying to approach writing this history differently. As I suggest later, self-hate and alienation are the scorned targets not only of prideful but also of much antipride activism, and they often overlap in the affirmation of the healthy self. I also want to make the related point that although shaming remains a powerful activist strategy, it is not the same as sitting within shame, a fact also noted by Love.

95. For a discussion of queer archives and the place of feelings within them, see Cvetkovich, *An Archive of Feelings*.

96. In *Moving Politics*, Gould highlights how ACT UP activists turned shame into shaming to mixed effect.

97. I only list in the bibliography those interviews that I ultimately used; I conducted an additional six interviews that did not make it into the final project.

98. The tension between individual intention and collective action serves as testimony to the wide influence of liberal political ideals. Although the individual choices that activists made are significant, especially as they pressed themselves into public view and reflected the viewpoints of those who would replicate strategies and visions in organizations that followed, my approach diverges from those that buffer collective actions from criticism by contextualizing individuals' motives or from those that suggest individual intention to be the primary lens for understanding political movements. My method does not seek to dispense with the question of responsibility or agency nor to deny the significance of experience; rather, I focus my lens on group actions over individual intentions, while highlighting original participants' perspectives.

99. See Francesca Polletta, *Freedom Is an Endless Meeting: Democracy in American Social Movements* (Chicago: University of Chicago Press, 2002).

100. It is important to note that this book is organized around case studies of activist organizations rather than intellectual debates within print sources. Although I include examples from these sources, I do not review the full editorial history of the politics of violence and neighborhood.

101. Archives less frequently hold the papers of groups whose members were primarily women of color or were far-left identified. This is a reflection of archives' collecting tendencies as well as the distrust felt by marginalized peoples and movements. As I discuss in chapter 3, many women of color and radicals moved between movements; this too contributes to the absence of such sources in LGBT archives. I will also add here that I noted authorship of documents cited here when that information was missing in the archives but revealed to me through interviews and I was able to confirm that the attribution was likely correct.

102. For an analysis of how the politics of AIDS has affected queer political organizing, see Sarah Schulman, *The Gentrification of the Mind: Witness to a Lost Imagination* (Berkeley: University of California Press, 2012).

103. Here it is worth mentioning that while there is long-term continuity provided by members who later became staff, the membership itself changes quite frequently. As a result, I primarily interviewed individuals on staff who also had been members.

104. On the mixed dynamics of representation, see Gayatri Chakravorty Spivak, "Can the Subaltern Speak?," in *Marxism and the Interpretation of Culture*, ed. Carey Nelson and Lawrence Grossberg (Urbana: University of Illinois Press, 1988), 271–313. For different approaches to the ethnography of social movements, see Michael Burawoy et al., *Ethnography Unbound: Power and Resistance in the Modern Metropolis* (Berkeley: University of California Press, 1991); June Nash, ed. *Social Movements: An Anthropological Reader* (Malden, MA: Blackwell, 2005); Jeff Goodwin and James M. Jasper, eds. *The Social Movements Reader: Cases and Concepts*, 2nd ed. (Malden, MA: Blackwell, 2009).

105. For a recent critique of the terms of equality in LGBT/queer politics, see the writings of the collective Against Equality at www.againstequality.org. Their written archive is organized around three themes: marriage, the military, and prison. Also see the individual writings of Yasmin Nair, a member of the collective, at www.yasminnair.net.

106. One exception is the history of the feminist left, which has critiqued the family if not sexual normalization. For a fuller discussion of the sexual politics of the left in the United States, see Svati P. Shah, "Sexuality and 'The Left': Thoughts on Intersections and Visceral Others," *Scholar and the Feminist Online* 7, no. 3 (2009), http://sfonline.barnard.edu/sexecon/shah_01.htm. For an analysis of the continuity between liberalism and Marxism in the treatment of identity see Ferguson, *Aberrations in Black*.

107. Wendy Brown, "Neoliberalism and the End of Liberal Democracy," *Theory and Event* 7, no. 1 (2003), http://muse.jhu.edu/journals/theory_and_event/v007/7.1brown.html.

108. Frantz Fanon, *The Wretched of the Earth*, trans. Constance Farrington (1965; New York: Grove, 2005).

109. This is not to idealize bodily autonomy nor to stigmatize immobility, but to value self-determination. See McRuer, *Crip Theory*.

110. Gilmore, *Golden Gulag*, 28.

111. Studs Terkel, "An Interview with James Baldwin," in *Conversations with James Baldwin*, ed. Fred L. Standley and Louis H. Pratt (Jackson: University Press of Mississippi, 1989), 21.

112. Terkel, "An Interview with James Baldwin," 21.

113. Butler discusses the issue of nonviolence throughout the chapter "The Question of Social Transformation" in *Undoing Gender*, 204–31.

114. For a history of safe sex see the documentary, *Sex in an Epidemic* (directed by Jean Carlomusto, 2010), as well as the book from which the documentary takes its title: Richard Berkowitz and Michael Callen, *How to Have Sex in an Epidemic: One Approach*

(New York: News from the Front Publications, 1983). Michael Shernoff, a former member of a safe streets patrol discussed in chapter 2, is included in the documentary discussing the term *safer sex*.

115. See Douglas Crimp, *Melancholia and Moralism: Essays on AIDS and Queer Politics* (Cambridge: MIT Press, 2002).

116. Tim Dean, *Unlimited Intimacy: Reflections on the Subculture of Barebacking* (Chicago: University of Chicago Press, 2009), 60, 62. Noting that all activities involve some risk, Dean posits the acceptance of sexual risk as a challenge to "'health' as an instrument of power" and its morality and responsibility mandates (63).

117. Anthony Giddens, "Risk and Responsibility," *Modern Law Review* 62, no. 1 (1999): 3.

118. Ulrich Beck, *Risk Society: Toward a New Modernity* (London: Sage, 1992).

119. Randy Martin, *The Financialization of Everyday Life* (Philadelphia: Temple University Press, 2002).

120. It is interesting that many safe streets activists moved into public health advocacy and approached AIDS via risk reduction. Michael Shernoff and Hank Wilson, two 1970s safe streets activists whom I interviewed, later became, respectively, the author of the only book on barebacking aside from Tim Dean (Michael Shernoff, *Without Condoms: Unprotected Sex, Gay Men, and Barebacking* [New York: Routledge, 2005]) and a zealous campaigner against poppers (Hank Wilson and John Lauritsen, *Death Rush: Poppers and AIDS* [New York: Pagan, 1986]). Both men passed away soon after I interviewed them.

121. As I clarify later, the homophile movement's ability to advocate for inclusion in public programs was distinct from the types of state funding that the antiviolence movement would achieve.

122. Although I name the pairing of violence and criminality as most central here, these dynamics regarding legitimacy are also instructive for understanding debates about gay marriage. Marriage is not only an institution of exclusion but also one of discipline—in particular of women, poor people, and people of color. It is a structure that people have been forced to enter in order to receive benefits, avoid criminal status, or achieve legitimation. For a group to demand entry into such an institution is to authorize that discipline and its structures of exclusion, even if the group seeking entry includes members who have been punished by or suffered from their previous exclusion from it. For a more detailed critique, see Farrow, "Is Gay Marriage Anti-Black?"

123. See Valentine, *Imagining Transgender*; Spade, *Normal Life*; Gayle Salamon, *Assuming a Body: Transgender and Rhetorics of Materiality* (New York: Columbia University Press, 2010).

124. D'Emilio, "Capitalism and Gay Identity."

125. Butler, *Undoing Gender*, 23.

126. Butler, *Undoing Gender*, 13.

127. This contention is also central to Valentine's argument. Because so much transgender activism since the 1990s has been organized around the claim that trans people are uniquely vulnerable to violence, this warrants a fuller treatment than I can provide here. Spade (*Normal Life*), Salamon (*Assuming a Body*), Halberstam (*In a Queer Time and Place*), and Valentine (*Imagining Transgender*) have all discussed related issues.

128. Peter Osborne and Lynne Segal, "Gender as Performance: An Interview with Judith Butler," *Radical Philosophy* 67 (Summer 1994): 38. This is not to idealize ACT UP but to hold it as one cited example; there are multiple forms of AIDS and antipoverty activism that have pushed in this direction. The Treatment Action Coalition in South Africa

is another organization that has pursued creative and militant forms of protest based on highlighted vulnerability. This is also a feature of the long legacy of hunger-strike activism; one recent example is the Mapuche nation in Chile (see Macarena Gómez-Barris, "Mapuche Hunger Acts: Epistemology of the Decolonial," *Transmodernity* 1, no. 3 [2012], http://www.escholarship.org/uc/item/6305p8vr).

129. James Baldwin, *Nobody Knows My Name* (New York: Dell, 1961), 117.

130. Lisa Duggan writes: "In responding to pathologizing representations of sexual minorities as violent or dangerous, it is important to resist the countermove of representing exclusion as innocence violated or nobility scorned. The moral terms of such melodramas limited the scope of political resistances in the United States throughout the twentieth century. At the start of the twenty-first, we need new narratives to claim greater equality without qualification or exclusion" (*Sapphic Slashers: Sex, Violence, and American Modernity* [Durham: Duke University Press, 2000], 200). I offer this as one such story.

131. I borrow the "not yet" from Muñoz's use of Ernest Bloch in *Cruising Utopia*.

1. "The White Ghetto"

Epigraph: Tom Ramsay, untitled and undated document, Box 15, Folder 4, Donald S. Lucas Papers, Gay, Lesbian, Bisexual, Transgender Historical Society, San Francisco, CA (hereafter Don Lucas Papers, GLBTHS).

1. *Report of the National Advisory Commission on Civil Disorders* (New York: Bantam, 1968), 396. It was best known as the Kerner Report, named after the commission's chair, Governor Otto Kerner Jr. of Illinois. See also David Boesel and Peter H. Rossi, eds., *Cities under Siege: An Anatomy of the Ghetto Riots, 1964–1968* (New York: Basic Books, 1971); Nikhil Pal Singh, *Black Is a Country: Race and the Unfinished Struggle for Democracy* (Cambridge: Harvard University Press, 2004).

2. The phrases *maximum feasible participation* and *community control* were central to War on Poverty rhetoric. For an insider discussion of the War on Poverty, see Daniel P. Moynihan, *Maximum Feasible Misunderstanding: Community Action in the War on Poverty* (New York: Free Press, 1970). For critical perspectives see Ralph M. Kramer, *Participation of the Poor: Comparative Community Case Studies in the War on Poverty* (Englewood Cliffs, NJ: Prentice Hall, 1969); Frances Fox Piven and Richard A. Cloward, *Poor People's Movements: Why They Succeed, How They Fail* (New York: Vintage, 1977), and *Regulating the Poor: The Functions of Public Welfare*, updated ed. (New York: Vintage, 1993); Alice O'Connor, *Poverty Knowledge: Social Science, Social Policy, and the Poor in Twentieth-Century U.S. History* (Princeton: Princeton University Press, 2001); Noel A. Cazenave, *Impossible Democracy: The Unlikely Success of the War on Poverty Community Action Programs* (Albany: State University of New York Press, 2007); Alyosha Goldstein, *Poverty in Common: The Politics of Community Action during the American Century* (Durham: Duke University Press, 2012). For a close look at San Francisco, see Kramer, *Participation of the Poor*; Daniel Crowe, *Prophets of Rage: The Black Freedom Struggle in San Francisco, 1945–1969* (New York: Garland, 2000). For nearby Oakland, see Robert O. Self, *American Babylon: Race and the Struggle for Postwar Oakland* (Princeton: Princeton University Press, 2003); Christopher Rhomberg, *No There There: Race, Class, and Political Community in Oakland* (Berkeley: University of California Press, 2004); Alondra Nelson, *Body and Soul: The Black Panther Party and the Fight against Medical Discrimination* (Minneapolis: University of Minnesota, 2011). Kramer's detailed study of the San Francisco EOC discusses the Central City campaign within the context of the citywide program but does not name the leading participation of homophile advocates.

3. The Mattachine Society was originally called the Mattachine Foundation. This overview is based in John D'Emilio, *Sexual Politics, Sexual Communities: The Making of a Homosexual Minority in the United States, 1940–1970* (Chicago: University of Chicago Press, 1983). Despite earlier challenges in the United States and Europe to the criminalization of sodomy and the stigma of same-sex desire, historians generally regard the U.S. homophile movement as the starting point for sustained lesbian and gay activism. Also see Mark Blasius and Shane Phelan, eds., *We Are Everywhere: A Historical Sourcebook of Gay and Lesbian Politics* (New York: Routledge, 1997).

4. For an overview of lesbian and gay life and examples of violence in the early to mid-twentieth-century United States, see Allan Bérubé, *Coming Out under Fire: The History of Gay Men and Women in World War Two* (New York: Free Press, 1990); Elizabeth Lapovsky Kennedy and Madeline Davis, *Boots of Leather, Slippers of Gold: The History of a Lesbian Community* (New York: Penguin, 1994); George Chauncey, *Gay New York: Gender, Urban Culture, and the Making of the Gay Male World, 1890–1940* (New York: Basic Books, 1994); Donna Penn, "The Sexualized Women: The Lesbian, the Prostitute and the Containment of Female Sexuality In Postwar America," in *Not June Cleaver: Women and Gender in Postwar America, 1945–1960*, ed. Joanne Meyerowitz (Philadelphia: Temple University Press, 1994), 358–81; Brett Beemyn, ed., *Creating a Place for Ourselves: Lesbian, Gay, and Bisexual Community Histories* (New York: Routledge, 1997); Lisa Duggan, *Sapphic Slashers: Sex, Violence, and American Modernity* (Durham: Duke University Press, 2000); and Nan Alamilla Boyd, *Wide Open Town: A History of Queer San Francisco to 1965* (Berkeley: University of California Press, 2005).

5. Thus the time line for the increased safety of lesbians and gay men must be reconsidered. For example, John Howard's *Men Like That: A Southern Queer History* (Chicago: University of Chicago Press, 1999) contrasts the violence directed at civil rights activists during the 1960s in Mississippi—in which charges of sexual deviancy were invoked—with the relative protection afforded to gay white men during the 1950s, which is often considered the height of antigay sentiment. Duggan's *Sapphic Slashers* also shows how the white supremacy that fueled racial violence in the late nineteenth century was entwined with dominant narratives of gender and sexual transgression.

6. See Margot Canaday, *The Straight State: Sexuality and Citizenship in Twentieth-Century America* (Princeton: Princeton University Press, 2009).

7. For example, homophile members invested in public relations campaigns to improve views on homosexuality reached out to writers such as Christopher Isherwood and the psychologist Evelyn Hooker (see D'Emilio, *Sexual Politics, Sexual Communities*, 73). Boyd elaborates: "Homophile organizations encouraged members to be visible only as they complied with the law and embraced the limited entitlements of loyal citizenship—they eschewed overt or outlaw characters such as cross-dressers and sex offenders" (*Wide Open Town*, 174).

8. Kennedy and Davis, *Boots of Leather, Slippers of Gold*, 93.

9. Boyd, *Wide Open Town*, especially 87 and 108–47.

10. See D'Emilio, *Sexual Politics, Sexual Communities*, 192–95; Boyd, *Wide Open Town*, 231–36. The attorneys were acquitted on February 11, 1965 ("Mardi Gras Ball Attorneys Acquitted," *Vector*, February 1965, 1, Periodicals, Gay, Lesbian, Bisexual, Transgender Historical Society, San Francisco, CA). Although these kinds of conflicts existed in other cities, few gained equal publicity or provided the same traction for future organized political response. One of the few other events that did gain some publicity and that led to a formal response was the 1967 police raid on the Los Angeles Black Cat bar. Members of the homophile organization Personal Rights in Defense and Education worked

with the leftist organization the Right of Assembly and Movement Committee to plan coordinated protests indicting the Los Angeles Police Department's brutality (see Lillian Faderman and Stuart Timmons, *Gay L.A.: A History of Sexual Outlaws, Power Politics, and Lipstick Lesbians* [New York: Basic Books, 2006], 154–58; Emily Hobson, "Policing Gay L.A.: Mapping Racial Divides in the Homophile Era, 1950–1967," in *The Rising Tide of Color: Race, Radicalism, and Repression on the Pacific Coast and Beyond*, ed. Moon-Ho Jung [Seattle: University of Washington Press, forthcoming]).

11. Lewis E. Durham stayed at Glide until 1972, and Robert Theodore (Ted) Mc-Ilvenna remained active in sexual politics for years to come. For more information on both men, as well as other figures associated with Glide, see "Urban Specialist Pastors and Their Supporters," *Vanguard Revisited* [Megan Rohrer], Saturday, October 17, 2009, http://vanguardrevisited.blogspot.com/2009/10/urban-specialist-pastors-and-their .html. The Glide Urban Center and its Young Adult Project had helped to organize a conference called The Young Adult in the Metropolis, on October 5–9, 1964. See the conference booklet in Box 14, Folder 22, Don Lucas Papers, GLBTHS.

12. Del Martin and Phyllis Lyon, *Lesbian/Woman* (San Francisco: Glide, 1972).

13. Chester Hartman with Sarah Carnochan, *City for Sale: The Transformation of San Francisco*, rev. and updated ed. (Berkeley: University of California Press, 2002), 8.

14. For more descriptions of the area and some of these political contexts, see Chester Hartman, *Yerba Buena: Land Grab and Community Resistance in San Francisco* (San Francisco: Glide, 1974); Kathleen Connell and Paul Gabriel, "The Power of Broken Hearts: The Origin and Evolution of the Folsom Street Fair," http://folsomstreetfair .org/history/; Gayle Rubin, "The Miracle Mile: South of Market and Gay Male Leather, 1962–1997," in *Reclaiming San Francisco: History, Politics, Culture*, ed. James Brooks, Chris Carlsson, and Nancy J. Peters (San Francisco: City Lights, 1998), 247–72; Members of the Gay and Lesbian Historical Society of Northern California, "MTF Transgender Activism in the Tenderloin and Beyond, 1966–1975," GLQ 4, no. 2 (1998): 349–72; *Screaming Queens: The Riot at Compton's Cafeteria* (directed by Susan Stryker and Victor Silverman, 2005); and the finding aids, oral histories, and other materials produced by Martin Meeker and Paul Gabriel as part of the GLBTHS.

15. Hartman, *City for Sale*, 8.

16. See John Mollenkopf, *The Contested City* (Princeton: Princeton University Press, 1983); Hartman, *City for Sale*; Crowe, *Prophets of Rage*. A1 and A2 were but the most recent examples of displacement in San Francisco's Western Addition. Earlier displacements included that of the Ohlone people at the end of the eighteenth century and the forced removal and internment of Japanese Americans during World War II (the latter was also aided by the designation of the Western Addition as a slum; see Sandra C. Taylor, *Jewel of the Desert: Japanese American Internment at Topaz* [Berkeley: University of California Press, 1993]).

17. Baldwin made this comment in an interview with the psychologist Kenneth Clark in the 1963 documentary *The Negro and the American Promise* (directed by Fred Barzyk and produced by Henry Morgenthau III). The interview followed a tour Baldwin had taken of the Western Addition and Bayview–Hunters Point neighborhoods that had been filmed by San Francisco's KQED television station ("Take This Hammer," San Francisco Bay Area Television Archive, https://diva.sfsu.edu/collections/sfbatv/bundles/187041). In the film, Orville Luster, the executive director of the organization Youth for Service, leads the tour and clarifies the fact that by "redevelopment" he means "removal of Negroes." The term "Negro removal" can be considered part of the history of the African American left and press relabeling of policies that negatively affected African Americans.

The New Deal was referred to as "the raw deal," and the National Recovery Act of 1933 as "the Negro run around." See Joe William Trotter Jr., "From a Raw Deal to a New Deal? 1929–1945," in *To Make Our World Anew: A History of African Americans*, ed. Robin D. G. Kelley and Earl H. Lewis (Oxford: Oxford University Press, 2000), 409–44.

18. See James Sobredo, "From Manila Bay to Daly City: Filipinos in San Francisco," in *Reclaiming San Francisco: History, Politics, Culture*, ed. James Brooks, Chris Carlsson, and Nancy J. Peters (San Francisco: City Lights, 1998), 273–86.

19. Members of the Gay and Lesbian Historical Society of Northern California, "MTF Transgender Activism in the Tenderloin and Beyond," 31. See also Susan Stryker, *Transgender History* (Berkeley, CA: Seal, 2008).

20. The Fillmore is a section of the Western Addition, but the two names are often used interchangeably. Urban renewal efforts were in large part responsible for the rhetorical shift from the *Fillmore* to *Western Addition*. The use of the name Fillmore indexes the neighborhood's African American population in particular. For the sake of clarity, I primarily use the name Western Addition.

21. Some sources refer to *the* Central City and others drop the article. Activist sources tend to favor the former and city sources opt for the latter; since this history focuses on social movement perspectives, I have chosen to use the article for consistency, although I sometimes omit it as well.

22. See Timothy J. Gilfoyle, *City of Eros: New York City, Prostitution, and the Commercialization of Sex, 1790–1920* (New York: W. W. Norton, 1992); Kevin Mumford, *Interzones: Black/White Sex Districts in Chicago and New York in the Early Twentieth Century* (New York: Columbia University Press, 1997); Nayan Shah, *Contagious Divides: Epidemics and Race in San Francisco's Chinatown* (Berkeley: University of California Press, 2001); Chauncey, *Gay New York*.

23. Rev. Edward Hansen, "Night Ministry in the Tenderloin," October 13, 1965, Ed Hansen Papers, Gay, Lesbian, Bisexual, Transgender Historical Society, San Francisco, CA (hereafter Ed Hansen Papers, GLBTHS). This piece might have been part of a sermon, since it resembled another document titled "The Church and the Tenderloin" that Hansen later described as such in a letter home.

24. Georg Simmel, "The Metropolis and Mental Life" (1903), in *The Blackwell City Reader*, 2nd ed., ed. Gary Bridge and Sophie Watson (Malden, MA: Wiley-Blackwell, 2010), 103–10.

25. Simmel, "The Metropolis and Mental Life," 108.

26. Jonathan Bell's *California Crucible: The Forging of Modern American Liberalism* (Philadelphia: University of Pennsylvania Press, 2012) and Martin Meeker's "The Queerly Disadvantaged and the Making of San Francisco's War on Poverty, 1964–1967," *Pacific Historical Review* 81, no. 1 (2012): 21–59, both discuss this same campaign, focusing on the participation of gay activists, but these publications came out too late for me to fully integrate them into my argument. I discuss Jonathan Bell, "'To Strive for Economic and Social Justice': Welfare, Sexuality, and Liberal Politics in San Francisco in the 1960s," *Journal of Policy History* 22, no. 2 (2010), which is revised in *California Crucible*, later in this chapter and I have integrated references to Meeker's essay in my notes. Bell's book situates this campaign within the broader context of modern liberalism, arguing for the significance of California in developing a politics that sought to unite economic and civil rights interests and that included a broad diversity of groups, and he analyzes the history of gay rights alongside the politics of welfare. Meeker focuses on the assertion of a minority identity in the campaign, and he gives the most detailed context for the operation of San Francisco's Economic Opportunity Council

and the individual perspectives of key players (he also draws on Kramer, *The Partici-pation of the Poor*). Ultimately, Bell analyzes the debates in San Francisco as a way to understand the emergence of modern liberalism in the United States more generally. In contrast, Meeker and I focus more specifically on its significance for understanding the formal lesbian and gay movement that followed. (Meeker also analyzes the place of this campaign in the history of San Francisco municipal politics.) Nonetheless, Meeker and I come to different understandings about what this means for the landscape of LGBT politics more generally.

27. Kramer, *Participation of the Poor*, 53.

28. The group was first called the North and South of Market Target Area Commit-tee and later named the Central City Citizens Committee, which was also referred to as the Central City Citizens Council. Both versions of the name were written up with inconsistent punctuation: sometimes "Citizen's," other times "Citizens," and still other times "Citizens'." This is also the case for the organization Citizens Alert, which I discuss later in the chapter, as well as for the neighborhood Hunters Point, the official name of which has also changed over time. For the sake of consistency, I have chosen to use no apostrophe for all three organizations and the neighborhood throughout the book, and to try to preserve the given punctuation when quoting primary sources.

29. Mentioned by Lucas in an interview with Paul Gabriel. See transcript of Paul Gabriel interview with Don Lucas, December 30, 1996–February 28, 1998 (ten sessions), vol. 1, p. 251, Oral History Collection 97-032, Gay, Lesbian, Bisexual, Transgender His-torical Society, San Francisco, CA (hereafter Gabriel interview with Lucas, Oral History Collection, GLBTHS).

30. Central City Citizens' Committee, "The Central City Ghetto of San Francisco," Box 15, Folder 6, Don Lucas Papers, GLBTHS. Although this report is undated, a docu-ment labeled CC-TLC-66 (Box 15, Folder 26, ibid.) suggests it was released in November 1965.

31. Rev. Edward Hansen, Mark Forrester, and Rev. Fred Bird, "The Tenderloin Ghetto: The Young Reject in Our Society," Box 15, Folder 7, Don Lucas Papers, GLBTHS. The release date of January 12, 1966, was announced in a document labeled CC-TLC-66 (Box 15, Folder 26, ibid.). "The Tenderloin Ghetto" was also to be accompanied by "A Funding Proposal for the Tenderloin Project," 1966, Box 15, Folder 26, ibid. Later in this chapter, I discuss another version of the "Tenderloin Ghetto" report titled "The White Ghetto."

32. Letter from Ed Hansen to his parents, March 27, 1966, Ed Hansen Papers, GLBTHS. Hansen reported that the first meeting had been held the previous Monday. A report of that meeting can be found in "Minutes of the T.L.C.," March 21, 1966, Box 20, Folder 21, Don Lucas Papers, GLBTHS. The Tenderloin Committee, "Proposal for Confronting the Tenderloin Problem," 1966, Box 15, Folder 1, Don Lucas Papers, GLBTHS.

33. The Tenderloin Committee, "Proposal for Confronting the Tenderloin Problem."

34. The Mattachine Society, "Proposal for Confronting the Tenderloin Problem," 1966, Box 15, Folder 1, Don Lucas Papers, GLBTHS.

35. The Mattachine Society, "Proposal for Confronting the Tenderloin Problem."

36. The Tenderloin Committee, "Proposal for Confronting the Tenderloin Problem."

37. Donovan Bess, "The Cops Vs. City's Sin Jungle," *San Francisco Chronicle*, February 25, 1966; Donovan Bess, "Tenderloin's Exiles of Sin," *San Francisco Chronicle*, February 24, 1966 (above the masthead read: "S.F. Sin Survey: A Neon Sex Jungle"); Donovan Bess, "In the Tenderloin Underground: Stories of 'Boys for Sale,'" *San Francisco Chronicle*, March 2, 1966 (all clippings are in Ed Hansen Papers, GLBTHS).

38. "The Tenderloin Report Rejected," *Cruise News and World Report*, May 1966, "Guy Strait Publications, 1961–1967," San Francisco/Bay Area Gay and Lesbian Microfilm Serial Collection, Gay, Lesbian, Bisexual, Transgender Historical Society, San Francisco, CA. The article indicated that members of the Council on Religion and the Homosexual had rejected the report, accusing it of provoking police violence. The writer (presumably Strait) also concurred with the suspicions of Carlos Lara, owner of a popular Tenderloin hangout called Chukkers, that Mattachine members were exploiting the area for the benefits of federal money or simply as spectacle. Nonetheless, it is important to note that many business owners act out of economic interests despite familiarity with local marginalized figures. The claim that activists or reformers are outsiders has long been made to support the status quo, even if it may appear more culturally competent.

39. In 1972 the Methodist youth magazine *motive* published two issues (albeit their last) on gay liberation and lesbian feminism. See David Hollinger, "After Cloven Tongues of Fire: Ecumenical Protestantism and the Modern American Encounter with Diversity," *Journal of American History* 98, no. 1 (2011): 21–48.

40. Gunnar Myrdal, *An American Dilemma: The Negro Problem and Modern Democracy* (1944; Piscataway, NJ: Transaction, 1995); also see Alice O'Connor's assessment in *Poverty Knowledge*, 98.

41. See Daryl Michael Scott, *Contempt and Pity: Social Policy and the Image of the Damaged Black Psyche, 1880–1996* (Chapel Hill: University of North Carolina Press, 1997).

42. For example, the work of Kenneth Clark, the social psychologist, was cited in the *Brown v. Board of Education*, 347 U.S. 483 (1954) decision. A longer list of examples would include Kenneth B. Clark, *Dark Ghetto: Dilemmas of Social Power* (New York: Harper, 1965); E. Franklin Frazier, *The Negro Family in the United States* (Chicago: University of Chicago Press, 1939); and W. E. B. Du Bois, *The Philadelphia Negro* (1899; Philadelphia: University of Pennsylvania Press, 1995).

43. Joanne Meyerowitz, "'How Common Culture Shapes the Separate Lives': Sexuality, Race, and Mid-Twentieth Century Social Constructionist Thought," *Journal of American History* 96, no. 4 (2010): 1069. Meyerowitz shows how the historiography of racial and homosexual advocacy maps two trajectories: on the one hand, a challenge to biologically deterministic theories of race through an emphasis on culture and behavior and, on the other hand, a renouncing of psychological cures for homosexuality. Instead, Meyerowitz traces the overlaps between these areas of study and social intervention. The homosexuality studies focused more on parenting than on society, but both lines of research ultimately looked at the mutual influence of each. That said, some researchers did name homosexuality as a problem and treated it as a negative response to dominant social ideology; in some cases, homosexuals were theorized to be like racists who suffered from "incomplete" personalities (1076) or like those damaged by new American gender roles (1078–79).

44. See Jennifer Terry, *An American Obsession: Science, Medicine, and Homosexuality in Modern Society* (Chicago: University of Chicago Press, 1999); Chad Heap, *Slumming: Sexual and Racial Encounters in American Nightlife, 1885–1940* (Chicago: University of Chicago Press, 2009).

45. The term "tangle of pathology" is the heading of chapter 4 of *The Negro Family: The Case for National Action*. The full report can be found on the website of the U.S. Department of Labor: http://www.dol.gov/oasam/programs/history/moynchapter1.htm.

46. The concept of the "culture of poverty" is credited to the anthropologist Oscar Lewis's description of a "subculture of poverty" in his book *Five Families: Mexican Case Studies in the Culture of Poverty* (New York: Basic Books, 1959).

47. Kevin Mumford, "Untangling Pathology: The Moynihan Report and Homosexual Damage, 1965–1975," *Journal of Policy History* 24, no. 1 (2012): 53–73.

48. Richard A. Cloward and Lloyd E. Ohlin, *Delinquency and Opportunity: A Theory of Delinquent Gangs* (New York: Free Press, 1960).

49. In some contexts, black nationalism became associated with psychosis even as some scholars, such as Kenneth Clark, were more ambivalent about it. See Scott, *Contempt and Pity*; O'Connor, *Poverty Knowledge*; Jonathan Metzl, *The Protest Psychosis: How Schizophrenia Became a Black Disease* (Boston: Beacon, 2010). For context on the tensions between liberal and nationalist black politics, see Singh, *Black Is a Country*. It is also important to note that Black Power, too, would draw on the language of psychology; see, for example, Stokely Carmichael's October 29, 1966, "Black Power" speech in Berkeley, California (the audio and a transcription of the speech are available on the website of American RadioWorks of American Public Media: http://americanradioworks.publicradio.org/features/sayitplain/scarmichael.html). The differences and resonances between racial liberal versus black nationalist understandings of the psychic injuries of racism are worth exploring more, and suggest their shared frameworks as analyzed in Roderick A. Ferguson, *Aberrations in Black: Toward a Queer of Color Critique* (Minneapolis: University of Minnesota Press, 2004).

50. Edward Hansen, Fred Bird, Mark Forrester, and Victor J. Des Marais Jr., "The White Ghetto: Youth and Young Adults in the Tenderloin Area of Downtown San Francisco," Box 15, Folder 5, Don Lucas Papers, GLBTHS. This item is also in Ed Hansen Papers [attached to cover letter dated February 1, 1966], GLBTHS. The cover letter demonstrates that it was used to reach out for support and was signed by Hansen and Forrester.

51. Among the statistics cited about the area were that 41 percent of its families made less than $4,000 a year (which, the report noted, was the lowest of all of San Francisco's War on Poverty target areas); 67 percent of the residents of North of Market [the area just north of Market Street that included the Tenderloin] and 42 percent of those of South of Market were single adults not living with relatives and earning well below the poverty line; the area had the city's highest rate of single parents, infant mortality, juvenile delinquency, and elderly people, as well as the highest percentage of unemployment of all EOC areas, at 11.5–19 percent; and that it had crisis levels of crowded housing and poor education. The report also cited 6.4 percent of the area's residents as "Negro," 6 percent as having a Spanish surname, and 5.1 percent as other nonwhite (presumably many people in the latter two categories were Filipino). Central City Citizens' Committee, "The Central City Ghetto of San Francisco," Box 15, Folder 6, Don Lucas Papers, GLBTHS.

52. Connell and Gabriel, "The Power of Broken Hearts."

53. See Thomas Sugrue, *The Origins of the Urban Crisis: Race and Inequality in Postwar Detroit* (Princeton: Princeton University Press, 1996); George Lipsitz, *The Possessive Investment in Whiteness: How White People Profit from Identity Politics* (Philadelphia: Temple University Press, 1998); Daniel Martinez HoSang, *Racial Propositions: Ballot Initiatives and the Making of Postwar California* (Berkeley: University of California Press, 2010).

54. HoSang, *Racial Propositions*, 16–19.

55. For a brief discussion of these dynamics, see Meeker, "The Queerly Disadvantaged." Also, in a letter the Mattachine Society sent to other homophile organizations during the campaign, they wrote, "We know it [the Office of Economic Opportunity] has already employed many leaders of the Civil Rights movement in the U.S., and that these people, now on a government payroll, are going to be less vociferous, providing the benefits to the people that are proposed in the program actually filter down to where

they DO benefit the poor." The letter also clarified that other homophile activists should be mindful that the language of the report was chosen strategically, and that "eminent psychiatrists" were helping them make their writing "more validly scientific." Letter from Mattachine Society to Organizations in the Homophile Movement, March 21, 1966, Box 19, Folder 15, Phyllis Lyon and Del Martin Papers, Gay, Lesbian, Bisexual, Transgender Historical Society, San Francisco, CA (hereafter Lyon Martin Papers, GLBTHS).

56. Ed Hansen, "Dear Dads & Moms & Brothers & Sisters-in-law," letter, January 24, 1966, Ed Hansen Papers, GLBTHS. Here it is worth repeating the Mattachine Society's own investment in psychological research as well (see "San Jose Researchers in Psychology Project," *Town Talk*, August 15, 1965 [Periodicals, GLBTHS]).

57. Joanne Meyerowitz and Susan Stryker each showcase transsexual organizations that were part of Glide and linked to War on Poverty initiatives, in particular COG (standing for either or both Conversion Our Goal or Change: Our Goal) and, less so, the California Advancement for Transsexuals Society. This suggests the possibility of an early model for affirmative identification for transsexuals through urban uplift as well, although in later years, medicine more than neighborhood would provide a context for this consolidation. See Meyerowitz, *How Sex Changed: A History of Transsexuality in the United States* (Cambridge: Harvard University Press, 2004); Stryker, *Transgender History*.

58. Canaday, *The Straight State*, 134.

59. Michael Omi and Howard Winant, *Racial Formation in the United States* (New York: Routledge, 1986).

60. HoSang, *Racial Propositions*, 20.

61. HoSang, *Racial Propositions*, 20.

62. In short time, the press would begin to clarify that the viability of a "gay ghetto" depended explicitly on responsible and regular gay rental (rather than social use) patterns. See Larry Carlson, "The Gay Rental," *Vector*, April–May 1968, 16–17, and Hector Simms, "New York Gay Ghettos," *Gay*, December 15, 1969, 4–5 (Periodicals, GLBTHS).

63. Khalil Gibran Muhammad discusses the North/South distinction as part of his detailed history of how criminality has been ascribed to African Americans and how the accusation and use of violence has operated in making that correlation (*The Condemnation of Blackness: Race, Crime, and the Making of Modern Urban America* [Cambridge: Harvard University Press, 2010]). Also, Scott describes research on so-called black rage in the mid-1960s (*Contempt and Pity*) and Metzl shows that black men during the late civil rights era were commonly diagnosed as having schizophrenia, which was considered by then to include a propensity to violence (*The Protest Psychosis*).

64. Scott, *Contempt and Pity*; Muhammad, *The Condemnation of Blackness*.

65. In many of his speeches Martin Luther King Jr. spoke of the limits of the idea of "maladjustment." Following is an excerpt of one such speech that he gave at the annual convention of the American Psychological Association (APA) in 1967, which was later published in *Journal of Social Issues* 24, No. 1 (1968), and is reprinted on the APA's website (http://www.apa.org/monitor/features/king-challenge.aspx). "You who are in the field of psychology have given us a great word. It is the word maladjusted. This word is probably used more than any other word in psychology. It is a good word; certainly it is good that in dealing with what the word implies you are declaring that destructive maladjustment should be destroyed. You are saying that all must seek the well-adjusted life in order to avoid neurotic and schizophrenic personalities. But on the other hand, I am sure that we will recognize that there are some things in our society, some things in our world, to which we should never be adjusted. There are some things concerning which we must always be maladjusted if we are to be people of good will. We must

never adjust ourselves to racial discrimination and racial segregation. We must never adjust ourselves to religious bigotry. We must never adjust ourselves to economic conditions that take necessities from the many to give luxuries to the few. We must never adjust ourselves to the madness of militarism, and the self-defeating effects of physical violence."

66. See James Polchin,"'Why Do They Strike Us?': Representing Violence and Sexuality, 1930–1950," PhD diss., New York University, 2002; Gayle Salamon, *Assuming a Body: Transgender and Rhetorics of Materiality* (New York: Columbia University Press, 2010).

67. Thank-you letters from Calvin Colt, Chairman of the Central City Citizen's Council, to Eduard Anderson, Chairman of the Mission Community Action Board, and to Joseph Wong, Chairman of the Chinatown Board, both dated March 18, 1966, Box 15, Folder 2, Don Lucas Papers, GLBTHS.

68. Letter from Ed Hansen to his parents, March 27, 1966, Ed Hansen Papers, GLBTHS.

69. The implications of the limited funds would be compounded in later years, when the federal government continued to scale back poverty funding and shifted to the Demonstration Cities and Metropolitan Development Act, best known as the Model Cities Program. Like the Community Action Program, Model Cities were to pick target areas for community-based programs to fight poverty and neighborhood blight. Unlike the Community Action Program, the Model Cities Program was administered by the Department of Housing and Urban Development and, in many places, supplanted existing institutions of community-based planning. See June Thomas Manning, "Model Cities Revisited: Issues of Race and Empowerment," in *Urban Planning and the African-American Community: In the Shadows*, ed. June Thomas Manning and Martha Ritzdorf (Thousand Oaks, CA: Sage, 1997), 143–63.

70. See Jeff Andrews, Acting Chairman, Western Addition Area Board, "Statement to the Economic Opportunity Council," November 1966, Box 13, Folder 13, Don Lucas Papers, GLBTHS. Wilfred Ussery was ousted from the Western Addition board for political reasons (he was later reinstated); he also served as the second national chairman of the Congress of Racial Equality. The statement by Andrews about his dismissal cited the "alleged anti-white racist indoctrination given staff members by Mr. N. Shabazz," an activist involved in campaigns across the city. Conflict also erupted around a purported incident of violence at an EOC meeting that resulted in the temporary stepping down of Judge Joseph Kennedy of the San Francisco Municipal Court, who had been chairman of the San Francisco EOC and was the second African American judge to serve in San Francisco (see EOC *Newsletter of the Economic Opportunity Council of San Francisco* ["published weekly to keep management informed of progressive action in the War on Poverty"], August 30, 1968, Box 12, Folder 13, Don Lucas Papers, GLBTHS). For further discussions of these incidents, also see Crowe, *Prophets of Rage*.

71. "Chairman Retires Under Fire: Heeds Pleas to Return," EOC *Newsletter of the Economic Opportunity Council of San Francisco*, August 30, 1968, Box 12, Folder 13, Don Lucas Papers, GLBTHS.

72. For a look at this event, see "1966 Hunters Point Rebellion: Recollections of Harold Brooks and Thomas Fleming," *San Francisco Bay View*, September 27, 2011, http://sfbayview .com/2011/1966-hunters-point-rebellion-recollections-of-harold-brooks-and-thomas -fleming/.

73. For a general discussion of the charged internal racial politics of the Western Addition board, see the correspondence between Arthur H. Coleman and Wilfred Ussery (December 29, 1966, and January 3, 1967). Other forms of conflict are nodded to in the meeting minutes of the San Francisco EOC Executive Committee, December 5 and 7,

1966, and January 4 and February 1, 1967, in Box 12, Folder 3, Don Lucas Papers, GLBTHS. Also see Kramer, *Participation of the Poor*; Crowe, *Prophets of Rage*.

74. For contextual information on Genie Bowie, see transcript, pp. 200–202, 281–82, Gabriel interview with Lucas, Oral History Collection, GLBTHS; for an example of her work in the Central City see Genie Bowie, "W Word for the 'Word': The Beauty of a Black People," *Central City Word*, February 7, 1968, Box 14, Folder 11, Don Lucas Papers, GLBTHS. For some of the critiques of Bowie and her defense against such accusations, see memos to Don Lucas and Don Ganoung dated July 22, 1968, from Don Lucas dated July 23, 1968, and other memos in Box 14, Folder 10, ibid. These critiques were presumably deemed unfounded since the interview with Lucas cited above also suggests that Bowie may have taken up Lucas's position in the Central City after he left.

75. A prior vote in March 2012 had rejected the target area. Ed Hansen's letter home about the May meeting suggested it was voted in unanimously: 24–0 (Hansen letter to parents, May 30, 1966, Ed Hansen Papers, GLBTHS). Meeker's extensive research within the EOC materials suggests a divided vote. For the most detailed discussions of internal EOC dynamics see Meeker, "The Queerly Disadvantaged," and Kramer, *Participation of the Poor*.

76. This success granted the area designation as a target area plus $125,000, support for an interim area board, and approval for at least $100,000 worth of social programs (Ed Hansen, letter to parents, May 30, 1966, Ed Hansen Papers, GLBTHS).

77. Organization flow chart, Box 13, Folder 1, Don Lucas Papers, GLBTHS. (Community Action Agencies were a part of the Community Action Program.)

78. O'Connor, *Poverty Knowledge*, 132.

79. O'Connor, *Poverty Knowledge*, 132.

80. For an analysis of the Community Action Program in the frame of empire, especially the language of underdevelopment, see Goldstein, *Poverty in Common*.

81. Wendell E. Pritchett, *Robert Clifton Weaver and the American City: The Life and Times of an Urban Reformer* (Chicago: University of Chicago Press, 2008), 252–54.

82. "CRH 'A Brief of Injustices' Published," *Vector*, September 1965, 9. Articles by Forrester often had freewheeling analyses of sexual and racial inequality, arguing that both "the Negro" and "the homosexuals" were social totems (Mark Forrester, "Totems," *Vector*, January 1965, 5), for the redistribution of power to social minorities (Mark Forrester, "A Nation of Sleepwalkers," *Vector*, August 1965, 4), and in support of Saul Alinsky's methods (Mark Forrester, "Alinsky Says 'Act,'" *Vector*, November 1965, 4).

83. John D'Emilio interview with Mark Forrester, December 9, 1976, Tape #A00467, Audiovisual Materials, International Gay Information Center Collection, Manuscripts and Archives Division, New York Public Library, New York, New York.

84. Martin D. Meeker Jr. writes: "the organization ceased to exist for all intents and purposes in 1967" ("Behind the Mask of Respectability: Reconsidering the Mattachine Society and Male Homophile Practice, 1950s and 1960s," *Journal of the History of Sexuality* 10, no. 1 [2001]: 111). On Mattachine's support, see endorsement letter from Harold L. Call, president, and Donald S. Lucas, executive secretary, Mattachine Society, n.d., in support of the fifth target area designation (Box 15, Folder 1, Don Lucas Papers, GLBTHS).

85. Transcript of Paul Gabriel interview with Bill Beardemphal [sic] and John De-Leon, August 11, 1997, p. 3, Oral History Collection # 97-030, Gay, Lesbian, Bisexual, Transgender Historical Society, San Francisco (hereafter Gabriel interview with Beardemphal [sic] and DeLeon, Oral History Collection, GLBTHS).

86. Boyd, *Wide Open Town*, 227–28.

87. Meeker, "Behind the Mask of Respectability." Although I interpret this dynamic

differently than Meeker does, I agree with his and Marc Stein's assessments that the homophile movement has been painted as conservative with too broad a brush (Marc Stein, *City of Sisterly and Brotherly Loves: Lesbian and Gay Philadelphia* [Chicago: University of Chicago Press, 2000]).

88. Stein, *City of Sisterly and Brotherly Loves*, 11.

89. Jacquelyn Dowd Hall, "The Long Civil Rights Movement and the Political Uses of the Past," *Journal of American History* 91, no. 4 (2005): 1233–63.

90. See Siobhan B. Somerville, "Queer *Loving*," GLQ 11, no. 3 (2005): 355–70; Janet E. Halley, "'Like Race' Arguments," in *What's Left of Theory: New Work on the Politics of Literary Theory*, ed. Judith Butler, John Guillory, and Kendall Thomas (New York: Routledge, 2000), 40–74.

91. O'Connor, *Poverty Knowledge*, 153–54.

92. Bell, "'To Strive for Economic and Social Justice,'" 218. Also see Felicia Kornbluh, *The Battle for Welfare Rights: Politics and Poverty in Modern America* (Philadelphia: University of Pennsylvania Press, 2007).

93. Nelson describes how nearby Oakland-based Black Panther activists crafted a "close-quarters critique of the War on Poverty," using their participation in antipoverty programs as a place to design alternatives, collect material resources, and build a base (*Body and Soul*, 55). Also see Self, *American Babylon*.

94. Ed Hansen letter to parents, July 25, 1966, Ed Hansen Papers, GLBTHS.

95. "Rev. Hansen Leaves," *Vanguard*, Issue 1 (1966); "New Plan for Tenderloin," *San Francisco Progress*, February 1–2, 1967 (clipping in Box 16, Folder 21, Don Lucas Papers, GLBTHS); "Attention! Tenderloin Meeting," flier, Box 15, Folder 1, ibid. Also see Stryker, *Transgender History*; Members of the Gay and Lesbian Historical Society of Northern California, "MTF Transgender Activism in the Tenderloin and Beyond."

96. Transcript, pp. 249–52, Gabriel interview with Lucas, Oral History Collection, GLBTHS.

97. Document, "EOC Position on CAP Memos #23 & #24," July 27, 1966, Box 20, Folder 1, Don Lucas Papers, GLBTHS.

98. Block quote is from "EOC Position on CAP Memos #23 & #24." For the decision to accept funds under protest, see untitled piece signed by Calvin B. Colt, chairman, Interim Area Board, August 16, 1966 published in *Vanguard*, Issue 1 (1966): n.p. The issue also included information about the new Community Action Program rules, prepared by John J. Colvin, vice pres. Vanguard (*Vanguard*, Issue 1 [1966]: n.p.). In a letter dated November 13, 1968, Don Lucas wrote to John Dukes, executive director of the San Francisco EOC, requesting a waiver of the rule so as to pay the maximum end of the pay scale to a key neighborhood participant in the Central City, Margaret "Peggy" Ann Galvez. Galvez, described as a single mother of three, worked in the intake and referral unit of the Central City area board (Box 13, Folder 15, Don Lucas Papers, GLBTHS).

99. Alinsky referenced this exact phrase in an interview with William F. Buckley Jr. on Buckley's show *Firing Line* ("Mobilizing the Poor," December 11, 1967, New York, Program 079, *Firing Line* Archives, Hoover Institution Library and Archives, Stanford, CA, available online at http://hoohila.stanford.edu/firingline/programView2 .php?programID=99). His more detailed discussion of the program as "political pornography" can also be found in Saul D. Alinsky, "The War on Poverty—Political Pornography," *Journal of Social Issues* 21, no. 1 (1965): 41–47.

100. According to Manuel Castells, in the Mission during these years, nationalists accused Alinsky-trained leaders of "using a Latino image . . . to win power in city hall for a non-Latino organization." Manuel Castells, "City and Culture: The San Francisco Expe-

rience," in *The City and the Grassroots: A Cross-Cultural Theory of Urban Social Movements* (Berkeley: University of California, 1983), 106–37, 116. Castells adds that this was a common feature of Alinsky campaigns. On the Mission, also see John Mollenkopf, "Neighborhood Mobilization and Urban Development: Boston and San Francisco, 1968–1978," *International Journal of Urban and Regional Research* 5, no. 1 (1981): 15–39.

101. Mark Forrester, "A Workplan for Community Organization," May 24, 1966, Box 15, Folder 4, Don Lucas Papers, GLBTHS. Forrester's views and confrontational strategies were considered by many to be too radical and by others as an expression of a difficult personality. For testimonies to Forrester's contested style of supervising, advocacy, and teamwork, see the materials collected in Box 20, Folder 4, ibid. Despite this, Don Lucas appreciated Forrester's work even as they diverged ideologically. Lucas explained: "We never saw eye to eye always, but we always worked together" (transcript, p. 253, Gabriel interview with Lucas, Oral History Collection, GLBTHS). Don Ganoung, assistant director of the Central City Multi-Service Center, who was also affiliated with Glide, tended to be sympathetic to Forrester's plans, but he found Forrester divisive and difficult. Although there were many complaints about Forrester, his own problems with others were even more numerous—especially in his highly supervised approach to "bottom-up" organizing. For example, Forrester considered one Central City Multi-Service Center aide as eligible for a permanent position on "the condition that he undertake whatever form of therapy we [Lucas and Forrester] can arrange" (Mark Forrester, memorandum addressed to Calvin Colt, area director, and Don Lucas, administrative assistant, on "Staff Activities in Area Organization from Feb. 6th to Feb. 9th, 1967," Box 13, Folder 14, Don Lucas Papers, GLBTHS). Forrester also designed many evaluation forms to supervise his staff (see "Central City Multi-Service Center Staff Platform Evaluation," Box 13, Folder 13, ibid.).

102. This was earlier suggested by "The Tenderloin Report Rejected," *Cruise News and World Report*, May 1966, and repeated by varied individuals.

103. For example, the board argued that cuts to the 1966–67 Office of Economic Opportunity budget, which reduced funds by at least 30 percent, left money for staff and little else. The August 16, 1966, memo from Central City EOC Board Director Calvin Colt, reprinted in the first issue of *Vanguard*, explained: "The headquarters and staff will provide the operational base by which funds for badly needed projects for the Central City's poor can be obtained. The anti-poverty program has almost no money itself and will have little for the foreseeable future. The program will only be a tool used by the poor of the Central City to get help from other sources. In that, at least, we will be somewhat better off than before. . . . But only slightly so. More than money, what this program will need is the help of every low-income resident of the area to involve himself as far as his energy and resources allow. This will be a real self-help program if he does. There will be no handout of cash; there will be no big payrolls; there will be no easy road to affluence. There will be only hard work and considerable frustration available to those who want to help themselves out of poverty" (*Vanguard*, Issue 1 [1966]: n.p.).

104. Identified as a letter from Gaylan [?]einstock, former Senior Assistant Area organizer at Central City, to Mark Forrester, the Central City Area Organization Supervisor, "I Quit!!!!!!!!!!!!," *Gadfly* 1, no. 12 (circa December 1967), Box 20, Folder 23, Don Lucas Papers, GLBTHS.

105. An undated issue of the *Gadfly* referenced the new federal rules, and the October 23, 1967, issue explained the San Francisco regulations. The December issue solicited donations to support the defense of Huey P. Newton ("!!!!! IF YOU CAN RAISE SOME MONEY FOR FREEDOM!!!!!!!," *Gadfly* 1, no. 12 [circa December 1967]), Box 20, Folder 23, Don Lucas Papers, GLBTHS).

106. Reference to Tom Ramsay's affiliation is found in the administration update of the weekly publication of the Central City Multi-Service Center: "Administration," *House Organ*, February 12, 1968, p. 5, Box 14, Folder 11, Don Lucas Papers, GLBTHS.

107. "SNCC Speaker at Guild," *Town Talk*, September 15, 1965.

108. Meeting minutes from the Central City Planning Council record a discussion as to whether "mass-based" was a "'red flag' phrase" (Minutes of the Meeting of the Planning Council, April 4, 1968, Box 13, Folder 10, Don Lucas Papers, GLBTHS).

109. For more in-depth discussions of how War on Poverty programs both cultivated and constrained radical critique, see Self, *American Babylon*; Nelson, *Body and Soul*; Piven and Cloward, *Regulating the Poor*; Goldstein, *Poverty in Common*; George Lipsitz, *A Life in the Struggle: Ivory Perry and the Culture of Opposition* (Philadelphia: Temple University Press, 1995); Robert Bauman, *Race and the War on Poverty: From Watts to East L.A.* (Norman: University of Oklahoma Press, 2008). As I suggest at the end of this chapter, these contradictions could also have negative personal effects and limit the actions of activists. Lipsitz well describes this dynamic in his study of the St. Louis activist Ivory Perry: "The federal effort to combat poverty in America enabled Ivory Perry to emerge as an organic intellectual, to secure an economic base and a receptive constituency for direct action protests. But it also trapped him in the contradictions of American politics, imposing significant limits on his attempts to build a coalition capable of solving the problems of his community" (*A Life in the Struggle*, 135).

110. Robert Edward Cruz and Michael B. Music, public notice from the San Francisco Neighborhood Legal Assistance Foundation, October 18, 1973, Box 20, Folder 8, Tavern Guild of San Francisco Records, Gay, Lesbian, Bisexual, Transgender Historical Society, San Francisco, CA (hereafter Tavern Guild Records, GLBTHS).

111. I believe that Sandigan was linked to the International Institute of San Francisco; the Pilipino Organizing Committee was a community-based group in the Central City's South of Market.

112. Central City Citizens Council Organizing Council, memorandum to "All Central City Community Organizations and Citizens, All Central City Filipino Organizations, and All San Francisco Gay Organizations," subject "Looking Ahead," October 26, 1973, Box 20, Folder 8, Tavern Guild Records, GLBTHS. For a full list of the groups receiving services from the Central City Multi-Service Center, see the Central City Citizens Council Mailing List, November 8, 1973 (ibid.). The memos described strong affinities between gay and Filipino groups.

113. See Josh Sides, *Erotic City: Sexual Revolutions and the Making of Modern San Francisco* (New York: Oxford University Press, 2009); Crowe, *Prophets of Rage*.

114. It is worth noting that Beardemphl, in his interview with Paul Gabriel, specifically cites Asian (American)s as among those SIR was not interested in collaborating with via the EOC program, suggesting that the dynamics with Filipinos in the Central City area were so contested (Gabriel interview with Beardemphal [*sic*] and DeLeon, p. 3, Oral History Collection, GLBTHS).

115. Boyd, *Wide Open Town*, 218.

116. J. Campbell Bruce, "Cahill's Stand on Prostitution Hit," *San Francisco Chronicle*, August 21, 1968; "Criticism of Proposal for Law against Streetwalkers," *San Francisco Progress*, August 28–29, 1968, clippings in Box 16, Folder 21, Don Lucas Papers, GLBTHS.

117. Mark Forrester, press release by Tenderloin Committee, announcing event for August 15, 1968, Box 42, Folder 22, Lyon Martin Papers, GLBTHS.

118. Minutes of the Central City Police Community Relations Committee, February 14, 1967, Box 10, Folder 8, Don Lucas Papers, GLBTHS.

119. See Richard Rogers, executive director, Family Service Agency of San Francisco, letter to Calvin Brook Colt, area director, EOC, August 25, 1967, Box 13, Folder 14, Don Lucas Papers, GLBTHS; Herbert Donaldson, chief counsel, San Francisco Neighborhood Legal Assistance Foundation, letter to Calvin Colt, Center City E.O.C., August 28, 1967, Box 13, Folder 14, ibid. Donaldson also called for a "social and economic alternative" rather than a policing solution in the form of arrests of prostitutes and homosexuals. As Connell and Gabriel note in their essay on the Folsom Street Fair, Donaldson was hired by Lucas, had been arrested at California Hall, and would later become the first openly gay judge in California ("The Power of Broken Hearts").

120. For critiques of such see, for example, "The Biggest Farce in March: Police Community Relations Meeting," *Vanguard* 1, no. 6 [probably circa 1967]: 25–26. Central City activists also complained when Chief Cahill unilaterally installed the chairman of the Central City Police Community Relations, local hotel manager William Popham. See Charles Clay, director of the Central City Hospitality House, letter, [recipient unclear; appears to be addressed to the police commissioner] May 13, 1968, Box 42, Folder 11, Lyon Martin Papers, GLBTHS.

121. Council on Religion and the Homosexual, "A Brief of Injustices," 1965, Box 10, Folder 5, Don Lucas Papers, GLBTHS.

122. "Need for Communication Stressed: S.F.P.D. Blackstone Addresses SIR," *Vector*, July 1966, 1. For more on Blackstone, see Paul Gabriel, "Elliott Blackstone: Man of the Year 2000," program for the 15th Anniversary Celebration of the Gay, Lesbian, Bisexual, Transgender Historical Society of Northern California, October 5, 2000 (in author's possession); Members of the Gay and Lesbian Historical Society of Northern California, "MTF Transgender Activism In the Tenderloin and Beyond"; *Screaming Queens* (directed by Stryker and Silverman).

123. "'Pocket Lawyer' Ready" and "Homophile Alert System," *Vector*, September 1965, 1, 3. Also see "Homophile Alert System," flier with return to address as that of William E. Beardemphl, former director of SIR, Box 15, Folder 9, Don Lucas Papers, GLBTHS.

124. One sidebar titled "Police Brutality" read: "While the local papers reported with banner headlines an alleged beating of 3 police officers while they were checking out a North Beach 'topless' club, not one word was mentioned of the alleged beating of 3 teenagers by 10 policemen at a local police station. The youth were being questioned after leaving a bowling alley last Saturday night. No charges were placed against the boys. Two days after the event, SIR was informed about the incident. The ACLU and CRH were contacted. All three organizations are investigating the matter" (*Vector*, June 1965, 3).

125. "Citizen Alert Goals and Purposes Ready," *Vector*, November 1965, 3. Also see "Citizens Alert, A Brief History," circa 1968, Box 42, Folder 15, Lyon Martin Papers, GLBTHS.

126. The Committee of Racial Equality was the earlier name of the Congress of Racial Equality, a name sometimes still used—especially in local contexts.

127. "Citizen's Alert System," flier, n.d., Box 15, Folder 9, Don Lucas Papers, GLBTHS (also in Box 19, Folder 3, Tavern Guild Records, GLBTHS).

128. Marcia Gallo looks at the central role of the Daughters of Bilitis in Citizens Alert in *Different Daughters: A History of the Daughters of Bilitis and the Rise of the Lesbian Rights Movement* (Emeryville, CA: Seal, 2006).

129. There were other campaigns, such as José Sarria's run for supervisor, that involved individual cross-race participation, but none that mobilized diverse constituencies.

130. Del Martin and Phyllis Lyon, interview by author, San Francisco, August 2004. Don Lucas also affirmed this position in an interview conducted by Susan Stryker in

1997 (Transcript of Susan Stryker interview of Donald Lucas, June 13, 1997, p. 16, Oral History Collection 97-035, Gay, Lesbian, Bisexual, and Transgender Historical Society, San Francisco, CA). Also see Gallo, *Different Daughters*.

131. Fliers announcing rallies, n.d., Box 15, Folder 9, Don Lucas Papers, GLBTHS.

132. "Citizen's Alert Training Session," flier, n.d., Box 15, Folder 9, Don Lucas Papers, GLBTHS.

133. "Citizens Alert" (circa 1968), Box 42, Folder 24, Lyon Martin Papers, GLBTHS.

134. The names come from two undated lists of people considered for and then elected to the Board of Directors of Citizens Alert, Box 15, Folder 9, Don Lucas Papers, GLBTHS.

135. "Citizens Alert Is Underway: Volunteers Needed for Office," *Town Talk*, October–November 1965.

136. Citizens Alert, "First Annual Report, August 1965–December 1966," Box 42, Folder 24, Lyon Martin Papers, GLBTHS.

137. Citizens Alert, "First Annual Report."

138. "Statistical Abstract of Information Contained in the Files of Citizens Alert between October 1965 and June 1968 [draft and final versions]," Box 42, Folder 20, Lyon Martin Papers, GLBTHS.

139. "Cops Loathe Brutality, Hate Queers Equally," *Town Talk*, October–November, 1965.

140. Citizens Alert, "Better Police-Community Relations Concern You: Eight Point Program for Better Police-Community Relations in San Francisco," August 1968, Box 42, Folder 20, Lyon Martin Papers, GLBTHS.

141. Del Martin, "Williams Pledges Help," *Vector*, August 1969, 12.

142. Del Martin, "Police Power and Proposition I," *Vector*, June 1970, 6–7. In later years, Martin would come out against obscenity from a feminist position.

143. See "Meeting of Committee for Conference on Jail Reform, 'Rehabilitation or Revenge,'" March 12, 1970, Box 42, Folder 18, Lyon Martin Papers, GLBTHS.

144. P. Lane, "National Legal Defense Fund Becomes a Reality," *Vector*, April 1967, 9.

145. Letterhead of the New York City Review Board Conference, Box 3, Folder 7, Mattachine Society of New York, Records, Manuscripts and Archives Division, New York Public Library, New York, New York (hereafter Mattachine Society Records, NYPL). This group was different from Bayard Rustin's Civilian Complaint Review Board, which primarily organized African Americans in Harlem. See Marge Friedlander, head of the New York City Review Board Conference, letter to Bayard Rustin, January 10, 1966, Box 3, Folder 7, ibid. For a history of the citywide struggles for the Citizen's Committee for a Complaint Review Board, see Algernon D. Black, *The People and the Police* (New York: McGraw-Hill, 1968).

146. See Marge Friedlander, letter to Rep. Theodore Weiss, February 10 [1966?], explaining the risks homosexuals would face with public exposure (Box 3, Folder 7, Mattachine Society Records, NYPL).

147. For example, in a letter to William Stringfellow, a civil rights attorney, and Frank Patton Jr., a religious activist, Marge Friedlander wrote: "It is our view that a CCRB should concern itself with more than police brutality and excessive-use-of-force (against Negroes *and* whites). It should address itself to *all* instance[s] of police malpractice violative of human dignity and constitutional rights. Among other things, a CCRB should provide redress for homosexuals subjected to police harassment and abuse under the sodomy and vagrancy statutes. Pending statutory reform, the law enforcement methodology under the status concerned needs drastic overhaul. To my knowledge, NYC and

Rochester, NY are the only cities where the CCRB focus is solely police brutality" (August 16, 1965, Box 3, Folder 7, Mattachine Society Records, NYPL). It is important to note that police-community relations were a part of a new nationwide movement for commissions on human rights, a movement that was also active in San Francisco.

148. An open letter from Rev. Cecil Williams, then chair of Citizens Alert, defined police brutality with a long list of aggressive police strategies that included abusive language as well as the threat and actual use of violence. Open letter from the Reverend A. Cecil Williams, July 22, 1968, Box 42, Folder 16, Lyon Martin Papers, GLBTHS.

149. W. E. Beardemphl, "Don't Mess with Mona," *Vector*, August 1967, 5.

150. Del Martin, "Hospitality House Harassed," *Vector*, February 1970, 5.

151. Del Martin, "Examiner Accused of Yellow Journalism," *Vector*, January 1970, 7.

152. Del Martin, "Cop Is Honored," *Vector*, April 1970, 10.

153. Del Martin, "Know Your I.D. Requirement," *Vector*, May 1970, 8.

154. In addition to above citations see, for example, the following items by Del Martin: "Gays and Cops Face to Face," *Vector*, July 1970, 12; "Coincidence Reigns Supreme in the SFPD," *Vector*, August 1970, 12; "Banned in Frisco," *Vector*, September 1970, 13.

155. Del Martin, "Coincidence Reigns Supreme in the SFPD."

156. Del Martin, "Police Power and Proposition 1."

157. Del Martin, "Columnist Resigns: Blasts Male Chauvinism," *Vector*, October 1970, 35.

158. Martin, "Columnist Resigns," 36.

159. Martin, "Columnist Resigns," 37; also see S. Willer, president of the Daughters of Bilitis, "The Lesbian, the Homosexual, and the Homophile Movement," *Vector*, October 1966, 8; Del Martin, "Women's Rights and S.I.R.," *Vector*, September 1969, 14.

160. Del Martin, "Columnist Resigns."

161. Del Martin, "Sexism and Lesbians," *Vector*, January 1971, 28.

162. Somerville, "Queer Loving."

163. Ed Hansen served as a pastor at the Hollywood United Methodist Church in Southern California for many years before retiring. Mark Forrester remained an activist until he died in the 1980s. Don Lucas continued to work in social services for some years; he passed away in 2003. Phyllis Lyon and Del Martin remained very active in lesbian and gay politics for decades founding and participating in numerous lesbian and gay organizations and institutions; they were the first same-sex couple to be married in San Francisco in 2008 after it was briefly legalized in the state of California. Del Martin passed away later that year; Phyllis Lyon still lives in San Francisco.

164. The play on words in the title of this section is meant to signal both that the organization Vanguard often referred to its members as "street" youth or people (a common phrase used to describe those active in informal economies) and that those on the street were considered a kind of political vanguard.

165. One supporter appears to have been Lawrence (Larry) Mamiya, youth minister and member of the Student Nonviolent Coordinating Committee (see *Vanguard Revisited* [Megan Rohrer], "Urban Specialist Pastors and Their Supporters").

166. The title of the magazine was either *V* (which usually appeared on the cover) or *Vanguard* (as appeared in the table of contents). I have referred to it here as *Vanguard*. The founding of the organization Vanguard was also announced in "Young Rejects Form Own Organization," *Cruise News and World Report*, July 1966.

167. "From the Press Release," *Vanguard* 1, no. 2 (October 1966): n.p.

168. "We Protest," flier, circa 1966, Box 11, Folder 17, Don Lucas Papers, GLBTHS.

169. Jean-Paul Marat, "Exploitation," *Vanguard*, Issue 1 (1966): n.p.

170. Mark Forrester, "Central City: Profile of Despair," *Vanguard* Issue 1 (1966): n.p.

171. "The Black Race vs. the White Race OR the Human Race vs. Ignorance and Superstition," *Vanguard* 1, no. 6 [probably circa 1967]: n.p. The article also railed against Governor Ronald Reagan and President Johnson as attacking antipoverty programs and working people. For speculation on police involvement in drug trade, see untitled commentary in *Vanguard* 1, no. 3 (November 1966): n.p. For one of many examples of sexually explicit drawings in the publication, see the picture accompanying the article "Summary of the Tenderloin Problem," *Vanguard* 1, no. 9 [probably circa 1967]: n.p.

172. "Young Homos Picket Compton's Restaurant," *Cruise News and World Report*, August 1966.

173. To the mainstream eye, this still made the group deviant. An article about Glide Church in the *Wall Street Journal* cited Vanguard as "a group of young male prostitutes" to emphasize Glide's nonconventional approach (Howard Merry, "Tenderloin Ministry: A 'Secularized' Church Pursues Its Mission in Unorthodox Causes," *Wall Street Journal*, March 13, 1967, reprinted in an undated brochure produced by and about Glide, Box 19, Folder 11, Lyon Martin Papers, GLBTHS).

174. J.-P. Marat, "The Views of Vanguard," *Cruise News and World Report*, October 1966.

175. Doug Patrick, "President's Page," *Vanguard* 1, no. 5 [probably circa 1967]: n.p.

176. "The Biggest Farce in March: Police Community Relations Meeting," *Vanguard* 1, no. 6 [probably circa 1967]: 25.

177. A group of Vanguard members, led by the former organization's president, Doug Patrick, and vice president, Carolyn V. "Frosty" Smith, left Vanguard for Los Angeles in a huff. Their departure was proclaimed in an April 1967 memo to "The Membership of Vanguard the Youth Organization" with the subject line "Your own failing and the loss of a Great Idea." They declared: "God Damn the Tenderloin Youth" (*Vanguard* 1, no. 7 [probably circa 1967]: 32). The Street Prophets was announced in the next issue.

178. "Street Prophets Prediction," *Vanguard* 1, no. 8 [probably circa 1967]: 10.

179. For a brilliant theoretical and ethnographic look at the limits of liberal ideas of agency in analyzing political activity, see Saba Mahmood, *Politics of Piety: The Islamic Revival and the Feminist Subject* (Princeton: Princeton University Press, 2005).

180. Denise Ferreira da Silva, *Toward a Global Idea of Race* (Minneapolis: University of Minnesota Press, 2007).

181. Piven and Cloward, *Regulating the Poor*, especially 256–86.

182. Piven and Cloward, *Poor People's Movements*, 465.

183. As the article cited in note 62 argued, in late 1969 neighborhoods like Times Square and public places like parks and the subway could not count as "gay ghettos," for their "gay legions are primarily transient than permanent." The article suggested instead that "A gay ghetto, therefore, may be defined as a particular area where a very heavy concentration of homosexuals actually live and frequently pay rent" (Simms, "New York Gay Ghettos," 4).

184. Here it is helpful to remark again on some of the differences between New York and San Francisco. In both places, War on Poverty Community Action Agencies were centered in racialized sites of urban poverty (such as Harlem and Bedford-Stuyvesant, in New York, and the Fillmore and Mission District in San Francisco). Yet unlike San Francisco, where the bohemian North Beach abutted the impoverished Tenderloin, in New York, Greenwich Village was considerably south of the similarly seedy Times Square. The development dramas of Greenwich Village during these years were primar-

ily on behalf of the Village's middle-class residents—most notably the activities of the famed champion of antirenewal, Jane Jacobs—and did not link up with the needs of street kids and gay bar culture. This narrative thus complicates the view of many historians who contrast New York's militancy with San Francisco's accommodationism in the Mattachines of the 1960s. New York activists' hard-edged principles did not always include systematic, cross-constituency base building although they were uncompromising in pursuing a gay-focused agenda. And although the New Yorkers' demand for privacy did refuse a kind of drive toward visibility, it did so by affirming the very framework of exposure as the most salient for homosexuals.

185. It is worth noting that although these dynamics were unique in their depth of elaboration in San Francisco, they were not unfamiliar in other cities. For example, in 1972 religious figures joined with gay activists to found Gay House in Minneapolis, which addressed marginalized youth and drew on Model City funds ("Federal Funds for 'Gay House' Blasted," *Gay*, February 21, 1972, 16; "'Gay House' Proceeds," *Gay*, March 6, 1972; Erik Larsson, "Hoods Crash Midwest Gay House," *Gay*, March 20, 1972, 1).

186. The argument that sexual politics are primarily one of "recognition" and not economic redistribution is made in Nancy Fraser, "Social Justice in the Age of Identity Politics: Redistribution, Recognition, and Participation," in Nancy Fraser and Axel Honneth, *Redistribution or Recognition? A Political-Philosophical Exchange* (London: Verso, 2003), 7–109, and Nancy Fraser, "Heterosexism, Misrecognition, and Capitalism: A Response to Judith Butler," *Social Text* 53–54 (Winter–Spring 1998): 279–89. In this case study, the refusal to see street violence experienced by, for example, lesbian sex workers or the brutalization of black gender nonconforming men by the police as a gay political issue would mean that gay is recognized only after race, gender, and class features are "taken out."

2. Butterflies, Whistles, and Fists

1. "A New 'Polk Street' Comes Alive," photos by Jim Briggs, *Vector*, July 1971, 30.

2. For histories of the growth of the Castro, see Manuel Castells, "City and Culture: The San Francisco Experience," in Manuel Castells, *The City and the Grassroots: A Cross-Cultural Theory of Urban Social Movements* (Berkeley: University of California Press, 1983), 97–172. Timothy Stewart-Winter, "The Castro: Origins to the Age of Milk," *Gay and Lesbian Review*, January–February 2009, 12–15. Imperator Properties, which was located in what would become the commercial core of the Castro, began running advertisements in *Vector* with the motto "Serving the Community" as early as February 1965.

3. "Mission District—New Gay Power," *Vector*, August 1971, 21. The article notes a rise of police activity in Dolores Park, a divider between the Castro and Mission, but concludes that the political power of the Tavern Guild helped thwart dire consequences. For a discussion of police harassment South of Market, see Gayle Rubin, "The Miracle Mile: South of Market and Gay Male Leather, 1962–1997," in *Reclaiming San Francisco: History, Politics, Culture*, ed. James Brooks, Chris Carlsson, and Nancy J. Peters (San Francisco: City Lights, 1998), 247–72.

4. To repeat, this is not a totalizing claim. Street violence was surely a topic of conversation, and it was occasionally featured in the gay press. But the number of published articles about street violence and crime in publications like *Vector* were markedly fewer than those about police abuse.

5. See, as one example, Elizabeth A. Armstrong, *Forging Gay Identities: Organizing Sexuality in San Francisco, 1950–1994* (Chicago: University of Chicago Press, 2002).

6. Leo Laurence, "Gay Revolution," *Vector*, April 1969, 11. John D'Emilio suggests that Laurence was "radicalized" by witnessing the battles between police and protesters during the 1968 Democratic Convention in Chicago (*Sexual Politics, Sexual Communities: The Making of a Homosexual Minority in the United States, 1940–1970* [Chicago: University of Chicago Press, 1983], 230–31). Jim Kepner, a homophile activist and founder of the ONE Institute's National Gay and Lesbian Archives, indicated to Donn Teal that police had gassed Laurence (*The Gay Militants: How Gay Liberation Began in America, 1969–1971* [1971; New York: St. Martin's, 1995]).

7. Committee for Homosexual Freedom flier, late 1969, Carton 8, Gay Movement, 1969–1982, Social Protest Collection, Bancroft Library, University of California, Berkeley. Emily Hobson describes these and other activities of the committee in *Lavender and Red: Race, Empire, and Solidarity in the Gay and Lesbian Left* (Berkeley: University of California Press, forthcoming).

8. The Sexual Freedom League was an almost exclusively heterosexual group opposed to dominant sexual mores. Its members supported the rights of homosexuals despite the organization director's dubious claims that "the only threat that the homosexual gives to the straight society is where and when he might un-zip his pants" and that gays were responsible for their own underrepresentation within the league (Thomas W. Palmer, "Sexual Freedom League: A Gay Invasion," *Vector*, April 1969, 5).

9. D'Emilio, *Sexual Politics, Sexual Communities*; Terence Kissack, "Freaking Fag Revolutionaries: New York's Gay Liberation Front, 1969–1971," *Radical History Review* 62 (Spring 1995): 104–35.

10. In *Forging Gay Identities*, Armstrong suggests that the omission of a reference to Stonewall shows how separate the gay liberation scenes in New York and San Francisco were from each other. Although that is true, the fact that the riots were described as a "protest" (in scare quotes) also underscores the growing contempt of *Vector*—and, by extension, the Society for Individual Rights—for gay radicalism on both coasts ("Greenwich Village," *Vector*, October 1969, 4). It is also worth investigating the reason why many other uprisings, such as the riot at Compton's Cafeteria, did not spur organizing as Stonewall did. Some authors suggest that it might be because in 1966 models of radical action were less available, or because trans people did not represent the homophile movement's privileged constituency (see Elizabeth Armstrong and Susanna M. Crage, "Meaning and Memory: The Making of the Stonewall Myth," *American Sociological Review* 71, no. 5 [2006]: 724–51 and Susan Stryker, *Transgender History* [Berkeley, CA: Seal, 2008]). I would add an analysis of location. Although in 1966 the Tenderloin was the closest thing San Francisco had to a gay neighborhood, that fact was still based on the neighborhood's uses, and its identity was linked to sex work and transience. Greenwich Village in 1969 was a very different place: a middle-class residential neighborhood home to gay people and the counterculture. Thus the riot at Compton's in San Francisco might not have escalated because it did not invite extensive middle-class participation and subsequent media attention. There had been a major crackdown on sex work and homosexual cruising in New York's Times Square and Greenwich Village in 1966. Although gay residents of Greenwich Village as a whole organized a community meeting that succeeded in curtailing homosexual entrapment, their focus was arguably as much the Village as it was Times Square (D'Emilio, *Sexual Politics, Sexual Communities*, 206–7).

11. Kissack, "Freaking Fag Revolutionaries," 107.

12. Kissack, "Freaking Fag Revolutionaries," 115.

13. Arrested in April 1969, the Panther 21 were members of the New York Black Panther Party who were accused of plotting to blow up various public spaces in New York.

On May 13, 1971, they were acquitted in a trial that lasted less than one hour (Peter L. Zimroth, *Perversions of Justice: The Prosecution and Acquittal of the Panther 21* [New York: Viking, 1974]).

14. For examples of GLF prison and police activism and the group's desire to collaborate with the Black Panther Party, see "Gay People Help Plan New World," *Gay Flames*, September 11, 1970; the entire issue of *Gay Flames*, November 14, 1970; and "U.S. Justice = Gay Is Guilty," *Gay Flames*, December 14, 1970.

15. "Gay People Help Plan New World," *Gay Flames*. I discuss the activities of the Third World Gay Revolution further in chapter 3. See also Duchess Harris and Adam Waterman, "Babylon Is Burning, Or Race, Gender, and Sexuality at the Revolutionary People's Constitutional Convention," *Journal of Intergroup Relations* 27, no. 2 (2000): 17–33.

16. "Working Paper for the Revolutionary People's Constitutional Convention," in *Out of the Closets: Voices of Gay Liberation*, 20th anniversary edition (2nd ed.), ed. Karla Jay and Allen Young (New York: New York University Press, 1992), 348.

17. Carl Wittman, "A Gay Manifesto," in *Out of the Closets*, ed. Jay and Young, 330–42. Carl Wittman had been active in Students for a Democratic Society and, with Tom Hayden, wrote "An Interracial Movement of the Poor" in 1963, which was distributed in brochure form. The original, full title of Wittman's manifesto was "Refugees from Amerika: A Gay Manifesto," and it was published in leftist papers across the country in the early 1970s. In the year of its publication, the Red Butterfly Cell of the GLF distributed it, yet they also criticized "coming out" as individualistic and were concerned about Wittman's rejection of socialism. See Toby Marotta, *The Politics of Homosexuality* (Boston: Houghton Mifflin, 1981).

18. Wittman, "A Gay Manifesto," 335, 340–41.

19. Wittman, "A Gay Manifesto," 330, 339–41.

20. In the early 1970s, Wittman moved to Wolf Creek, Oregon. He eventually relocated to Durham, North Carolina, where he died from AIDS-related illness in 1986. Mab Segrest provides a moving testimony about his life through his last years in *Memoir of a Race Traitor* (Cambridge, MA: South End, 1994).

21. The internal colonialism thesis has many roots; one is based on the national question as posed by Vladimir Lenin and taken up by Josef Stalin. Among Third World Leftists in the United States during the 1970s, Mao Zedong and Che Guevara were most influential. See Robin D. G. Kelley, *Freedom Dreams: The Black Radical Imagination* (Boston: Beacon, 2002); Cynthia A. Young, *Soul Power: Culture, Radicalism, and the Making of a U.S. Third World Left* (Durham: Duke University Press, 2006); Laura Pulido, *Black, Brown, Yellow, and Left: Radical Activism in Los Angeles* (Berkeley: University of California Press, 2006); Max Elbaum, *Revolution in the Air: Sixties Radicals Turn to Lenin, Mao, and Che* (New York: Verso, 2006).

22. Emily Hobson, "Imagining Alliance: Queer Anti-Imperialism and Race in California, 1966–1990," PhD diss., University of Southern California, 2009, 120–28.

23. Scott Morgensen, "Arrival at Home: Radical Faerie Configurations of Sexuality and Place," *GLQ* 15, no. 1 (2008): 67–96.

24. Charles P. Thorp[e], "I.D., Leadership and Violence," in *Out of the Closets*, ed. Jay and Young, 352–63.

25. The GAA looked to expand local political representation by supporting individual candidates and efforts to shape public opinion, explicitly eschewing the GLF's advocacy of broad political agendas. In *The Politics of Homosexuality*, Marotta notes that positions within the GAA were divided between "political" and "cultural" reformers. Although

their strategies often diverged, the two groups shared a focus on a gay-specific agenda. For analyses of the split from GLF, also see Kissack, "Freaking Fag Revolutionaries"; Teal, *The Gay Militants*; and John D'Emilio, "After Stonewall," in John D'Emilio, *Making Trouble: Essays on Gay History, Politics, and the University* (New York: Routledge, 1992), 234–75.

26. For a broader analysis of gay debates about Cuba, see Ian Keith Lekus, "Queer Harvests: Homosexuality, the U.S. New Left, and the Venceremos Brigades to Cuba," *Radical History Review* 89 (2004): 57–91.

27. For an example of its geography, in 1974 the GAA organized a "Freedom Ride" to the Bronx, Brooklyn, and Queens in search of nongay support for passage of the city's first gay civil rights bill, called Intro 475. The GAA proved unsuccessful in garnering the support necessary for passing Intro 475 (a version would eventually pass in 1986), and by then the group's membership was already beginning to dwindle.

28. Michael Schiavi, *Celluloid Activist: The Life and Times of Vito Russo* (Madison: University of Wisconsin Press, 2011), 84.

29. Steven Capsuto, *Alternate Channels: The Uncensored Story of Gay and Lesbian Images on Radio and Television* (New York: Ballantine, 2000), 94–95, 103–4. For additional discussion of the strategy of "zaps," see Marotta, *The Politics of Homosexuality*.

30. Broshears was rumored to have been a former lover of David Ferrie, who may have had a connection to Lee Harvey Oswald; Broshears was briefly held for threats to assassinate President Johnson; and he was reported to have been a good friend of Oliver Sipple, who knocked the gun out of the hand of Sara Jane Moore, the would-be assassin of President Ford (in fact, this report, first made by famed *San Francisco Chronicle* columnist Herb Caen, became the target of a "outing" lawsuit by Sipple almost ten years later). Before arriving in San Francisco, Broshears served time for having had sex with a minor; evidence suggests this was routine antigay targeting. For information on the connection to Sipple see David Luzer, "The Gay Man Who Saved Ford's Life," *Gay and Lesbian Review Worldwide* 16, no. 4 (July–August 2009), http://www.glreview.com /article.php?articleid=161. For all other details about Broshears's life mentioned here see the obituary, George Mendenhall, "Heaven Can't Wait! Broshears Gets Final Call," *Bay Area Reporter*, January 14, 1982.

31. Broshears was also described as a pastor of Christ Church of God in the clipping "March Movie," *Advocate* July 21–August 3, 1971. The clipping is Document #24, GAA Notebook 1, Box B, Raymond Broshears Papers, Gay, Lesbian, Bisexual, Transgender Historical Society, San Francisco, CA (hereafter Raymond Broshears Papers, GLBTHS). For additional church affiliations see Mendenhall, "Heaven Can't Wait!"

32. The rumor became community folklore (Randy Alfred, interview by author, San Francisco, August 11, 2004). Broshears kept clippings and letters that testified to various people's dislike of him, including a postal gram of unknown origin that named "The Committee to Run Ray Broshears Out of Town." Broshears also kept copies of his own letters in which he complained of misrepresentation (see letters in 1978, Correspondence Box, Carton 4, Raymond Broshears Papers, GLBTHS). The gay novelist and playwright Daniel Curzon wrote a story about Broshears called "The Reverend Rat," which was never published ("The Reverend Rat," Box 3 [Manuscripts], Daniel Curzon Papers, Gay, Lesbian, Bisexual, Transgender Historical Society Collection, San Francisco Public Library, San Francisco, CA). Broshears's obituary in the *Bay Area Reporter* was actually accompanied by an additional piece titled "Broshears' Death Brings Community Reactions," that ranged from tributes to "no comment" to expressions of confusion to declarations that he was destructive (*Bay Area Reporter*, January 14, 1982).

33. An article in the *Advocate* announcing the start of the Lavender Panthers ("Lavender Panthers Fight Back," *Advocate*, August 1, 1973) mentions the Lavender Patrol in Seattle and the Lavender Raiders in Florida. Evidence of these groups' existence would be worth exploring. Nonetheless, the attention paid to the Lavender Panthers was unique.

34. "New GAA Forms in S.F. as Splintered GLF fades," *Advocate*, June 22, 1971. (Broshears also claimed to have been involved in the founding of San Francisco's GLF; see "History of Christopher Street West-S.F.," *Gay Pride*, San Francisco, June 25, 1972, Periodicals, GLBTHS. The byline for the article is the Christopher Street West-SF Parade Committee, but *Gay Pride* was one of Broshears's publications, the piece is clearly written in his style, and it features a huge photo of him in the center.) The name of the GAA was registered with the state of California on May 17, 1971 (see State of California, Office of the Secretary of State, Form #23613, Document #4, GAA Notebook 1, Box B, Raymond Broshears Papers, GLBTHS). The GAA later became the GLA, the Gay Liberation Alliance.

35. In the draft version of the GAA Constitution (listed as adopted May 12, 1971), the organization was restricted to "any Gay person who is in agreement with the purposes of the Gay Activists Alliance as specified by the Preamble and Constitution" (Document #5, GAA Notebook 1, Box B, Raymond Broshears Papers, GLBTHS). An undated booklet titled "Gay Activists Alliance San Francisco" claims that the organization had an open membership policy and a "single issue" focus that indicated that "trans-sexualism" is closely related to homosexual issues and thus a theme on which the group would work (GAA Notebook 1, Box B, ibid.). This booklet suggests that the group relaxed its membership policy, perhaps following bad publicity about the initial policy of "no straights." Members of the Society for Individual Rights, many of whom were reportedly excited about joining the organization because of its gay-focused agenda, left over the gay-only membership policy ("Gay Lib Splits" and "No Straights!," *Berkeley Barb*, May 14–20, 1971, clippings included in Document #9, GAA Notebook 1, Box B, ibid.).

36. Of the many organizations that Broshears reportedly ran during that period—such as the Central City Neighbors Association, Old Folks Defense Lead, Helping Hands Services, Central City/Tenderloin Independent Democrats, and Gay Liberation Alliance—the majority were in the Tenderloin and dedicated to fighting redevelopment, policing, or the alienation of the elderly and the poor. In a review of Broshears's files, letterheads representing no fewer than nineteen organizations name him as the director and provide one of two phone numbers and three addresses for him. Hence it is difficult to determine what was an active group and what was just a publicity vehicle (Cartons 2 and 4, Raymond Broshears Papers, GLBTHS). In addition, Broshears ran numerous publications, including the *Crusader, Gay Crusader, San Francisco Crusader, Gay Pride, Gay Pride Crusader,* and *Gay Focus*. For most all articles in these publications, there are no authors listed but they were presumably penned by Broshears.

37. According to Susan Stryker and Joanne Meyerowitz, the California Advancement for Transsexuals Society was a small and contested organization that may have been defunct by this point. References to the groups' collaboration may, thus, refer to the participation of specific individuals associated with each organization (see Stryker, *Transgender History*; Joanne Meyerowitz, *How Sex Changed: A History of Transsexuality in the United States* [Cambridge: Harvard University Press, 2004]; "CATS and GAA," *Berkeley Barb*, September 3, 1971, [Clipping, Document #51, GAA Notebook 1, Box B, Raymond Broshears Papers, GLBTHS]). A letter from Rt. Rev. Gerard O. Dunkin, president of the society, to Ray Broshears, president, GAA, dated August 20, 1971, also affirmed the groups' partnership (Document #59, GAA Notebook 1, Box B, ibid.).

38. For a study of the invention of the category of "chronic homelessness" years later, see Craig Willse, "Neoliberal Biopolitics and the Invention of Chronic Homelessness," *Economy and Society* 39, no. 2 (2010): 155–84.

39. Quoted in Ian Young, "Mikhail Itkin: Tales of a Bishopric," *Gay and Lesbian Review Worldwide*, November–December 2010, 26–27. I have distilled much of this profile of Itkin from Young's article.

40. Young describes Itkin as able to "inspire visceral distaste," quoting someone who described him as having a "lack of personal charisma" (Young, "Mikhail Itkin," 27).

41. For the quotes on the banning of Socialist Workers Party members from the GAA, see "S.F. Gay Activists Alliance Out 'Trotskyites' in Purge," *Advocate*, December 8, 1971 (Clipping, Document #103, GAA Notebook 1, Box B, Ray Broshears Papers, GLBTHS). On the list of "enemy" organizations, see "Transsexuals Victory," *Berkeley Barb*, August 27, 1971 (Clipping, Document 51, GAA Notebook 1, Box B, ibid.). The modeling groups presumably were, in part, fronts for escort services, which Broshears reviled. The Alan Stanford Modeling Group and Dial-a-Model appear to have been run by Alan Stanford, who was also identified as a monsignor because he had been ordained as a Roman Catholic priest in Rochester, New York, in 1959 and was active in a Catholic Streets Ministry (see "About Our Pastor and Counselor; Msgr. Alan Stanford," flier in Bishop Alan Stanford File, Carton 1, ibid.). The *San Francisco Chronicle* reported that lesbians claimed that they were not allowed to speak at the parade by Broshears (Larry Liebert, "S.F.'s Lively Gay Parade," *San Francisco Chronicle*, June 26, 1972 [Clipping, Document #210, GAA Notebook 1, Box B, ibid.]). Broshears's actions were often in the name of "street queens" and "prostitutes" and against vice squad members; the general opposition to the police is evident in many documents listed later, such as those related to the short-lived Coalition against Police Brutality (flier, Carton 2, unmarked folder, ibid.).

42. "Gay Guerillas Hit Beaux Arts Ball," *Berkeley Barb*, October 29–November 4, 1971 (Clipping, Document #85, Notebook 1, Box B, Ray Broshears Papers, GLBTHS). Broshears is reported to have addressed each guest at a Society for Individual Rights party as "fascist pig" ("No Sir," *Good Times*, January 28, 1972; "Gay Militants Zap S.I.R. Dinner," *Bay Area Reporter*, February 1, 1972 [Clipping, Document #133, GAA Notebook 1, Box B, ibid.]).

43. Letter of commendation from Elliott Blackstone for Raymond Broshears, August 5, 1969, Carton 2, GLBTHS.

44. The quote is from "Transsexuals Victory." Other examples of antipolice actions include fliers such as "GAA Presents: Downtown Citizens Police Community Relations Coalition Meeting" and "GAA 'Zap' Letter #4: Help! Murder! 6 Slain within 5 Days! SFPD Looks Other Way??" as well as a booklet, "Gay Activist: SFPD Wages War on Gays" (GAA Notebook 1, Box B, Raymond Broshears Papers, GLBTHS). How many of these actions actually occurred or featured more than Broshears alone is unknown. Broshears had also launched a crusade against the military some years earlier when he served a symbolic restraining order against officers located at the Presidio base (Jack Viets, "Pastor's War on Presidio: 'Brutality,'" *San Francisco Chronicle*, September 22, 1969). Broshears also seems to have filed with the support of the GAA a restraining order on behalf of himself and "Homosexual Citizens of San Francisco County" against three members of the San Francisco Police Department—Donald M. Scott, chief of police; Gerald Shaughnessy, chief of special services; and William Conroy, commander of the city prison—so that they would stop "assaulting, harassing or arresting plaintiffs" mentally or physically (Box A, Raymond Broshears Papers, GLBTHS). The GAA was also involved in a "Work-In" to protest federal discrimination. The action included members of the Society for Individual Rights and many other groups ("Federal Building 'Work-In' Protests US Hir-

ing Policy," *Advocate*, July 7–20, 1971 [Clipping, Document #12, GAA Notebook 1, Box B, ibid.]). This was also covered in the *Berkeley Barb* and *Vector*. In addition, Broshears was on the vanguard of efforts to push the Society for Individual Rights to investigate police misconduct ("SIR's Staid Stand on Swine," *Berkeley Barb*, July 8, 1971 [Clipping, Document #33, GAA Notebook 1, Box B, ibid.]); to protest evictions ("Drag Queens Ousted from Majority of Hotels! Serious Housing Shortage Exists!" [unnumbered document, Notebook 1, Box B, ibid.]); and he even officiated at the marriage of two members of the Women's Army Corps (Mitchell Thomas, "WACs Wed Each Other," *San Francisco Chronicle*, February 22, 1973 [Clipping, Notebook 1, Box B, ibid.]).

45. The "Purple Panther Division" of "street people" based in the Tenderloin was originally a part of the GAA ("Rev. Broshears Quits as Head of SF GAA," *Advocate,* January 5, 1972 [Clipping, Document #113, Box B, Raymond Broshears Papers, GLBTHS]). Although the Lavender Panthers initially intended to patrol Eureka Valley, inclusive of the Castro, they ultimately focused on the Tenderloin.

46. "Lavender Panthers Protect Gays," *Rolling Stone*, September 27, 1973, 7; "The Lavender Panthers," *Time*, October 8, 1973, 73; "Gay Vigilantes to Fight Back," *San Francisco Examiner*, July 7, 1973 (Clippings, Notebook 1, Box B, Raymond Broshears Papers, GLBTHS). Also see John T. Parker, "The Lavender Panthers: Vigilante Justice on the Sexual Frontier," *Coast*, April 1974, 29–31.

47. In contrast, in Oakland the Gay Men's Political Action Group was also founded in 1973 and provided support for the campaigns of Bobby Seale for mayor and Elaine Brown for City Council. This is discussed in Hobson, *Lavender and Red.*

48. See Alondra Nelson, *Body and Soul: The Black Panther Party and the Fight against Medical Discrimination* (Minneapolis: University of Minnesota, 2011).

49. "Lavender Panthers Protect Gays," 7; "The Lavender Panthers," 30. In the latter article Broshears used a racial epithet to describe those black people he considered a threat.

50. "Rev. Ray Beaten," *Gay Crusader*, August–September 1973.

51. "Gays Beaten & Shot!; Jimmy Lorton 'Sally' Beaten; Vice Cops Shoot Down Two Gays," *Gay Crusader*, August–September 1973, 1.

52. "Gay Vigilantes to Fight Back."

53. "The Lavender Panthers," 73.

54. "Gay Groups Opposed to Retaliation," and O'Hara, "Question Man: Your Reaction to the Lavender Panthers?," *San Francisco Examiner*, July 11, 1973 (clippings included in Ray Broshears Papers, GLBTHS).

55. Parker, "The Lavender Panthers," 30.

56. "GAA/ Lavender Panthers," *Gay Crusader*, December–January 1973–74. For earlier purges (postdating the Trotskyite purge), see "Lavender Panther Growl Heard around the World," *Gay Crusader*, October–November 1973.

57. "The Have-Nots Attack (Sometimes Physically) The 'Haves!'" *Crusader: Voice of West Coast Gay Liberation*, May 1975.

58. See the collected correspondence, legal papers, fliers, and other documents in Carton 4, Raymond Broshears Papers, GLBTHS. Also see Mendenhall, "Heaven Can't Wait!"

59. See Ward Churchill and Jim Vander Wall, *The COINTELPRO Papers: Documents from the FBI's Secret Wars against Dissent in the United States* (Cambridge, MA: South End, 2001).

60. Mendenhall, "Heaven Can't Wait!"

61. Herbert Caen published this column in the *San Francisco Chronicle* on September

24, 1975. As mentioned in note 30, the Caen piece became the grounds of a lengthy lawsuit that Sipple filed against the City of San Francisco for exposing his private life as a homosexual. His case eventually failed, in part because of the time he had spent in the Tenderloin and Castro, which were noted as "the well-known gay sections of San Francisco" (David Luzer, "The Gay Man Who Saved Ford's Life").

62. Arguably, the media coverage of the Black Panthers was sensationalized at the same time as it helped to dramatize the stark social conditions that the party sought to challenge.

63. Sasha Gregory, "S.F. Harassment Data Gathered," *Advocate*, May 24, 1972 (Document #189, Notebook 1, Box B, Raymond Broshears Papers, GLBTHS). In 1972 a key target of critique was the building of a downtown Hilton hotel.

64. "?Finis?: Lavender Panthers Disbanded . . . ????," *Crusader*, July 1974. (Note that this issue of the publication dropped the word *gay* from its title in an effort to resist "the ghettoization of those of us who are of same-sex persuasion.")

65. Fliers titled "Old Folks Lunch," "Old Folks Lobbying," and "Teddy Roosevelt Republican Club." In addition, Broshears's correspondence files include many complaints about drugs and modeling in the late 1970s (Carton 4, Raymond Broshears Papers, GLBTHS).

66. George Mendenhall, "Heaven Can't Wait!"

67. It would be interesting to know if the founding of BAGL was influenced by the New York GAA, which in 1973 sent out "firemen" to build GAAs nationwide. See Marotta, *The Politics of Homosexuality*, 322. For additional information on BAGL, see *Gay Sunshine: A Journal of Gay Liberation* 24 (1975): n.p. (clipping in Gay Sunshine Ephemera File, San Francisco LGBT Groups Ephemera Collection, GLBTHS; Hal Offen, "Gay Liberation Growing with BAGL," *Voice of the Gay Students Coalition*, April 18, 1975, clipping in BAGL Ephemera File, San Francisco LGBT Groups Ephemera Collection, GLBTHS [hereafter BAGL Ephemera File, GLBTHS]).

68. BAGL, "Can Gay People Get it Together in San Francisco?," flier, n.d. (probably 1975), BAGL Ephemera File, GLBTHS.

69. Randy Alfred interview by author, San Francisco, August 11, 2004; fliers titled "Progressive Gay Caucus—Principles of Unity" and "Gay Action," BAGL Ephemera File, GLBTHS.

70. "Progressive Gay Caucus—Principles of Unity."

71. BAGL, "Second Annual BAGL Birthday Party: So What Has BAGL Done?," flier, n.d., BAGL Ephemera file, GLBTHS. For a more elaborate explanation of the Progressive Caucus stance on imperialism, see "Progressive Gay Caucus—Principles of Unity."

72. "Gay Action"; also see Hal Offen, "Waves from the Left," *San Francisco Sentinel*, November 18, 1976; Randy Alfred, "Waves from the Left," *San Francisco Sentinel*, December 16, 1976. These debates played out through the statements by each group, with the Progressive Caucus focused on the problem of imperialism and the need to consider the special issues affecting effeminate men, transsexuals, women, and people of color, and Gay Action focused on unity and more achievable, gay-centered reforms. Members of the Progressive Caucus were also outspoken advocates of the practice of criticism/self-criticism, discussed in the next chapter.

73. Ron Lanza, "Butterfly Brigade: Love and Rage," *San Francisco Sentinel*, June 30, 1977. Hank Wilson suggested that there had been a prior effort to distribute whistles, led by a man named Chris Perry (Hank Wilson interview by author, San Francisco, August 9, 2004). I did not manage to collect more information about that effort. The Butterfly Brigade also made plans to patrol parts of South of Market (the intersection of 8th and Howard Streets), Polk Street (at California), and Cole Valley (at Haight and Cole

Streets). After running one patrol and failing to get broader community support, the group stopped these efforts ("A List of Dates and Places for Butterfly Brigade Street-Watch and Public Outreach Program," Box 1, Butterfly Bridgade Folder 1, Randy Alfred Subject Files and Sound Recordings, Gay, Lesbian, Bisexual, Transgender Historical Society, San Francisco, CA (hereafter Randy Alfred Files, GLBTHS). Most of the articles cited here are included as clippings in Box 1, Butterfly Brigade Folder 2, Randy Alfred Files, GLBTHS.

74. Castells, "City and Culture: The San Francisco Experience," 145–51.

75. In other words, Castells did not necessarily count homes in this territory whose residents were women, did not vote for gay candidates, or lived with children or other relatives.

76. The description of the membership and activities of the Butterfly Brigade is culled from the author's interviews with Randy Alfred (San Francisco, August 11, 2004), Hank Wilson (San Francisco, August 9, 2004), Ben Gardiner (San Francisco, August 16, 2004), and Ali Marrero (Alameda, CA, July 28, 2008); the article, Hank Wilson and Harley Kohler, "Butterfly Brigade: Not about to Disband," *San Francisco Sentinel*, July 14, 1977; and a video recording of a panel discussion of former Brigade members held at the San Francisco Public Library in June 2002, on file at the Gay, Lesbian, Bisexual, Transgender Historical Society, San Francisco, CA. Also see John Bryan, "Castro Gays Mass to Thwart Thugs," *Berkeley Barb*, December 3–9, 1976, and "San Francisco Police Approve Butterfly Brigade," *Pacific Coast Times*, August 19–September 1, 1977, in addition to previously cited materials.

77. The biographical information on Assunta Femia comes from Arthur Evans, "Poet Assunta Femia Dies," *Bay Area Reporter*, November 9, 2006, http://ebar.com/news/article.php?sec=news&article=1318. Another Faerie associated with the Brigade was Jamal Redwing (see Steve Rubenstein, "CB Patrol Protects SF Gays," *San Francisco Chronicle*, January 24, 1977). For a discussion of Redwing's art, see Scott Morgensen, *The Spaces between Us: Queer Settler Colonialism and Indigenous Decolonization* (Minneapolis: University of Minnesota Press, 2011).

78. Ali Marrero interview by author, Alameda, CA, July 28, 2008.

79. "Gay Action: Notice of Anti-Gay Conduct," fliers, various dates in 1977, Box 1, Butterfly Brigade Folder 1, Randy Alfred Files, GLBTHS.

80. Of approximately ninety index cards, two noted white assailants, six noted assailants of color, and five noted mixed-race groups. The cards and letters are filed in the Box 1, Butterfly Brigade Folder 1, Randy Alfred Papers, GLBTHS. It is important to note that in the *San Francisco Sentinel*, Alfred was mindful to systematically note white assailants (Randy Alfred, "Anti-Gay Violence: Any Time, Any Place," *San Francisco Sentinel*, June 30, 1977).

81. Randy Alfred interview by author, San Francisco, August 11, 2004.

82. On May 5, 1982, years after the Butterfly Brigade had officially disbanded, its former member Ben Gardiner would send out a press release announcing "Butterfly Whistle Month" as proclaimed by Dianne Feinstein, then mayor of San Francisco. An undated press release also from Gardiner declared that Butterfly whistles were being provided to the first two groups of refugees from Cuba to arrive in San Francisco, funded by the Tavern Guild (Box 1, Butterfly Brigade Folder 1, Randy Alfred Files, GLBTHS).

83. Hank Wilson interview by author, San Francisco, August 9, 2004.

84. Ben Gardiner interview by author, San Francisco, August 16, 2004. The lesbian activist Ruth Mahaney was not a formal member of the Butterfly Brigade, but she shared the following memory: "The Butterfly Brigade and the whistle campaign was also a way

of not turning to 'the Man.' You know, not turning to the cops, but to police ourselves and each other, and help each other out. . . . I remember . . . our favorite stories that we told again and again. . . . I remember one in Collingwood Park. There were a lot of beatings in Collingwood Park. And I remember one where a guy, you know, was walking his dog or something in Collingwood Park and got attacked by . . . a gang of young kids. And somebody saw it from their apartment, and threw open the window and blew his whistle. And suddenly, all the windows flew open, and whistles were, like, everywhere, and it was this din around the park that just echoed against the buildings. And the kids, like, froze and ran" (Ruth Mahaney interview by author, San Francisco, July 16, 2008).

85. "Opinion: Self-Discipline in Gay Community," *San Francisco Examiner*, June 27, 1977 (Box 1, Butterfly Brigade Folder 2, Randy Alfred Files, GLBTHS).

86. Randy Shilts, *The Mayor of Castro Street: The Life and Times of Harvey Milk* (New York: St. Martin's, 1982), 175.

87. See Lanza, "Butterfly Brigade: Love and Rage," for a disavowal of masculinism. During interviews, former members also critiqued the use of masculine prerogative.

88. Gardiner explained: "Some people [would say], 'Who wants the pigs? Who would want to have anything to do with the pigs? Wait a minute. They came and arrested the people we talked about the other night, remember? Oh, yeah. But they have to do that. They're pigs. We don't want them.' And most people got the idea that the police were willing to help us and we didn't have to invite them over to our house" (Ben Gardiner interview by author, San Francisco, August 16, 2004).

89. Hank Wilson interview by author, San Francisco, August 9, 2004.

90. Shilts, *The Mayor of Castro Street*, 175.

91. For a discussion of self-management and the risk of violence, see Gail Mason, *The Spectacle of Violence: Homophobia, Gender, and Knowledge* (London: Routledge, 2002), 80–83. Mason builds on the work of Michel Foucault here, highlighting how the very ideal of visibility might provide for one's regulation. What is important to acknowledge is that activists cast visibility in the terms of choice (i.e., passing) and not as a means to interrogate the kinds of identity formations in play.

92. Castells, "City and Culture: The San Francisco Experience," n142, 410.

93. In fact, patroller Randy Alfred published an article on the topic just a few years later: "Will the Real Clone Please Stand Out?" *Advocate* 338, March 18, 1982. Also see Martin P. Levine, *Gay Macho: The Life and Death of the Homosexual Clone*, ed. Michael S. Kimmel (New York: New York University Press, 1998).

94. Alfred estimated them to be between nineteen and twenty-three and primarily from Bay Area suburbs, with some from among the white ethnic groups slowly leaving the Castro for other San Francisco neighborhoods and areas outside the city (Randy Alfred interview by author, San Francisco, August 11, 2004).

95. For example, Gardiner pointed to the problem of economic violence coming from young, low-income black men from the Western Addition (Ben Gardiner interview by author, San Francisco, August 16, 2004). Alfred noted the history of violence in Dolores Park, a divider between the Mission and the Castro, although he clarified that this was mostly sexual harassment against women and should not be presumed to be committed by Latino men (Randy Alfred interview by author, San Francisco, August 11, 2004).

96. Ali Marrero interview by author, Alameda, CA, July 28, 2008.

97. In some interviews, people remember Marrero playing this role; others remember it being she and friends of Hillsborough doing it.

98. Gayle Rubin, "Thinking Sex," in *The Lesbian and Gay Studies Reader*, ed. Henry Abelove, Michele Aina Barele, and David M. Halperin (New York: Routledge, 1993), 24.

99. See Wayne Friday, vice president of the Tavern Guild of San Francisco, letter to Randy Alfred, March 15, 1977, donating $100 for the Richard Heakin Memorial Community Defense Committee (Butterfly Brigade) and Alfred's thank-you letter dated March 20, 1977 (Box 1, Butterfly Brigade Folder 1, Randy Alfred Files, GLBTHS). The folder also contains thank-you letters from Alfred to the Castro Village Association and Castro Village Jewelers, dated February 10, 1977. From 1976 to 1983, the People's Fund gave funds to gay individuals in need. It operated under the sponsorship of the Pride Foundation and was run by the Council of Emperors, originally founded by José Sarria and Bob Ross, who was the founder and publisher of the *Bay Area Reporter*. The People's Fund provided the economic support for Robert Hillsborough's funeral (Finding Aid, People's Fund Records, Collection 1988–06, Gay, Lesbian, Bisexual, Transgender Historical Society Collection, San Francisco Public Library, San Francisco; at the time I consulted this collection, the folder about Hillsborough was not on site, so I refer to the finding aid description of it here). The People's Fund also held a fund-raiser auction to raise money for walkie-talkies for the Butterfly Brigade on August 18, 1977 (program announcement, Box 1, Butterfly Brigade Folder 1, Randy Alfred Files, GLBTHS). For the Golden Gate Business Association's consideration of later community safety campaigns, see the association director's Meeting Minutes of February 19, 1980 (Folder 8) and June 25, 1981 (Folder 9), Golden Gate Business Association Records, Gay, Lesbian, Bisexual, Transgender Historical Society Collection, San Francisco Public Library, San Francisco.

100. David Garland, *The Culture of Control: Crime and Social Order in Contemporary Society* (Chicago: University of Chicago Press, 2001), 16.

101. Garland, *The Culture of Control*, 16.

102. George L. Kelling and James Q. Wilson, "Broken Windows: The Police and Neighborhood Safety," *Atlantic*, March 1, 1982, 29–38. This essay describes Kelling's work with the Police Foundation during the mid-1970s and his study of walking patrols in Newark, New Jersey.

103. *Plexus* reported at least 3,000 women; other informal sources suggest more. See "Take Back the Night Conference . . . and March," *Plexus*, January 1979.

104. Judith Butler discusses how pornography and antigay language have been asserted as examples of hate speech, speech acts that both lead to an effect and are the effect in itself. Butler explores the rhetorical and political limits of advocating for the legal regulation of speech as violence, from the variable power of speech to act, dependent on who is speaking, to the inherent nonequivalence of terms likened to each other through the use of metaphor. Here I am most interested in Butler's brief analysis of how Catharine MacKinnon, in arguing for the regulation of pornography, constitutes the visual field of pornography as an injurious speech act that promises and realizes the threat it carries. This provides a link between safe streets patrols' emphasis on antigay language and looks and the new anticrime theories of the 1970s. Activists followed MacKinnon's primary understanding of pornography as that which orders those addressed to do as it shows. Yet as Butler explains, MacKinnon goes on to assert the visual field as conduct that violates women's right to equality unto itself and thus should be regulated. Butler criticizes this as a misunderstanding of the work of "visual depiction," which she argues is ultimately a phantasmatic representation of social norms that are otherwise unrealizable. Judith Butler, *Excitable Speech: A Politics of the Performative* (New York: Routledge, 1997), 4, 47–52, 65–69. See also J. L. Austin, *How to Do Things with Words* (Cambridge: Harvard University Press, 1962).

105. Susan Brownmiller, *In Our Times: Memoir of a Revolution* (New York: Dial, 1999). Other feminists argued that a cleanup of Times Square would do more to target than

protect lesbians, gay men, and prostitutes and would make people of color most vulnerable. See, for example, a letter to the editor from Marjorie Ackerman, Quinn Bevan, Cathy Cockrell, Eileen Kane, Doris Lunden, and Marty Pottenger to the lesbian feminist newspaper *Plexus*, February 1980. For an analysis of these marches in the context of urban politics during this time, see Claire Bond Potter, "Taking Back Times Square: Feminist Repertoires and the Transformation of Urban Space in Late Second Wave Feminism," *Radical History Review* 113 (Spring 2012): 67–80.

106. Marge Piercy, preface to *Take Back the Night: Women on Pornography*, ed. Laura Lederer (New York: William Morrow, 1980), 7.

107. George Kelling cites his research from the 1970s in "'Broken Windows' and the Culture War: A Response to Selected Critiques," in *Crime, Disorder and Community Safety*, ed. Roger Matthews and John Pitts (London: Routledge, 2001), 120–44. Although the "broken windows" theory provided the rationale for quality-of-life policing, it was just one of many analyses with diverse political roots that sought to correlate environment and behavior. The Chicago School sociologists provide one example; another has been suggested by Kwame Holmes, who cites a genealogy of scholarship and activism by black liberals and radicals—from Kenneth B. Clark (*Dark Ghetto: Dilemmas of Social Power* [New York: Harper, 1965]) to Kwame Ture [Stokely Carmichael] and Charles Hamilton (*Black Power: The Politics of Liberation* [1967; New York: Vintage, 2001] that saw "municipal neglect to produce environmental conditions that loudly communicate to residents their lack of worth or value, a psychological message that . . . encourages violent crime" (personal email communication, June 17, 2012).

108. Deviant city street culture might best be described as "periperformative," Eve Kosofsky Sedgwick's term to describe what is nearby the explicit speech act. Sedgwick uses this concept as a way to spatialize the performative; it captures the everyday and signals that which *acts out of place* (*Touching Feeling: Affect, Pedagogy, Performativity* [Durham: Duke University Press, 2003]).

109. Khalil Gibran Muhammad, *The Condemnation of Blackness: Race, Crime, and the Making of Modern Urban America* (Cambridge: Harvard University Press, 2010).

110. I acknowledge that hateful epithets can, and often do, signal violence to come. Nonetheless, such scenes of threat must be analyzed in their broadest social contexts and not just one in which the effects of hate are substituted for violence itself.

111. Hank Wilson and Ron Lanza would later collaborate in running a series of single-room-occupancy hotels in the Tenderloin that provided harm-reduction-based services to low-income people living with AIDS and launched other HIV/AIDS programs in the Tenderloin; they also cofounded Valencia Rose Café, a gay cabaret and performance space in the Mission. In later years, when describing his work in the Tenderloin, Wilson cited violence and negligence as a problem of the police and explained that this drove many of his efforts to reform police training. He also helped to spearhead a lesbian and gay speakers bureau that tackled violence by educating young people in city schools. Wilson dedicated the last years of his life to fighting gay men's use of poppers; he died in 2008. Randy Alfred went on to publish a series of articles exposing negligence that led to murderous fires in gay bars and wrote a famed indictment of the CBS show "Gay Power, Gay Politics" that had represented gay life in the Castro as narcissistic and destructive. Alfred was a founding member of the National Lesbian and Gay Journalists Association. Today, he remains a journalist in San Francisco, and he has been diligent in collecting and presenting gay history in conjunction with the Gay, Lesbian, Bisexual, Transgender Historical Society. Ali Marrero would stay active in city-run safe streets campaigns and both Latino/a and lesbian activism, including Gente (profiled in the next chapter) and Dykes on Bikes; af-

ter over thirty years of living and working in San Francisco's Mission District as an HIV and drug treatment counselor, she has now retired in the area. Ben Gardiner remained central to neighborhood activism in the Duboce Triangle area, near the Castro, and also became an AIDS activist; he ran the first computerized AIDS bulletin. He passed away in 2010.

112. "Speculators Get out of Our Neighborhood!," flier, n.d. BAGL Ephemera File, GLBTHS. Lesbian and Gay Action also joined this action. I am unsure if this organization is connected to the Gay Action group that gave birth to the Butterfly Brigade.

113. "What Hotel Fight Means to Gays," *San Francisco Sentinel*, February 24, 1977. See also James Sobredo, "From Manila Bay to Daly City: Filipinos in San Francisco," in *Reclaiming San Francisco: History, Politics, Culture*, ed. James Brooks, Chris Carlsson, and Nancy J. Peters (San Francisco: City Lights, 1998), 273–86.

114. The description of SMASH is based on an article by Michael Shernoff, "Early Gay Activism in Chelsea: Building a Queer Neighborhood," LGNY, July 6, 1997 (Shernoff remembers the patrol as founded in the summer of 1978; media coverage suggests it was the summer of 1976); Michael Shernoff interview by author, New York, September 13, 2004; a video in which the founders of SMASH, Louis Weingarden and Larry Durham, were interviewed by Myron Berger (a journalist for the *Villager*) on the short-lived gay public-access television program *Emerald City* ("The Emerald City," Pilot Episode A, Summer 1976, Emerald City Tapes [Television Program], National Archives of Lesbian, Gay, Bisexual, and Transgender History, Lesbian, Gay, Bisexual, and Transgender Community Center, New York, NY); and a series of articles including Myron Berger, "Gays Organize Vigilante Action," *Villager*, August 12, 1976; Myron Berger, "SMASH and Kids at Summit," *Villager*, August 19, 1976; and Myron Berger, "Friendly Persuasion Works," *Villager*, August 26, 1976.

115. Shernoff, "Early Gay Activism in Chelsea."

116. Shernoff, "Early Gay Activism in Chelsea."

117. For a longer biography of Weingarden, see the Estate Project for Artists with AIDS, "Louis Weingarden," http://www.artistswithaids.org/artforms/music/catalogue /weingarden.html. Weingarden passed away in 1989, as did Shernoff in 2008. I did not find information on Larry Durham.

118. Birney Jarvis, "Volunteer Squads: The Gay Crime Fighters," *San Francisco Chronicle*, June 5, 1978; "Citizen Squad Patrols Folsom," *Bay Area Reporter*, June 11, 1978.

119. "The Emerald City," Pilot Episode A. For a similar argument, see Eric Weissman, "Kids Who Attack Gays," *Christopher Street*, August 1978, 9–13.

120. For example, see Shernoff, "Early Gay Activism in Chelsea."

121. My presumption that the killer was white is due to many descriptive features of an article about the case, including a quote from a teacher who said that the killer's crowd had "'a thing' against blacks and Puerto Ricans" (quoted in Dan Oppenheimer, "Aftermath of a Tragedy," *Villager*, June 24, 1976) and that the article referred to other members of the group he hung out with as white. Otherwise this article and other media coverage of this event for the most part occluded the explicit mention of race, which also suggests that they were white. This is rarely the case in media representations of violence done by people of color. Also see Dan Oppenheimer, "Youth Confesses to Fatal Stabbing," *Villager*, June 17, 1976.

122. The call for police to "do their job" is quoted in Steve Simon, "Washington Square Tragedy," *Villager*, September 16, 1976. The language of "undesirables" getting out of "our parks" is in Earl Jay Perel, "Police Manipulations," letter to the editor, *Villager*, September 16, 1976.

123. Simon, "Washington Square Tragedy." The residents continued to protest after the youth attackers were convicted; see Adam Blumenthal, "Angry Rally Follows Riot Convictions," *Villager*, March 23, 1978.

124. See, for example, Jerry Podair, *The Strike That Changed New York: Blacks, Whites, and the Ocean Hill–Brownsville Crisis* (New Haven: Yale University Press, 2002); Joshua Freeman, *Working-Class New York: Life and Labor since World War II* (New York: New Press, 2000).

125. Berger, "Friendly Persuasion Works," *Villager*, August 26, 1976; Shernoff, "Early Gay Activism in Chelsea."

126. Lee Rainwater and William L. Yancey, *The Moynihan Report and the Politics of Controversy* (Cambridge: MIT Press, 1967).

127. Kenneth T. Smith, "Homophobia: A Tentative Personality Profile," *Psychological Reports* 29 (1971): 1091–94; George Weinberg, *Society and the Healthy Homosexual* (New York: St. Martin's, 1972). There is some debate as to who coined the term, since both authors claim to have first used it in the late 1960s.

128. Daniel Wickberg, "Homophobia: On the Cultural History of an Idea," *Critical Inquiry* 27 (August 2000): 42–57.

129. Michael Shernoff interview by author, New York, September 13, 2004.

130. On April 18, 1972, the Mattachine Society held a public forum with Weinberg called "Society and the Healthy Homosexual," which was covered in the June 1972 *New York Mattachine Times*. Weinberg's book was also affirmatively reviewed in the gay press; see, for example, Thane Hampten, "By Far the Best Book!" *Gay*, March 6, 1972.

131. George Weinberg, "The Homophobic Scale," *Gay*, August 30, 1971. Also see George Weinberg, "What Is the Gay Activists Alliance Really Doing?," *Gay*, March 6, 1972.

132. As many have pointed out, this concept does not account for the broad cultural and legal rejections of homosexuality that undermine the assumption that homophobia is necessarily irrational. For a comprehensive review of the literature and an alternative model of understanding and responding to antigay sentiment, see Gregory M. Herek, "Beyond 'Homophobia': A Social Psychological Perspective on Attitudes towards Lesbians and Gay Men," in *Bashers, Baiters and Bigots: Homophobia in American Society*, ed. Jay DeCecco (New York: Harrington Park, 1985), 1–22.

133. The assumption that racial alienation and poverty drive violence and sexual deviance was also manifested in liberal social science research on prison rape during these years. Although Regina Kunzel argues that lesbian and gay prison activism of the 1970s mostly avoided explicit discussions of race (as did the activists profiled here), the move to recast rape as violence rather than sex might also have produced readings by white gay activists of black-on-white rape as a political response. See Kunzel, *Criminal Intimacy: Prison and the Uneven History of Modern American Sexuality* (Chicago: University of Chicago Press, 2008).

134. Whitman, "A Gay Manifesto," 340.

135. Weinberg, *Society and the Healthy Homosexual*, 83. See also Daryl Michael Scott's discussion of black self-hate in *Contempt and Pity: Social Policy and the Image of the Damaged Black Psyche, 1880–1996* (Chapel Hill: University of North Carolina Press, 1997).

136. For information on the early efforts of the Chelsea Gay Association, see David Behrens, "Joining against Crime," *Newsday*, November 29, 1982. The organization is discussed more in chapter 4.

137. Josh Sides, *Erotic City: Sexual Revolutions and the Making of Modern San Francisco* (New York: Oxford University Press, 2009), 141–73.

138. Sides, *Erotic City*, 161.

139. Sides, *Erotic City*, 142.

140. Perhaps most significant, Josh Sides affirmatively notes the legacy of the Butterfly Brigade and the founding of Community United Against Violence as informed by this sentiment about Latino homophobia: "Gay men defended themselves in the Castro by organizing the Butterfly Brigade, a group that detained suspects in antigay attacks. But it was an uphill battle. Dolores Park—across the street from the historic Mission Dolores—had become 'a hotspot of antigay harassment by Latinos,' according to Dick Stingel, head of the gay organization Community United Against Violence" (*Erotic City*, 164). This is an example of how the very fact of self-policing in a mostly white gay neighborhood would be broadly interpreted as productive of these dynamics, regardless of activists' stated objectives to the contrary.

141. The concept of a "racial project" is drawn from Michael Omi and Howard Winant, *Racial Formation in the United States: From the 1960s to the 1990s*, 2nd ed. (New York: Routledge, 1994).

142. Isaac William Martin, *The Permanent Tax Revolt: How the Property Tax Transformed American Politics* (Stanford: Stanford University Press, 2008).

3. "Count the Contradictions"

Epigraph: From the theme song "That's Contradictions!" (sung to the tune of "That's Entertainment!"). The song was part of the skit "Count the Contradictions," written by Lesbians Against Police Violence around 1980 (Skits and Lyrics Folder, Meg Barnett Collection of Lesbians Against Police Violence Records, Gay, Lesbian, Bisexual, Transgender Historical Society, San Francisco (hereafter Meg Barnett Collection, GLBTHS).

1. Wages Due Lesbians was founded in 1975 in Britain as part of the international effort to demand economic remuneration for housework known as Wages Due Housework.

2. The San Francisco Office of Citizen Complaints was instituted after the 1982 election.

3. The group was first called the Women's Coalition Against Police Violence and later changed its name (Lois Helmbold interview by author, Oakland, CA, July 25, 2008; also see documents in Lois Helmbold personal collection). Also see "Principles of Unity, Women's Coalition Against Police Violence," March 21, 1979, History and Structure of LAPV Folder, Meg Barnett Collection, GLBTHS. Here the group's members stated explicitly: "We do not work with the police." They also indicated that the group was to be lesbian focused but open to all women's participation. The history of LAPV here is based on the author's interviews with Meg Barnett (also known as Maggie Jochild) via telephone, September 8 and 15, 2004; Laura Hahn (pseudonym) via telephone, 2004; Pamela David, San Francisco, July 9, 2008; and Lois Helmbold, Oakland, CA, July 25, 2008; as well as the following written materials: Meg Barnett, "Chronological Timeline and Herstory of Lesbians Against Police Violence," unpublished document (Meg Barnett personal collection), and untitled and undated documents in History and Structure of LAPV Folder, Meg Barnett Collection, GLBTHS and the ephemeral materials in Lois Helmbold's personal collection that she discussed with me during our interview. I am tremendously grateful for the generosity of those who spoke with me, especially Maggie Jochild, for her razor-sharp memory, smarts, and humor. For her own perspective on LAPV, see http://maggiesmetawatershed .blogspot.com/2008/05/white-night-riot-21-may-1979-and.html.

4. Many of the women I interviewed noted how strong gender divisions were during these years.

5. Proposition 13 linked property tax rates to acquisition rather than market value. As cited in the last chapter, Isaac Martin shows how this movement began as populist

campaign with varied political roots but was taken up by conservative politics to support big business interests. See Martin, *The Permanent Tax Revolt: How the Property Tax Transformed American Politics* (Stanford: Stanford University Press, 2008); Jack Citrin and Isaac Martin, eds., *After the Tax Revolt: California's Proposition 13 Turns 30* (Berkeley, CA: Berkeley Public Policy Press, 2009). For a more detailed discussion of lesbian and gay leftists' opposition to Propositions 6, 7, and 13, see Emily Hobson, "Imagining Alliance: Queer Anti-Imperialism and Race in California, 1966–1990," PhD diss., University of Southern California, 2009, and *Lavender and Red: Race, Empire, and Solidarity in the Gay and Lesbian Left* (Berkeley: University of California Press, forthcoming).

6. "Gays Launch Major Offensive to Defeat Family Protection Act; Denounce 'Bullying' Tactics and Legitimizing of Anti-Gay Violence," National Gay Task Force (NGTF) press release, June 17, 1981, Box 36, Folder 199, National Gay and Lesbian Task Force Records (Collection 7301), Rare and Manuscript Collections, Kroch Library, Cornell University (hereafter NGLTF Records, Cornell); "NGTF Gears up to Challenge the New Right," NGTF press release, August 20, 1981, Box 36, Folder 202, ibid.

7. "NGTF targets 50 largest cities regarding police hiring practices," NGTF press release, April 8, 1982, Box 36, Folder 230, NGLTF Records, Cornell; "NGTF Urges Support for Statewide Independent Civilian Review Boards," NGTF press release, May 28, 1984, Box 36, Folder 305, ibid.

8. This chapter focuses on the activities of three mostly lesbian organizations that organized in response to violence and gentrification around 1980: the Third World Gay Coalition, Dykes Against Racism Everywhere, and Lesbians Against Police Violence. But I want to note here other organizations that might be considered fellow travelers, especially later in the decade. These include the San Francisco Bay Area–based chapter of the Alliance Against Women's Oppression, which was at the frontlines of multi-issue approaches to gender and racial justice in the Bay Area that also attempted to integrate issues of homosexuality into their development of a political line during the 1980s. (I consulted the group's records at the Women of Color Resource Center in Oakland. They were donated in 2012 to the Sophia Smith Collection at Smith College.) Other relevant organizations from New York during the 1980s that I do not discuss in detail include the Coalition Against Racism, Anti-Semitism, Sexism, and Heterosexism and Asian Lesbians of the East Coast, and, from San Francisco, Bay Area Black Lesbians and Gays. These organizations joined already existing groups that began in the 1970s (which I name in the first part of this chapter), such as Salsa Soul Sisters and El Comité Homosexual Latinamericano in New York and the Gay Latino Alliance and the Third World Gay Caucus in San Francisco.

9. National lesbian and gay organizations also challenged the proposed Family Protection Act, but as a form of policy opposition rather than as part of broad-based campaigns. See "Gays Launch Major Offensive to Defeat Family Protection Act."

10. See John D'Emilio, foreword to *Out of the Closets: Voices of Gay Liberation*, ed. Karla Jay and Allen Young, 20th anniversary edition, 2nd ed. (New York: New York University Press, 1992), xi–xxix; Martin Duberman, *Stonewall* (New York: Plume, 1993); Terence Kissack, "Freaking Fag Revolutionaries: New York's Gay Liberation Front, 1969–1971," *Radical History Review* 62 (Spring 1995): 104–35.

11. Karla Jay, *Tales of the Lavender Menace: A Memoir of Liberation* (New York: Basic Books, 1999), 76.

12. Many of these organizations are discussed in more detail in Stephan L. Cohen, *The Gay Liberation Youth Movement in New York: "An Army of Lovers Cannot Fail"* (New York: Routledge, 2008). It is unclear whether Bubbles Rose's last name was Lee or Marie.

Cohen's book uses Lee. But in an interview with STAR member Marsha P. Johnson, she uses "Marie" (it is worth noting that the same interview transcribes Johnson's first name as Marcia). For the reference to Marie and more information about STAR, see "Rapping with a Street Transvestite Revolutionary: An Interview with Marcia Johnson," in *Out of the Closets: Voices of Gay Liberation*, ed. Jay and Young, 112–20.

13. On Salsa Soul Sisters, see Alice Y. Hom, "Unifying Differences: Lesbian of Color Community Building in Los Angeles and New York, 1970s-1980s," PhD diss., University of California, Los Angeles, 2011. El Comité Homosexual Latinamericano is mentioned in Luis Aponte-Parés, "Outside/In: Crossing Queer and Latino Boundaries," in *Mambo Montage: The Latinization of New York*, ed. Augustín Laó-Montes and Arlene Davila (New York: Columbia University Press, 2001), 363–86.

14. On Gay American Indians, see Scott Morgensen, *The Spaces between Us: Queer Settler Colonialism and Indigenous Decolonization* (Minneapolis: University of Minnesota Press, 2011). On the Gay Latino Alliance, see Horacio N. Roque-Ramirez, "'That's *My* Place!': Negotiating Racial, Gender, and Sexual Politics in San Francisco's Gay Latino Alliance, 1973–1983," *Journal of the History of Sexuality* 12, no. 2 (2003): 224–48. (Roque-Ramirez notes that the organization changed its name in 1976 or 1977 to Gay Latina/Latino Alliance, although many members continued to use its original title.) On Asian American Feminists, see Trinity A. Ordona, "Asian Lesbians in San Francisco: Struggles to Create a Safe Space, 1970s–1980s," in *Asian/Pacific Islander American Women: A Historical Anthology*, ed. Shirley Hune and Gail Nomura (New York: New York University Press, 2003), 319–34. The Third World Gay Caucus was associated with Bay Area Gay Liberation (BAGL) but also had an independent trajectory.

15. See Amin Ghaziani, *The Dividends of Dissent: How Conflict and Culture Work in Lesbian and Gay Marches on Washington* (Chicago: University of Chicago Press, 2008).

16. Third World Gay Revolution, "What We Want, What We Believe," in *Out of the Closets*, ed. Jay and Young, 363–67.

17. K. [Abram J.] Lewis, "Gays Are Revolting! Multi-Issue Organizing in the Gay Liberation Front, 1969–1972," BA thesis, Columbia University, 2006.

18. See "Gay People Help Plan New World," *Gay Flames*, September 11, 1970.

19. "The Oppressed Shall Not Become the Oppressors," cited in Donn Teal, *The Gay Militants: How Gay Liberation Began in America, 1969–1971* (1971; New York: St. Martin's, 1995), 194.

20. Huey P. Newton, "The Women's Liberation and Gay Liberation Movements," August 15, 1970, http://www.historyisaweapon.com/defcon1/newtonq.html.

21. In an interview, Marsha P. Johnson of Street Transvestite Action Revolutionaries made it clear that the biggest threats trans women arrested for prostitution faced were from the police, and that straight prisoners would often court trans prisoners for sexual favors. These requests for sex could be coercive or violent, but not always; furthermore, for some women this was a dynamic continuous with what they experienced outside the jails. See Interview with Marcia [*sic*] P. Johnson, "Rapping with a Street Transvestite Revolutionary."

22. "Black Gay Caucus: Black Is Beautiful, Gay Is Good, Come Join Us!!!," n.d., Black Gay Caucus Ephemera File, San Francisco LGBT Groups Ephemera Collection, Gay, Lesbian, Bisexual, Transgender Historical Society, San Francisco, CA.

23. "Double carding" is the practice of requiring two forms of identification before entering a bar. See for example the "New York" update in the newsletter of BWMT which describes an ongoing campaign to protect Blues, a "Black gay/Transpersons' bar near Times Square," and two lesbian bars, Déjà Vu and the Duchess, with a variable clien-

tele of lesbians of color, from police harassment; it also discusses activist challenges to the Ice Palace, a gay club, for its discriminatory policies (BWMT *Quarterly*, Winter 1982, Newsletter Collection, Gay, Lesbian, Bisexual, Transgender Historical Society, San Francisco, CA [hereafter Newsletters, GLBTHS]). For an example of a campaign against the exclusion of "effeminate," "Third World," "elderly," and "other" (that is, political) men, see the flier titled "Have You Been Clubbed by the Club Baths?," announcing an action sponsored by BAGL and the affiliated Black Gay Caucus, n.d., BAGL Ephemera File, San Francisco LGBT Groups Ephemera Collection, Gay, Lesbian, Bisexual, Transgender Historical Society, San Francisco, CA. Black lesbians also took on racist bar practices at Bay Area lesbian bars (see letters to the editor, ONYX: *Black Lesbian Newsletter*, April–May 1983, Newsletters, GLBTHS) as well as in New York (see fliers announcing actions in Dykes Against Racism Everywhere Organization File, Lesbian Herstory Archives, Brooklyn, NY).

24. Cohen, *The Gay Liberation Youth Movement in New York*.

25. Cherríe Moraga and Gloria Anzaldúa, eds., *This Bridge Called My Back: Writings by Radical Women of Color* (Latham, NY: Kitchen Table: Women of Color Press, [1981] 1983); also see Barbara Smith, ed., *Home Girls: A Black Feminist Anthology* (New York: Kitchen Table: Women of Color Press, 1983) and Barbara Smith, "A Press of Our Own Kitchen Table: Women of Color Press," *Frontiers: A Journal of Women Studies* 10, no. 3 (1989): 11–13.

26. For an overview of many leftist organizations during this period and their stances on lesbian and gay issues as well, see Max Elbaum, *Revolution in the Air: Sixties Radicals Turn to Lenin, Mao and Che* (New York: Verso, 2006).

27. For more details, see Hobson, *Lavender and Red*.

28. In many ways, the collective echoed the Third World Women's Alliance of the late 1960s, which was an expansion of the Black Women's Alliance, a working group in the Student Nonviolent Coordinating Committee. For more on the history of the Combahee River Collective, see Kimberly Springer, *Living for the Revolution: Black Feminist Organizations, 1968–1980* (Durham: Duke University Press, 2005); Winifred Breines, *The Trouble between Us: An Uneasy History of White and Black Women in the Feminist Movement* (New York: Oxford University Press, 2006).

29. Combahee River Collective, "A Black Feminist Statement," in *This Bridge Called My Back: Writings by Radical Women of Color*, ed. Cherríe Moraga and Gloria Anzaldúa (Latham, NY: Kitchen Table: Women of Color Press, [1981] 1983), 210.

30. Combahee River Collective, "A Black Feminist Statement," 214.

31. The pamphlet, titled "Six, 7, 8 Black Women: Why Did They Die?" was reproduced in an issue of the magazine *Radical America*. Along with the pamphlet was a brief article without clear attribution titled, "Why Did They Die? A Document of Black Feminism," *Radical America* (November–December 1979): 40–49. Also included in Combahee River Collective Organization File, Lesbian Herstory Archives.

32. Grace Kyungwon Hong, *The Ruptures of American Capital: Women of Color Feminism and the Culture of Immigrant Labor* (Minneapolis: University of Minnesota Press, 2006), xxxiii.

33. For an analytic genealogy of antiracist feminist antiviolence activism from that period, see Emily Thuma, "Not a Wedge, but a Bridge: Prisons, Feminist Activism, and the Politics of Gendered Violence, 1968–1987," PhD diss., New York University, 2011.

34. "Why Did They Die?," 42.

35. The following are some of the sources that reproduced or discussed the statement: Zillah Eisenstein, ed., *Capitalist Patriarchy and the Case for Socialist Feminism*

(New York: Monthly Review, 1978); Moraga and Anzaldúa, eds., *This Bridge Called My Back*; Sara Bennett and Joan Gibbs, eds., *Top Ranking: A Collection of Articles on Racism and Classism in the Lesbian Community* (New York: Come!Unity, 1980). It was also featured as a letter in the June 1979 issue of *Off Our Backs*. Clearly engaging with the statement was Barbara Smith's essay "Notes for Yet Another Paper on Black Feminism, Or Will the Real Enemy Please Stand Up," published in *Conditions* 2, no. 2 (1979): 123–27.

36. It is worth noting here that Boston, in general, had an active scene of multi-issue, antiracist lesbian and gay activism throughout the 1980s. Much of that activism circulated around the newspaper *Gay Community News*, which was one of the few sources to report not only on these issues in Boston, but on leftist lesbian and gay organizations across the country. For a history of that publication, see Amy Hoffman, *An Army of Ex-Lovers: My Life at the Gay Community News* (Amherst: University of Massachusetts Press, 2007).

37. In referring to 1970s Brooklyn, Suleiman Osman writes: "In brochures, newspapers, and real estate guides, the area had become 'Brownstone Brooklyn'—a constellation of revitalized townhouse districts including Clinton Hill, Park Slope, and Prospect Heights. Brownstoners, however, believed they were involved in something more than a renovation fad. Brownstoning was a cultural revolt against sameness, conformity, and bureaucracy" (*The Invention of Brownstone Brooklyn: Gentrification and the Search for Authenticity in Postwar New York* [New York: Oxford University Press, 2011], 5).

38. In the second issue of the gay magazine *Christopher Street*, the editors celebrated scholarship that named the leadership roles of gay men in urban revitalization during that time: "Out & Around: Brownstoning," *Christopher Street*, August 1976, 3. In *The Invention of Brownstone Brooklyn*, Osman does not focus on lesbian and gay male participation in this phenomenon, instead citing long-standing middle-class gay communities in other parts of Brooklyn that he argues served to facilitate cross-class exchanges. This argument is somewhat similar to one made by Samuel R. Delany about the history of Times Square (*Times Square Red, Times Square Blue* [New York: New York University Press, 1999]).

39. For an excellent discussion of this debate, see Roque-Ramirez, "'That's My Place!'" Roque-Ramirez also notes that some members of the Gay Latino Alliance called gay Latinos who supported Carol Silver, the candidate favored by most gay whites, "sellouts" (246).

40. Quoted in Susan Cohen, "Decade of Change Apparent in S.F. Street's Gay Lifestyle" *San Jose Mercury News*, September, 4, 1979 (clipping in Box 1, Folder 3, Golden Gate Business Association Records, San Francisco Public Library, San Francisco, CA).

41. For an emblematic example in New York, see David Behrens, "Joining against Crime," *Newsday*, November 29, 1982. The *Tomorrow with Tom Snyder* episode is on a video held by the GLBTHS.

42. A wide variety of opinions were featured in the pages of the BWMT newsletter. One example of the economic argument was made by a black letter writer identified as "L" (*BWMT Quarterly*, Spring 1981). The editors of the newsletter agreed: "Isn't much, if not most, Black criminal activities, whether against White or other Blacks, economically motivated, the 'have-nots' going after the 'haves'?" Also see a letter from a Bostonian identified as "R" in *BWMT Newsletter* (later renamed *BWMT Quarterly*), November 1980: "One Black politician even introduced an anti-gentrification (= anti-faggot) bill in the legislature to prevent Gays from buying property in his South End constituency, but the issue was not pressed since this same politician also solicits the Gay vote" (Newsletters, GLBTHS).

43. The Third World Gay Coalition did not use an acronym, but I have adopted one for clarity here.

44. For more on Reclamation Site No. 1, see Peter Siskind, "'Rockefeller's Vietnam'? Black Politics and Urban Development in Harlem, 1969–1974," paper, Gotham History Festival, October 6, 2001, http://www.gothamcenter.org/festival/2001/confpapers/siskind .pdf.

45. Today Lenn Keller continues to live in the San Francisco Bay Area. For years she has balanced arts, activism, and public health work. She is currently completing a documentary about butch/femme cultures.

46. As I noted in chapter 1, the Fillmore is a part of the Western Addition, but the name is also used to represent the entire neighborhood. In each chapter, I defer to the usage in the majority of primary sources; in this chapter that is *Fillmore*.

47. Lenn Keller interview by author, San Pablo, CA, March 18, 2011, and materials in personal collection of Lenn Keller, San Pablo, CA. Randy Alfred covered some of the community meetings during this time, writing that "anti-gay hostility rankled in some black neighborhoods as a portion of that community's leadership openly expressed their homophobia at a series of meetings dealing with the city's housing crunch" (Randy Alfred, "Why the Lid Blew Off," *Berkeley Barb*, May 24–June 6, 1979).

48. "Third World Gay Coalition: Community Organizing for Nonviolent Mediation," document, n.d., personal collection of Lenn Keller.

49. "Third World Gay Coalition."

50. "Third World Gay Coalition."

51. Helen Keller, "Third World Gay Denied $$," *Plexus*, November 1979.

52. Erika Huggins, letter to Ida Strickland, June 2, 1979; open letter from Ron Dellums, May 30, 1979; E. Kitch Childs letter to the TWGC, May 27, 1979; Luz Guerra letter to the Board of the Third World Fund, May 30, 1979 (all, personal collection of Lenn Keller).

53. "Failed Kidnap Attempt: Black Youths Attack *Sentinel* Publisher at Home," *San Francisco Sentinel*, August 8, 1980.

54. "Blacks vs. Gays," BWMT *Newsletter*, September–October 1980.

55. Castells, "City and Culture: The San Francisco Experience," 139. The link between gay community growth and the rise of the service-sector economy is discussed by Castells; and by Lawrence Knopp and Mickey Lauria, "Toward an Analysis of the Role of Gay Communities in the Urban Renaissance," *Urban Geography* 6, no. 2 (1985): 152–69; and by Lawrence Knopp, "Some Theoretical Implications of Gay Involvement in an Urban Land Market," *Political Geography Quarterly* 9, no. 4 (1990): 337–52. Also see Stephen Quilley, "Constructing Manchester's 'New Urban Village': Gay Space in the Entrepreneurial City," in *Queers in Space: Communities/Public Places/Sites of Resistance*, ed. G. Brent Ingram, Anne Marie Bouthillette, and Yvette Retter (Seattle: Bay, 1997), 275–94.

56. Jeffrey Escoffier, "The Political Economy of the Closet: Notes Toward an Economic History of Gay and Lesbian Life Before Stonewall," in *Homo Economics: Capitalism, Community, and Lesbian and Gay Life*, ed. Amy Gluckman and Betsy Reed (New York: Routledge, 1997), 131.

57. Escoffier, "The Political Economy of the Closet," 129, 131.

58. Around 1981 the activist group the Media Alliance sponsored an event titled "Hispanic-Gay Violence: A Media War?," which featured members of the San Francisco Police Department, Harvey Milk Democratic Club, and Mission Community Legal Defense, among others ("Media Alliance Presents . . . Hispanic-Gay Violence: A Media War?" flier [ca. 1981], Women's Building Ephemera, San Francisco LGBT Groups Ephemera Collection, Gay, Lesbian, Bisexual, Transgender Historical Society, San Francisco, CA).

59. Interview with Pamela David, San Francisco, CA, July 9, 2008.

60. A member whom I did not interview is featured under a pseudonym in Becky Thompson, *A Promise and a Way of Life: White Anti-Racist Organizing* (Minneapolis: University of Minnesota Press, 2001). She is described as a white Jewish lesbian from South Africa who, in addition to being a member of LAPV, was active in an organization of white allies to a black liberation organization that is not named in the book. I also interviewed one member who chose to keep her personal history and identity private.

61. Although much of LAPV's activism focused on the Mission, this was not the residential base for all of its members, many of whom lived in the East Bay. Lois Helmbold noted this in my interview with her, Oakland, CA, July 25, 2008.

62. There are two versions of this skit, with almost identical scripts but with divergent spellings and labeling of characters. Although not recorded in the archives, interviews and informal correspondence suggest that the coauthors of the skit were Joan Annsfire and another woman. I managed to reach Annsfire, who affirmed her coauthorship of many of the skits LAPV produced. I did not succeed in getting in touch with the other woman, so have chosen to protect her privacy here.

63. The White (Night) Riot refers to the confrontation on May 21, 1979, between lesbian and gay activists and the police following the conviction of former San Francisco supervisor Dan White just for manslaughter, despite having murdered Supervisor Harvey Milk and Mayor George Moscone at point-blank range. After the riot, the police raided and destroyed a popular gay bar, the Elephant Walk, in what was considered revenge. (LAPV also did a skit about this and the police investigation that followed, which they performed in gay bars ["Grand Jury's Coming to Town," Skits and Lyrics Folder, Meg Barnett Collection, GLBTHS]; Pamela David also discussed this in her interview with me.) The Peg's Place reference is to an incident in March 1979 when off-duty officers celebrating the engagement of former police officer Bernard Shaw to Patty Hearst barged into the lesbian bar Peg's Place and harassed patrons. Despite damage to the bar and injury to the owners, police failed to arrest their colleagues. Here it is also worth mentioning that the opening song in a draft of another skit on police violence was to be sung to a big star with SFPD (San Francisco Police Department) emblazoned on it: "When you wish upon this star / Makes a difference who you are / Hookers, queers, Black, Latinos / Will get screwed" (untitled draft, September 3, 1979, Lyrics and Scripts Folder, Meg Barnett Collection, GLBTHS).

64. See Legal Committee Meeting Minutes, February 28, 1979, Meeting Minutes February–April 1979 Folder, Meg Barnett Collection, GLBTHS.

65. Marjorie Heins, *Strictly Ghetto Property: The Story of Los Siete de la Raza* (Berkeley, CA: Ramparts Press, 1972); Center for Research on Criminal Justice, *The Iron Fist and the Velvet Glove: An Analysis of the U.S. Police*, expanded and rev. ed. (Berkeley, CA: Center for Research on Criminal Justice, 1977). The dedication of the latter reads: "This book is dedicated to the people of the United States and throughout the world fighting against exploitation and oppression and struggling for socialism." The discussion of these reading groups is based on Meg Barnett interviews with author (September 8 and 15, 2004, via telephone) as well as the "suggested mandatory readings" in Legal Committee Meeting Minutes, March 14, 1979, Meeting Minutes February–April 1979 Folder, Meg Barnett Collection, GLBTHS.

66. See Louis Althusser, *For Marx*, trans. Ben Brewster (New York: Vintage, 1970).

67. Andrew Ross discusses the "subterranean influence" of late Maoist thought associated with the Cultural Revolution on politics in the United States since the 1970s

in his "Mao Zedong's Impact on Cultural Politics in the West," *Cultural Politics* 1, no. 1 (2005): 5–22.

68. Gay activists appropriated ideas such as Maoism more as metaphor than doctrine, a dynamic that Robin D. G. Kelley and Betsy Esch also identify in the Black Panthers' use of Mao (see "Black Like Mao: Red China and Black Revolution," *Souls* 1, no. 4 [Fall 1999]: 6–41). This Maoism diverged from official Chinese policy as well as the positions of a good number of U.S. Maoists at the time, many of whom were antigay. For a more detailed discussion of this dynamic, see Ordona, "Asian Lesbians in San Francisco."

69. This was also a feature of the "No on 6 and 7" campaign, which sometimes kept the categories *gay* and *black* separate, understanding Proposition 6 to most affect lesbians and gay men (racially unidentified, but white by default) and Proposition 7 to most affect African Americans (sexually unidentified, but straight by default). Activists called for a united fight against the rise of fascism or the scapegoating of the marginalized, but they more often accused the state of exciting hostilities between gays and African Americans, a key strategy that nonetheless often left black lesbians and gay men out. One flier read: "Proposition 7 *also* affects gay people. According to the 'special circumstances' any murder involving oral copulation or sodomy would be punishable by death. Although a large number of Californians, gay and not gay, frequently engage in these 'felonies,' we know how the law would be used" ("Don't Be Fooled by Propositions Six and Seven," n.d., Proposition 6 Folder, Stonewall Records, 1989–90, Gay, Lesbian, Bisexual, Transgender Historical Society, San Francisco, CA [hereafter Stonewall Records, GLBTHS]). That said, the Third World Gay Caucus associated with the organization Stonewall (a separate organization than the Third World Gay Coalition discussed in this chapter) also organized around these issues in ways that may have merged rather than parsed these interests ("Vote No on 6 and 7," flier from the Third World Gay Caucus, Stonewall Records, GLBTHS). Also see African People's Solidarity Committee, "No on 6 and 7," brochure, Proposition 7 Folder, Stonewall Records, GLBTHS.

70. "What Makes Racism So Difficult to Talk about Anyway?" and "Non-Confrontation of Racism in a Group of White Women That Claim to Be Anti-Racist," Workshops Folder, Meg Barnett Collection, GLBTHS. On the limits of the antiracist paradigm, see Sara Ahmed, "Declarations of Whiteness: The Non-Performativity of Anti-Racism," *Borderlands E-Journal* 3, no. 2 (2004): http://www.borderlands.net.au/vol3no2_2004/ahmed_declarations.htm. Although Ahmed's essay focuses on the admissions of institutions, her analysis that antiracist declarations fail to do what they claim to do (racism is not challenged through the discursive recentering of the white subject) is also useful for examining the grassroots expressions of antiracist politics. For other critiques of the language of antiracism, see Mimi Thi Nguyen, "Riot Grrrl, Race, and Revival," *Women and Performance* 22 (July–November 2012): 173–96; and Jodi Melamed, *Represent and Destroy: Rationalizing Violence in the New Racial Capitalism* (Minneapolis: University of Minnesota Press, 2011).

71. This is close to an argument made by Andrew Ross, yet his diagnosis of the so-called culture wars of the 1980s feels a bit more dismissive of movements often called identity politics (Ross, "Mao Zedong's Impact on Cultural Politics in the West"). But the influence of Maoism on queer activists and on thinkers central to the emerging field of queer theory, including Guy Hocquenghem, Michel Foucault, and Louis Althusser, suggests this as an important area for more inquiry. For work in this direction, see Camille Robcis, "'China in Our Heads': Althusser, Maoism, and Structuralism," *Social Text* 30, no. 1 (2012): 51–69.

72. In the decades that followed LAPV's tenure, its members continued to fight for gender, sexual, racial, and economic justice through a wide mix of activist approaches: Meg Barnett (Maggie Jochild) joined the group called the Pleiades and organized among lesbian incest survivors; in later years, she continued doing lesbian and disability activism in Austin, Texas. She now writes a blog titled Maggie's Meta Watershed (maggiesmetawatershed.blogspot.com/), which features detailed and astute history and political analysis. Pamela David continued to be involved in local, municipal, and national organizing, including serving as an organizer of the 1987 LGBT March on Washington, advisor to Jesse Jackson's 1988 presidential campaign, and head of the San Francisco Mayor's Office of Community Development in the 1990s. She is now the executive director of the Walter and Elise Haas Fund. After earning her doctorate in history at Stanford, Lois Helmbold taught for many years at San Jose State University, while continuing to advocate for women's studies programs. She has published in labor history and on the intersections of gender, race, and class in women's history, and she was the chair of the Women's Studies Department at the University of Nevada, Las Vegas, before retiring. Joan Annsfire held a variety of jobs in the years after LAPV, as she struggled in workplaces as an out lesbian and an active supporter of workers rights. She eventually found job security as a drafter for the San Francisco Water Department and later became a librarian, working at the James Hormel Gay and Lesbian Center at the San Francisco Public Library until she retired in 2012. She began writing in a more sustained fashion in the 1990s, publishing poetry and short stories, many about lesbian life and activism in the San Francisco Bay Area from the 1970s and 1980s. She has published in *Harrington Lesbian Literary Quarterly, Sinister Wisdom,* and *SoMa Literary Review,* and in anthologies that include *Milk and Honey: A Celebration of Jewish Lesbian Poetry,* ed. Julie Enszer (New York: A Midsummer's Night Press, 2011), among many more. After a break from formal activism, she became an active member of Occupy Oakland.

73. Castells, "City and Culture: The San Francisco Experience," 140.

74. Tamar Rothenberg, "'And She Told Two Friends': Lesbians Creating Urban Social Space," in *Mapping Desire: Geographies of Sexualities,* ed. David Bell and Gill Valentine (London: Routledge, 1995), 165–81. The *new middle class* is a contested term that refers to the rise of the professional and managerial class during this period, whose members' relationship to property distinguishes them from both the capitalist class (whose members own the means of production) and the exploited working class. See David Ley, *The New Middle Class and the Remaking of the Central City* (New York: Oxford University Press, 1997). For more contemporary work on lesbian and gay communities and gentrification see Japonica Brown-Saracino, *A Neighborhood That Never Changes: Gentrification, Social Preservation, and the Search for Authenticity* (Chicago: University of Chicago Press, 2010).

75. Damaris Rose, "Rethinking Gentrification: Beyond the Uneven Development of Marxist Urban Theory," *Environment and Planning D: Society and Space* 2, no. 1 (1984): 65.

76. "Contradictory class location" is a phrase used by Erik Olin Wright in *Class, Crisis, and the State* (London: Verso, 1978).

77. Joan Gibbs interview by author, Brooklyn, NY, June 26, 2009. Also see "Stop Cruising/Stop Media Racism," flier, and DARE, "How Do We Work?," introductory brochure, n.d.; Dykes against Racism Everywhere Organization File, Lesbian Herstory Archives, Brooklyn, NY (hereafter DARE File, LHA).

78. Gibbs interview by author, Brooklyn, NY, June 26, 2009.

79. "Bacall's Demo Wins 'Apology' for Racism," *Woman News,* June 1982 (clipping); Joyce Hunter, "Demonstration at Bacall's," *New York City News,* May 12, 1982 (clipping);

"Stop Cruising/Stop Media Racism," flier (circa 1980); "Did you Know That . . . ," flier (on the Family Protection Act, n.d.); "Not Yet Uhuru: The Struggle against Apartheid," flier, 1982; Lesbians United to Defeat the Klan, flier (circa late 1979 or early 1980); "Hiss With Us!," flier, n.d.; Inside Out Educational Forum flier (also announcing participation in "Free Dessie Woods: Smash Colonial Violence" event, May 12, 1980); untitled flier noting collaboration with the Organization of Asian Women and with Casa Nicaragua, 1981; "Support the Laurel Mississippi Strikers," flier, 1980; "Fight the Right," flier, 1981; "DARE Submits Petitions in Support of Voting Rights Act," press release, February 4, 1982; "Fight for Reproductive Freedom/Fight for the Liberation of *all Women*," flier, 1981; "Many Fronts, One Struggle: An Evening of Solidarity with Native American Women" (cosponsors were Asian Lesbians of the East Coast, Third World Women's Archives, Salsa Soul Sisters, Women Free Women in Prison, Jewish Lesbian/Feminist Group, and DARE), flier, n.d.; "Forum on the Resurgence of the Right" (with Frances Beale, Nine Reimer, and DARE), flier, n.d. (ca. 1980); "DARE Lesbian Pride Week Forum: The Lesbian Community and the Police," flier, 1980; public letter on behalf of the Anti-Police Abuse Coalition, 1984; "The Police: A Forum and Speakout for the Lesbian and Gay Male Communities," flier, 1983; "Fight the Right," flier announcing a meeting to be held July 1, 1980. All materials cited in this note were made by DARE unless otherwise noted and are included in DARE File, LHA. The group was divided into the following committees: racism in media, police brutality, housing and urban removal (gentrification), and women in prison.

80. Dykes Against Racism Everywhere, "Hiss With Us!" flier, n.d., DARE File, LHA.

81. Dykes Against Racism Everywhere, public letter on behalf of the Anti-Police Abuse Coalition, 1984, DARE File, LHA.

82. Although I did not have the opportunity to interview Bulkin, her participation in DARE is mentioned in Thompson, *A Promise and a Way of Life.*

83. Sara Bennett and Joan Gibbs, "Racism and Classism in the Lesbian Community: Towards the Building of a Radical Autonomous Lesbian Movement," in *Top Ranking: A Collection of Articles on Racism and Classism in the Lesbian Community*, ed. Joan Gibbs and Sara Bennett (New York: Come! Unity Press, 1980), 1–30.

84. Bennett and Gibbs, "Racism and Classism in the Lesbian Community," 2–3.

85. In addition to citing the Combahee River Collective, Gibbs and Bennett also cite an organization called Zulema in San Francisco.

86. For an example of lesbians of color making land claims, see La Luz, "Third World Warriors—Earth Trust Collective," *Lesbian Connection* 4, no. 3 (1978): 15. David Harvey adapts Marx's concept of primitive accumulation to describe the strategy of accumulation by dispossession essential to contemporary capitalist strategies (*The New Imperialism* [New York: Oxford University Press, 2005]).

87. Rose, "Rethinking Gentrification," esp. 49. See also Neil Smith, *The New Urban Frontier: Gentrification and the Revanchist City* (London: Routledge, 1996).

88. Smith's argument might be best summarized as follows: Although house value is measured by a labor theory of value—both to construct the house and to maintain it—a house's sale price also reflects ground rent, which is not a product of labor per se. Capitalized ground rent is the amount that an owner can get under "present land use," generally in the form of rent (for landlords) or added to the house's value in the sale price (for owner occupiers). Yet the present is always in flux, and thus landowners also bank on "potential ground rents" that might commandeer a higher price should the land be used under its "highest and best use." It is this "rent gap" that is the cornerstone of gentrification to Smith (N. Smith, *The New Urban Frontier*, 61–62).

89. Section "Why an Anti-Racist Lesbian Group?," in DARE brochure, n.d. DARE File, LHA.

90. DARE, Open Letter/Untitled Statement [begins; "DARE recently received information . . ."] flier, n.d. (ca. 1983). It is worth noting here that although DARE did not conduct systematic activism under the rubric of trans issues, this statement did discuss how gentrification also negatively impacts "transvestites," especially those people who did sex work and socialized along those areas near the waterfront in Greenwich Village.

91. Grace Kyungwon Hong and Roderick A. Ferguson, "Introduction," in *Strange Affinities: The Gender and Sexual Politics of Comparative Racialization,* ed. Grace Kyungwon Hong and Roderick A. Ferguson (Durham: Duke University Press, 2011), 9.

92. Lawrence Knopp, "Gentrification and Gay Neighborhood Formation in New Orleans: A Case Study," in *Homo Economics: Capitalism, Community, and Lesbian and Gay Life,* ed. Amy Gluckman and Betsy Reed (New York: Routledge, 1997), 56. In the Marigny, the cumulative effect of gay property owners changed the culture of the neighborhood, but the displacement associated with gentrification began once developers arrived on the scene.

93. Rose, "Rethinking Gentrification," 67–69.

94. Smith, *The New Urban Frontier,* 101.

95. The chapter subsection title "DARE to Struggle, DARE to Win" is taken from DARE, "Stop Cruising, Stop Media Racism," flier, n.d. DARE File, LHA.

96. In one flier the Prairie Fire Organizing Committee featured a whistle with the tagline "Who's Attacking Who? Blow the Whistle on Urban Genocide" (June 1980); it described the situation of gentrification in the Mission and Fillmore as "forced relocation" programs and "urban genocide" and explicitly criticized the new safe streets organization Community United Against Violence, discussed in the next chapter. The flier also called the citizen review board a "sham," adding: "White gays who settle in the Fillmore and then organize to 'Blow the Whistle on Crime' are helping to build a police state consciousness and apparatus." Also see flier titled "Gay Liberation—1981: What Are We Fightig For?" (All items cited in this note are in Prairie Fire Organizing Committee Ephemera, San Francisco LGBT Groups Ephemera Collection, Gay, Lesbian, Bisexual, Transgender Historical Society, San Francisco, CA. For a discussion of the Gay Latino Alliance, see Roque-Ramirez, "That's *My* Place!")

97. See "Draft-Organizational Statement" and "1/10/79 Stonewall Discusses Racism," 1979, Organizational Papers, Minutes, etc. Folder, Stonewall Records, GLBTHS. The meeting minutes of Stonewall suggest that the group made efforts to collaborate with LAPV and shared that group's concern with an implicit racism that both organizations detected in the incipient Community United Against Violence (see July 23, 1979, Meeting Minutes, ibid.). Founded after the May 21st riot, Stonewall also staged a 1979 guerrilla theater production about the housing crisis and rent control (see "Draft-Organizational Statement"). For more information on Stonewall, as well as on the 1980 Lavender Left Conference in which they participated, see Hobson, *Lavender and Red.*

98. Ali Marrero interview by author, Alameda, CA, July 28, 2008; Women in Prison, "Dykes behind Bars," *DYKE,* Winter 1975–76: 14–17. DARE also collaborated with Women Free Women in Prison which published *No More Cages: A Bi-Monthly Women's Prison Newsletter.* For a more thorough history of lesbian feminist antiprison organizing in this period, see Thuma, "'Not a Wedge, but a Bridge.'"

99. The members of the Coalition against Racism, Anti-Semitism, Sexism, and Heterosexism included participants from DARE and BWMT, and is noted in Sarah Schulman, *My American History: Lesbian and Gay Life during the Reagan/Bush Years* (New York: Routledge, 1994), 71.

100. Cherríe Moraga, "Preface," in *This Bridge Called My Back: Writings by Radical Women of Color*, ed. Cherríe Moraga and Gloria Anzaldúa (Latham, NY: Kitchen Table: Women of Color Press [1981] 1983), xiii–xix.

101. Hong, *The Ruptures of American Capital*, xi–xii. The introduction to Hong and Ferguson, eds., *Strange Affinities*, also analyzes this scene from the introduction to *This Bridge Called My Back* to model the "heterotopic mode of comparison."

102. Moraga, "Preface," xiv.

103. Hong, *The Ruptures of American Capital*, xi.

104. The case was also written about in *Azalea*; see Claudette Furlonge, "Why Joanne?" *Azalea*, Spring 1978, 3–9.

105. Marrero interview by author, Alameda, CA, July 28, 2008.

106. sudi mae, "We Have to Be Our Own Spark: An Interview with 'Gente' Third-World Lesbian Softball Team," *Tide*, July 1974.

107. mae, "We Have to Be Our Own Spark."

108. New York update, BWMT *Quarterly*, Winter 1982. Also see the materials in the Committee for the Visibility of the Other Black Woman Organization File, Lesbian Herstory Archives.

109. Vivienne Walker-Crawford, "How to Fight Back," *Black Lesbian Newsletter*, August 1982; Eileen Gaines, "The Need for a Black Lesbian Front," *Black Lesbian Newsletter*, August 1982; Helen L. Keller, "Open Letter to the Black Lesbian Community," ONYX: *Black Lesbian Newsletter*, 1984, 4.

110. Although I interviewed Gibbs, we discussed DARE more than *Azalea*. For a history of *Azalea* see Hom, "Unifying Differences."

111. Linda J. Brown, "Foundations: Why the Cultural is the Political: Validity, Purpose to Womyn who are working for political and societal change thru cultural levels," *Azalea*, Spring/Summer 1981, 4.

112. Brown, "Foundations," 5.

113. By *contradictions of community*, I mean to signal two different yet related concepts—the embracing of the contradictions between political tactics that might be deemed contradictory to each other and the highlighting of the contradictions of a liberalism that imagines remedy through multiculturalism. For a sustained critique of the concept of community, see Miranda Joseph, *Against the Romance of Community* (Minneapolis: University of Minnesota Press, 2002).

114. Anne Enke, *Finding the Movement: Sexuality, Contested Space, and Feminist Activism* (Durham: Duke University Press, 2007), 9. Ghaziani also considers the role of process in political ideology formation. He adopts a "resinous culture framework" to show how the often mundane tasks of political organizing provide the means by which broader cultural understandings are made (*The Dividends of Dissent*, 315).

115. Most of my interviews with lesbian feminists from this period featured stories of political debates between lovers, requests that I promise not to reveal the whereabouts of individuals to their exes (and some feminists declined public interviews for, I suspect, the same reasons), and both painful and humorous memories of lost romances and health and friendship challenges.

116. One other example is showcased by Clyde Woods's groundbreaking work on "blues epistemology" as a counternarrative to the dominant planning history of the Mississippi Delta. Woods rejects standard periodization and describes the aesthetic and everyday practices of African Americans who fought land-based economies of exploitation. He elaborates this history as adopting an approach counter to instrumentalist modes of social explanation and dedicated to claims to place. It is in an adaption of this

model that we might best understand alternative political visions of sexual identity in the city. Clyde Woods, *Development Arrested: Blues and Plantation Power in the Mississippi Delta* (London: Verso, 1998). See also Chela Sandoval, *Methodology of the Oppressed* (Minneapolis: University of Minnesota Press, 2000).

117. For a discussion of use versus exchange values in the urban land market, see John R. Logan and Harvey L. Molotch, *Urban Fortunes: The Political Economy of Place* (Berkeley: University of California Press, 1987), 99–146.

4. Visibility and Victimization

Epigraph: Community United Against Violence flier [part of a volunteer manual], n.d. Box 48, Folders 25 and 26, National Gay and Lesbian Task Force Records (Collection 7301), Rare and Manuscript Collections, Kroch Library, Cornell University (hereafter NGLTF Records, Cornell). Also in CUAV File, LGBT Groups Ephemera Collection, GLBTHS.

1. Valerie Jenness and Kendal Broad, *Hate Crimes: New Social Movements and the Politics of Violence* (New York: Aldine de Gruyter, 1997), 103–5. With the exception of CUAV, almost all antiviolence organizations during the 1980s were led by men.

2. David Valentine, *Imagining Transgender: An Ethnography of a Category* (Durham: Duke University Press, 2007).

3. See Jenness and Broad, *Hate Crimes*; Nancy A. Matthews, *Confronting Rape: The Feminist Anti-Rape Movement and the State* (New York: Routledge, 1994); Maria Bevacqua, *Rape on the Public Agenda: Feminism and the Politics of Sexual Assault* (Boston: Northeastern University Press, 2000); Kristin Bumiller, *In an Abusive State: How Neoliberalism Appropriated the Feminist Movement against Sexual Violence* (Durham: Duke University Press, 2008).

4. The literatures on the two movements is also distinct, with each rarely citing the other. Jenness and Broad also note this fact in *Hate Crimes*, which provides one of the few detailed and historical treatments of U.S.-based LGBT antiviolence activism. The literature on hate crime and hate speech in general, and on the causes and impacts of anti-LGBT violence in particular, is more extensive and cited elsewhere in this chapter. There is also some historical and sociological literature on the LGBT antiviolence movement in England and Australia. See, for example, Gail Mason, *The Spectacle of Violence: Homophobia, Gender, and Knowledge* (London: Routledge, 2002); Leslie Moran and Beverly Skeggs, with Paul Tyrer and Karen Corteen, *Sexuality and the Politics of Violence* (London: Routledge, 2004).

5. Jenness and Broad, *Hate Crimes*, 31–36.

6. See Markus Dirk Dubber, *Victims in the War on Crime: The Use and Abuse of Victims' Rights* (New York: New York University Press, 2002); Valerie Jenness and Ryken Grattet, *Making Hate a Crime: From Social Movement to Law Enforcement* (New York: Russell Sage Foundation, 2001).

7. The National Gay and Lesbian Task Force was originally called the National Gay Task Force, and the Anti-Violence Project was first called the Violence Project. I try to use each name when appropriate.

8. Michael Shernoff interview by author, New York, September 13, 2004; Ben Gardiner interview by author, San Francisco, August 16, 2004; Jenness and Broad, *Hate Crimes*; David M. Wertheimer, "Treatment and Service Interventions for Lesbian and Gay Male Crime Victims," in *Hate Crimes: Confronting Violence against Lesbians and Gay Men*, ed. Gregory M. Herek and Kevin T. Berrill (Newbury Park, CA: Sage, 1992), 227–40; Gregory M. Herek, "The Community Response to Violence in San Francisco: An Interview with Wenny Kusuma, Lester Olmstead-Rose, and Jill Tregor," in *Hate Crimes*, ed.

Herek and Berrill, 241–57; David Wertheimer, "The Emergence of a Gay and Lesbian Anti-violence Movement," in *Creating Change: Sexuality, Public Policy, and Civil Rights*, ed. John D'Emilio, William B. Turner, and Urvashi Vaid (New York: St. Martin's, 2000), 261–79.

9. An early CUAV proposal was the Urban Crime Prevention Program and the Community Halt Assault Project, which was to include a "victim/witness assistance component, a community dispute settlement component, a property crime victimization component, and an arson monitoring component, in that order of priority" (concept paper, n.d. [ca. 1980], Carton 8, Community Halt Assault Project Folder, Community United Against Violence Organization Records, Gay, Lesbian, Bisexual, Transgender Historical Society, San Francisco, CA [hereafter CUAV Records, GLBTHS]). Target areas included all or parts of the Castro, Corona Heights, Haight, Fillmore, Mission, and Noe Valley. Written materials suggest that the members were actively debating if and how race should be integrated into their efforts (see Dick Stingel, "A Presentation by Community United Against Violence to the Police, Fire, and Public Safety Committee of the San Francisco County Board of Supervisors," October 10, 1980, Community Halt Assault Project Folder, CUAV Records, GLBTHS).

10. The CGA-advertised whistle campaign was hosted by the East Village Lesbian and Gay Neighbors Association and sponsored by CUAV ("Whistle Campaign," *Chelsea Gay Association Newsletter*, December 1979, Vertical File, National Archive of Lesbian, Gay, Bisexual, and Transgender History, Lesbian, Gay, Bisexual, and Transgender Community Center, New York; also see David Behrens, "Joining against Crime," *Newsday*, November 29, 1982).

11. "Community United Against Violence Volunteer Manual," n.d., Box 46, Folder 12 (also see Box 48, Folder 25), NGLTF Records, Cornell.

12. In this chapter I discuss both the New York Anti-Violence Project and the Anti-Violence Project of the National Gay and Lesbian Task Force. The former still exists and is typically referred to as AVP, the latter no longer exists and rarely used the acronym. Thus, I use the acronym for the New York organization and write out Anti-Violence Project for the now-defunct program within NGLTF.

13. Wertheimer, "The Emergence of a Gay and Lesbian Antiviolence Movement," 268.

14. Wertheimer, "The Emergence of a Gay and Lesbian Antiviolence Movement," 276.

15. On the tax exemption, see "Fund for Human Dignity Receives Tax-Deductible Status: Internal Revenue Service Policy Concerning Gay Organizations Is Reversed," NGTF press release, August 9, 1977, Box 36, Folder 1, NGLTF Records, Cornell. On the funding of Crisisline, see "Fund Receives Crisisline Grant from AT&T Foundation: First Corporate Support," NGTF press release, November 25, 1985, Box 37, Folder 29, ibid. A grant for the same amount had been received from the Playboy Foundation in 1980, see "Playboy Awards Large Grant for Gay Rights," NGTF press release, November 11, 1980, Box 36, Folder 171, ibid. Later Playboy money was used for an antiviolence booklet, Minutes, July 26, 1990, Box 46, Folder 3, NGLTF Records, Cornell.

16. "NGLTF Receives Major Grant for Anti-Violence Work," NGLTF press release, February 7, 1991, Box 37, Folder 76, NGLTF Records, Cornell.

17. Gene Royale, executive director, Centro de Cambio, memo to Dick Stingel, chair, Board of Directors, Community United Against Violence, Carton 1, Board of Directors Meeting, April 1981 Folder, CUAV Records, GLBTHS. The memo describes "Community Assistance Teams," the exact purpose of which is unclear, but Ron Wickliffe (identified in an article as the treasurer—and a member of the board of directors—of CUAV) suggested that the collaboration between the two organizations was "to have straight

Latinos [the assumed membership of Centro de Cambio] join us [CUAV members] on street patrol" (Ron Wickliffe, "Queer Bashers Meet Resistance in the Streets of San Francisco," WIN: *Peace and Freedom through Non-Violent Action*, August 15, 1981, 15 [clipping in Violence against People File, Gay, Lesbian, Bisexual, Transgender Historical Society, San Francisco]).

18. Behrens, "Joining against Crime."

19. Chief of Police Cornelius P. Murphy, Police Department, City and County of San Francisco, letter to James Andrew Nicholas, Community United Against Violence, April 7, 1980, Carton 8, unnumbered and unnamed orange folder, CUAV Records, GLBTHS.

20. In April 1980 officers were directed to, when appropriate, "place in the narrative of an assault report the statement 'Incident may be gay-related'; and complete the sentence with the appropriate information." In order to determine what might be gay-related, officers were asked to be attentive to reported antigay remarks or statements rather than individuals' identities (Information Bulletin 80–57, San Francisco Police Department, April 23, 1980, CUAV Records, GLBTHS). In a later meeting, the CUAV board noted that the agreement to make such indications in the narrative was not being honored by the police (Board Meeting Minutes, May 28, 1981 Folder, Carton 1, ibid.).

21. Chief of Police Cornelius P. Murphy, Police Department, City and County of San Francisco, letter to James Andrew Nicholas, Community United Against Violence, April 7, 1980, Carton 8, unnumbered and unnamed orange folder, CUAV Records, GLBTHS.

22. CUAV also worked on citywide campaigns, but its patrols and whistle distribution focused on those areas with a large residential and/or social gay- and lesbian-identified populations. This included at least temporary projects in places like South of Market.

23. Bruce Voeller, "My Days on the Task Force," *Christopher Street*, October–November 1979, 55–65.

24. John D'Emilio "Organizational Tales: Interpreting the NGLTF Story," in *Creating Change*, ed. D'Emilio, Turner, and Vaid, 469–86; "NGTF Begins New Anti-Violence Effort," NGTF press release, February 10, 1982, Box 5, Folder 7, Larry Bush Papers (Collection 7316), Rare and Manuscript Collections, Kroch Library, Cornell University (hereafter Bush Papers, Cornell).

25. "The NGTF Violence Project," booklet, n.d. n.p. (probably late 1982), Box 5, Folder 9, Bush Papers, Cornell.

26. "The NGTF Violence Project," n.p.

27. "NGTF Toll-Free 'Crisisline' Telephone Number 800-221-7044," NGTF press release, October 15, 1982, Box 5, Folder 7, Bush Papers, Cornell. Also see NGTF, "Stop Anti-Gay Violence!: Call the Crisisline," flier, n.d., Box 5, Folder 9, ibid.

28. "NGTF Crisisline Hours Change: AIDS Calls Predominate in FIRST THREE MONTHS," NGTF press release, January 26, 1983, Box 36, Folder 255, NGLTF Records, Cornell.

29. "NGLTF—A History," n.d. and Memorandom to Members, Strategic Plan Work Group of NGLTF, from Bill Bailey, co-chair, regarding Minutes from New York Meeting, April 22–33, dated May 6, both in Box 46, Folder 32, NGLTF Records, Cornell. Also see Memo, December 20, 1982, from Kevin, re: Crisisline Stats for Fund Focus, Box 46, Folder 12, ibid. D'Emilio also vaguely alludes to bad publicity during these years in "Organizational Tales."

30. "NGTF Documents Epidemic of Anti-Gay/Lesbian Violence," NGTF press release, October 19, 1983, Box 36, Folder 275, NGLTF Records, Cornell. The press release further detailed that there had been 1,682 incidents of harassment, threats, and attacks reported to Crisisline and twelve local projects.

31. "NGTF at Federal Hearings on Police Misconduct, Family Violence," NGTF press

release, December 12, 1983, Box 8, Folder 5, Bush Papers, Cornell. (Also in Box 36, Folder 280, NGLTF Records.) See also James Credle, "November 28, 1983: Police Brutality: The Continual Erosion of Our Most Basic Rights," in *Speaking for Our Lives: Historical Speeches and Rhetoric for Gay and Lesbian Rights (1892–2000)*, ed. Robert B. Ridinger (Binghamton, NY: Haworth Press, 2004), 423–27. Jean O'Leary, co-executive director of the NGTF, had testified before the U.S. Commission on Civil Rights on police practices in 1978 ("Statement by Jean O'Leary," December 12, 1978, Box 5, Folder 5, Bush Papers, Cornell).

32. "Criminal Justice Subcommittee, Hearing on Police Practices," Testimony Submitted by Kevin Berrill, Violence Project director, National Gay Task Force, November 28, 1983, Box 9, Folder 19, Bush Papers, Cornell.

33. "NGTF Urges Support for Statewide Independent Civilian Review Boards," NGTF press release, May 28, 1984, Box 36, Folder 305, and "National Gay Task Force Opens Its Crisisline to Lesbian/Gay Youth," NGTF press release, March 1, 1984, Box 36, Folder 292, NGLTF Records, Cornell.

34. "The NGTF Violence Project 1984," n.d., Box 8, Folder 5, Bush Papers, Cornell.

35. James B. Jacobs and Kimberly Potter, *Hate Crimes: Criminal Law and Identity Politics* (New York: Oxford University Press, 1998), 4.

36. Jenness and Grattet, *Making Hate a Crime*, 6; for full discussion see chapter "The Emergence of an Anti-Hate-Crime Movement and the Construction of an Epidemic of Violence." Also see Grattet and Jenness, "The Birth and Maturation of Hate Crime Policy in the United States," in *Hate and Bias Crime: A Reader*, ed. Barbara Perry (New York: Routledge, 2003), 389–408 and Jenness and Broad, *Hate Crimes*.

37. Donald P. Green, Laurence H. McFalls, and Jennifer K. Smith, "Hate Crime: An Emergent Research Agenda," in *Hate and Bias Crime*, ed. Perry, 27–28.

38. See Carolyn Petrosino, "Connecting the Past to the Future: Hate Crime in America," in *Hate and Bias Crime*, ed. Perry, 9–26; Colin Flint, ed., *Spaces of Hate: Geographies of Discrimination and Intolerance in the U.S.A.* (New York: Routledge, 2004).

39. The defendant and his friends had left the movie *Mississippi Burning*, about the history of state-based and vigilante antiblack violence that had, in part, led to the passage of subsequent civil rights bills.

40. See Judith Butler, *Excitable Speech: A Politics of the Performative* (New York: Routledge, 1997), 43–70; Mari Matsuda, *Where Is Your Body? And Other Essays on Race, Gender, and the Law* (Boston: Beacon, 1996); Kimberlé Crenshaw, Neil Gotanda, Gary Peller, and Kendall Thomas, eds., *Critical Race Theory: The Key Writings That Formed the Movement* (New York: New Press, 1996).

41. See National Gay and Lesbian Task Force, "Hate Crimes Protection Timeline," http://www.thetaskforce.org/issues/hate_crimes_main_page/timeline. Peri Jude Radecic, then legislative head of the NGLTF, was allowed to bring seven people with her to the signing. Explained as an effort at representativeness, she brought a Midwest activist to represent grassroots lobbyists and organizers, a gay Republican, a lesbian survivor of a brutal hate crime, a Senate staffer, the NGLTF's media director, and the director of the Anti-Violence Project (Peri Jude Radecic, "An Open Letter of Gratitude to Gays and Lesbians on the Historic Passage of the Federal Hate Crimes Law," April 24, 1990, NGLTF Press Release, Box 37, Folder 45, NGLTF Records, Cornell). Later, Radecic also noted the presence of law authorities and the demographic diversity of the group; a press release additionally indicated that activist Urvashi Vaid had originally planned to come but was denied entry into the White House due to her recent attendance at an anti-Bush AIDS rally ("Candidate Slams Black Gays and Lesbians at D.C. Mayoral Forum;

Task Force Blasts Prejudiced Remarks," NGLTF press release, May 1, 1990, Box 37, Folder 46, ibid.).

42. For a comprehensive list of hate and bias crime statutes, see the appendices to Barbara Perry, ed., *Hate and Bias Crime: A Reader* (New York: Routledge, 2003). It is worth noting here that antimask laws, sometimes used to counter hate groups such as the Ku Klux Klan, are at other times used to criminalize protesters as well as gender nonconforming people.

43. Dubber, *Victims in the War on Crime*, 1.

44. Quoted in Jacobs and Potter, *Hate Crimes*, 77.

45. It was declared unconstitutional in 2000 in *U.S. v. Morrison* for exceeding congressional powers under the Commerce and Equal Protection Clauses of the Fourteenth Amendment (see David Altschiller, *Hate Crimes*, 2nd ed. [Santa Barbara, CA: ABC-CLIO, 2005]). For a discussion of the contradictory response to the funding for domestic violence activism sponsored by the Violence against Women Act, see Kimberlé Williams Crenshaw, "Mapping the Margins: Intersectionality, Identity Politics, and Violence against Women of Color," in *Critical Race Theory*, ed. Crenshaw, Gotanda, Peller, and Thomas, 357–83; Matsuda, *Where Is Your Body?*; Bevacqua, *Rape on the Public Agenda*; Matthews, *Confronting Rape*; Emily Thuma, "Not a Wedge, but a Bridge: Prisons, Feminist Activism, and the Politics of Gendered Violence, 1968–1987," PhD diss., New York University, 2011.

46. A prime example is Jacobs and Potter, *Hate Crimes*.

47. Chai Feldblum, "The Federal Gay Rights Bill: From Bella to ENDA," in *Creating Change*, ed. D'Emilio, Turner, and Vaid, 149–87.

48. See "Close to Home: Developing Innovative, Community-Based Responses to Anti-LGBT Violence," "Corrupting Justice: A Primer for LGBT Communities on Racism, Violence, Human Degradation and the Prison-Industrial Complex" (both available at http://www.prisonpolicy.org/factsheets.html); "In the Killing Fields of the State: Why the Death Penalty Is a Queer Issue" (http://www.prisonpolicy.org/scans/death-penalty-brief.pdf); "In a Time of Broken Bones: A Call to Dialogue on Hate Violence and the Limitations of Hate Crime Legislation" (https://afsc.org/document/time-broken-bones); and "AFSC's Position on the Local Law Enforcement Enhancement Act (LLEEA)" (described in David Kirby, "No Friends of the Hate-Crimes Bill: The Gay-Friendly Quakers Come out against the Federal Bill," *Advocate*, October 1, 2001, 34). Most of these reports were written by or under the leadership of the writer and activist Kay Whitlock.

49. INCITE! Women of Color against Violence, "Gender Violence and the Prison Industrial Complex," 2001, http://www.incite-national.org/index.php?s=92.

50. Chandan Reddy, *Freedom with Violence: Race, Sexuality, and the U.S. State* (Durham: Duke University Press, 2011), 17.

51. For information on the transformation of CUAV see Morgan Bassichis, "Reclaiming Queer & Trans Safety," in *The Revolution Starts at Home: Confronting Intimate Violence within Activist Communities*, ed. Ching-In Chen, Jai Dulani, and Leah Lakshmi Piepzna-Samarasinha (Brooklyn: South End Press, 2011), 5–24; for the goals of ALP's SOS Collective see "Safe Outside the System: SOS Collective," http://dev.alp.org/whatwedo/organizing/sos.

52. Jacobs and Potter, *Hate Crimes*, 5.

53. Butler, *Excitable Speech*, 102.

54. For example, Wendy Brown contends that it is an attachment to particular injuries that causes people to hold hate speech as "responsible for a whole domain of suffering" (*Politics out of History* [Princeton: Princeton University Press, 2001], 57). Also see

Wendy Brown, *States of Injury: Power and Freedom in Late Modernity* (Princeton: Princeton University Press, 1995).

55. This is a separate statistic from anti-Semitic violence. See Karen Franklin, "Good Intentions: The Enforcement of Hate Crime Penalty Enhancement Statutes," *American Behavioral Scientist* 46 (2002), 159–60. Jill Tregor, an early activist with CUAV who later led the organization Intergroup Clearinghouse, cited the use of hate crime designations by white people as an "abuse" of their original intention (see Jacobs and Potter, *Hate Crimes*, 134).

56. Franklin, "Good Intentions," 162–63.

57. Crenshaw, "Mapping the Margins," 357.

58. Sexual orientation was also excluded from a New York State Senate Special Task Force on Vandalism, Religious Desecration and Other Acts of Bigotry, headed by State Senator Norman Levy, a Republican. See "New York State Senate Special Task Force on Vandalism, Religious Desecration and Other Acts of Bigotry Refuses to Examine Anti-Gay Bigotry," NGTF press release, March 22, 1983, Box 5, Folder 8, Bush Papers, Cornell.

59. For example: "NGTF Documents Epidemic of Anti-Gay/Lesbian Violence." Also, as Grattet and Jenness point out in "The Birth and Maturation of Hate Crime Policy in the United States," this differed from other efforts to expand the categories of inclusion that did not have such sustained advocacy, such as campaigns to include octogenarians or the elderly in general, union members, children, and police officers. Important, too, is the fact that the victims' rights movement was slow to join the hate crime campaign. Dubber argues that this is because the "paradigmatic" victim of a hate crime is black, and the main figures of the victims' rights movement are white (*Victims in the War on Crime*, 177).

60. "The NGTF Violence Project," booklet.

61. See Martin F. Manalansan, "Homophobia at New York's Gay Central," in *Homophobia: Lust and Loathing across Time and Space*, ed. David A. B. Murray (Durham: Duke University Press, 2009), 34–47.

62. Wertheimer, "The Emergence of a Gay and Lesbian Antiviolence Movement," 263.

63. Gregory M. Herek, "Comments on the Hate Crimes Statistics Bill," n.d., Box 54, Folder 1, NGTLF Records, Cornell. Kevin Berrill of the NGLTF also argued that these issues should be a part of police response. In a draft of a speech he indicated that when officers encounter examples of violence that might have been hate-motivated, they should refrain from asking people if they are lesbian or gay and instead ask less directed questions that include: "This is a gay neighborhood, and people around here get attacked because of that. Was there anything in the attack that might point in that direction?" Kevin Berrill, "Confronting Violence against Lesbians and Gay Men," unpublished talk, n.d., Box 57, Folder 44, ibid.

64. Letter from Kevin Berrill to Bar Owner/Manager, May 1983, Box 61, Folder 27, NGTLF Records, Cornell.

65. "5 Boro Demonstration!," flier, circa January 1990, Box 48, Folder 2, NGTLF Records, Cornell. [Listed as "Coordinated by New York City Gay and Lesbian Anti-Violence Project, In conjunction with Dr. Marjorie Hill, Liaison to the Mayor & Dennis deLeon, Commissioner of Human Rights and Lesbian/Gay Organizations in Each Borough."]

66. Memo from the Gay and Lesbian Community Action Council of Minneapolis to the Anti-Violence Project, February 11, 1991, Box 61, Folder 5, NGTLF Records,Cornell.

67. Letter to Business Owners and Oak Lawn Residents, from DGA [Dallas Gay Alliance] Anti-Violence Project, n.d., Box 48, Folder 4, NGTLF Records, Cornell.

68. NGTLF Public Policy Program, Goals, and Objectives, 1991 Budget Proposal, Box

46, Folder 3, NGTLF Records, Cornell; Urvashi Vaid, *Virtual Equality: The Mainstreaming of Gay and Lesbian Liberation* (New York: Anchor, 1995).

69. "NGTLF Violence Project Director Berrill Elected to NOVA Board; Violence Project Obtains \$10,000 Grant," NGTLF press release, October 14, 1986, Box 46, Folder 47; and Kevin Berrill, memo to NGTLF Board Program Committee, March 22, 1991, Box 46, Folder 21, NGTLF Records, Cornell.

70. "US Civil Rights Commission Responds to NGTF Lobbying on Violence," NGTF press release, February 27, 1985, Box 37, Folder 7, NGTLF Records, Cornell.

71. See Marvin E. Wolfgang and Franco Ferracuti, "The Subculture of Violence," in *Criminological Theories: Bridging the Past to the Future*, ed. Suzette Cote (1969; Thousand Oaks, CA: Sage, 2002), 88–95.

72. See Marvin E. Wolfgang, Robert M. Figlio, and Thorsten Sellin, *Delinquency in a Birth Cohort* (1972; Chicago, University of Chicago Press, 1987).

73. Dr. Martin Wolfgang's Testimony to the Subcommittee on Criminal Justice of the House Judiciary Committee, October 9, 1986, Box 57, Folder 49, NGTLF Records, Cornell.

74. Examples of articles collected by the organization include Lawrence Sherman, "Neighborhood Safety," National Institute of Justice Crime File Study Guide, n.d. (on neighborhood watches, and that cited James Q. Wilson, Charles A. Murray, and Wesley Skogan); Deb Wheeler, "Cops Back on the Beat in the Village," *Villager*, November 7, 1985 (on the inauguration of a Community Patrol Officer Program in New York); Citizens Committee for New York City, "The Block Booster Project," page insert in *Citizens Report, The Newsletter of the Citizens Committee for New York City* 11, no. 1 (Winter 1987) (on an initiative funded by the Ford Foundation), all in Box 48, Folder 4, NGTLF Records, Cornell.

75. Again, it is worth repeating here that evidence such as this—testifying to the director of the Anti-Violence Project's own investment in narrative evidence even as reporting protocols narrowed—demonstrates why this history should be interpreted not as an expression of individuals' goals but of broader social shifts. See Letter from Kevin Berrill to Linettes, February 10, 1986, Box 46, Folder 12, NGTLF Records, Cornell.

76. Kevin Berrill, "Personal and Community Safety," 1992, p. 6, NGLTF Policy Institute, Box 48, Folder 21, NGLTF Records, Cornell.

77. Kevin Berrill, "Reaching out to Victims of Hate Violence," speech, n.d. (marked as intended for conference on April 17, 1988), Box 57, Folder 44, NGTLF Records, Cornell.

78. Moran and Skeggs, *Sexuality and the Politics of Violence*, 57.

79. Moran and Skeggs, *Sexuality and the Politics of Violence*, 54.

80. Memorandom to Members, Strategic Plan Work Group, NGTLF, from Bill Bailey, co-chair, on Minutes from New York Meeting, April 22–33, dated May 6, 1989, p. 5, Box 46, Folder 32, NGLTF Records, Cornell.

81. Quoted in notes titled "Discussion with Kevin Berrill about Anti-Violence Project" [no author], August 27 [no year], Box 46, Folder 23, NGLTF Records, Cornell.

82. Moran and Skeggs, *Sexuality and the Politics of Violence*, 19.

83. Kevin Berrill, "Confronting Violence against Lesbians and Gay Men," n.d., "talking point" in unpublished talk, Box 57, Folder 44, NGTLF Records, Cornell.

84. Gregory M. Herek and Kevin T. Berrill, "Introduction," in *Hate Crimes: Confronting Violence against Lesbians and Gay Men*, ed. Gregory M. Herek and Kevin T. Berrill (Newbury Park, CA: Sage, 1992), 8.

85. For instance, in 1986 Berrill drafted a letter to the editor of *New York Native*, taking the paper to task for coverage of an antigay crime that "may help to perpetuate racist stereotypes about criminals and victims." His letter also emphasized the importance of

paying attention to antigay violence outside Greenwich Village and Chelsea. Nonetheless, his conclusion—"What most Americans are not aware of is that blacks are much more likely than whites to be victims of violent crimes; black men, in particular, are seven times more likely than their white counterparts to be victims of homicide"—still sustains the construction of antigay violence as individualized crime (Kevin Berrill, letter to *New York Native*, January 20, 1986, Box 51, Folder 5, NGTLF Records, Cornell). It is interesting, though, that Berrill wrote the letter at the encouragement of Craig G. Harris, who highlighted that the issue at stake was how it left unrecognizable the vulnerabilities of lesbians and gay men of color and "the fact that homophobia, AIDS backlash, etc. has not caused people of color to attack the white gay male population of NYC physically—no more so than the mainstream straight community" (letter from Craig Harris to Kevin Berrill, December 31, 1985, Box 51, Folder 5, ibid.). Harris was a gay black activist who was involved in AIDS activism before he died early in the 1990s. His analysis of violence and threat as marked by dynamics of power and vulnerability rather than as crime category is striking; furthermore, it reflects the ongoing political critiques being made by people of color–centered lesbian and gay organizing described in the last chapter. Berrill's letter does not appear to have been published, although in that same week a letter from David Wertheimer, then executive director of AVP (whom Harris also contacted), was published. Wertheimer wrote a letter more similar to Berrill's: "Not all victims of homophobic assault are white and male. In fact, if you are poor, female, and/or a person of color in New York City, you stand a considerably higher chance of becoming a victim of crime" (*New York Native*, January 20–26, 1986). Many thanks to Abby Tallmer for background information on Harris.

86. A letter from attorney James B. Levin to Richard Dadey, executive director of the Empire State Pride Agenda, June 3, 1991 read: "Also, the emphasis on the Bias Related Violence bill seems misplaced. We were originally asked to support it rather than the more important lesbian/gay civil rights bill because it would be easy to pass. (I supported it although I object to bills which increase penalties as a means to deter crime. I don't believe that such penalties ever work.) Now, however, I find that for five years no one has paid any serious attention to the lesbian and gay rights bill while all the attention goes on the bias related violence bill which really hasn't been so easy to pass. Wouldn't it be possible to make a clear statement that the chief objective of PRIDE is gay civil rights and that bias-related violence is a secondary issue?" (Box 4, Folder 21, Empire State Pride Agenda Collection, Rare and Manuscript Collections, Kroch Library, Cornell University).

87. The NGTLF Hate Crime Statistics Act lobby packet included the following statement: "This is not a back-door gay rights bill. Including sexual orientation does not address the issue of whether sexual orientation is or should be a protected class. This is a separate issue for Congress to address and the courts to decide. Amendments, such as those proposed by Senator Jesse Helms, are an attempt to steer floor debate into the area of lesbian and gay civil rights" (NGTLF, "Hate Crime Statistics Lobbying Packet," n.d. [ca. 1989/1990], Box 54, Folder 31, NGTLF Records, Cornell).

88. Examples include "We speak today of one such challenge—the war of terror and hate being waged against gay and lesbian Americans and others who, because of their identity or beliefs, are perceived to be legitimate targets for abuse" and "Each anti-gay attack is an act of terrorism intended to drive us back into the isolation and self hatred of the closet," both from Kevin Berrill, "Statement to the Media on the NGTLF Policy Institute Report, Anti-gay/lesbian Violence, Victimization, and Defamation in 1990," March 6 1991, Box 37, Folder 82, NGTLF Records, Cornell. This statement made antigay violence parallel to anti-Arab, anti-Semitic, and other forms of hate.

89. "The NGTF Violence Project—1983 Report," Box 46, Folder 29, NGTLF Records, Cornell.

90. The phrase "rising tide of hate violence" appears in Kevin Berrill, letter to Steven Freeman of the ADL, January 22, 1988 (Box 106, Folder 6, NGTLF Records, Cornell).

91. Testimony on Bill 8–168, the Bias-Related Crime Act of 1989, submitted to the Judiciary Committee of the City Council of the District of Columbia by Kevin Berrill, Director, Anti-Violence Project, National Gay and Lesbian Task Force, 8 June 1989, Box 57, Folder 45, NGTLF Records, Cornell. "Siege" is also used in Kevin Berrill, "Testimony on Anti-Gay Discrimination and Violence," submitted to Raleigh Human Resources and Human Relations Advisory Committee, August 12, 1987, Box 57, Folder 46, ibid.

92. For an analysis of such an analogy, see Jakobsen, "Queers Are Like Jews, Aren't They? Analogy and Alliance Politics," in Queer Theory and the Jewish Question, ed. Daniel Boyarin, Daniel Itzkovitz, and Ann Pellegrini (New York: Columbia University Press, 2003).

93. "Hate Crime: A Training Video for Police Officers," 1990, Box 290, NGTLF Records, Cornell.

94. See side-by-side articles, "New Jersey Lawmen Train in Israel" and "Hate Crime: A Police Training Video," ADL Law Enforcement Bulletin, Spring 1992, clipping in Box 106, Folder 6, NGTLF Records, Cornell.

95. The ADL's model legislation is included as the first item in Appendix One of Barbara Perry, ed., Hate and Bias Crime: A Reader, 481–82.

96. Kevin Berrill submitted testimony to the Committee on the Judiciary Subcommittee on the Constitution: "As you know, the administration has taken special exception to the federal collection of data on vandalism, trespass and threat. We believe these data are necessary because such crimes are both serious and frequent. According to the NIJ study, vandalism is among the most commonly reported forms of hate violence. Reports issued by the Anti-Defamation League of B'nai B'rith, the National Gay and Lesbian Task Force, and other groups also show that threats, vandalism, and trespass are among the most frequent hate crimes." Testimony on Federal Hate Crime Statistics Collection Submitted to the Senate Judiciary Committee Subcommittee on the Constitution, June 21, 1988. Box 54, Folder 34, NGLTF Records, Cornell.

97. "'Task Force Opposes Persian Gulf War' Position Paper Released, Says Gays and Lesbians 'Detrimentally Affected' by Conflict," NGTLF press release, January 30, 1991, Box 37, Folder 74, NGTLF Records, Cornell.

98. ADL of B'nai B'rith, "1991 Audit of Anti-Semitic Incidents," Box 52, Folder 32, NGTLF Records, Cornell.

99. "ADL Opposed a National Education Association Report That Claims the US Was Institutionally Racist," NGTF press release, October 23, 1981, Box 106, Folder 6, NGTLF Records, Cornell.

100. For example, in West Hollywood members of the local Queer Nation began a street patrol (Hugo Martin, "Gay Form Patrols to Battle Hate Crimes," Los Angeles Times, December 3, 1991) and then a few years later the West Hollywood Sheriff's Department began its own program, the Community Oriented Bashing Recognition and Abatement program (Louise Hoyt, "COBRA Strikes Out at Gay-Bashers," Hollywood Independent, Wednesday, July 14, 1993). Other patrols included the Pink Angels in Chicago (Don Terry, "'Pink Angels' Battle Anti-Gay Crime," New York Times, April 7, 1992), the Pynk Patrol in Boston, the Q Patrol in Seattle, and another Q Patrol in Houston, Texas, which was joined by a police sting operation (Susan Hightower, "Murder Leads to Protection for Gays," Los Angeles Times, March 22, 1992). (Clippings in ONE Subject Files Collection, ONE National Gay and Lesbian Archives, Los Angeles, CA.)

101. "Pink Panther Loses Use of Name," *Wall Street Journal*, October 4, 1991; "Pink Panther Booted Out of Gay Group," *New York Post*, October 4, 1991. (Clippings in Box 48, Folder 4, NGLTF Records, Cornell).

102. The San Francisco Street Patrol explained that one of their differences from Queer Nation were not only that they did not make decisions by consensus, but that they also did not wear Queers Bash Back stickers because those might suggest vigilantism. The San Francisco Street Patrol also noted that many of its members were dedicated to stopping violent crime and not to the political messages of Queer Nation (see Undated Press Release, Box 1, Publicity—Press Releases Folder 9, SF Street Patrol Records, Gay, Lesbian, Bisexual, Transgender Historical Society, San Francisco).

103. Lauren Berlant with Elizabeth Freeman, "Queer Nationality," in Lauren Berlant, *The Queen of America Goes to Washington City: Essays on Sex and Citizenship* (Durham: Duke University Press, 1997), 156.

104. The Street Patrol was also accused of copyright violation by a San Francisco resident, who had designed a coiled snake from a triangle with the phrase "Don't Tread on Moi" (Dennis Conkin, "Queer Nation Street Patrol Accused of Copyright Violation," *Bay Area Reporter*, May 16, 1991, reprinted in *Street Patrol News*, May 22, 1991, Box 48, Folder 4, NGTLF Records, Cornell).

105. Curtis Sliwa and Murray Schwartz, *Street Smart: The Guardian Angel Guide to Safe Living* (Reading, MA: Addison-Wesley, 1982), 1. An accompanying photo of two young men, one black and the other not racially identifiable, sitting on a street curb with an empty forty-ounce beer bottle is captioned "Some inner-city youths, unable to find summer jobs, hang out in public areas, waiting—and sometimes looking—for trouble."

106. In fact, years earlier, in 1980, Supervisor Carol Silver (who won the contested election mentioned in chapter 3), wrote an open letter to the *Bay Area Reporter* arguing for more policing in San Francisco's Mission District and Dolores Park and also calling to unite the by-then-defunct Butterfly Brigade with the newly founded Guardian Angels in New York. She further explained, "We must ask ourselves, both individually and collectively, what we have done to reach out to these kids whose self-esteem is so low that they can only achieve a sense of power and self-worth by victimizing someone perceived to be more vulnerable than themselves. These are our youth—and they are ours, whether you color them brown or black or pink, or emotionally disturbed to mentally retarded" (Carol Ruth Silver, "An Open Letter Re: Anti-Gay Violence," *Bay Area Reporter*, December 4, 1980).

107. The membership package of the San Francisco Street Patrol included the following warning that denounced vigilantism: "We are not politically correct. We are not a consensus organization. We are not vigilantes. We are not a gang. If you have a problem with these or any of these rules, please go away rapidly." It later noted that vigilantism would result in expulsion (Membership Booklet, Box 1, Membership Folder [1/6], 1993, SF Street Patrol Records, GLBTHS). This is also reprinted in Sara Miles, "The Fabulous Fight Back: On the Streets after Dark to Confront Gay Bashers," *Out/Look* (Summer 1992), 57.

108. "Some Questions and Answers about Street Patrol," flier in Membership Booklet, and published in *Street Patrol News*, May 29, 1991. The flier goes on to explain that the street patrol's entire "political agenda" was restricted to stopping violent attacks on the bases of people's sexual orientation. Regarding the group's relationship with the police, the flier noted: "Upon apprehending a basher, we have only three options: kill him, let him go, or detain him until the police arrive and then remand him into their custody. This last option, commonly known as 'citizen's arrest', seems to us the only practical one of the three."

109. One newsletter item said: "Style points to Dary for cruising the head of the [Hate Crimes] unit and inviting her out for coffee" (*Street Patrol Newsletter*, January 31, 1992, Box 48, Folder 4, NGTLF Records, Cornell).

110. "The Law, Our Hope and Salvation," *Street Patrol Newsletter*, November 15, 1991, NGTLF Records, Cornell.

111. For reference to the kiosk see *Street Patrol Newsletter*, January 31, 1992, Box 48, Folder 4, NGTLF Records, Cornell. For references to the plan for faster response, see minutes from a meeting between members of Street Patrol and police officers at the Mission Station, dated December 23, 1991, San Francisco, reprinted in that same issue of the newsletter. The term *mutants* was apparently borrowed from the Guardian Angels (Miles, "The Fabulous Fight Back," 58).

112. Adam Z, "Walking on the Wild Side: A Few Handy Hints on How to Avoid Getting Your Ass Kicked by Crazed Heterosexist Slime," *Street Patrol Newsletter*, October 4, 1991; Box 48, Folder 4, NGTLF Records, Cornell. (Note: Box 48, Folder 4 of this collection includes mostly loose sheets of paper. As a result, the citation of newsletter dates represents a best approximation within a three-month period.)

113. Michael C. Botkin, "Street Patrol Thwarts Gay Bashing in Castro," *Bay Area Reporter*, clipping in Box 48, Folder 4, NGTLF Records, Cornell.

114. Ellen Twiname, "Defending Ourselves," *Frighten the Horses*, Spring 1991, 12–14, clipping reprint in Box 48, Folder 4, NGTLF Records, Cornell. Despite this, the San Francisco Street Patrol did sometimes make different claims, as in one flier in which members wrote: "Street Patrol is not out to enforce the law and clean up the streets, nor are we claiming the Castro as 'our turf.' Rather, Street Patrol intends to make the Castro a place where Queer people can hang out without being targeted for violence attack," flier, n.d., Box 1, Publicity-fliers Folder [1/8], SF Street Patrol Records, GLBTHS.

115. See "National News," *Street Patrol Newsletter*, October 4, 1991, Box 48, Folder 4, NGTLF Records, Cornell. Later, a San Francisco Street Patrol member identified as Dani indicated in a letter to the Vet's Council Members that s/he was trying to reach out to other groups to make a national network, including the Christopher Street Patrol and Outwatch in New York, but hadn't yet made contact (letter [ca. 1993], Box 1, Miscellaneous SFSP material folder [1/14], San Francisco Street Patrol Records, GLBTHS). A proposal called the Confederation of Anti-Violence Street Patrols later emerged.

116. In addition to the ones named earlier, another patrol of that era was Streetcats (sometimes spelled Street Cats) in Los Angeles. It was founded in March 1991 and eventually came to San Francisco in 1993. They paid patrollers $5–$6 per hour and were led by Don Fass. See Don Fass, "Streetcats Roar Back," *San Francisco Bay Times*, May 20, 1993 and Caroline Harding, "Superman's Dead, but . . . ," *Los Angeles Times Magazine* (clippings in Box 1, Street Cats in LA and SF folder [1/15] 1993, San Francisco Street Patrol Records, GLBTHS). Also see materials on the Street Cats patrol in Gay Bashing, ONE Subject File Collection, ONE National Gay and Lesbian Archives, Los Angeles. The San Francisco Street Patrol and Street Cats clashed, especially over the latter's use of paid members, a jeep, mace, and—reportedly—a stun gun. The Street Patrol released an open letter on May 1, 1993, questioning the ethics and strategies of the Street Cats; another letter to Don Fass, August 15, 1993, also complained of verbal harassment by Street Cats (in Street Cats in LA and SF folder, San Francisco Street Patrol Records, GLBTHS).

117. "Pink Panthers," flier, n.d., Box 48, Folder 21, NGTLF Records, Cornell.

118. Alisa Solomon, "Fired Up: Should Gays Carry Guns?," *Village Voice*, November

27, 1990. The title refers to Larry Kramer's proposal that the Pink Panthers should carry guns.

119. The presentation was described as "interventionist" in Edward Eihauge, "San Francisco's Queer Street Patrol," *Ideas and Action*, n.d. (ca. late 1991; published by Workers Solidarity Alliance in San Francisco, clipping in Box 1, Publicity—publications with articles about SFSP Folder [1/10], 1993, SF Street Patrol Records, GLBTHS). This article also notes that the Christopher Street Patrol was so disliked that its members needed to reach out to recruit gay people.

120. See "Christopher Street Patrol 'Street Awareness Series' Offers Video/Panel on Bias-Related Crime on Wednesday October 24th, 8pm at Dugout," n.d. press release included in *Street Patroller*, September 27, 1990; also see updates in *Street Patroller*, October 9, 1990, for discussion of collaboration with East Villagers against Crack (Box 48, Folder 4, NGTLF Records, Cornell).

121. John Voelcker, Nina Reyes, and Andrew Miller, "Panthers and Angels Arrive on Christopher Street," *Outweek*, August 22, 1990, 18.

122. Christopher Street Patrol, "A Report to Our Neighbors," *Street Patroller*, July 24, 1991, Box 48, Folder 4, NGTLF Records, Cornell.

123. "Christopher St. Is a Special Place: Let's Work Together to Keep It That Way," flier, n.d., Box 48, Folder 4, NGTLF Records, Cornell.

124. In one newsletter, the San Francisco Street Patrol profiled other San Francisco–based, nongay street patrols of those years; representatives of the groups sat together on a panel organized by the Coalition for San Francisco Neighborhoods. The other groups included Safe Streets (a group of residents and homeowners in the Mission), Residents against Druggies (a resident patrol against those they described as "crack-heads," based in Haight Ashbury), Natoma and Vicinity Neighbors (a racially diverse group of residents and merchants patrolling a small section of the Mission), and the Lexington Look Outs (a crime control patrol also in the Mission). The members of these groups all wore uniforms and carried radios. See *San Francisco Street Patrol Newszine*, September 1993, in Street Patrol News, Periodicals, Gay, Lesbian, Bisexual, Transgender Historical Society, San Francisco. In another newsletter, the Street Patrol profiled a straight member who had joined because of his desire for experience that would help him become a police officer ("Meet Kenton Hoover! Patroller O' the Month—July!," *San Francisco Street Patrol Newszine*, July–August, 1993, ibid.).

125. Cathy Cohen, "Punks, Bulldaggers, and Welfare Queens: The Radical Potential of Queer Politics?," *GLQ* 3, no. 4 (1997): 448.

126. In a letter to the editor of an unnamed paper dated November 5, 1991 (and reproduced in an issue of the *Street Patrol Newsletter*), Jo Meyertons, a coordinator of the patrol, wrote: "In 1990 C.U.A.V. [Community United Against Violence]'s own staff statistician reported that 25% of San Francisco's reported bashings occurred in the Castro, which is the area we primarily patrol. In the first half of 1991, C.U.A.V. reported that this figure had dropped to 19%. This period of time coincides with the existence of our Street Patrol. To my knowledge, no other relevant variable in the area has changed. Mere coincidence? We don't think so. We intervene in violent situations several times a month, and have deterred an immeasurable number of bashings simply by being a visible force. Street Patrol STOPS THE VIOLENCE" (*Street Patrol Newsletter* [most likely from Nov. 15, 1991, issue], Box 48, Folder 4, NGTLF Records, Cornell).

127. Berlant and Freeman, "Queer Nationality," 157.

128. Lisa Duggan, "Making it Perfectly Queer," in Duggan and Hunter, *Sex Wars: Sexual Dissent and Political Culture* (New York: Routledge, 1995), 160–61.

129. In this way, the dynamic of constituting the commonplace idea that antigay violence is first and foremost a crime aligns with the making of criminal categories and crisis outlined by Stuart Hall et al., *Policing the Crisis: Mugging, the State, and Law and Order* (London: Palgrave Macmillan, 1978).

5. "Canaries of the Creative Age"

Epigraph: Dave Poster and Elaine Goldman, "Gay Youth Gone Wild: Something Has Got to Change," *Villager*, September 21–27, 2005. Emphasis added.

1. Denny Lee, "Street Fight," *New York Times*, March 31, 2001.

2. On quality-of-life politics in New York, see Tanya Erzen, "Turnstile Jumpers and Broken Windows: Policing Disorder in New York City," in *Zero Tolerance: Quality of Life and the New Police Brutality in New York City*, ed. Andrea McArdle and Tanya Erzen (New York: New York University Press, 2001), 19–49.

3. As noted in the last chapter, the Christopher Street Patrol collaborated on a few occasions with the Anti-Violence Project in the 1990s. This was not so in the 2000s, but many individual lesbian and gay residents and activists did come out to support the patrol.

4. See, in particular, Gary J. Gates and Jason Ost, *The Gay and Lesbian Atlas* (Washington, D.C.: Urban Institute Press, 2004).

5. Richard Florida, *The Rise of the Creative Class, and How It's Transforming Work, Leisure, Community, and Everyday Life* (New York: Basic Books, 2002). Florida's ideas have been roundly challenged and he has since revised his position a bit.

6. Gates is quoted in Christopher Swope, "Chasing the Rainbow: Is a Gay Population an Engine of Urban Revival? Cities Are Beginning to Think So," *Governing*, August 2003 (http://www.governing.com/topics/economic-dev/Chasing-The-Rainbow.html).

7. Florida, *The Rise of the Creative Class*, 256. The phrase "canaries of the creative age" is attributed to Gary Gates, while the use of the phrase "last frontier" in this context is Florida's. Gates's full study, done with Jason Ost, demonstrates that gays and lesbians live everywhere, not only in concentrated gay enclaves. I do not mean to suggest that he affirms the primacy of gay enclaves, but I am drawing attention to the kinds of terms used to characterize gay neighborhood life (Gates and Ost, *The Gay and Lesbian Atlas*).

8. Florida, *The Rise of the Creative Class*, 262–63.

9. For one history of bohemianism in Greenwich Village, see Sally Banes, *Greenwich Village 1963: Avant-Garde Performance and the Effervescent Body* (Durham: Duke University Press, 1993). As Fred Moten shows (*In the Break: The Aesthetics of the Black Radical Tradition* [Minneapolis: University of Minnesota Press, 2003]), Banes's vision of bohemian Greenwich Village also reveals stark racial exclusions. For a discussion of urban redevelopment and bohemianism, see Richard Lloyd, *Neo-Bohemia: Art and Commerce in the Postindustrial City* (New York: Routledge, 2005).

10. Wendy Brown, "Neoliberalism and the End of Liberal Democracy," *Theory and Event* 7, no. 1 (2003), http://muse.jhu.edu/login?auth=0&type=summary&url=/journals/theory_and_event/v007/7.1brown.html; David Harvey, *A Brief History of Neoliberalism* (New York: Oxford University Press, 2007).

11. Lisa Duggan, *The Twilight of Equality? Neoliberalism, Cultural Politics, and the Attack on Democracy* (Boston: Beacon, 2004).

12. Jodi Melamed, *Represent and Destroy: Rationalizing Violence in the New Racial Capitalism* (Minneapolis: University of Minnesota Press, 2011).

13. My thinking on the politics of lifestyle has been shaped by ongoing conversations about race, representation, and real estate with Eva Hageman. Many of these ideas ap-

peared in "Realty TV: Reality Television and the Value of 'Lifestyle,'" a paper she presented at the Critical Ethnic Studies conference, Riverside, CA, March 11, 2011.

14. Alexandra Chasin argues that during the 1990s many lesbian and gay activist goals were transformed into consumer demands (*Selling Out: The Gay and Lesbian Movement Goes to Market* [New York: St. Martin's, 2000]).

15. For a helpful overview of New York City's governing structure and community boards, including their purpose and policies, see the page "About Community Boards" posted on the website of the Mayor's Community Affairs Unit (http://www.nyc.gov /html/cau/html/cb/about.shtml).

16. Jane Jacobs, *The Death and Life of Great American Cities* (New York: Vintage, [1961] 1992), 50–54.

17. Jacobs, *The Death and Life of Great American Cities*, 35, 68.

18. Deyan Sudjic, *100 Mile City* (New York: Harcourt Brace, 1992); Marshall Berman, *All That Is Solid Melts into Air: The Experience of Modernity* (New York: Penguin, 1988).

19. Marc Stein, *City of Sisterly and Brotherly Loves: Lesbian and Gay Philadelphia* (Chicago: University of Chicago Press, 2000), 85.

20. Andrew Ross, *The Celebration Chronicles: Life, Liberty, and the Pursuit of Property Value in Disney's New Town* (New York: Ballantine, 2000); Samuel R. Delany, *Times Square Red, Times Square Blue* (New York: New York University Press, 1999).

21. Throughout the 1960s city administrators dismissed community plans in low-income neighborhoods as too ambitious or contested. One example was the plan put forth by the Architects Renewal Committee for Harlem. See Richard Plunz, *A History of Housing in New York City* (New York: Columbia University Press, 1990); also see, "Community-based Planning Milestones," in "The Livable City: Community-Based Planning, Building on Local Knowledge" [brochure], ed. Jocelyne Chait (New York: Municipal Art Society, Fall 2002) (in author's possession).

22. My timeline is adapted from the "Livable City" brochure.

23. Todd W. Bressi, ed., *Planning and Zoning New York City: Yesterday, Today and Tomorrow* (New Brunswick, NJ: Center for Urban Policy Research, Rutgers University, 1993).

24. For some, the 1961 revision was a de facto comprehensive plan in line with the top-down programs of the urban renewal era, and it handed Manhattan over to real estate developers. For a stinging critique of the law and the developer-led drive of manufacturing out of lower Manhattan, see Robert Fitch, *The Assassination of New York* (London: Verso, 1993).

25. Community councils had existed since 1951, but they did not have the same power as the boards. See Tom Angotti (with Ron Schiffman), "The Roots of Community-Based Planning in New York City," in "The Livable City," 2.

26. John R. Fawcett, "The Will to Plan: Community-Initiated Planning in New York City," Planning Center, Municipal Art Society of New York, Winter 1989–90; Jocelyne Chait, "The State of 197-a Planning in New York City," Municipal Art Society Planning Center, Fall 1998 (both items in author's possession).

27. Chait, "The State of 197-a Planning"; also see Julie Sze, *Noxious New York: The Racial Politics of Urban Health and Environmental Justice* (Cambridge: MIT Press, 2006).

28. The Campaign for Community Based Planning, "Planning for All New Yorkers: An Atlas of Community Based Plans" (with interactive digital map), Municipal Art Society, http://myciti.mas.org/atlas/.

29. The Comprehensive Plan was published in 1992 ("New York City Comprehensive Waterfront Plan: Reclaiming the City's Edge," Department of City Planning, City of

New York, Summer 1992); the Manhattan section was released in 1993 and revised in 1997 ("Plan for the Manhattan Waterfront: New York City Comprehensive Waterfront Plan," Department of City Planning, City of New York, Winter 1993, and "Comprehensive Manhattan Waterfront Plan: A 197-a Plan as modified and adopted by the City Planning Commission and the City Council," Department of City Planning, City of New York, Summer 1997). All items in author's possession.

30. "The History of the Hudson River Park," n.d. (http://www.gothamgazette.com /iotw/hudson/doc2.shtml)

31. Hudson River Park Conservancy, "Hudson River Park Concept and Financial Plan," n.d., 12 (in author's possession).

32. The governor and mayor each appointed five members of HRPT's board; three other members were chosen by the Manhattan Borough president with input from Community Boards 1, 2, and 4. An example of sponsored private development that conformed with regulations was the Chelsea Piers, a sporting facility in Community Board 4.

33. Hudson River Park Conservancy, "Hudson River Park Concept and Financial Plan," 41.

34. City Planning Commission, "Document # N 950604 NPM," February 5, 1997, Calendar No. 35, "Comprehensive Manhattan Waterfront Plan," Section 2, n.p.

35. CB2 also supported the preservation of Piers 49 and 51 for wildlife conservation and Pier 54 for historic purposes, as well as the cleanup of the Gansevoort Peninsula, a sanitation truck garage. The board also requested a dog run in the Gansevoort Peninsula. See "Recommendations," in "Comprehensive Manhattan Waterfront Plan," 143.

36. City of New York Community Board No. 2 Manhattan Waterfront Committee Meeting Minutes, March 1, 1999, Community Board No. 2 Offices, New York. At different times during these years this committee was variably referred to as the Waterfront Committee; the Parks, Waterfront, Recreation, and Open Space Committee; and the Parks and Waterfront Committee.

37. HRPT held a ribbon-cutting ceremony to celebrate the opening of the first phase of the park (City of New York Community Board No. 2 Manhattan Waterfront Committee Meeting Minutes, September 23, 1999, Community Board No. 2 Offices, New York).

38. For a fantastic analysis of *Times Square*, see Mimi Thi Nguyen, *Punk Planet* 62 (July–August 2004): 94–97. threadandcircuits.wordpress.com/tag/times-square/.

39. On *Paris Is Burning*, see bell hooks, "Is Paris Burning?," *Black Looks: Race and Representation* (Boston: South End, 1992), 145–56; Phillip Brian Harper, "'The Subversive Edge': *Paris Is Burning*, Social Critique, and the Limits of Subjective Agency," *Diacritics* 24, nos. 2–3 (1994): 90–103; Chandan Reddy, "Home, House, and Nonidentity: *Paris Is Burning*," in *Burning Down the House: Recycling Domesticity*, ed. Rosemary George (Boulder, CO: Westview, 1997), 355–79; Lucas Hilderbrand, *Paris Is Burning: A Queer Film Classic* (Vancouver: Arsenal Pulp, forthcoming).

40. For an excellent reading of *The Salt Mines* and *The Transformation*, see Robert McRuer, *Crip Theory: Cultural Signs of Queerness and Disability* (New York: New York University Press, 2006).

41. The exact numbers are 74.8 percent white, 14.6 percent Asian American, 5.7 percent of Hispanic origin, 2.4 percent African American, 2 percent mixed race, 0.3 percent other race non-Hispanic, and 0.1 percent American Indian and Alaska Native. The public assistance measure includes Aid to Families with Dependent Children, Home Relief, Supplemental Security Income, and Medicaid. Information reported in Department of City Planning, "Community District Needs: Manhattan, Fiscal Years 2002/2003," Department of City Planning, City of New York, 28 (in author's possession).

42. According to one article, the space was converted into a unit renting for $7,000 a month (Denny Lee, "Street Fight," *New York Times*, March 31, 2001).

43. For example, the bar Two Potato mentioned in this book's introduction was forced to leave after residents complained (Lee, "Street Fight").

44. One exception was Sex Panic, a group founded in 1997. Central to its campaigns was opposition to zoning and public health policies that restricted sex businesses and clubs, including those in Greenwich Village. Many of its members were queer academics—including Michael Warner, who wrote about these issues in *The Trouble with Normal: Sex, Politics, and the Ethics of Queer Life* (New York: Free Press, 1999). I discuss Warner's analysis at the end of this chapter.

45. David Dunlap, "PATH Project Unloved in the Village," *New York Times*, June 20, 2002.

46. The northern end of the territory under the jurisdiction of CB2 is known as the meat packing district for its mostly bygone industrial purposes. It later became a hot market for condominium development. Although it was doubtful that historical preservation status would save the meat packing industry, many hoped it might put a limit on the number of new condominium developments. A prime example of how historical preservation has been used to promote gentrification is represented in the film *Flag Wars*, dir. Linda Good Bryant and Laura Poitras (New York: Praxis Films, 2003).

47. One resident reportedly complained that the new PATH exits would lead to "people from New Jersey disgorging in the community" (quoted in Richard Goldstein, "Street Hassle: New Skool versus Old School in Greenwich Village," *Village Voice*, April 24–30, 2002).

48. In addition to my interviews, sources for the history I have outlined include Justin Anton Rosado, "Corroding Our Quality of Life," in *That's Revolting! Queer Strategies for Resisting Assimilation*, ed. Mattilda Bernstein Sycamore (New York: Soft Scull, 2004), 287–302, and the website of the Audre Lorde Project: http://alp.org/.

49. In 1997, Abner Louima was brutalized by New York City police officers outside a nightclub in Brooklyn. Two years later, in 1999, the unarmed Amadou Diallo was shot and killed by four police officers who were later acquitted at trial. Both incidents inspired widespread and sustained activism against police violence in New York City.

50. See Dayo F. Gore, Tamara Jones, and Joo-Hyun Kang, "Organizing at the Intersections: A Roundtable Discussion of Police Brutality through the Lens of Race, Class, and Sexual Identities," in *Zero Tolerance*, ed. McArdle and Erzen, 251–69.

51. Bran Fenner interview by author, New York, June 2, 2006.

52. In later years, Community United Against Violence would begin a radical transformation to tighten its focus on racial justice and question the use of state punishment solutions; it would also move from the Castro to the Mission (see Morgan Bassichis, "Reclaiming Queer & Trans Safety," in *The Revolution Starts at Home: Confronting Intimate Violence within Activist Communities*, ed. Ching-In Chen, Jai Dulani, and Leah Lakshmi Piepzna-Samarasinha [Brooklyn, NY: South End, 2011], 3–24).

53. Here I am referring to the linked campaigns against sexual and racial violence in the South, especially by activists like Mandy Carter, Mab Segrest, and other founders of Southerners on New Ground.

54. Bran Fenner interview by author, New York, June 2, 2006; Krystal Portalatin interview by author, New York, July 21, 2009.

55. Vogue is a style of dance performance developed within black and Latino queer subcultures that grew in popularity during the 1980s and 1990s. Vogue performances are often staged within ball culture—a network of competitive performances between members of different "houses."

56. Krystal Portalatin interview by author, New York, July 21, 2009.

57. José Esteban Muñoz, *Cruising Utopia: The Then and There of Queer Futurity* (New York: New York University Press, 2009), 91.

58. As Elizabeth Freeman puts it, "time can be money only when it is turned into space, quantity, and/or measure" (*Time Binds: Queer Temporalities, Queer Histories* [Durham: Duke University Press, 2010], 54).

59. At the very end of the documentary, Justin Rosado, a member of FIERCE, reads a poem that concludes: "Our blood is sunken into your streets, and when we rise above your clouds of money, once again I'll be there, staring into your eyes, letting you know I will never leave."

60. Erzen, "Turnstile Jumpers and Broken Windows."

61. "Police Meeting," in "News . . . from Council Member Christine C. Quinn," flier, n.d. (early 2002), author's personal collection. Also attached to this document was a letter addressed to Ronald Shiftan, executive director of the Port Authority of New York and New Jersey, opposing new PATH exits, dated January 2002.

62. Deborah J. Glick, publicly distributed letter to Police Commissioner Raymond Kelly, January 25, 2001 [*sic*; it was 2002], author's personal collection. It was accompanied by a copy of a letter to the editor of the *New York Times,* from Glick, "West Village Crime," *New York Times,* January 26, 2002.

63. City of New York Community Board No. 2 Manhattan, open letter to Detective Michael Singer, Community Relations, Sixth Police Precinct, and Julius Lang, Coordinator, Midtown Community Court, c.c. to New York State Senator Thomas Duane, New York State Assembly Member Deborah Glick, Council Member Kathryn Freed, Council Member Margarita Lopez, Council Member Christine Quinn, Manhattan Borough President C. Virginia Fields, from Aubrey Lees, Chair, Community Board 2, Manhattan, November 30, 2001, author's personal collection.

64. Here I am referring to Arizona Senate Bill 1070 (the Support Our Law Enforcement and Safe Neighborhoods Act) passed in 2010. The law forbids local agencies from restricting the full enforcement of federal immigration laws; in this way, the law hopes to create the conditions that would force people to leave.

65. Robert F. Worth, "Tolerance in Village Wears Thin," *New York Times,* January 19, 2001. This article is also cited by Goldstein ("Street Hassle"), who provides a sharp reading of its editorial biases.

66. St. Vincent's has since been closed, and there are rumors that its buildings will be turned into condominiums.

67. All quotes from Community Board No. 2 General Meeting, St. Vincent's Hospital, New York, February 12, 2002, author's field notes.

68 Lee, "Street Fight."

69. Community Board No. 2 General Meeting, St. Vincent's Hospital, New York, February 12, 2002, author's field notes.

70. FIERCE, "Quality of Life Forum Update," flier, n.d., author's personal collection.

71. Community Board No. 2 General Meeting, St. Vincent's Hospital, New York, February 12, 2002, author's field notes.

72. Sixth Police Precinct Community Council Meeting, Our Lady of Pompeii Church, Father Demo Hall, New York, April 24, 2002, author's field notes.

73. Sixth Police Precinct Community Council Meeting, Our Lady of Pompeii Church, Father Demo Hall, New York, December 18, 2002, author's field notes.

74. Sixth Police Precinct Community Council Meeting, Our Lady of Pompeii Church, Father Demo Hall, New York, September 25, 2002, author's field notes.

75. The camera program was an informal proposal of Jessica Berk from Residents in Distress; it does not appear to have been officially pursued.

76. Sixth Precinct Community Council Meeting, Our Lady of Pompeii Church, Father Demo Hall, New York, November 20, 2002, author's field notes.

77. Fenner interview by author, New York, June 2, 2006.

78. See Judith Halberstam, *In a Queer Time and Place: Transgender Bodies, Subcultural Lives* (New York: New York University Press, 2005); Karen Tongson, *Relocations: Queer Suburban Imaginaries* (New York: New York University Press, 2011); Scott Herring, *Another Country: Queer Anti-Urbanism* (New York: New York University Press, 2010). For other critiques of spatial queer politics, see John Howard, *Men Like That: A Southern Queer History* (Chicago: University of Chicago Press, 1999); Martin F. Manalansan, *Global Divas: Filipino Gay Men in the Diaspora* (Durham: Duke University Press, 2003); Jasbir K. Puar, ed., "Queer Tourism: Geographies of Globalization," special issue, GLQ 8, nos. 1–2 (2002).

79. "FIERCE Info about LGBT Youth *FROM* LGBT Youth," flier, n.d., author's personal collection.

80. One of FIERCE's partners has been the Urban Justice Center, which has done research on and provided legal assistance to homeless LGBT youth through its Peter Cicchino Youth Program (Urban Justice Center, Projects: Peter Cicchino Youth, http://www.urbanjustice.org/ujc/projects/peter.html), and the Ali Forney Center, an advocacy and social service organization for LGBT youth that sponsors emergency and transitional living and a drop-in center (http://www.aliforneycenter.org/). The director of the center, Carl Siciliano, spoke at community board hearings (see Carl Siciliano, "Progress Report 2006: Youth: At Long Last, Progress on Homeless LGBT Youth," *Gay City News*, March 2–8, 2006).

81. Jay Jeffries, "Gay Youth Should Accept Pier 54," letter to the editor, *Villager*, March 15–21, 2006.

82. Daisy Hernandez, "Young and Out: Anything but Safe," *Colorlines*, Winter 2004; also available at http://www.daisyhernandez.com/2009/11/28/young-and-out-anything-but-safe/.

83. For an analysis of this mobilizing effort, see Zenzele Isoke, *Urban Black Women and the Politics of Resistance* (New York: Palgrave Macmillan, 2013).

84. FIERCE, "How Do You Define QUALITY OF LIFE?," flier, n.d., author's personal collection.

85. "Why Did They Die? A Document of Black Feminism," *Radical America* (November–December 1979): 41. The piece was included with the Combahee River Collective's pamphlet titled, "Six, 7, 8 Black Women: Why Did They Die?"

86. Sixth Precinct Community Council Meeting, Our Lady of Pompeii Church, Father Demo Hall, New York, November 20, 2002, author's field notes.

87. I remember the ejaculation comments from the first large community meeting held at St. Vincent's hospital on February 12, 2002. FIERCE activists cited the comment in their "Quality of Life Forum Update," flier, n.d., author's personal collection. I do not believe that the doorknob action was envisioned as a direct response to this claim, but it did work as such a retort.

88. In the minutes of the full board meeting of CB2 on July 18, 2002, the LGBT subcommittee included a declaration that was eventually passed by a majority of CB2 board members condemning citizen patrol groups, calling them "vigilante" and arguing that the police and social service agencies were better equipped to address "the problems that have been plaguing the West Village as a result of the clash between local residents

and those members of the LGBT community who come to the area" (on file in CB2 offices, New York).

89. Indeed, in the years I conducted my research and afterward, FIERCE and its political campaigns have been popular topics for students, researchers, and journalists. We often came to learn from and participate in the fight against the privatization of queer space, but we also sometimes came with the claim of expertise, the promise of technical assistance, and the dream of a finished thesis, article, or book. As I described in this book's introduction, I decided that I would do my research as someone allied with the organization; this decision defined the mode and extent of my participation.

90. See Halberstam's critiques of the dominant "epistemology of youth" in LGBT political organizing (*In a Queer Time and Place*).

91. Meeting between members of the Sixth Precinct and members of FIERCE sponsored by CB2 at the LGBT Community Center, New York, June 20, 2005, author's field notes. Residents also complained about PEP officers who were reported to have harassed reporters, politicians, and residents for activities such as taking photographs, collecting signatures, or walking dogs. See Lincoln Anderson, "Trust Is Peppered with Questions about Park PEP's," *Villager*, October 12–18, 2005.

92. Anderson, "Trust Is Peppered with Questions about Park PEP's."

93. Quoted in Duncan Osborne, "Piers Fears Go Racial: With No Christopher Street Solution, Community Board Faults LGBT Youth of Color," *Gay City News*, March 9–15, 2006.

94. Albert Amateau, "Queer Youth and Residents Still at Odds on Park Use," *Villager*, December 14–20, 2005. The second quote is from Florent Morellet, the former owner of a restaurant that had shared his first name and a big supporter of the historic preservation efforts in the meat-packing district to control condominium development.

95. Lincoln Anderson, "Gate May Be Closed to Gays in Park's Crowd-Control Plan," *Villager*, October 26–November 1, 2005; Daniel Wallace, "Gay Youth Slam Trust's Christopher St. Gates Plan," *Villager*, November 9–15, 2005; Duncan Osborne, "Christopher St. Late Night Flap," *Gay City News*, November 10–16, 2005; Ida C. Benedetto, "FIERCE Organizes to Keep Christopher St. Pier Open," *New York City Indymedia*, December 8, 2005; Duncan Osborne, "No Resolution on Pier Closing," *Gay City News*, December 8–14, 2005; James Withers, "A Ruckus over Christopher Street," NewYorkBlade.com, December 9, 2005; B. Baumer, "Pier Pressure," *City Limits*, December 12, 2005; Victoria Foltz, "Board Wants Earlier Pier 45 Curfew," *Washington Square News*, March 7, 2006; Kristen Lombardi, "'Gay and Loud': The New Battle over Queer Kids' Ruckus in Greenwich Village," *Village Voice*, March 21, 2006.

96. Lincoln Anderson, "Pier 54 Proposal for Gay Youth in Park Doesn't Float," *Villager*, March 8–14, 2006; Duncan Osborne, "Christopher Street Pier Rules Unchanged," *Gay City News*, March 30–April 5, 2006; Lincoln Anderson, "C.B. 2 Challenges Pier Kids to Be on Best Behavior," *Villager*, March 29–April 4, 2006.

97. Quoted in Anderson, "C.B. 2 Challenges Pier Kids to Be on Best Behavior" (emphasis added).

98. Moreover, this effort was grounded in a politics of "love" (Anderson, "C.B. 2 Challenges Pier Kids to Be on Best Behavior"). For another approach to the politics of love, see Chela Sandoval, *Methodology of the Oppressed* (Minneapolis: University of Minnesota Press, 2000).

99. Krystal Portalatin interview by author, New York, July 21, 2009.

100. The enforcement of racial covenants is among the most well known. See Thomas

Sugrue, *The Origins of the Urban Crisis: Race and Inequality in Postwar Detroit* (Princeton: Princeton University Press, 1996); George Lipsitz, *The Possessive Investment in Whiteness: How White People Profit from Identity Politics* (Philadelphia: Temple University Press, 1998).

101. The other waterfront tract's median income was $72,418; the two core neighborhoods had median incomes of $58,202 and $57,567 (information reported in Department of City Planning, "Community District Needs: Manhattan, Fiscal Years 2002/2003").

102. The New York State Mitchell-Lama Housing Program was developed in 1955 to help secure affordable housing for middle-income New Yorkers. Developers were given low-interest mortgages and tax exemptions. In exchange, units were reserved for those within designated income guidelines. After twenty years, owners had the option to "buy out" of their agreements and rent the units at market rates. Many took this option and forced long-term tenants out of their homes and neighborhoods.

103. Judith C. Lack, "Dispute Still Rages as West Village Houses Meets Its Sales Test," *New York Times*, August 18, 1974. Also see Carter B. Horsley, "The Making of a City Neighborhood," *New York Times*, December 24, 1978.

104. For discussions of racial capitalism, see Cedric Robinson, *Black Marxism: The Making of the Black Radical Tradition* (London: Zed, 1983); Clyde Woods, *Development Arrested: Blues and Plantation Power in the Mississippi Delta* (London: Verso, 1998); Ruth Wilson Gilmore, *Golden Gulag: Prisons, Surplus, Crisis, and Opposition in Globalizing California* (Berkeley: University of California Press, 2007). In one article, Arthur Schwartz, identified as then chair of CB2's Committee on Waterfront, Parks, Recreation, and Open Space, noted the low number of residents who attended the community board meeting supporting the establishment of an earlier curfew (see Osborne, "No Resolution on Pier Closing"); this suggests that residents' interests were not uniform, and that those opposing youth were simply the most outspoken.

105. Cheryl Harris, "Whiteness as Property," in *Critical Race Theory: The Key Writings that Formed the Movement,* ed. Kimberlé Crenshaw, Neil Gotanda, Gary Peller, and Kendall Thomas (New York: New Press, 1995), 279.

106. Jeffrey Escoffier, "The Political Economy of the Closet: Notes toward an Economic History of Gay and Lesbian Life Before Stonewall," in *Homo Economics: Capitalism, Community, and Lesbian and Gay Life,* ed. Amy Gluckman and Betsy Reed (New York: Routledge, 1997), 129.

107. To borrow a phrase from Georg Lukács, it "penetrat[es] the veil of reification" (*History and Class Consciousness: Studies in Marxist Dialectics*, trans. Rodney Livingstone [Cambridge: MIT Press, 1971], 86).

108. Many activists and popular commentators describe the situation in Greenwich Village as gentrification. I would argue that this story is not one of gentrification in the classic definition of displacing residents and business, but instead one of displacing neighborhood users. This recognition marks the fact that not all gay enclaves involve active displacement, but they might still be the site of ideology and policy construction that works to similar if not the same effect. Robert W. Bailey notes that many gay enclaves have not produced displacement (*Gay Politics, Urban Politics: Identity and Economics in the Urban Setting* [New York: Columbia University Press, 1999]).

109. I do not mean to idealize this plan. As the students in Arlene Holpp Scala's "Lesbian Lives" class at William Paterson University pointed out to me, the public housing still stands at the periphery of the city and is disproportionately sited near red light districts. This plan also places sex industries near the airport. That was a feature of Mayor Giuliani's sex entertainment rezoning, too, but in this plan because both are downtown, the effect is quite different!

110. Anderson, "Gate May Be Closed to Gays in Park's Crowd-Control Plan."

111. The white paper was delivered in tandem with a spoof of the *Wizard of Oz* and a photographic series of imagined future uses.

112. FIERCE, "LGBTQ Youth of Color Win Seat on Hudson River Park Trust Advisory Council," press release, September 29, 2009, http://www.fiercenyc.org/media/docs /8661_HRPT_AdvisoryCouncilVictoryRelease.pdf; City of New York, Office of the Mayor, "Mayor Bloomberg Appoints Members of City's Commission for Lesbian, Gay, Bisexual, Transgender and Questioning Runaway and Homeless Youth," press release, October 5, 2009, http://www.fiercenyc.org/media/docs/6683_LGBTQRHYCommission PressRelease-FINAL-Oct52009.pdf.

113. Arlene Dávila, *Barrio Dreams: Puerto Ricans, Latinos, and the Neoliberal City* (Berkeley: University of California Press, 2004), 211, 212.

114. Warner's chapter builds on an earlier piece written by him and Lauren Berlant, "Sex in Public." In that piece, Berlant and Warner argue that the exclusivity of privacy forces queers into dangerous territories—empty regions open for the violence of "gay-bashers and other criminals." The authors' example is the Greenwich Village waterfront. In this telling, the queer use of the piers represents a secondary displacement, one that has followed the affirmative territorialization of the core of Greenwich Village by lesbians and gay men in the face of national heteronormativity. Berlant and Warner argue that gay spaces throughout the United States are indebted to a public sex culture outside of national ideals of familial intimacy, in which public sex spawns community then commerce and eventually a political base. They write: "No group is more dependent on this kind of pattern in urban space than queers. If we could not concentrate a publicly accessible culture somewhere, we would always be outnumbered and overwhelmed. And because what brings us together is sexual culture, there are very few places in the world that have assembled much of a queer population without a base in sex commerce" (Lauren Berlant and Michael Warner, "Sex in Public," *Critical Inquiry* 24, no. 2 [1998]: 563).

115. Harper, "The Subversive Edge"; hooks, "Is Paris Burning?"

116. Warner is right on the money, so to speak, when he writes: "Large numbers of lesbians and gay men . . . embrace a politics of privatization that offers them both property value and an affirmation of identity in a language of respectability and mainstream acceptance" (Warner, *The Trouble with Normal*, 164). My point is simply to highlight the fact that some white lesbians and gay men supported the campaign although they did not own property and did not identify with all forms of middle-class respectability. Most of the activities emphasized in residents' campaigns were noise, loitering, and general rowdiness. Those bars and clubs that were most targeted were either cited because they failed to keep patrons inside and quiet or because residents rejected those patrons if they appeared in the neighborhood at all. In virtually all cases, those targeted were people of color. This is not to downplay the damages of zoning and public health regulations or to deny that many of the people who hung out on the piers participated in public sex. But it is clear that this is as much an investment in whiteness as it is in gay respectability. (Or, in other words, gay respectability depends on whiteness.) It is the targeting of forms of queer intimacy that exceed public sex per se (and that are suggested by Berlant and Warner in "Sex in Public") that are most salient for understanding the dynamics in Greenwich Village today.

117. As Bailey argues in *Gay Politics, Urban Politics*, gay enclaves are rarely identified only by their status as gay, and they are often renter-based economies. Bailey shows that despite the central role that gay men played in patterns of gentrification in certain areas during the 1970s and 1980s, this has not been a uniform process, nor has it produced

uniform political economic effects. But Bailey agrees that gay men have indelibly shaped certain aspects of dominant gay discourse that has then been used to limit understandings of gay space, and they have ignored other formations of gay community and density. He thus puts forth the idea of gay space as less a territory than a field.

118. See Jennifer Reck, "Be Queer . . . but not Here! Queer and Transgender Youth, the Castro 'Mecca,' and Spatial Gay Politics," PhD diss., University of California, Santa Cruz, 2005; Amy Donovan, "Telling Me Different: An Ethnography of Homeless Youth in San Francisco," PhD diss., New School for Social Research, 2002.

119. Joey Plaster discusses and historicizes sit/lie in "Imagined Conversations and Activist Lineages: Public Histories of Queer Homeless Youth Organizing and the Policing of Public Space in San Francisco's Tenderloin, 1960s and Present," *Radical History Review* 113 (Spring 2012): 99–109.

120. Martin F. Manalansan, "Race, Violence, and Neoliberal Spatial Politics in the Global City," *Social Text* 23, nos. 3–4 (2005): 141–55.

121. See Judith Halberstam, *Queer Art of Failure* (Durham: Duke University Press, 2011); J. K. Gibson-Graham, *The End of Capitalism (As We Knew It): A Feminist Critique of Political Economy* (Minneapolis: University of Minnesota Press, 1996).

122. Some of these changes are common to organizations that adopt the nonprofit (501c3) form, but FIERCE has tried to maintain open-ended strategies while meeting the reporting demands of official nonprofit status throughout its history.

Conclusion

1. Martin D. Meeker Jr., *Contacts Desired: Gay and Lesbian Communications and Community, 1940s–1970s* (Chicago: University of Chicago Press, 2006).

2. Miranda Joseph, *Against the Romance of Community* (Minneapolis: University of Minnesota Press, 2002).

3. The media coverage of violence has also come and gone and has corresponded significantly with new developments in lesbian and gay activism.

4. See Joseph Massad, *Desiring Arabs* (Chicago: University of Chicago Press, 2007), and "Re-Orienting Desire: The Gay International and the Arab World," *Public Culture* 14, no. 2 (2002): 361–85. Massad's assessment of the international human rights movement is quite sweeping and does not consistently engage local activist efforts. That noted, the core of his critique of the cultural imperialism of much international human rights discourse and mainstream LGBT politics is useful.

5. This is despite the claim in the *New York Times* that the "culture of poverty" thesis is only recently experiencing a "come back" (Patricia Cohen, "'Culture of Poverty' Makes a Comeback," *New York Times*, October 17, 2010).

6. Carlos Ulises Decena, *Tacit Subjects: Belonging and Same-Sex Desire among Dominican Immigrant Men* (Durham: Duke University Press, 2011).

7. Alyosha Goldstein, *Poverty in Common: The Politics of Community Action during the American Century* (Durham: Duke University Press, 2012). In *Poverty Knowledge: Social Science, Social Policy, and the Poor in Twentieth-Century U.S. History* (Princeton: Princeton University Press, 2001), Alice O'Connor also reminds us that this move ran in tandem with historical scholarship—exemplified by the work of Richard Hofstadter—that saw the so-called premodern worldview of rural traditionalism as shared by those living in urban poverty and that equated both with a reactionary political sensibility. This, O'Connor argues, joined other social scientific research that advocated for the exportation of U.S.-based psychological studies to examine global inequality, and, I argue, provides an important framework for understanding future research on the interpretation

of what would be understood as homophobia in international human rights advocacy for sexual minorities.

8. Kath Weston, "Get Thee to a Big City: Sexual Imaginary and the Great Gay Migration," *GLQ* 2, no. 3 (1995): 253–77. Suburbs also figured as a point of departure due to their supposedly asphyxiating culture of conformity, rather than of poverty, a move that prefigured gay cosmopolitanism, as the patterns of suburbanization would change.

9. As Chandan Reddy shows, this has absolved the U.S. state of responsibility for the human needs created by official policy based on, for example, family sanctity ("Asian Diasporas, Neoliberalism, and Family: Reviewing the Case for Homosexual Asylum in the Context of Family Rights," *Social Text* 84–85, vol. 23, nos. 3–4 [2005]: 101–19). Also see Jasbir K. Puar, *Terrorist Assemblages: Homonationalism in Queer Times* (Durham: Duke University Press, 2007) and Fatima El-Tayeb, *European Others: Queering Ethnicity in Postnational Europe* (Minneapolis: University of Minnesota Press, 2011).

10. David Palumbo-Liu, Bruce Robbins, and Nirvana Tanoukhi, eds., *Immanuel Wallerstein and the Problem of the World: System, Scale, Culture* (Durham: Duke University Press, 2011). On the global politics of punishment, see Ruth Wilson Gilmore, "Globalization and U.S. Prison Growth: From Military Keynesianism to Post-Keynesian Militarism," *Race and Class* 40, nos. 2–3 (1998–99): 177–88, and *Golden Gulag: Prisons, Surplus, Crisis, and Opposition in Globalizing California* (Berkeley: University of California Press, 2007).

11. See Nayan Shah, *Stranger Intimacy: Contesting Race, Sexuality, and the Law in the North American West* (Berkeley: University of California Press, 2011).

12. See S. M. Amadae, *Rationalizing Capitalist Democracy: The Cold War Origins of Rational Choice Liberalism* (Chicago: University of Chicago Press, 2003)—especially the chapter "Consolidating Rational Choice Liberalism, 1970–2000," in which Amadae unpacks the rational choice inflections in the arguments of both John Rawls and Amartya Sen.

13. Thus it is important to critique not only the terms of violence and safety, but also rationality and subjectification. Michel Foucault, *History of Sexuality*, vol. 1, trans. Robert Hurley (New York: Pantheon, 1978); Gilles Deleuze and Félix Guattari, *A Thousand Plateaus*, trans. Brian Massumi (London: Continuum, 2004); Cathy Cohen, "Deviance as Resistance: A New Research Agenda for the Study of Black Politics," *Du Bois Review* 1, no. 1 (2004): 27–45. Here it is worth repeating that although I concur with Cohen that a model of resistance is limited if it is disconnected from the precise ways in which individuals negotiate access to power, as I mentioned in my introduction, I remain more ambivalent than she is about what uncovering intent might reveal or do, especially insofar as the relationship between desire and intent—as well as the clarity of one's objectives and goals—is often unstable.

Epilogue

1. Here I intentionally refer to the District of Columbia rather than Washington to note the dynamics of two very different cities in one. As Derek Musgrove writes, "A consistent theme in the city's history is the separation between 'Washington' and 'D.C.'—between the gleaming white marble monumental city, populated by out-of-town lawmakers and tourists, and the neighborhoods; between the disproportionately rich, white, and powerful, and the black, poor, and powerless" ("A KING for Washington and D.C.," *East of the River Magazine*, August 2011, 17).

2. Washington, D.C., has the third most extreme income gap among major U.S. cities. The wealthiest fifth of the city makes twenty-nine times more than the poorest fifth

(see Caitlin Biegler, "A Big Gap: Income Inequality in the District Remains One of the Highest in the Nation," D.C. Fiscal Policy Institute, March 7, 2012, http://www.D.C.fpi .org/a-big-gap-income-inequality-in-the-district-remains-one-of-the-highest-in-the -nation). From 2000 to 2010, D.C.'s black population dropped by 11 percent, as the non-Hispanic white population grew by almost a third (see Carol Morello and Dan Keating, "Number of Black D.C. Residents Plummets as Majority Status Slips Away," *Washington Post*, March 24, 2011).

3. For a study of the entwined history of black and LGBT/queer Washington, D.C., see Kwame Holmes, "Chocolate to Rainbow City: The Dialectics of Black and Gay Community Formation in Postwar Washington, D.C., 1946–1978," PhD diss., University of Illinois at Urbana-Champaign, 2011. For a study of the gentrification of Columbia Heights, see Justin Maher, "The Capital of Diversity: Difference, Development, and Place-Making in Washington, D.C.," PhD diss., University of Maryland, College Park, 2011.

4. They also partner with the Rainbow Response, an organization that fights intimate partner violence within the LGBT community, and the DC Center, a local community center (see GLOV Partners page on their website: http://www.glovdc.org/partners .html).

5. See Alliance for a Safe & Diverse D.C., *Move Along Report: Policing Sex Work in Washington, D.C.* (Washington, D.C.: Different Avenues, 2008).

6. On Chicago see Yasmin Nair, "March Highlights Boystown Tensions," *Windy City Times*, June 25, 2008. On the group Check It in D.C. see Courtland Milloy, "Gay Black Youths Go from Attacked to Attackers," *Washington Post*, September 27, 2011. Although Milloy's coverage is not totally unsympathetic, that of others was less so. See Shani Hilton, "The Black Gay Gang at Gallery Place," *Washington City Paper*, September 28, 2011. So-called lesbian gangs in the Washington D.C. area first got attention from Bill O'Reilly in 2007; the Southern Poverty Law Center subsequently posted a rebuke (see Susy Buchanan and David Holthouse, "The Oh-Really Factor: Fox 'Expert' Decries Bogus Lesbian Gangs," *Intelligence Report* 127 [Fall 2007] [http://www.splcenter.org/get-informed/intelligence-report/browse-all-issues/2007/fall/the-oh-really -factor#.UYrXuIJAt6o]). The Newark Seven (later known as the Jersey Four) are a group of black lesbians who received draconian sentences in New York for what they described as an act of self-defense. For an overview of the case, see Imani Henry, "Lesbians Sentenced for Self-Defense," *Workers World*, June 21, 2007, http://www.workers.org/2007 /us/nj4-0628/. Also see the forthcoming documentary *Out in the Night*, directed by Blair Doroshwalther. In Minneapolis, CeCe McDonald is a trans woman who was sentenced for manslaughter after defending herself from attack. Kenyon Farrow provides a helpful analysis of the politics of self-defense in "CeCe McDonald Deserves Our Support, 'Innocent' or Not," *Colorlines*, May 4, 2012, http://colorlines.com/archives/2012/05 /cece_mcdonald_and_the_high_cost_of_black_and_trans_self-defense.html.

7. D.C. was the site of one of the earliest Black Pride celebrations and, as cited earlier, was reported by Gallup in 2013 to be the U.S. city with the highest percentage of LGBT self-identified residents.

BIBLIOGRAPHY

Interviews by the Author

Randy Alfred; August 11, 2004, San Francisco, CA.
Meg Barnett (Maggie Jochild); September 8 and 15, 2004, via telephone.
Pamela David; July 9, 2008, San Francisco, CA.
Bran Fenner; June 2, 2006, New York, NY.
Ben Gardiner; August 16, 2004, San Francisco, CA.
Joan Gibbs; June 26, 2009, Brooklyn, NY.
Laura Hahn (pseudonym); 2004, via telephone.
Lois Helmbold; July 25, 2008, Oakland, CA.
Lenn Keller; March 18, 2011, San Pablo, CA.
Ruth Mahaney; July 16, 2008, San Francisco, CA.
Ali Marrero; July 28, 2008, Alameda, CA.
Del Martin and Phyllis Lyon; August 2004, San Francisco, CA.
Krystal Portalatin; July 21, 2009, New York, NY.
Michael Shernoff; September 13, 2004, New York, NY.
Hank Wilson; August 9, 2004, San Francisco, CA.

Archival Sources

Bancroft Library, University of California, Berkeley, CA
    Social Protest Collection

Gay, Lesbian, Bisexual, Transgender Historical Society, San Francisco, CA
    Randy Alfred Subject Files and Sound Recordings (1991-24)
    Meg Barnett Collection of Lesbians Against Police Violence Records (1989-05)
    Raymond Broshears Papers (1996-03)
    Community United Against Violence (CUAV) Records (1996-33)
    Ed Hansen Papers (1998-37)
    Donald S. Lucas Papers (1997-25)
    Phyllis Lyon and Del Martin Papers (1993-13)
    Newsletters Collection
    Oral History Collection
    Periodicals Collection

San Francisco/Bay Area Gay and Lesbian Serial Collection (Microfilm)
San Francisco LGBT Groups Ephemera Collection
San Francisco Street Patrol Records and Artifacts (1998-17)
Stonewall Records (1989–2009)
Tavern Guild of San Francisco Records (1995-02)
Video Collection
Violence against People Vertical File
San Francisco Women's Building Records (1996-15)

James C. Hormel Gay and Lesbian Center, San Francisco Public Library, San Francisco, CA
Daniel Curzon Papers (GLC 52)
Golden Gate Business Association Records (1990-06) (GLBTHS Collection)
People's Fund Records (1988-06) (GLBTHS Collection)

Division of Rare and Manuscript Collections, Kroch Library, Cornell University, Ithaca, NY (Human Sexuality Collection)
Empire State Pride Agenda Records (7630)
National Gay and Lesbian Task Force Records (7301)
Larry Bush Papers (7316)

National Archives of Lesbian, Gay, Bisexual, and Transgender History, Lesbian, Gay, Bisexual, and Transgender Community Center, New York, NY
Vertical File (Chelsea Gay Association Newsletters)
Emerald City Tapes (Television Program)

Lesbian Herstory Archives, Brooklyn, NY
Combahee River Collective Organization File
Committee for the Visibility of the Other Black Woman Organization File
Dykes Against Racism Everywhere Organization File
Salsa Soul Sisters, Third World Wimmin, Inc. Organization File
Barbara Smith Papers

Manuscripts and Archives Division, New York Public Library, New York, NY
International Gay Information Center Collection, Audio Visual Materials
Mattachine Society, Inc., of New York Records

ONE National Gay and Lesbian Archives, University of Southern California Libraries, Los Angeles, CA
ONE Subject Files Collection

Women of Color Resource Center, Oakland, CA
Alliance Against Women's Oppression Records
Third World Women's Alliance Records
(In 2012 these collections were donated to the Sophia Smith Collection at Smith College, Northampton, MA.)

Private and Institutional Collections

Meg Barnett (Maggie Jochild), Austin, TX
Christina Hanhardt, Washington, DC
Lois Helmbold, Las Vegas, NV
Lenn Keller, Oakland, CA
Community Board No. 2 Offices, New York, NY

Selected Newsletters, Newspapers, and Magazines

Advocate
Bay Area Reporter
Berkeley Barb
Black Lesbian Newsletter (later renamed
  ONYX: Black Lesbian Newsletter)
BWMT Newsletter (later renamed BWMT
  Quarterly)
Christopher Street
Cruise News and World Report
Crusader
DYKE
Gay
Gay City News

Gay Crusader
Gay Flames
New York Blade
New York Times
Plexus
San Francisco Sentinel
Street Patrol News
Street Patrol Newsletter
Town Talk
Vanguard
Vector
Villager

Moving Image Sources

The Exiles. Directed by Kent MacKenzie. Los Angeles: UCLA Film and Television Archive, 1961.

Fenced Out! Produced and Directed by FIERCE/New Neutral Zone. New York: Paper Tiger Television, 2001.

Flag Wars. Directed by Linda Goode Bryant and Laura Poitras. New York: Praxis Films, 2003.

The Negro and the American Promise. Produced by Henry Morgenthau III and Directed by Fred Barzyk. Boston: WGBH, 1963, http://www.pbs.org/wgbh/amex/mlk/sfeature /sf_video.html.

Screaming Queens: The Riot at Compton's Cafeteria. Directed by Susan Stryker and Victor Silverman. San Francisco: Independent Television Service, 2005.

Sex in an Epidemic. Directed by Jean Carlomusto. USA, 2010.

"Take This Hammer" (1964), archival news footage, San Francisco Bay Area Television Archive, https://diva.sfsu.edu/collections/sfbatv/bundles/187041.

Secondary Sources

Abraham, Julie. *Metropolitan Lovers: The Homosexuality of Cities.* Minneapolis: University of Minnesota Press, 2009.

Ahmed, Sara. "Declarations of Whiteness: The Non-Performativity of Anti-Racism." *Borderlands E-Journal* 3, no. 2 (2004), http://www.borderlands.net.au/vol3no2 _2004/ahmed_declarations.htm.

Althusser, Louis. *For Marx.* Translated by Ben Brewster. New York: Vintage, 1970.

Altschiller, David. *Hate Crimes.* 2nd ed. Santa Barbara, CA: ABC-CLIO, 2005.

Amadae, S. M. *Rationalizing Capitalist Democracy: The Cold War Origins of Rational Choice Liberalism.* Chicago: University of Chicago Press, 2003.

Aponte-Parés, Luis. "Outside/In: Crossing Queer and Latino Boundaries." In *Mambo Montage: The Latinization of New York*, edited by Augustín Laó-Montes and Arlene Davila, 363–86. New York: Columbia University Press, 2001.

Armstrong, Elizabeth A. *Forging Gay Identities: Organizing Sexuality in San Francisco, 1950–1994.* Chicago: University of Chicago Press, 2002.

Armstrong, Elizabeth A., and Susanna M. Crage. "Meaning and Memory: The Making of the Stonewall Myth." *American Sociological Review* 71, no. 5 (2006): 724–51.

Austin, J. L. *How to Do Things with Words.* Cambridge: Harvard University Press, 1962.

Bailey, Robert W. *Gay Politics, Urban Politics: Identity and Economics in the Urban Setting.* New York: Columbia University Press, 1999.

Baldwin, James. *Nobody Knows My Name.* New York: Dell, 1961.

Banes, Sally. *Greenwich Village 1963: Avant-Garde Performance and the Effervescent Body.* Durham: Duke University Press, 1993.

Bassichis, Morgan. "Reclaiming Queer & Trans Safety." In *The Revolution Starts at Home: Confronting Intimate Violence within Activist Communities,* edited by Ching-In Chen, Jai Dulani, and Leah Lakshmi Piepzna-Samarasinha, 3–24. Brooklyn, NY: South End, 2011.

Bauman, Robert. *Race and the War on Poverty: From Watts to East L.A.* Norman: University of Oklahoma Press, 2008.

Beck, Ulrich. *Risk Society: Toward a New Modernity.* London: Sage, 1992.

Beckett, Katherine. *Making Crime Pay: Law and Order in Contemporary American Politics.* New York: Oxford University Press, 1997.

Beemyn, Brett, ed. *Creating a Place for Ourselves: Lesbian, Gay, and Bisexual Community Histories.* New York: Routledge, 1997.

Bell, Jonathan. *California Crucible: The Forging of Modern American Liberalism.* Philadelphia: University of Pennsylvania Press, 2012.

———. "'To Strive for Economic and Social Justice': Welfare, Sexuality, and Liberal Politics in San Francisco in the 1960s." *Journal of Policy History* 22, no. 2 (2010): 192–225.

Bennett, Sara, and Joan Gibbs, "Racism and Classism in the Lesbian Community: Towards the Building of a Radical Autonomous Lesbian Movement." In *Top Ranking: A Collection of Articles on Racism and Classism in the Lesbian Community,* edited by Joan Gibbs and Sara Bennett, 1–30. New York: Come!Unity, 1980.

Berkowitz, Richard, and Michael Callen, *How to Have Sex in an Epidemic: One Approach.* New York: News from the Front Publications, 1983.

Berlant, Lauren, with Elizabeth Freeman. "Queer Nationality." In Lauren Berlant, *The Queen of America Goes to Washington City: Essays on Sex and Citizenship,* 145–74. Durham: Duke University Press, 1997.

Berlant, Lauren, and Michael Warner. "Sex in Public." *Critical Inquiry* 24, no. 2 (1998): 547–66.

Berman, Marshall. *All That Is Solid Melts into Air: The Experience of Modernity.* New York: Penguin, 1988.

Bérubé, Allan. *Coming Out under Fire: The History of Gay Men and Women in World War Two.* New York: Free Press, 1990.

Bevacqua, Maria. *Rape on the Public Agenda: Feminism and the Politics of Sexual Assault.* Boston: Northeastern University Press, 2000.

Black, Algernon D. *The People and the Police.* New York: McGraw-Hill, 1968.

Blasius, Mark, and Shane Phelan, eds. *We Are Everywhere: A Historical Sourcebook of Gay and Lesbian Politics.* New York: Routledge, 1997.

Boesel, David, and Peter H. Rossi, eds. *Cities under Siege: An Anatomy of the Ghetto Riots, 1964–1968.* New York: Basic Books, 1971.

Boyd, Nan Alamilla. *Wide Open Town: A History of Queer San Francisco to 1965.* Berkeley: University of California Press, 2005.

Bravmann, Scott. *Queer Fictions of the Past: History, Culture, and Difference.* Cambridge: Cambridge University Press, 1997.

Breines, Winifred. *The Trouble between Us: An Uneasy History of White and Black Women in the Feminist Movement.* New York: Oxford University Press, 2006.

Brenner, Neil, and Nik Theodore, eds. *Spaces of Neoliberalism: Urban Restructuring in North America and Western Europe*. Malden, MA: Blackwell, 2003.

Bressi, Todd W., ed. *Planning and Zoning New York City: Yesterday, Today and Tomorrow*. New Brunswick, NJ: Center for Urban Policy Research, Rutgers University, 1993.

Brown, Wendy. "Neo-liberalism and the End of Liberal Democracy." *Theory and Event* 7, no. 1 (2003); http://muse.jhu.edu/login?auth=0&type=summary&url=/journals/theory_and_event/v007/7.1brown.html.

———. *Politics out of History*. Princeton: Princeton University Press, 2001.

———. *States of Injury: Power and Freedom in Late Modernity*. Princeton: Princeton University Press, 1995.

Brown-Saracino, Japonica. *A Neighborhood that Never Changes: Gentrification, Social Preservation, and the Search for Authenticity*. Chicago: University of Chicago Press, 2010.

Brownmiller, Susan. *In Our Times: Memoir of a Revolution*. New York: Dial, 1999.

Bumiller, Kristin. *In an Abusive State: How Neoliberalism Appropriated the Feminist Movement against Sexual Violence*. Durham: Duke University Press, 2008.

Burawoy, Michael, et al. *Ethnography Unbound: Power and Resistance in the Modern Metropolis*. Berkeley: University of California Press, 1991.

Butler, Judith. *Excitable Speech: A Politics of the Performative*. New York: Routledge, 1997.

———. *Undoing Gender*. New York: Routledge, 2004.

Canaday, Margot. *The Straight State: Sexuality and Citizenship in Twentieth Century America*. Princeton: Princeton University Press, 2009.

Capsuto, Steven. *Alternate Channels: The Uncensored Story of Gay and Lesbian Images on Radio and Television*. New York: Ballantine, 2000.

Carby, Hazel V. "Policing the Black Woman's Body in an Urban Context." *Critical Inquiry* 18, no. 4 (1992): 738–55.

Carter, David. *Stonewall: The Riots that Sparked the Gay Revolution*. New York: St. Martin's, 2004.

Castells, Manuel. "City and Culture: The San Francisco Experience." In Manuel Castells, *The City and the Grassroots: A Cross-Cultural Theory of Urban Social Movements*, 97–172. Berkeley: University of California Press, 1983.

Cazenave, Noel A. *Impossible Democracy: The Unlikely Success of the War on Poverty Community Action Programs*. Albany: State University of New York Press, 2007.

Center for Research on Criminal Justice. *The Iron Fist and the Velvet Glove: An Analysis of the U.S. Police*. Expanded and rev. ed. Berkeley, CA: Center for Research on Criminal Justice, 1977.

Chasin, Alexandra. *Selling Out: The Gay and Lesbian Movement Goes to Market*. New York: St. Martin's, 2000.

Chauncey, George. *Gay New York: Gender, Urban Culture, and the Making of the Gay Male World, 1890–1940*. New York: Basic Books, 1994.

Chicago Gay Liberation. "Working Paper for the Revolutionary People's Constitutional Convention." In *Out of the Closets: Voices of Gay Liberation*, 20th anniversary edition (2nd ed.), 346–52. New York: New York University Press, 1992.

Chisholm, Diane. *Queer Constellations: Subcultural Space in the Wake of the City*. Minneapolis: University of Minnesota Press, 2005.

Chuh, Kandice. *Imagine Otherwise: On Asian Americanist Critique*. Durham: Duke University Press, 2003.

Churchill, Ward, and Jim Vander Wall. *The COINTELPRO Papers: Documents from the

FBI's Secret Wars against Dissent in the United States. Cambridge, MA: South End, 2001.

Citrin, Jack, and Isaac Martin, eds. *After the Tax Revolt: California's Proposition 13 Turns 30*. Berkeley, CA: Berkeley Public Policy Press, 2009.

Clark, Kenneth B. *Dark Ghetto: Dilemmas of Social Power*. New York: Harper, 1965.

Cloward, Richard A., and Lloyd E. Ohlin. *Delinquency and Opportunity: A Theory of Delinquent Gangs*. New York: Free Press, 1960.

Cohen, Cathy. "Deviance as Resistance: A New Research Agenda for the Study of Black Politics." *Du Bois Review* 1, no. 1 (2004): 27–45.

———. "Punks, Bulldaggers, and Welfare Queens: The Radical Potential of Queer Politics?" *GLQ* 3, no. 4 (1997): 437–65.

Cohen, Stephan L. *The Gay Liberation Youth Movement in New York: "An Army of Lovers Cannot Fail."* New York: Routledge, 2008.

Connell, Kathleen, and Paul Gabriel, "The Power of Broken Hearts: The Origin and Evolution of the Folsom Street Fair." http://folsomstreetfair.org/history/.

Conrad, Ryan, ed. *Against Equality: Queer Critiques of Gay Marriage*. With an introduction by Yasmin Nair. Lewiston, ME: Against Equality Publishing Collective, 2010.

Credle, James. "November 28, 1983: Police Brutality: The Continual Erosion of Our Most Basic Rights." In *Speaking for Our Lives: Historical Speeches and Rhetoric for Gay and Lesbian Rights (1892–2000)*, edited by Robert B. Ridinger, 423–27. Binghamton, NY: Haworth Press, 2004.

Crenshaw, Kimberlé Williams. "Mapping the Margins: Intersectionality, Identity Politics, and Violence against Women of Color." In *Critical Race Theory: The Key Writings That Formed the Movement*, edited by Kimberlé Crenshaw, Neil Gotanda, Gary Peller, and Kendall Thomas, 357–83. New York: New Press, 1996.

Crenshaw, Kimberlé, Neil Gotanda, Gary Peller, and Kendall Thomas, eds. *Critical Race Theory: The Key Writings That Formed the Movement*. New York: New Press, 1996.

Crimp, Douglas. *Melancholia and Moralism: Essays on AIDS and Queer Politics*. Cambridge: MIT Press, 2002.

Cronin, Thomas E., Tania Z. Cronin, and Michael E. Milakovich. *U.S. v. Crime in the Streets*. Bloomington: Indiana University Press, 1981.

Crowe, Daniel. *Prophets of Rage: The Black Freedom Struggle in San Francisco, 1945–1969*. New York: Garland, 2000.

Cvetkovich, Ann. *An Archive of Feelings: Trauma, Sexuality, and Lesbian Public Cultures*. Durham: Duke University Press, 2003.

Dangerous Bedfellows Collective. *Policing Public Sex: Queer Politics and the Future of AIDS Activism*. Boston: South End, 1996.

Da Silva, Denise Ferreira. *Toward a Global Idea of Race*. Minneapolis: University of Minnesota Press, 2007.

Dávila, Arlene. *Barrio Dreams: Puerto Ricans, Latinos, and the Neoliberal City*. Berkeley: University of California Press, 2004.

Dean, Tim. *Unlimited Intimacy: Reflections on the Subculture of Barebacking*. Chicago: University of Chicago Press, 2009.

Decena, Carlos Ulises. *Tacit Subjects: Belonging and Same-Sex Desire among Dominican Immigrant Men*. Durham: Duke University Press, 2011.

Delany, Samuel R. *Times Square Red, Times Square Blue*. New York: New York University Press, 1999.

Deleuze, Gilles, and Félix Guattari. *A Thousand Plateaus*. Translated by Brian Massumi. London: Continuum, 2004.

D'Emilio, John. Foreword to *Out of the Closets: Voices of Gay Liberation*, edited by Karla Jay and Allen Young. 20th anniversary edition (2nd ed.), xi–xxix. New York: New York University Press, 1992.

———. "After Stonewall." In John D'Emilio, *Making Trouble: Essays on Gay History, Politics, and the University*, 234–75. New York: Routledge, 1992.

———. "Capitalism and Gay Identity." In *Powers of Desire: The Politics of Sexuality*, edited by Ann Snitow, Christine Stansell, and Sharon Thompson, 100–113. New York: Monthly Review Press, 1983.

———. "Organizational Tales: Interpreting the NGLTF Story." In *Creating Change: Sexuality, Public Policy, and Civil Rights*, edited by John D'Emilio, William B. Turner, and Urvashi Vaid, 469–86. New York: St. Martin's, 2000.

———. *Sexual Politics, Sexual Communities: The Making of a Homosexual Minority in the United States, 1940–1970*. Chicago: University of Chicago Press, 1983.

———. "Stonewall: Myth and Meaning." In John D'Emilio, *The World Turned: Essays on Gay History, Politics, and Culture*, 146–53. Durham: Duke University Press, 2002.

Different Avenues. *Move Along Report: Policing Sex Work in Washington D.C.* Washington, DC: Different Avenues, 2008.

Donovan, Amy. "Telling Me Different: An Ethnography of Homeless Youth in San Francisco." PhD diss., New School for Social Research, 2002.

Dubber, Markus Dirk. *Victims in the War on Crime: The Use and Abuse of Victims' Rights.* New York: New York University Press, 2002.

Duberman, Martin. *Stonewall*. New York: Plume, 1993.

Du Bois, W. E. B. 1899. *The Philadelphia Negro*. Philadelphia: University of Pennsylvania Press, 1995.

Duggan, Lisa. "Making It Perfectly Queer." In Lisa Duggan and Nan D. Hunter, *Sex Wars: Sexual Dissent and Political Culture*, 155–72. New York: Routledge, 1995.

———. *Sapphic Slashers: Sex, Violence, and American Modernity*. Durham: Duke University Press, 2000.

———. *The Twilight of Equality? Neoliberalism, Cultural Politics, and the Attack on Democracy*. Boston: Beacon, 2004.

Eisenstein, Zillah, ed. *Capitalist Patriarchy and the Case for Socialist Feminism*. New York: Monthly Review, 1978.

Elbaum, Max. *Revolution in the Air: Sixties Radicals Turn to Lenin, Mao and Che*. New York: Verso, 2006.

El-Tayeb, Fatima. *European Others: Queering Ethnicity in Postnational Europe*. Minneapolis: University of Minnesota Press, 2011.

Eng, David L. *The Feeling of Kinship: Queer Liberalism and the Racialization of Intimacy*. Durham: Duke University Press, 2010.

Enke, Anne. *Finding the Movement: Sexuality, Contested Space, and Feminist Activism*. Durham: Duke University Press, 2007.

Erzen, Tanya. "Turnstile Jumpers and Broken Windows: Policing Disorder in New York City." In *Zero Tolerance: Quality of Life and the New Police Brutality in New York City*, edited by Andrea McArdle and Tanya Erzen, 19–49. New York: New York University Press, 2001.

Eskridge, William. *Gay Law: Challenging the Apartheid of the Closet*. Cambridge: Harvard University Press, 1999.

Faderman, Lillian, and Stuart Timmons. *Gay L.A.: A History of Sexual Outlaws, Power Politics, and Lipstick Lesbians*. New York: Basic Books, 2006.

Fanon, Frantz. 1965. *The Wretched of the Earth*. Translated by Constance Farrington. New York: Grove, 2005.

Farrow, Kenyon. "Is Gay Marriage Anti-Black?" 2004. http://kenyonfarrow.com/2005/06/14/is-gay-marriage-anti-black/.

Feldblum, Chai R. "The Federal Gay Rights Bill: From Bella to ENDA." In *Creating Change: Sexuality, Public Policy, and Civil Rights*, edited by John D'Emilio, William B. Turner, and Urvashi Vaid, 149–87. New York: St. Martin's, 2000.

Ferguson, Roderick A. *Aberrations in Black: Toward a Queer of Color Critique*. Minneapolis: University of Minnesota Press, 2004.

Fetner, Tina. *How the Religious Right Shaped Lesbian and Gay Activism*. Minneapolis: University of Minnesota Press, 2008.

Fitch, Robert. *The Assassination of New York*. London: Verso, 1993.

Flamm, Michael. *Law and Order: Street Crime, Civil Unrest, and the Crisis of Liberalism in the 1960s*. New York: Columbia University Press, 2005.

Fleischer, Doris Zames, and Frieda Zames. *The Disability Rights Movement: From Charity to Confrontation*. Philadelphia: Temple University Press, 2001.

Flint, Colin, ed. *Spaces of Hate: Geographies of Discrimination and Intolerance in the U.S.A.* New York: Routledge, 2004.

Florida, Richard. *The Rise of the Creative Class, and How It's Transforming Work, Leisure, Community, and Everyday Life*. New York: Basic Books, 2002.

Foucault, Michel. *History of Sexuality*. Vol. 1. Translated by Robert Hurley. New York: Pantheon, 1978.

Franklin, Karen. "Good Intentions: The Enforcement of Hate Crime Penalty Enhancement Statutes," *American Behavioral Scientist* 46 (2002): 154–72.

Fraser, Nancy. "Heterosexism, Misrecognition, and Capitalism: A Response to Judith Butler." *Social Text* 53–54 (Winter–Spring 1998): 279–89.

———. "Social Justice in the Age of Identity Politics: Redistribution, Recognition, and Participation." In Nancy Fraser and Axel Honneth, *Redistribution or Recognition? A Political-Philosophical Exchange* (London: Verso, 2003), 7–109.

Frazier, E. Franklin. *The Negro Family in the United States*. Chicago: University of Chicago Press, 1939.

Freeman, Elizabeth. *Time Binds: Queer Temporalities, Queer Histories*. Durham: Duke University Press, 2010.

Freeman, Joshua. *Working-Class New York: Life and Labor since World War II*. New York: New Press, 2000.

Friedland, Roger. *Power and Crisis in the City*. London: Schocken, 1983.

Fugikawa, Laura Sachiko. "Domestic Containment: Japanese Americans, Native Americans, and the Cultural Politics of Relocation." PhD diss., University of Southern California, 2011.

Gallo, Marcia. *Different Daughters: A History of the Daughters of Bilitis and the Rise of the Lesbian Rights Movement*. Emeryville, CA: Seal, 2006.

Garland, David. *The Culture of Control: Crime and Social Order in Contemporary Society*. Chicago: University of Chicago Press, 2001.

Garrison, Jim. *On the Trail of the Assassins: My Investigation and Prosecution of the Murder of President Kennedy*. New York: Sheridan Square Press, 1988.

Gates, Gary J., and Jason Ost. *The Gay and Lesbian Atlas*. Washington, DC: Urban Institute Press, 2004.

Geertz, Clifford. "Thick Description: Toward an Interpretive Theory of Culture." In

Clifford Geertz, *The Interpretation of Cultures: Selected Essays*, 3–32. New York: Basic Books, 1973.

Ghaziani, Amin. *The Dividends of Dissent: How Conflict and Culture Work in Lesbian and Gay Marches on Washington*. Chicago: University of Chicago Press, 2008.

———. "There Goes the Gayborhood?" *Contexts* 9, no. 3 (2010): 64–66.

Gibson-Graham, J. K. *The End of Capitalism (As We Knew It): A Feminist Critique of Political Economy*. Minneapolis: University of Minnesota Press, 1996.

Giddens, Anthony. "Risk and Responsibility." *Modern Law Review* 62, no. 1 (1999): 1–10.

Gilfoyle, Timothy J. *City of Eros: New York City, Prostitution, and the Commercialization of Sex, 1790–1920*. New York: W. W. Norton, 1992.

Gilmore, Ruth Wilson. "Globalization and U.S. Prison Growth: From Military Keynesianism to Post-Keynesian Militarism." *Race and Class* 40, nos. 2–3 (1998–99): 177–88.

———. *Golden Gulag: Prisons, Surplus, Crisis, and Opposition in Globalizing California*. Berkeley: University of California Press, 2007.

Giroux, Henry A. "Racial Injustice and Disposable Youth in the Age of Zero Tolerance." *Qualitative Studies in Education* 16, no. 4 (2003): 553–65.

Goldstein, Alyosha. *Poverty in Common: The Politics of Community Action during the American Century*. Durham: Duke University Press, 2012.

Gómez-Barris, Macarena. "Mapuche Hunger Acts: Epistemology of the Decolonial." *Transmodernity* 1, no. 3 (2012). http://www.escholarship.org/uc/item/6305p8vr.

Goodwin, Jeff, and James M. Jasper, eds. *The Social Movements Reader: Cases and Concepts*. 2nd ed. Malden, MA: Blackwell, 2009.

Gore, Dayo F., Tamara Jones, Joo-Hyun Kang. "Organizing at the Intersections: A Roundtable Discussion of Police Brutality through the Lens of Race, Class, and Sexual Identities." In *Zero Tolerance: Quality of Life and the New Police Brutality in New York City*, edited by Andrea McArdle and Tanya Erzen, 251–69. New York: New York University Press, 2001.

Gould, Deborah B. *Moving Politics: Emotion and ACT UP's Fight against AIDS*. Chicago: University of Chicago Press, 2009.

Grattet, Ryken, and Valerie Jenness. "The Birth and Maturation of Hate Crime Policy in the United States." In *Hate and Bias Crime: A Reader*, edited by Barbara Perry, 389–408. New York: Routledge, 2003.

Gray, Mary. *Out in the Country: Youth, Media, and Queer Visibility in Rural America*. New York: New York University Press, 2009.

Green, Donald P., Laurence H. McFalls, and Jennifer K. Smith. "Hate Crime: An Emergent Research Agenda." In *Hate and Bias Crime: A Reader*, edited by Barbara Perry, 27–48. New York: Routledge, 2003.

Hackworth, Jason. *The Neoliberal City: Governance, Ideology, and Development in American Urbanism*. Ithaca: Cornell University Press, 2006.

Halberstam, Judith. *In a Queer Time and Place: Transgender Bodies, Subcultural Lives*. New York: New York University Press, 2005.

———. *Queer Art of Failure*. Durham: Duke University Press, 2011.

Hall, Jacquelyn Dowd. "The Long Civil Rights Movement and the Political Uses of the Past." *Journal of American History* 91, no. 4 (2005): 1233–63.

Hall, Stuart, et al. *Policing the Crisis: Mugging, the State, and Law and Order*. London: Palgrave Macmillan, 1978.

Halley, Janet E. "'Like Race' Arguments." In *What's Left of Theory: New Work on the*

Politics of Literary Theory, edited by Judith Butler, John Guillory, and Kendall Thomas, 40–74. New York: Routledge, 2000.

Halley, Janet E., and Wendy Brown, eds. *Left Legalism/Left Critique*. Durham: Duke University Press, 2002.

Haritaworn, Jin. "Colorful Bodies in the Multikulti Metropolis: Vitality, Victimology and Transgressive Citizenship in Berlin." In *Transgender Migrations: The Bodies, Borders, and Politics of Transition*, edited by Trystan Cotton, 11–31. New York: Routledge, 2012.

———. "Queer Injuries: The Racial Politics of 'Homophobic Hate Crime' in Germany." *Social Justice* 37, no. 1 (2010–11): 69–87.

Haritaworn, Jin, with Tamsila Tauqir and Esra Erdem. "Gay Imperialism: Gender and Sexuality Discourse in the 'War on Terror.'" In *Out of Place*, edited by Adi Kuntsman and Esperanza Miyake, 71–95. York, UK: Raw Nerve Books, 2008.

Harper, Phillip Brian. *Private Affairs: Critical Ventures in the Culture of Social Relations*. New York: New York University Press, 1999.

———. "'The Subversive Edge': *Paris Is Burning*, Social Critique, and the Limits of Subjective Agency." *Diacritics* 24, nos. 2–3 (1994): 90–103.

Harris, Cheryl. "Whiteness as Property." In *Critical Race Theory: The Key Writings that Formed the Movement*, edited by Kimberlé Crenshaw, Neil Gotanda, Gary Peller, and Kendall Thomas, 276–91. New York: New Press, 1995.

Harris, Dutchess, and Adam Waterman. "Babylon Is Burning, or Race, Gender, and Sexuality at the Revolutionary People's Constitutional Convention." *Journal of Intergroup Relations* 27, no. 2 (2000): 17–33.

Hartman, Chester, with Sarah Carnochan. *City for Sale: The Transformation of San Francisco*. Revised and updated edition. Berkeley: University of California Press, 2002.

Hartman, Chester. *Yerba Buena: Land Grab and Community Resistance in San Francisco*. San Francisco: Glide, 1974.

Harvey, David. *A Brief History of Neoliberalism*. New York: Oxford University Press, 2007.

———. "Globalization and the 'Spatial Fix.'" *Geographische Review* 2 (2001): 23–30.

———. *The New Imperialism*. New York: Oxford University Press, 2005.

———. *Spaces of Capital: Towards a Critical Geography*. New York: Routledge, 2001.

Hayden, Dolores. *Building Suburbia: Green Fields and Urban Growth, 1820–2000*. New York: Vintage, 2004.

Heap, Chad. *Slumming: Sexual and Racial Encounters in American Nightlife, 1885–1940*. Chicago: University of Chicago Press, 2009.

Heins, Marjorie. *Strictly Ghetto Property: The Story of Los Siete de la Raza*. Berkeley, CA: Ramparts Press, 1972.

Herek, Gregory M. "Beyond 'Homophobia': A Social Psychological Perspective on Attitudes Towards Lesbians and Gay Men." In *Bashers, Baiters and Bigots: Homophobia in American Society*, edited by Jay DeCecco, 1–22. New York: Harrington Park, 1985.

———. "The Community Response to Violence in San Francisco: An Interview with Wenny Kusuma, Lester Olmstead-Rose, and Jill Tregor." In *Hate Crimes: Confronting Violence against Lesbians and Gay Men*, edited by Gregory M. Herek and Kevin T. Berrill, 241–57. Newbury Park, CA: Sage, 1992.

Herek, Gregory M., and Kevin T. Berrill, eds. *Hate Crimes: Confronting Violence against Lesbians and Gay Men*. Newbury Park, CA: Sage, 1992.

Herring, Scott. *Another Country: Queer Anti-Urbanism*. New York: New York University Press, 2010.

Hilderbrand, Lucas. *Paris Is Burning: A Queer Film Classic*. Vancouver: Arsenal Pulp, forthcoming.

Hillman, Betty Luther. "'The Most Profoundly Revolutionary Act a Homosexual Can Engage In': Drag and the Politics of Gender Presentation in the San Francisco Liberation Movement, 1964–1972." *Journal of the History of Sexuality* 20, no. 1 (January 2011): 153–81.

Hobson, Emily. "Imagining Alliance: Queer Anti-Imperialism and Race in California, 1966–1990." PhD diss., University of Southern California, 2009.

———. *Lavender and Red: Race, Empire, and Solidarity in the Gay and Lesbian Left*. Berkeley: University of California Press, forthcoming.

———. "Policing Gay L.A.: Mapping Racial Divides in the Homophile Era, 1950–1967." In *The Rising Tide of Color: Race, Radicalism, and Repression on the Pacific Coast and Beyond*, edited by Moon-Ho Jung. Seattle: University of Washington Press, forthcoming.

Hoffman, Amy. *An Army of Ex-Lovers: My Life at the Gay Community News*. Amherst: University of Massachusetts Press, 2007.

Hollinger, David. "After Cloven Tongues of Fire: Ecumenical Protestantism and the Modern American Encounter with Diversity." *Journal of American History* 98, no. 1 (2011): 21–48.

Holmes, Kwame. "Chocolate to Rainbow City: The Dialectics of Black and Gay Community Formation in Postwar Washington, D.C., 1946–1978." PhD diss., University of Illinois at Urbana-Champaign, 2011.

Hom, Alice Y. "Unifying Differences: Lesbian of Color Community Building in Los Angeles and New York, 1970s–1980s." PhD diss., University of California, Los Angeles, 2011.

Hong, Grace Kyungwon. *The Ruptures of American Capital: Women of Color Feminism and the Culture of Immigrant Labor*. Minneapolis: University of Minnesota Press, 2006.

Hong, Grace Kyungwon, and Roderick A. Ferguson. "Introduction." In *Strange Affinities: The Gender and Sexual Politics of Comparative Racialization,* edited by Grace Kyungwon Hong and Roderick A. Ferguson, 1–22. Durham: Duke University Press, 2011.

hooks, bell. "Is Paris Burning?" In bell hooks, *Black Looks: Race and Representation*, 145–56. Boston: South End, 1992.

HoSang, Daniel Martinez. "Beyond Policy: Ideology, Race and the Reimagining of Youth." In *Beyond Resistance! Youth Activism and Community Change*, edited by Shawn Ginwright, Pedro Noguera, and Julio Cammarota, 3–20. New York: Routledge, 2006.

———. *Racial Propositions: Ballot Initiatives and the Making of Postwar California*. Berkeley: University of California Press, 2010.

Howard, John. *Men Like That: A Southern Queer History*. Chicago: University of Chicago Press, 1999.

Isoke, Zenzele. *Urban Black Women and the Politics of Resistance*. New York: Palgrave Macmillan, 2012.

Jacobs, James B., and Kimberly Potter. *Hate Crimes: Criminal Law and Identity Politics*. New York: Oxford University Press, 1998.

Jacobs, Jane. [1961] *The Death and Life of Great American Cities*. New York: Vintage, 1992.

Jakobsen, Janet R. "Queers Are Like Jews, Aren't They? Analogy and Alliance Politics." In *Queer Theory and the Jewish Question*, edited by Daniel Boyarin, Daniel Itzkovitz, and Ann Pellegrini, 64–89. New York: Columbia University Press, 2003.

Jay, Karla. *Tales of the Lavender Menace: A Memoir of Liberation*. New York: Basic Books, 1999.

Jay, Karla, and Allen Young, eds. *Out of the Closets: Voices of Gay Liberation*. 20th anniversary edition (2nd ed.). New York: New York University Press, 1992.

Jenness, Valerie, and Kendal Broad. *Hate Crimes: New Social Movements and the Politics of Violence*. New York: Aldine de Gruyter, 1997.

Jenness, Valerie, and Ryken Grattet. *Making Hate a Crime: From Social Movement to Law Enforcement*. New York: Russell Sage Foundation, 2001.

Joseph, Miranda. *Against the Romance of Community*. Minneapolis: University of Minnesota Press, 2002.

Kelley, Robin D. G. *Freedom Dreams: The Black Radical Imagination*. Boston: Beacon, 2002.

Kelley, Robin D. G., and Betsy Esch. "Black Like Mao: Red China and Black Revolution." *Souls* 1, no. 4 (Fall 1999): 6–41.

Kelling, George L. "'Broken Windows' and the Culture War: A Response to Selected Critiques." In *Crime, Disorder and Community Safety*, edited by Roger Matthews and John Pitts, 120–44. London: Routledge, 2001.

Kelling, George L., and James Q. Wilson. "Broken Windows: The Police and Neighborhood Safety." *Atlantic*, March 1, 1982, 29–38.

Kennedy, Elizabeth Lapovsky, and Madeline Davis. *Boots of Leather, Slippers of Gold: The History of a Lesbian Community*. New York: Penguin, 1994.

Kissack, Terence. "Freaking Fag Revolutionaries: New York's Gay Liberation Front, 1969–1971." *Radical History Review* 62 (Spring 1995): 104–35.

Knopp, Lawrence. "Gentrification and Gay Neighborhood Formation in New Orleans: A Case Study." In *Homo Economics: Capitalism, Community, and Lesbian and Gay Life*, edited by Amy Gluckman and Betsy Reed, 45–63. New York: Routledge, 1997.

———. "Some Theoretical Implications of Gay Involvement in an Urban Land Market." *Political Geography Quarterly* 9, no. 4 (1990): 337–52.

Knopp, Lawrence, and Mickey Lauria. "Toward an Analysis of the Role of Gay Communities in the Urban Renaissance." *Urban Geography* 6, no. 2 (1985): 152–69.

Kornbluh, Felicia. *The Battle for Welfare Rights: Politics and Poverty in Modern America*. Philadelphia: University of Pennsylvania Press, 2007.

Kramer, Ralph M. *Participation of the Poor: Comparative Community Case Studies in the War on Poverty*. Englewood Cliffs, NJ: Prentice Hall, 1969.

Kunzel, Regina. *Criminal Intimacy: Prison and the Uneven History of Modern American Sexuality*. Chicago: University of Chicago Press, 2008.

Levine, Martin P. *Gay Macho: The Life and Death of the Homosexual Clone*. Edited by Michael S. Kimmel. New York: New York University Press, 1998.

Lewis [Abram J.] "Gays Are Revolting! Multi-Issue Organizing in the Gay Liberation Front, 1969–1972." BA thesis, Columbia University, 2006.

Lewis, Oscar. *Five Families: Mexican Case Studies in the Culture of Poverty*. New York: Basic Books, 1959.

Ley, David. *The New Middle Class and the Remaking of the Central City*. New York: Oxford University Press, 1997.

Lipsitz, George. *A Life in the Struggle: Ivory Perry and the Culture of Opposition*. Philadelphia: Temple University Press, 1995.

———. *The Possessive Investment in Whiteness: How White People Profit from Identity Politics*. Philadelphia: Temple University Press, 1998.

Lloyd, Richard. *Neo-Bohemia: Art and Commerce in the Postindustrial City*. New York: Routledge, 2005.

Logan, John R., and Harvey L. Molotch. *Urban Fortunes: The Political Economy of Place*. Berkeley: University of California Press, 1987.

Love, Heather. *Feeling Backward: Loss and the Politics of Queer History*. Cambridge: Harvard University Press, 2007.

Lowe, Lisa. *Immigrant Acts: On Asian American Cultural Politics*. Durham: Duke University Press, 1996.

Luciano, Dana. *Arranging Grief: Sacred Time and the Body in Nineteenth Century America*. New York: New York University Press, 2007.

Lukács, Georg. *History and Class Consciousness: Studies in Marxist Dialectics*. Translated by Rodney Livingstone. Cambridge: MIT Press, 1971.

Maher, Justin. "The Capital of Diversity: Difference, Development, and Place-Making in Washington DC." PhD diss., University of Maryland, College Park, 2011.

Mahmood, Saba. *Politics of Piety: The Islamic Revival and the Feminist Subject*. Princeton: Princeton University Press, 2005.

Manalansan, Martin F. *Global Divas: Filipino Gay Men in the Diaspora*. Durham: Duke University Press, 2003.

———. "Homophobia at New York's Gay Central." In *Homophobia: Lust and Loathing across Time and Space*, edited by David A. B. Murray, 34–47. Durham: Duke University Press, 2009.

———. "Race, Violence, and Neoliberal Spatial Politics in the Global City." *Social Text* 23, nos. 3–4 (2005): 141–55.

Manning, June Thomas. "Model Cities Revisited: Issues of Race and Empowerment." In *Urban Planning and the African-American Community: In the Shadows*, edited by June Thomas Manning and Martha Ritzdorf, 143–63. Thousand Oaks, CA: Sage, 1997.

Marotta, Toby. *The Politics of Homosexuality*. Boston: Houghton Mifflin, 1981.

Martin, Del, and Phyllis Lyon. *Lesbian/Woman*. San Francisco: Glide, 1972.

Martin, Isaac William. *The Permanent Tax Revolt: How the Property Tax Transformed American Politics*. Stanford: Stanford University Press, 2008.

Martin, Randy. *The Financialization of Everyday Life*. Philadelphia: Temple University Press, 2002.

Mason, Gail. *The Spectacle of Violence: Homophobia, Gender, and Knowledge*. London: Routledge, 2002.

Massad, Joseph. *Desiring Arabs*. Chicago: University of Chicago Press, 2007.

———. "Re-Orienting Desire: The Gay International and the Arab World." *Public Culture* 14, no. 2 (2002): 361–85.

Matsuda, Mari. *Where Is Your Body? And Other Essays on Race, Gender, and the Law*. Boston: Beacon, 1996.

Matthews, Nancy A. *Confronting Rape: The Feminist Anti-Rape Movement and the State*. New York: Routledge, 1994.

McRuer, Robert. *Crip Theory: Cultural Signs of Queerness and Disability*. New York: New York University Press, 2006.

Meeker, Martin D., Jr. "Behind the Mask of Respectability: Reconsidering the Mattachine Society and Male Homophile Practice, 1950s and 1960s." *Journal of the History of Sexuality* 10, no. 1 (2001): 78–116.

———. *Contacts Desired: Gay and Lesbian Communications and Community, 1940s–1970s*. Chicago: University of Chicago Press, 2006.

———. "The Queerly Disadvantaged and the Making of San Francisco's War on Poverty, 1964–1967." *Pacific Historical Review* 81, no. 1 (2012): 21–59.

Melamed, Jodi. *Represent and Destroy: Rationalizing Violence in the New Racial Capitalism*. Minneapolis: University of Minnesota Press, 2011.

Members of the Gay and Lesbian Historical Society of Northern California. "MTF Transgender Activism in the Tenderloin and Beyond, 1966–1975." GLQ 4, no. 2 (1998): 349–72.

Menon, Madhavi. "Spurning Teleology in *Venus and Adonis*." GLQ 11, no. 4 (2005): 491–519.

Metzl, Jonathan. *The Protest Psychosis: How Schizophrenia Became a Black Disease*. Boston: Beacon, 2010.

Meyerowitz, Joanne. "'How Common Culture Shapes the Separate Lives': Sexuality, Race, and Mid-Twentieth Century Social Constructionist Thought." *Journal of American History* 96, no. 4 (2010): 1057–84.

———. *How Sex Changed: A History of Transsexuality in the United States*. Cambridge: Harvard University Press, 2004.

Miceli, Melinda. *Standing Out, Standing Together: The Social and Political Impact of Gay-Straight Alliances*. New York: Routledge, 2005.

Mogul, Joey, Andrea Ritchie, and Kay Whitlock. *Queer (In)Justice: The Criminalization of LGBT People in the United States*. Boston: Beacon, 2011.

Mollenkopf, John. *The Contested City*. Princeton: Princeton University Press, 1983.

———. "Neighborhood Mobilization and Urban Development: Boston and San Francisco, 1968–1978." *International Journal of Urban and Regional Research* 5, no. 1 (1981): 15–39.

Moraga, Cherríe, and Gloria Anzaldúa, eds. *This Bridge Called My Back: Writings by Radical Women of Color*. Latham, NY: Kitchen Table, 1983.

Moran, Leslie, and Beverly Skeggs, with Paul Tyrer and Karen Corteen. *Sexuality and the Politics of Violence*. London: Routledge, 2004.

Morgensen, Scott. "Arrival at Home: Radical Faerie Configurations of Sexuality and Place." GLQ 15, no. 1 (2008): 67–96.

———. *The Spaces between Us: Queer Settler Colonialism and Indigenous Decolonization*. Minneapolis: University of Minnesota Press, 2011.

Moten, Fred. *In the Break: The Aesthetics of the Black Radical Tradition*. Minneapolis: University of Minnesota Press, 2003.

Mountz, Sarah. "Revolving Doors: LGBTQ Youth at the Interface of the Child Welfare and Juvenile Justice Systems." *LGBTQ Policy Journal*, 2011, http://isites.harvard.edu/icb/icb.do?keyword=k78405&pageid=icb.page414421.

Moynihan, Daniel P. *Maximum Feasible Misunderstanding: Community Action in the War on Poverty*. New York: Free Press, 1970.

Muhammad, Khalil Gibran. *The Condemnation of Blackness: Race, Crime, and the Making of Modern Urban America*. Cambridge: Harvard University Press, 2010.

Mumford, Kevin. *Interzones: Black/White Sex Districts in Chicago and New York in the Early Twentieth Century*. New York: Columbia University Press, 1997.

———. *Newark: A History of Race, Rights, and Riots in America*. New York: New York University Press, 2007.

———. "Untangling Pathology: The Moynihan Report and Homosexual Damage, 1965–1975." *Journal of Policy History* 24, no. 1 (2012): 53–73.

Muñoz, José Esteban. *Cruising Utopia: The Then and There of Queer Futurity*. New York: New York University Press, 2009.

Munt, Sally. *Heroic Desire: Lesbian Identity and Cultural Space*. London: Cassell, 1998.

Murphy, Kevin P. "Gay Was Good: Progress, Homonormativity, and Oral History." In *Queer Twin Cities: Twin Cities GLBT Oral History Project*, edited by Kevin P. Murphy,

Jennifer L. Pierce, and Larry Knopp, 305–18. Minneapolis: University of Minnesota Press, 2010.

Myrdal, Gunnar. 1944. *An American Dilemma: The Negro Problem and Modern Democracy*. Piscataway, NJ: Transaction, 1995.

Nash, June, ed. *Social Movements: An Anthropological Reader*. Malden, MA: Blackwell, 2005.

Nast, Heidi J. "Queer Patriarchies, Queer Racisms, International." *Antipode* 34, no. 5 (2002): 874–909.

Nelson, Alondra. *Body and Soul: The Black Panther Party and the Fight against Medical Discrimination*. Minneapolis: University of Minnesota, 2011.

Nguyen, Mimi Thi. "Riot Grrrl, Race, and Revival." *Women and Performance: A Journal of Feminist Theory* 22, nos. 2–3 (2012): 173–96.

———. "Times Square." *Punk Planet* 62 (July–August 2004): 94–97. threadandcircuits.wordpress.com/tag/times-square/.

O'Connor, Alice. *Poverty Knowledge: Social Science, Social Policy, and the Poor in Twentieth-Century U.S. History*. Princeton: Princeton University Press, 2001.

Omi, Michael, and Howard Winant. *Racial Formation in the United States*. New York: Routledge, 1986.

Ordona, Trinity A. "Asian Lesbians in San Francisco: Struggles to Create a Safe Space, 1970s–1980s." In *Asian/Pacific Islander American Women: A Historical Anthology*, edited by Shirley Hune and Gail Nomura, 319–34. New York: New York University Press, 2003.

Osborne, Peter, and Lynne Segal. "Gender as Performance: An Interview with Judith Butler." *Radical Philosophy* 67 (Summer 1994): 32–39.

Osman, Suleiman. *The Invention of Brownstone Brooklyn: Gentrification and the Search for Authenticity in Postwar New York*. New York: Oxford University Press, 2011.

Palumbo-Liu, David, Bruce Robbins, and Nirvana Tanoukhi, eds. *Immanuel Wallerstein and the Problem of the World: System, Scale, Culture*. Durham: Duke University Press, 2011.

Park, Robert E., and Ernest W. Burgess. [1925] *The City: Suggestions for the Investigation of Human Behavior in the Urban Environment*. Chicago: University of Chicago Press, 1967; reprint 1984.

Patel, Geeta. "Risky Subjects: Insurance, Sexuality, and Capital." *Social Text* 24, no. 4 (2006): 25–65.

Penn, Donna. "The Sexualized Women: The Lesbian, the Prostitute and the Containment of Female Sexuality In Postwar America." In *Not June Cleaver: Women and Gender in Postwar America, 1945–1960*, edited by Joanne Meyerowitz, 358–81. Philadelphia: Temple University Press, 1994.

Perry, Barbara, ed. *Hate and Bias Crime: A Reader*. New York: Routledge, 2003.

Petrosino, Carolyn. "Connecting the Past to the Future: Hate Crime in America." In *Hate and Bias Crime: A Reader*, edited by Barbara Perry, 9–26. New York: Routledge, 2003.

Piercy, Marge. Preface to *Take Back the Night: Women on Pornography*, edited by Laura Lederer. New York: William Morrow, 1980.

Piven, Frances Fox, and Richard A. Cloward. *Poor People's Movements: Why They Succeed, How They Fail*. New York: Vintage, 1977.

———. *Regulating the Poor: The Functions of Public Welfare*. Updated ed. New York: Vintage, 1993.

Plaster, Joey. "Imagined Conversations and Activist Lineages: Public Histories of Queer

Homeless Youth Organizing and the Policing of Public Space in San Francisco's Tenderloin, 1960s and Present." *Radical History Review* 113 (Spring 2012): 99–109.

Plunz, Richard. *A History of Housing in New York City.* New York: Columbia University
Press, 1990.

Podair, Jerald. *The Strike That Changed New York: Blacks, Whites, and the Ocean Hill–
Brownsville Crisis.* New Haven: Yale University Press, 2002.

Polchin, James. "'Why Do They Strike Us?': Representing Violence and Sexuality,
1930–1950." PhD diss., New York University, 2002.

Polletta, Francesca. *Freedom Is an Endless Meeting: Democracy in American Social Movements.* Chicago: University of Chicago Press, 2002.

Poovey, Mary. "Figures of Arithmetic, Figures of Speech: The Discourse of Statistics
in the 1830s." In *Questions of Evidence: Proof, Practice, and Persuasion across the
Disciplines,* edited by James Chandler, Arnold I. Davidson, and Harry Harootunian,
401–21. Chicago: University of Chicago Press, 1994.

Potter, Claire Bond. "Taking Back Times Square: Feminist Repertoires and the Transformation of Urban Space in Late Second Wave Feminism." *Radical History Review*
113 (Spring 2012): 67–80.

Pritchett, Wendell E. *Robert Clifton Weaver and the American City: The Life and Times of
an Urban Reformer.* Chicago: University of Chicago Press, 2008.

Puar, Jasbir K., ed. "Queer Tourism: Geographies of Globalization." Special issue, GLQ
8, nos. 1–2 (2002).

———. *Terrorist Assemblages: Homonationalism in Queer Times.* Durham: Duke University Press, 2007.

Pulido, Laura. *Black, Brown, Yellow, and Left: Radical Activism in Los Angeles.* Berkeley:
University of California Press, 2006.

Quilley, Stephen. "Constructing Manchester's 'New Urban Village': Gay Space in
the Entrepreneurial City." In *Queers in Space: Communities/Public Places/Sites of
Resistance,* edited by Gordon Brent Ingram, Anne-Marie Bouthillette, and Yolanda
Retter, 275–94. Seattle: Bay, 1997.

Rainwater, Lee, and William L. Yancey. *The Moynihan Report and the Politics of Controversy.* Cambridge: MIT Press, 1967.

"Rapping with a Street Transvestite Revolutionary: An Interview with Marcia [*sic*]
Johnson." In *Out of the Closets: Voices of Gay Liberation,* 20th anniversary edition
(2nd ed.), edited by Karla Jay and Allen Young, 112–20. New York: New York University Press, 1992.

Reck, Jennifer. "Be Queer . . . but not Here! Queer and Transgender Youth, the Castro
'Mecca,' and Spatial Gay Politics." PhD diss., University of California, Santa Cruz, 2005.

Reddy, Chandan. "Asian Diasporas, Neoliberalism, and Family: Reviewing the Case
for Homosexual Asylum in the Context of Family Rights." *Social Text* 23, nos. 3–4
(2005): 101–19.

———. *Freedom with Violence: Race, Sexuality, and the U.S. State.* Durham: Duke University Press, 2011.

———. "Home, House, and Nonidentity: *Paris Is Burning.*" In *Burning Down the House:
Recycling Domesticity,* edited by Rosemary George, 355–79. Boulder, CO: Westview,
1997.

Rhomberg, Christopher. *No There There: Race, Class, and Political Community in Oakland.* Berkeley: University of California Press, 2004.

Robcis, Camille. "'China in Our Heads': Althusser, Maoism, and Structuralism." *Social
Text* 30, no. 1 (2012): 51–69.

Robinson, Cedric. *Black Marxism: The Making of the Black Radical Tradition*. London: Zed, 1983.

Roque-Ramirez, Horacio N. "'That's *My* Place!': Negotiating Racial, Gender, and Sexual Politics in San Francisco's Gay Latino Alliance, 1973–1983." *Journal of the History of Sexuality* 12, no. 2 (2003): 224–48.

Rosado, Justin Anton. "Corroding Our Quality of Life." In *That's Revolting! Queer Strategies for Resisting Assimilation*, edited by Mattilda Bernstein Sycamore, 287–302. New York: Soft Scull, 2004.

Rose, Damaris. "Rethinking Gentrification: Beyond the Uneven Development of Marxist Urban Theory." *Environment and Planning D: Society and Space* 2, no. 1 (1984): 47–74.

Ross, Andrew. *The Celebration Chronicles: Life, Liberty, and the Pursuit of Property Value in Disney's New Town*. New York: Ballantine, 2000.

———. "Mao Zedong's Impact on Cultural Politics in the West." *Cultural Politics* 1, no. 1 (2005): 5–22.

Ross, Marlon B. *Manning the Race: Reforming Black Men in the Jim Crow Era*. New York: New York University Press, 2004.

Rothenberg, Tamar. "'And She Told Two Friends': Lesbians Creating Urban Social Space." In *Mapping Desire: Geographies of Sexualities*, edited by David Bell and Gill Valentine, 165–81. London: Routledge, 1995.

Rubin, Gayle. "The Miracle Mile: South of Market and Gay Male Leather, 1962–1997." In *Reclaiming San Francisco: History, Politics, Culture*, edited by James Brooks, Chris Carlsson, and Nancy J. Peters, 247–72. San Francisco: City Lights, 1998.

———. "Thinking Sex." In *The Lesbian and Gay Studies Reader*, edited by Henry Abelove, Michèle Aina Barale, and David M. Halperin, 3–44. New York: Routledge, 1993.

Ruskola, Teemu. "Gay Rights versus Queer Theory." *Social Text* 23, nos. 3–4 (2005): 235–49.

Salamon, Gayle. *Assuming a Body: Transgender and Rhetorics of Materiality*. New York: Columbia University Press, 2010.

Sandoval, Chela. *Methodology of the Oppressed*. Minneapolis: University of Minnesota Press, 2000.

Schiavi, Michael. *Celluloid Activist: The Life and Times of Vito Russo*. Madison: University of Wisconsin Press, 2011.

Schneider, Eric. *Vampires, Dragons, and Egyptian Kings: Youth Gangs in Postwar New York*. Princeton: Princeton University Press, 1999.

Schulman, Sarah. *The Gentrification of the Mind: Witness to a Lost Imagination*. Berkeley: University of California Press, 2012.

———. *My American History: Lesbian and Gay Life during the Reagan/Bush Years*. New York: Routledge, 1994.

Scott, Daryl Michael. *Contempt and Pity: Social Policy and the Image of the Damaged Black Psyche, 1880–1996*. Chapel Hill: University of North Carolina Press, 1997.

Sears, Clare. "Electric Brilliancy: Cross-Dressing Law and Freak Show Displays in Nineteenth-Century San Francisco." *Women Studies Quarterly* 36, nos. 3–4 (2008): 170–87.

Sedgwick, Eve Kosofsky. *Touching Feeling: Affect, Pedagogy, Performativity*. Durham: Duke University Press, 2003.

Segrest, Mab. *Memoir of a Race Traitor*. Cambridge, MA: South End, 1994.

Self, Robert O. *American Babylon: Race and the Struggle for Postwar Oakland*. Princeton: Princeton University Press, 2003.

Shah, Nayan. *Contagious Divides: Epidemics and Race in San Francisco's Chinatown.* Berkeley: University of California Press, 2001.

———. *Stranger Intimacy: Contesting Race, Sexuality, and the Law in the North American West.* Berkeley: University of California Press, 2011.

Shah, Svati P. "Sexuality and 'The Left': Thoughts on Intersections and Visceral Others." *Scholar and the Feminist Online* 7, no. 3 (2009). http://sfonline.barnard.edu /sexecon/shah_01.htm.

Shernoff, Michael. *Without Condoms: Unprotected Sex, Gay Men, and Barebacking.* New York: Routledge, 2005.

Shilts, Randy. *The Mayor of Castro Street: The Life and Times of Harvey Milk.* New York: St. Martin's, 1982.

Sides, Josh. *Erotic City: Sexual Revolutions and the Making of Modern San Francisco.* New York: Oxford University Press, 2009.

Simmel, Georg. [1903] "The Metropolis and Mental Life." In *The Blackwell City Reader,* 2nd ed., edited by Gary Bridge and Sophie Watson, 103–10. Malden, MA: Wiley-Blackwell, 2010.

Singh, Nikhil Pal. *Black Is a Country: Race and the Unfinished Struggle for Democracy.* Cambridge: Harvard University Press, 2004.

Siskind, Peter. "'Rockefeller's Vietnam'? Black Politics and Urban Development in Harlem, 1969–1974." Paper, Gotham History Festival, October 6, 2001. http://www .gothamcenter.org/festival/2001/confpapers/siskind.pdf.

Skogan, Wesley. *Disorder and Decline: Crime and the Spiral of Decay in American Neighborhoods.* Berkeley: University of California Press, 1990.

Sliwa, Curtis, and Murray Schwartz. *Street Smart: The Guardian Angel Guide to Safe Living.* Reading, MA: Addison-Wesley, 1982.

Smith, Andrea. *Native Americans and the Christian Right: The Gendered Politics of Unlikely Alliances.* Durham: Duke University Press, 2008.

Smith, Barbara, ed. *Home Girls: A Black Feminist Anthology.* Latham, NY: Kitchen Table: Women of Color Press, 1983.

———. "Notes for Yet Another Paper on Black Feminism, or Will the Real Enemy Please Stand Up." *Conditions* 2, no. 2 (1979): 123–27.

———. "A Press of Our Own Kitchen Table: Women of Color Press," *Frontiers: A Journal of Women Studies* 10, no. 3 (1989): 11–13.

Smith, Kenneth T. "Homophobia: A Tentative Personality Profile." *Psychological Reports* 29 (1971): 1091–94.

Smith, Neil. *The New Urban Frontier: Gentrification and the Revanchist City.* London: Routledge, 1996.

Sobredo, James. "From Manila Bay to Daly City: Filipinos in San Francisco." In *Reclaiming San Francisco: History, Politics, Culture,* edited by James Brooks, Chris Carlsson, and Nancy J. Peters, 273–86. San Francisco: City Lights, 1998.

Somerville, Siobhan B. *Queering the Color Line: Race and the Invention of Homosexuality in American Culture.* Durham: Duke University Press, 2000.

———. "Queer *Loving.*" *GLQ* 11, no. 3 (2005): 355–70.

Spade, Dean. *Normal Life: Administrative Violence, Critical Trans Politics, and the Limits of the Law.* Cambridge, MA: South End, 2011.

Spivak, Gayatri Chakravorty. "Can the Subaltern Speak?" In *Marxism and the Interpretation of Culture,* edited by Carey Nelson and Lawrence Grossberg, 271–313. Urbana: University of Illinois Press, 1988.

Springer, Kimberly. *Living for the Revolution: Black Feminist Organizations, 1968–1980.* Durham: Duke University Press, 2005.

Stanko, Elizabeth A. "Victims R Us: The Life History of 'Fear of Crime' and the Politicisation of Violence." In *Crime, Risk and Insecurity: Law and Order in Everyday Life and Political Discourse,* edited by Tim Hope and Richard Sparks, 13–30. London: Routledge, 2000.

———. "Women, Crime, and Fear." *Annals of the American Academy of Political and Social Science* 539 (May 1995): 46–58.

Stanley, Eric A., and Nat Smith, eds. *Captive Genders: Trans Embodiment and the Prison Industrial Complex.* Oakland, CA: AK, 2011.

Stein, Marc. *City of Sisterly and Brotherly Loves: Lesbian and Gay Philadelphia, 1945–1972.* Chicago: University of Chicago Press, 2000.

Stewart-Winter, Timothy. "The Castro: Origins to the Age of Milk." *Gay and Lesbian Review,* January–February 2009, 12–15.

———. "Raids, Rights, and Rainbow Coalitions: Sexuality and Race in Chicago Politics, 1950–2000." PhD diss., University of Chicago, 2009.

Stryker, Susan. *Transgender History.* Berkeley, CA: Seal, 2008.

Sudjic, Deyan. *100 Mile City.* New York: Harcourt Brace, 1992.

Sugrue, Thomas. *The Origins of the Urban Crisis: Race and Inequality in Postwar Detroit.* Princeton: Princeton University Press, 1996.

Suran, Justin. "Coming Out against the War: Antimilitarism and the Politicization of Homosexuality in the Era of Vietnam." *American Quarterly* 53, no. 3 (2001): 452–88.

Sze, Julie. *Noxious New York: The Racial Politics of Urban Health and Environmental Justice.* Cambridge: MIT Press, 2006.

Taylor, Sandra C. *Jewel of the Desert: Japanese American Internment at Topaz.* Berkeley: University of California Press, 1993.

Teal, Donn. 1971. *The Gay Militants: How Gay Liberation Began in America, 1969–1971.* New York: St. Martin's, 1995.

Terkel, Studs. "An Interview with James Baldwin." In *Conversations with James Baldwin,* edited by Fred L. Standley and Louis H. Pratt. Jackson: University Press of Mississippi, 1989.

Terry, Jennifer. *An American Obsession: Science, Medicine, and Homosexuality in Modern Society.* Chicago: University of Chicago Press, 1999.

Third World Gay Revolution. "What We Want, What We Believe." In *Out of the Closets: Voices of Gay Liberation,* 20th anniversary edition (2nd ed.), edited by Karla Jay and Allen Young, 363–67. New York: New York University Press, 1992.

Thompson, Becky. *A Promise and a Way of Life: White Anti-Racist Organizing.* Minneapolis: University of Minnesota Press, 2001.

Thuma, Emily. "Not a Wedge, but a Bridge: Prisons, Feminist Activism, and the Politics of Gendered Violence, 1968–1987." PhD diss., New York University, 2011.

Tongson, Karen. *Relocations: Queer Suburban Imaginaries.* New York: New York University Press, 2011.

Trotter, Joe William, Jr. "From a Raw Deal to a New Deal? 1929–1945." In *To Make Our World Anew: A History of African Americans,* edited by Robin D. G. Kelley and Earl H. Lewis, 409–44. Oxford: Oxford University Press, 2000.

Ture, Kwame [Stokely Carmichael], and Charles Hamilton. 1967. *Black Power: The Politics of Liberation.* New York: Vintage, 2001.

Vaid, Urvashi. *Virtual Equality: The Mainstreaming of Gay and Lesbian Liberation.* New York: Anchor, 1995.

Valentine, David. *Imagining Transgender: An Ethnography of a Category.* Durham: Duke University Press, 2007.

Vogel, Shane. *The Scene of Harlem Cabaret: Race, Sexuality, Performance.* Chicago: University of Chicago Press, 2009.

Ward, Jane. *Respectably Queer: Diversity Culture in LGBT Activist Organizations.* Nashville, TN: Vanderbilt University Press, 2008.

Warner, Michael. *The Trouble with Normal: Sex, Politics, and the Ethics of Queer Life.* New York: Free Press, 1999.

Weinberg, George. *Society and the Healthy Homosexual.* New York: St. Martin's, 1972.

Wertheimer, David M. "The Emergence of a Gay and Lesbian Antiviolence Movement." In *Creating Change: Sexuality, Public Policy, and Civil Rights,* edited by John D'Emilio, William B. Turner, and Urvashi Vaid, 261–79. New York: St. Martin's, 2000.

———. "Treatment and Service Interventions for Lesbian and Gay Male Crime Victims," in *Hate Crimes: Confronting Violence against Lesbians and Gay Men,* edited by Gregory M. Herek and Kevin T. Berrill, 227–40. Newbury Park, CA: Sage, 1992.

Weston, Kath. "Get Thee to a Big City: Sexual Imaginary and the Great Gay Migration." *GLQ* 2, no. 3 (1995): 253–77.

Wickberg, Daniel. "Homophobia: On the Cultural History of an Idea." *Critical Inquiry* 27 (August 2000): 42–57.

Williams, Rhonda. *The Politics of Public Housing: Black Women's Struggles against Urban Inequality.* Oxford: Oxford University Press, 2004.

Willse, Craig. "Neoliberal Biopolitics and the Invention of Chronic Homelessness." *Economy and Society* 39, no. 2 (2010): 155–84.

Wilson, Elizabeth. *The Sphinx in the City: Urban Life, the Control of Disorder, and Women.* Berkeley: University of California Press, 1992.

Wilson, Hank, and John Lauritsen. *Death Rush: Poppers and AIDS.* New York: Pagan, 1986.

Wolfgang, Marvin E., and Franco Ferracuti. [1969] "The Subculture of Violence." In *Criminological Theories: Bridging the Past to the Future,* edited by Suzette Cote, 88–95. Thousand Oaks, CA: Sage, 2002.

Wolfgang, Marvin E., Robert M. Figlio, and Thorsten Sellin. 1972. *Delinquency in a Birth Cohort.* Chicago: University of Chicago Press, 1987.

Woods, Clyde. *Development Arrested: Blues and Plantation Power in the Mississippi Delta.* London: Verso, 1998.

Worley, Jennifer. "'Street Power' and the Claiming of Public Space: San Francisco's 'Vanguard' and Pre-Stonewall Queer Radicalism." In *Captive Genders: Trans Embodiment and the Prison Industrial Complex,* edited by Eric A. Stanley and Nat Smith, 41–56. Oakland, CA: AK, 2011.

Wright, Erik Olin. *Class, Crisis, and the State.* London: Verso, 1978.

Wright, Kai. *Drifting toward Love: Black, Brown, Gay, and Coming of Age on the Streets of New York.* Boston: Beacon, 2008.

Young, Cynthia A. *Soul Power: Culture, Radicalism, and the Making of a U.S. Third World Left.* Durham: Duke University Press, 2006.

Young, Ian. "Mikhail Itkin: Tales of a Bishopric." *Gay and Lesbian Review Worldwide,* November–December 2010, 26–27.

Zimroth, Peter L. *Perversions of Justice: The Prosecution and Acquittal of the Panther 21.* New York: Viking, 1974.

INDEX

Page numbers in *italics* refer to figures.

Abraham, Julie, 11
Advocate, 93, 269n33
Advocates for Gay Men of Color (New York), 194
African Americans, 12, 63, 79, 92, 197–98, 242n70, 290n116; absence in Gay Index, 187; African American bars, 5, 142, 161, 193, 214, 219; in Bayview-Hunters Point, 52, 68–69; black churches, 176; black women, 125–26, 131, 144, 149, 169, 236n22; blamed for homophobia, 113–14, 123, 223–24, 284n47; blamed for Proposition 8, 13; blamed for violence, 94, 133, 170–71, 180, 283n42; in Central City, 35; in Chelsea, 110–11; excluded from GI Bill, 50–51; in Greenwich Village, 202, 208; in Harlem, 262n145; hate crimes legislation and, 14, 157, 163, 296n59, 297n85; homophile movement and, 56, 61; kinship and, 47, 115, 242n71; LGBT people, 63, 236n22, 265n186, 286n69, 306n55; in Los Angeles, 36; mental illness attributed to, 254n49, 255n63; New Deal and, 250n17; policing of, 65, 71–72, 219; in South Park, 40, 65; terminology, 234n9; Third World Gay Coalition and, 131; violence against, 36–38, 68–69, 125–26, 169, 204, 277n121; in War on Poverty, 46–47, 49, 53–56, 65; in Washington, D.C., 227–29, 313n1; in Western Addition, 36, 52, 63, 68–69, 105, 129, 251n20, 274n95; youth, 2, 149, 171

African People's Socialist Party, 139
African People's Solidarity Committee, 139
Against Equality, 246n105. *See also* Nair, Yasmin
Ahmed, Sara, 286n70
AIDS activism, 26, 83–84, 246n102, 297n85; discrimination and, 110; risk reduction strategies, 247n120, 247n128, 276n111; vulnerability and 32. *See also* AIDS Coalition to Unleash Power; Crisisline; HIV/AIDS
AIDS Coalition to Unleash Power (ACT UP), 32, 213, 245n96, 247n128
Alan Stanford Modeling Group (San Francisco), 93, 270n41
Alfred, Randy, 273n76, 274n93, 274n94, 275n99; as journalist, 100–101, 276n111, 284n47; on violence, 273n80, 274n95
Alice B. Toklas Democratic Club (San Francisco), 56, 90
Alinsky, Saul, 20, 58, 60–61, 257n82, 258nn99–100
Alioto, Joseph, 53
Alliance Against Women's Oppression, 119, 148, 280n8
Alpine Liberation Front (ALF), 88–89
Althusser, Louis, 286n71
Amadae, S. M., 313n12
Amelia's (San Francisco), 117
American Bar Association, 170
American Civil Liberties Union (ACLU), 67, 170, 261n124
American Friends Service Committee, 68, 166. *See also* Whitlock, Kay

American Indian Center (San Francisco), 67

American Indian Movement (AIM), 80

American Jewish Congress, 170

American Nazi Party, 93, 141

American Psychiatric Association, 92, 113

American Psychological Association, 169, 255n65

analogies, 24, 37, 51, 175, 242n68, 253n43; between liberation struggles, 86, 93; between race and sexuality, 20–21, 37–58, 72–73, 75, 79

Annsfire, Joan, 135, 285n62, 287n72

anti-abortion movement, 116

anti-apartheid movement, 119, 142

Anti-Defamation League (D.C.), 228

Anti-Defamation League of B'nai B'rith (ADL), 24, 170, 299n96; fight with NAACP, 175–76; model hate crimes legislation, 157–58, 162–64, 167

anti-imperialist activism, 21–22, 86, 89, 139. See also black freedom movement; colonialism; imperialism; Third World decolonization movement

Anti-Police Abuse Coalition, 142, 148

antiracist activism, 17, 49, 123, 283n36, 286n70; lesbian feminist antiracist activism, 135, 139–42, 153. See also black freedom movement; Black Power movement; civil rights movement (African American)

antirape activism, 22, 101, 107–8; rape crisis centers, 164. See also rape; Violence Against Women Act

anti-Semitism, 24, 157, 176, 296n55, 298n88

antiwar movement, 57, 100, 121, 131, 135, 176

Appalachian Regional Commission, 55

Apuzzo, Virginia, 160

Aquarius cell, 122

Arab Americans, 157

archives: of book, 11–12, 26–28; exclusions, 246n101; queer archives, 245n95. See also individual archives

Arizona Senate Bill 1070, 201, 307n64

Armstrong, Elizabeth A., 266n10

art, 11; as activism, 125, 151–52; artists, 30, 110, 131, 142, 228. See also cultural production

Asian American Feminists (San Francisco), 122, 281n14

Asian Americans, 56, 149, 219, 260n114; Chinese Americans, 12, 68, 94, 109; Filipino Americans, 40, 49, 62–64, 109, 260n114; Japanese Americans, 68, 163, 250n16

Asian Lesbians of the East Coast (New York), 280n8

assimilation, 20; critiques of, 1, 86, 92–93, 97; in War on Poverty, 42, 44, 48, 50, 52, 73

AT&T, 159

Audre Lorde Project (ALP), 25, 166, 194, 196, 213

Austin, Texas, 135, 287n72

Azalea, 142, 151–52. See also Gibbs, Joan

Bacall's (New York), 141

back-to-the-city movement, 8–9, 145

Bailey, Robert W., 310n108, 311n117

Baldwin, James, 30, 33, 41, 250n17

Baraka, Amina, 204

Baraka, Amiri, 198, 204

Bar Nocetti, 5, 253n20

bars, 43, 81, 136, 193, 229, 264n184; exclusionary practices, 4, 122, 124, 142, 149–50, 281n23; fires in, 276n111; gentrification and, 26, 134; leather bars, 110; performances in, 140, 154; policing of, 180, 214, 219, 311n116; raids of, 38, 161, 233n2, 249n10, 285n63; street bars, 39; strip bars, 17, 96; studies of, 100, 169. See also individual bars

"bash back" slogans, 177, 180–82, 300n102

Bay Area Black Lesbians and Gays, 280n8

Bay Area Coalition against the Briggs Initiative, 135

Bay Area Gay Liberation (BAGL), 99, 104, 109, 272n67, 281n14, 281n23

Bay Area PoliceWatch, 195

Bay Area Rapid Transit (BART), 40, 136

Bay Area Reporter, 268n32, 275n99, 300n106

Bay View Community Center, 66, 68

Bayview-Hunters Point (San Francisco), 52–53, 250n17. See also Hunters Point

Beale, Frances, 142

criminalization, 49, 130, 158, 175, 224; of anti-LGBT violence, 9, 14–15, 18, 22–24, 31–32, 109; of blackness, 51, 255n63; of clothing, 163, 295n42; enhanced criminal penalties, 3–4, 165, 173, 229; marriage and, 247n122; police entrapment, 5, 38, 66, 70–72, 86, 108; privatization and, 188, 199, 201, 236n22; of racialized poor, 13, 37, 59, 78, 148; safe streets patrols and, 178–81; of sex work, 65, 74, 78, 212; of youth, 5–6, 219. *See also* crime statistics and documentation; criminology; death penalty; hate crimes legislation; law; prisons; quality-of-life laws; racial profiling; rational choice theory; zero tolerance policies

criminology, 9, 107, 167, 170–71. *See also* broken windows theory; crime statistics and documentation; culture of poverty thesis; rational choice theory

Crisisline, 159, 161, 171, 293n30

criticism/self-criticism, 140

Cruise News and World Report, 46

Cruising (film), 142, 192

Cruz, Robert Edward, 62

Cuba, 89, 268n26, 273n82

Cuite, Thomas, 90

cultural production, 11–12, 17, 57, 125, 136, 196. *See also* art

culture of poverty thesis, 4, 47, 132, 170–71, 312n5; basis for homophobia discourse, 21, 223–24; critiques of, 112–13; metronormativity and, 10; origin, 253n46

Curzon, Daniel, 268n32

Cvetkovich, Ann, 245n95

Cyril, Malkia, 199

Dallas Anti-Violence Project, 169–70

Daughters of Bilitis, 38, 40, 67, 71–72, 85, 261n128. *See also* Lyon, Phyllis; Martin, Del

David, Pamela, 135, 287n72

Dávila, Arlene, 217

Davis, Madeline, 11, 39

Davis, Sue, 117, *118*, 135, *136*

Dean, Tim, 30–31, 247n116, 247n120

death penalty, 10, 118, 165. *See also* Proposition 7

Defend Our Rights in the Streets / Super Queers United against Savage Heterosexism (DORIS SQUASH), 177

Déjà Vu (New York), 281n23

Delany, Samuel, 190, 283n38

Dellums, Ron, 132

D'Emilio, John, 11, 32, 55, 266n6

Deming, Barbara, 67

Department of Justice, 15, 162, 172, 227

Dial-a-Model, 93, 270n41

differential opportunity theory, 47, 54. *See also* Juvenile Delinquency and Youth Offences Control Act

disability, 191; in hate crimes legislation, 163–65; mental illness, 92, 113, 255n63. *See also* HIV/AIDS

disability activism, 96, 287n72

Dolores Park (San Francisco), 265n3, 274n95, 279n140, 300n106

Donaldson, Herbert, 65, 261n119

Door, The (New York), 216

Drug Enforcement Agency, 109

drugs, 17, 76, 185, 224; in anticrime campaigns, 2, 5, 45, 74; class and, 208; condemnations of, 96, 98, 200, 272n65, 302n120; explanations of, 50, 203; homosexuality and, 78; police participation in drug trade, 75; quality-of-life laws and, 178, 181–82; treatment, 276n111; users, 4, 35–36, 45, 50, 74–76, 78, 181, 203, 208. *See also* Drug Enforcement Agency

Dubber, Markus Dirk, 296n59

Du Bois, W. E. B., 51

Duchess (New York), 281n23

Duggan, Lisa, 10–11, 183, 240n56, 248n130, 249n5

Dupont Circle (Washington, D.C.), 228

Durham, Larry, 111

Durham, Lewis, 40, 250n11

Dykes Against Racism Everywhere (DARE), 124, *143*, 150–51, 196; antigentrification activism, 22, 119–20, 141–48, 154, 280n8; antiprison activism and, 289n98; trans issues and, 289n90. *See also* Bulkin, Elly; Gibbs, Joan

Dykes and Faggots Organized to Defeat Institutionalized Liberalism (DAFODIL), 148

Dykes on Bikes, 276n111. *See also* Marrero, Ali

East Bay, California, 100, 120, 285n61. *See also* Berkeley; Oakland
East Bay Action Coalition, 131
East Bay Gay Liberation Theatre, 85
East Village (New York City), 110, 128
East Village Lesbian and Gay Neighbors, 292n10
Economic Opportunity Act, 35
Economic Opportunity Council (San Francisco), 36, 41, 43–44, 49, 53, 56–57, 59–61, 67–68, 74, 248n2, 254n51, 256nn70–71
economics, 116, 214, 222, 242n67, 288n86; anticapitalist activism, 28, 86, 88, 99, 125, 146–49; criminalization and, 14–15, 74; deindustrialization, 111, 128, 304n24; economic crime, 171–72, 229, 274n95; economic exploitation, 77, 119, 143, 255n65; economic justice, 25, 147, 188, 195–96, 220, 287n72; economic rights, 251n26; financialization of everyday life, 31; funding for activism, 31, 66–67, 107, 132, 159, 273n82; informal economies, 197, 212, 217–18, 263n164; Keynesianism, 57–58, 187; morality and, 59; political economy of space, 40–42, 120, 134, 153, 190, 211; prisons and, 242n73; race and, 12, 23, 145; redistribution of wealth, 9, 37, 57–58, 78, 265n186; sexuality and, 6, 11, 145–46, 166; social welfare programs, 8, 13, 57, 189. *See also* class; gentrification; liberalism; neoliberalism; poverty; privatization; real estate; speculation
Education for Liberation Project, 214–15. *See also* Fenner, Bran
Ehrensaft-Hawley, Jesse, 194–95, 209
Eisenstein, Zillah, 127
El Comité Homosexual Latinoamericano (New York), 122
Elephant Walk (San Francisco), 285n63
Ella Baker Center for Human Rights, 195. *See also* Racial Justice 911; TransAction
Emmaus House (San Francisco), 97

Empire State Development Corporation, 191
Employment Non-Discrimination Act (ENDA), 165
Eng, David, 236n24
Engels, Friedrich, 11
Enke, Anne, 153, 243n83
entrapment, 5, 66, 70, 81, 108, 266n10; gay liberation movement and, 8; gender and, 38, 72; homophile movement and, 38
Equality Act, 165
Esch, Betsy, 286n68
Escoffier, Jeffrey, 134, 211

Fabulous Independent Educated Radicals for Community Empowerment (FIERCE), 4, 25, 28, 194–217, 201; actions, 205, 207, 213, 215, 216, 225; *Fenced Out* documentary, 197–99, 201, 234n10, 237n34, 241n58
Faggots and Class Struggle conference, 88
Fair Housing Act, 49
Family Protection Act, 119, 280n9
Family Service Agency, 65, 261n119
Fanon, Frantz, 29, 89
Farrow, Kenyon, 213, 242n71, 247n122, 314n6
Federal Bureau of Investigation (FBI), 90, 96, 163
Feinstein, Dianne, 71, 273n82
Femia, Assunta, 100, 104
feminism, 85, 153, 275n105, 290n115; black feminism, 120, 126, 132; Butterfly Brigade and, 100–101, 103; critique of the family, 246n106; empowerment and, 139; feminist anti-obscenity activism, 262n142; feminist anti-pornography activism, 108, 115; feminist antiprison activism, 289n98; feminist antiviolence activism, 9, 22, 101, 107–8, 156, 164, 181; history of, 243n83; Latina feminism, 132; lesbian feminism, 16, 97, 116, 125–26, 135; radical feminism, 1; socialist feminism, 32; at Stonewall, 121; targeted by Counter Intelligence Program, 96; women of color feminism, 147. *See also* gender; sexism; *This Bridge Called My Back*

NAACP Legal Defense Fund, 157, 165
Nair, Yasmin, 238n40, 246n105, 314n6
National Advisory Commission on Civil Disorders, 37, 106
National Anti-Klan Network. *See* Center for Democratic Renewal
National Anti-Racist Organizing Committee, 142
National Association for the Advancement of Colored People (NAACP), 68, 70, 157, 176
National Association of Public Interest Lawyers, 170
National Black Feminist Organization, 125
National Coalition of Anti-Violence Programs, 16, 174, 241n56
National Congress for Puerto Rican Rights. *See* Justice Committee
National Criminal Justice Association, 170
National Education Association, 176
National Gay and Lesbian Task Force, 24, 90, *174*, 196, 291n7; Fund for Human Dignity, 159–60; hate crimes legislation and, 157, 165, 169–76, 299n96
National Institute against Prejudice and Violence, 157
National Institute of Mental Health, 54
nationalism, 177, 224, 258n100; black nationalism, 51, 125, 254n49; revolutionary nationalism, 9, 21, 88–89
National Legal Defense Fund, 70
National Organization for Victim Assistance, 24, 162, 170
National Recovery Act, 250n17. *See also* New Deal
National Third World Gay and Lesbian Conference, 122
National Transsexual Counseling Unit, 122
Native Americans, 12, 92, 144, 149, 242n67. *See also* indigenous activism
Natoma and Vicinity Neighbors, 302n120
Neighborhood Legal Assistance Foundation, 62–63, 65, 97. *See also* Donaldson, Herbert
Nelson, Alondra, 258n93
neoliberalism, 7–9, 22, 25, 149, 239n43,
240n56; attacks on social institutions, 28–29; critiques of, 189, 210; neoliberal multiculturalism, 188; reshaping cities, 187, 224; social science research and, 222, 224–25. *See also* gentrification; prisons; privatization; Proposition 13; rational choice theory; rationalism; Reagan, Ronald; real estate; speculation; urban renewal
Nestle, Joan, 198
Newark, New Jersey, 2, 204, 235n11, 314n6
New Deal, 50, 57, 187, 250n17
New Left, 21, 37, 97, 121
New Neutral Zone, 193, 195; *Fenced Out* documentary, 197–99, 201, 234n10, 237n34, 241n58
New Orleans, Louisiana, 147, 236n24
New Right, 119
Newton, Huey P., 61, 93, 123, 259n105
New York, 70, 84–85, 112, 167, 196, 227, 229; community boards, 2, 6, 189–90, 217; contrasted with San Francisco, 264n184, 266n10; gay neighborhoods, 18, 239n45; gentrification in, 24, 110, 128, 212; hate crimes legislation and, 160, 170; map, 232; neoliberalism in, 187; public health boards, 218; role in LGBT history, 10–11, 16–17, 120–22, 243n81; safe streets patrols in, 82–83, 177–78. *See also individual neighborhoods, organizations, and publications*
New York Anti-Violence Project, 23, 157–62, 292n12; collaborations, 181–82, 228, 303n3; hate crimes legislation and, 167, 297n75
New York City Coalition Against Police Brutality (CAPB), 194
New York City Council, 90, 190, 236n30
New York City Human Resources Administration, 216
New York Civil Liberties Union, 70
New York Department of City Planning, 191, 207
New York Human Rights Commission, 110
New York PoliceWatch, 195
New York State Crime Victims Board, 159

New York State Senate Special Task Force on Vandalism, Religious Desecration and Other Acts of Bigotry, 296n58
New York University, 26 192
Ninja, Willi, 197
Nixon, Richard, 27, 62, 107
Nob Hill (Washington, D.C.), 229
normalization, 12, 78, 226; critiques of, 13, 28, 52, 58, 134, 246n106
Northampton, Massachusetts, 26
North Beach (San Francisco), 68, 108, 161n124, 264n184
North Texas State University, 135

Oakland, 97, 100, 122, 186, 271n47
Oakland Community Learning Center, 131
Oakland Community School, 132
O'Connor, Alice, 57, 312n7
Office of Economic Opportunity, 54, 61–62, 254n55, 259n103
Ohlin, Lloyd, 5, 47, 54
Old Folks Defense League, 98, 269n36. See also Broshears, Raymond
O'Leary, Jean, 294n31
Omi, Michael, 279n141
Omnibus Crime Control and Safe Streets Act, 37, 106
ONYX: Black Lesbian Newsletter, 150–51, 152
Open Society Institute, 159
Operation West Side, 203
Orthodox Episcopal Church of God, 91. See also Broshears, Raymond
Osman, Suleiman, 283nn37–38

Pacific Center for Human Growth, 131
Palestine, 176
Paper Tiger Television: Fenced Out documentary, 197–99, 201, 234n10, 237n34, 241n58
Paris Is Burning, 192, 218
Parker, Pat, 149
Pataki, George, 191
patriarchy, 86, 127, 141. See also sexism
Patrick, Doug, 76, 264n177
Patton, Frank, Jr., 262n147
Peg's Place, 285n63
People for the American Way, 170

People's Fund, 275n99
People's Guard, 98
People's Justice 2000, 194
Personal Rights in Defense and Education, 249n10
Philadelphia, Pennsylvania, 16, 90, 177, 180–81
Pilipino Organizing Committee, 63, 260n111
Pink Angels, 299n100
Pink Panthers, 24, 177, 180, 183, 299n101, 301n118
Piven, Frances Fox, 77–78
Pleiades, 287n72. See also Jochild, Maggie
Plexus, 132
Police Foundation, 170, 275n102
Police Precinct Community Council, 186, 202, 227
police violence, 21, 65–70, 128; activism against, 62, 64, 71–74, 85, 194; Black Panthers and, 94, 299n101; definition of, 263n148; Gay Activists Alliance and, 89, 93; gentrification and, 116, 141, 145, 148; homophile movement and, 11, 243; murder of community members, 53, 194, 306n49; targeting lesbians, 117, 135–38, 142, 151–52, 265n186; targeting people of color, 135–38, 142, 145, 151–52, 169, 197–99; targeting sex workers, 95; targeting trans women, 175, 195, 281n21. See also criminalization; entrapment; law; policing; racial profiling
policing, 3, 7, 13, 200, 210; alternatives to, 189–90, 203; antipolicing activism, 1, 15–16, 20; California Hall arrests, 36, 39, 55, 65–66; calls for more, 18, 227–28; colonialism and, 176; community police review boards, 69, 162, 289n96; community relations boards, 54, 65–70, 76, 91, 159–60, 262n147; documentation of violence, 110–11, 160; gay and lesbian officers, 104, 117, 162; involvement in drug trade, 75; know-your-rights trainings, 41; Marxist critiques of, 138–39; police watchdog groups, 20, 36–37, 41, 44; safe streets patrols and, 102–4, 146, 177–80; sensitivity trainings, 104,